# COMPARATIVE COMMENTARIES
ON
# PRIVATE INTERNATIONAL LAW
OR
# CONFLICT OF LAWS

BY

ARTHUR K. KUHN

MEMBER OF THE NEW YORK BAR
ASSOCIATE OF THE INSTITUTE OF INTERNATIONAL LAW

**Fred B. Rothman & Co.**
LITTLETON, COLORADO
1981

**Library of Congress Cataloging in Publication Data**

Kuhn, Arthur Kline, 1876-
Comparative commentaries on private international law, or, Conflict of laws.

Reprint. Originally published: New York : Macmillan, 1937.
Includes indexes.
1. Conflict of laws. I. Title. II. Title: Conflict of laws.
K7040.k83 1981 340.9 81-13873
ISBN 0-8377-0737-4 AACR2

Printed in the United States of America

The quality of this reprint is equivalent to the
quality of the original work.

Second Printing 2000.

Fred B. Rothman Publications

*a division of*
William S. Hein & Co., Inc.
Buffalo, New York

This book has been digitally archived to maintain
the quality of the original work
for future generations of legal researchers
by William S. Hein & Co., Inc

This volume is printed on acid-free paper by
William S. Hein & Co., Inc.

COMPARATIVE COMMENTARIES ON PRIVATE INTERNATIONAL LAW

THE MACMILLAN COMPANY
NEW YORK · BOSTON · CHICAGO · DALLAS
ATLANTA · SAN FRANCISCO

MACMILLAN & CO., LIMITED
LONDON · BOMBAY · CALCUTTA
MELBOURNE

THE MACMILLAN COMPANY
OF CANADA, LIMITED
TORONTO

# PREFACE

THE present work is an endeavor to present in a critical manner, and within reasonable compass, the legislation and jurisprudence of common-law jurisdictions relating to Private International Law, in parallel comparison with the principal systems of Europe and Latin America. The similarities of doctrine thus brought to light will often be found striking. The divergencies should also be frankly recognized. In the field of personal and family relations, many countries have adopted the principle of national law, which is foreign to English and American jurisprudence as a source of private law applicable to citizens abroad. Efforts to arrive at a compromise by international agreement are not likely to prove fruitful in an era of nationalism. Yet the world continues to grow smaller as the speed of travel and communication is accelerated and the science of jurisprudence must find ways for a just determination of the rights of private individuals where their transactions are subject to the competing laws of two or more states or countries.

The promulgation of the Restatement of the Law of Conflict of Laws by the American Law Institute in 1934, after a decade of research and discussion, was an event of great significance. It would be most unfortunate, however, if this step toward national uniformity in solving conflicts of law in jurisdictions of the United States were made the occasion for exaggerating the differences between the principles of English and American law and the principles recognized in this field in countries of the Roman tradition. English separatism is sometimes so greatly accentuated by legal commentators as to lead one to believe that the common law was evolved upon a different planet! This view is particularly unfortunate in respect to Private International Law because this branch of legal science is of comparatively recent origin and still in a formative stage. Story, recognized as a classical authority both in England and the United States, constantly referred to the Continental authorities of the seventeenth and eighteenth centuries and founded many of his doctrines upon their discussions.

The present work is designed to be useful both to the student and the practitioner. The comparative study of other systems must be the foundation of any further approaches toward international regulation. Even assuming that Private International Law continues to rest wholly upon a national basis, the practitioner must know the rules of conflict in foreign jurisdictions as well as in his own, because upon these rules may depend the choice of the forum and the application of the law. The principles of some of the most important foreign systems are here presented, parallel with the discussion of the English and the American law. It is needless to say that not all the foreign systems are referred to, nor could any single foreign system be presented with completeness. To attempt to do so would have unduly extended the scope of the present work. In adopting the comparative method, we have followed the example of the great master, Story, a century ago, with this difference, that where Story referred principally to the writings of foreign commentators, we have based the comparative comments also upon specific foreign legislation and the decisions of foreign courts.

Grateful acknowledgment is made to my wife for her assistance in reading the manuscript and for many helpful suggestions.

A. K. K.

CONTENTS

## LIST OF AUTHORITIES

Académie de Droit International, Recueil des Cours. 1923–
American Journal of International Law, 1907–
American Society of International Law, Proceedings of the, 1907–
Annuaire de l'Institut de Droit International. 1877–
Arminjon, P., Précis de droit international privé. 3 vols. 2nd ed. (1927–1935)
Bar, L. von, The Theory and Practice of Private International Law. Translated by G. R. Gillespie. 2nd ed. (1892)
Bate, J. Pawley, Notes on the Doctrine of Renvoi in Private International Law (1904)
Bates, L. T., The Divorce and Separation of Aliens in France (1929)
Baty, T., Polarized Law. Three Lectures on Conflicts of Law (1914)
Beale, J. H., A Treatise on the Conflict of Laws or Private International Law. Part I only (1916)
——, A Treatise on the Conflict of Laws. 3 vols. (1935)
——, The Law of Foreign Corporations and Taxation of Corporations both Foreign and Domestic (1904)
Bishop, J. P., New Commentaries on Marriage, Divorce and Separation. 2 vols. (1891)
Brissaud, J., History of French Public Law. Translated by J. W. Garner. Continental Legal History Series (1915)
British Year Book of International Law. 1920–
Brocher, C., Noveau Traité de droit international privé (1876)
Brunner, H., Sources of the Law of England; an Historical Introduction to the Study of English Law. Translated by W. Hastie (1888)
Bustamante y Sirven, A. S. de, Projet de Code de droit international privé (1925)
——, Code of Private International Law. English Translation in International Conferences of American States, 1889–1928 (1931) pp. 327–370
Buzzati, G. C., Trattato di diritto internazionale private secondo le Convenzioni dell' Aja. Vol. I. (1907)
Cardozo, B. N., The Paradoxes of Legal Science (1930)
Cheshire, G. C., Private International Law (1935)

Clunet, E., Journal de droit international privé. 1874–1922. Continued by André-Prudhomme. 1923–
Cooley, T. M., A Treatise on the Law of Torts, or the Wrongs which arise independently of Contracts. 3 vols. (1932)
Dernburg, H., Das bürgerliche Recht des Deutschen Reichs und Preussens (1902)
Dicey, A. V., A Digest of the Law of England with reference to the Conflict of Laws. 5th ed. by A. B. Keith (1932). The first edition of this work was published in 1896 with notes of American cases by John Bassett Moore.
Dickinson, J., Administrative Justice and the Supremacy of Law in the United States.
Digby, K. E., An Introduction to the History of the Law of Real Property. 4th ed. (1892)
Diena, G., Principi di diritto internazionale. 2 vols. (1914–1917) Vol. II: Diritto internazionale privato.
Fiore, P., Diritto internazionale privato. 4 vols. (1888–1903)
Flournoy, R. W., Jr., and Hudson, M. O., A Collection of Nationality Laws of Various Countries as contained in Constitutions, Statutes and Treaties (1929)
Foote, J. A., A Concise Treatise on Private International Law based on the Decisions in the English Courts. 5th ed. by H. H. L. Bellot (1925)
Goodrich, H. F., Handbook on the Conflict of Laws (1927)
Gray, J. C., The Nature and Sources of the Law (1900)
Grotius, H., De Jure Belli ac Pacis. Translated by F. W. Kelsey and others, with an Introduction by J. B. Scott. Series of Classics of International Law. 3 vols. (1925)
Haudek, W., Die Bedeutung des Parteiwillens im internationalen Privatrecht (1931)
Holland, T. E., The Elements of Jurisprudence, 11th ed. (1910)
Huebner, R., A History of Germanic Private Law. Translated by F. S. Philbrick. Continental Legal History Series (1918)
Hyde, C. C., International Law chiefly as interpreted and applied by the United States. 2 vols. (1922)
International Conferences of the American States, 1889–1928. Ed., J. B. Scott (1931)
Jenks, E., A Short History of English Law (1913)
Journal de Droit International Privé. See Clunet.
Kahn, F., Abhandlungen zum internationalen Privatrecht. 2 vols. (1928)
Kent, J., Commentaries on American Law. 4 vols. 14th ed. (1896)
Lainé, A., Introduction au Droit International Privé. 2 vols. (1888–1892)

Laurent, F., Le Droit Civil International. 8 vols. (1881)
Lewald, H., Das deutsche internationale Privatrecht (1931)
Livermore, S., Dissertations on the Questions which arise from the Contrariety of the Positive Laws of Different States and Nations. (1828)
Lorenzen, E. G., The Conflict of Laws relating to Bills and Notes (1919)
——, Cases on the Conflict of Laws, Selected from the Decisions of the English and American Courts. 3rd ed. (1932)
Maine, H. S., Ancient Law: in connection with the Early History of Society and its relation to Modern Ideas (1864)
Makarov, A. N., Das internationale Privatrecht der europäischen und aussereuropäishen Staaten. Part I. Die Quellen des internationalen Privatrechts (1929). In the series of Leske-Lowenfeld: Die Rechtsverfolgung im Internationalen Verkehr.
Melchior, F., Die Grundlagen des deutschen internationalen Privatrechts (1932).
Meili, F., International Civil and Commercial Law as founded upon Theory, Legislation and Practice. Translated and Supplemented with Additions of American and English Law by A. K. Kuhn (1905)
——, Internationales Civilprozessrecht (1906)
Meili, F., and Mamelok, A., Das internationale Privat- und Zivilprozessrecht auf Grund der Haager Konventionen (1911)
Minor, R. C., Conflict of Laws; or Private International Law (1901)
Miraglia, L., Comparative Legal Philosophy Applied to Legal Institutions. Translated by J. Lisle (1912). Modern Legal Philosophy Series.
Moore, J. B., A Digest of International Law. 8 vols. (1896)
Muirhead, J., Historical Introduction to the Private Law of Rome (2nd ed. 1899)
McNair, A. D., The Law of the Air (1932)
Niboyet, J. P., Manuel de Droit International Privé. 2nd ed. (1928)
Nussbaum, A., Deutsches Internationales Privatrecht (1932)
Phillimore, Sir R., Commentaries upon International Law, vol. iv: Private International Law or Comity. 3rd ed. (1889)
Phillipson, Coleman, The International Law and Custom of Ancient Greece and Rome. 2 vols. (1911)
Pillet, A., Traité pratique de droit international privé. 2 vols. (1923)
Pillet, A., and Niboyet, J. P., Manuel de droit international privé (1924)
Planiol, M., Traité élémentaire du Droit Civil. 3 vols. (3rd ed. 1905)
Restatement of the Law of Conflict of Laws as adopted and promulgated by the American Law Institute (1934)

——, New York Annotations prepared by E. E. Cheatham in co-operation with E. R. Finch and G. W. Murray (1935)
Revue de droit international et de législation comparée. 1869–
Rolin, A., Principes de droit international privé et appreciations aux diverses matières du Code civil. 3 vols. (1897)
Sanborn, F. R., The Origins of the Early English Maritime and Commercial Law (1930)
Savigny, F. C. von, Geschichte des römischen Rechts im Mittelalter. 7 vols. 2nd ed. 1834–1851.
——, System des heutigen-römischen Rechts (1849). Translated by W. Guthrie. 2nd ed. 1880.
Schnitzer, A. F., Handbuch des Internationalen Privatrechts, unter besonderer Berücksichtigung der Schweizerischen Gesetzgebung und Rechtsprechung (1937)
Sohm, R., The Institutes. A Textbook of the History and System of Roman Private Law. Translated by J. C. Ledlie. 2nd ed. 1901.
Story, J., Commentaries on the Conflict of Laws, Foreign and Domestic, in regard to Contracts, Rights, and Remedies, and especially in regard to Marriages, Divorces, Wills, Successions and Judgments. 8th ed. 1883.
Thompson, G. W., The Law of Wills. 2nd ed. (1936)
Udina, M., Droit international privé d'Italie (1930)
Valery, J., Manuel de Droit International Privé (1914)
Von Bar, L., Private International Law. Translated by G. R. Gillespie (1892)
Walker, G., Internationales Privatrecht (1924)
Weiss, André, Traité de droit international privé. 4 vols. (1892–1901) 2nd ed. 6 vols. (1907–1913)
——, Manuel de droit international privé (1925)
Westlake, J., A Treatise on Private International Law. 7th ed. by. N. Bentwich (1925)
Wharton, F., A Treatise on the Conflict of Laws, or Private International Law. 2 vols. 3rd ed. (1905)
Wigmore, J. H., The Anglo-American System of Evidence. 5 vols. (1923)
——, A Panorama of the World's Legal Systems. 3 vols. (1928)

# COMPARATIVE COMMENTARIES ON PRIVATE INTERNATIONAL LAW

## Chapter I

# HISTORICAL DEVELOPMENT

**Nomenclature.** Private International Law or The Conflict of Laws is that branch of legal science which seeks to determine the application of law when the administration of justice requires a choice between two or more systems of law. Objections have been raised to both the title "Private International Law" as well as to "The Conflict of Laws." However, both terms have now become too widely accepted to discard their use even in favor of some other term more scientifically accurate.[1]

**The Ancient World.** The obligation of determining the scope and application of laws confronted even the lawgivers and judges of tribes and peoples of the ancient world. Law was frequently considered to be of divine origin, with no clear line of demarcation between laws having to do with religious observance and those designed to regulate purely human relationships. And yet the peoples of the ancient world did not enforce the commandments of their own laws indiscriminately upon strangers within the gates. Grotius, always a scholarly commentator of the Scriptures, points out in his great work, *De Jure Belli ac*

[1] We have selected "Private International Law" as the principal title because of the obvious advantage, in a comparative work, of employing the term commonly accepted in most of the countries of the world. In the United States, the term most commonly used is "The Conflict of Laws," with the recognition of the term "Private International Law" as the alternative. Story adopted the former term doubtless through the subtitle used by Ulric Huber: *"De conflictu legum diversarum in diversis imperiis."* English writers, Phillimore, Foote, Westlake and Cheshire, use "Private International Law" without adding the alternative "Conflict of Laws." American writers, Wharton, Minor and Beale (in the preliminary volume of 1916), employ "Private International Law" as an alternative title. Among French writers, the term *Droit international privé* is employed as a comprehensive term, whereas *Conflits des lois* is commonly used as a subtitle to embrace the vast field of problems in which the possible application of foreign law is indicated for reasons other than the foreign status of a person or party. *Cf.* Pillet, *Traité pratique de droit int. privé* (1923), i, p. 7.

*Pacis,* that the Israelites did not consider all their laws to be equally applicable to sojourners or foreigners; and that only certain laws were considered to be of universal application.[2] The ancient Israelites distinguished two classes of aliens, the resident alien (*Ger Toshab*) and the sojourner or alien of passage (*Nochri*).[3]

The Egyptians often allowed foreign merchants to avail themselves of local judges of their own choice, and even of their own nationality, to regulate questions and settle differences arising out of mercantile transactions in accordance with their own foreign laws and customs.[4]

A special system of jurisdiction for aliens was developed in ancient Greece. The resident aliens (*Metoikoi*) were under the jurisdiction of special magistrates (*Zenodikai*) who tried civil suits in which such aliens were litigants. The principle of *lex loci contractus* was sometimes applied in settlements of conflicting claims due to differences of domicil or origin; at other times the defendant's domiciliary law was followed. The former principle seems to have been preferred. Frequently both jurisdiction and law were fixed by treaty.[5]

In the Roman world, the inhabitants of conquered territories were, in large measure, left in possession of their local institutions, laws and customs. Commerce was maintained on a wide scale among the various peoples of the Mediterranean basin, especially after the conquests of Lucullus. In the early days, down to the middle of the third century B.C., aliens had no legal capacity in the absence of a treaty of friendship between Rome and the nation of their origin. As commerce increased, the number of non-privileged aliens likewise multiplied. Beginning with 242 B.C., a special judge for aliens, a *praetor peregrinus,* was appointed, whose jurisdiction extended to disputes between aliens *inter sese* and between citizens and aliens. In his judicial capacity, he possessed unlimited authority for shaping and working out the law for transactions in which foreigners were interested.[6] The various edicts of the *praetor peregrinus* had the force of law and thus was developed the *jus gentium,* applicable to a special class of cases. This body of law was developed largely from foreign and pro-

[2] Bk. i, chap. 1, no. xvi, relying upon passages of both the Old and the New Testament and the classic commentators of both.

[3] Kassan, "Extraterritorial Jurisdiction in the Ancient World," in (1935) 29 Amer. Jour. of Int. Law 243.

[4] Coleman Phillipson, The International Law and Custom of Ancient Greece and Rome, (1911) i, p. 193.

[5] *Ibid.,* i, pp. 192–3, 200.

[6] Sohm, The Institutes (Ledlie's trans., 2nd ed., 1901) p. 80.

vincial sources and in the course of time exercised a powerful influence upon the *jus civile* itself.

The *jus gentium* of the Romans was not a system for solving conflicts of law. It was a special body of rules and customs applicable where alien litigants were involved. Its influence, however, extended further, and it soon became a vehicle by which the civil law itself could be reformed and liberalized. Its original function grew less important with the wider extension of Roman citizenship to the provinces. In the reign of Caracalla (A.D. 212–217) citizenship was extended to every inhabitant who was a member of a political community within the Empire. This development vastly reduced but did not entirely eliminate the field of probable conflicts.

The Justinian codes contain many passages in which a diversity of laws constitutes part of the problem to be solved. Roman jurisprudence developed rules for limiting the application of personal law in certain cases. In other cases the diversity grew out of differences between local customs rather than differences of personal status.[7] These local conflicts of law or of custom approach in some measure the problems of our own day, but the manner of their solution in the Roman world is still wrapped in obscurity. The reception of the Roman law in Europe caused certain of the Roman texts of the Justinian codes to be relied upon by those learned in the civil law, but the interpretation of the texts themselves became a source of dispute among judges and legal scholars for centuries.

**The Medieval Tribal Period.** When the northern European tribes succeeded in overrunning the western part of the Roman Empire, they did not attempt to impose their own laws upon the conquered territories. The reason for this is not far to seek. The laws of the conquerors were tribal in origin and the tribes had been migratory over a long period. A migratory group, of necessity, will carry with it the usages and customs common to the life of the tribe. The respect which it pays to the usages and customs of other tribes in dealing with the individuals with which it comes in contact is but another method of enforcing the application and the limits of its own law. Law thus becomes personal rather than territorial.

When the Goths, Burgundians, Franks and Lombards founded kingdoms in the countries formerly subject to the power of Rome, they continued the system under which they had formerly lived. Tribal custom remained the source of rights and obligations and adhered to

[7] Coleman Phillipson, (1911) p. 301.

the members of the tribe wherever they might go. Savigny informs us that the system did not originally include any duty of respect to the customs of the tribes of other individuals. This developed only after the various tribes were blended in more populous settlements. As kingdoms were set up, the internal condition of each then produced what could never have been brought about by any supposed benevolence toward foreigners. Curiously enough, recognition of the law of the vanquished Romans came before that of the other conquering Germanic tribes. But as one Germanic tribe succeeded another in establishing itself over a given territory, as for example, when the Franks succeeded the Lombards in Northern Italy, the recognition of personal law as such became an established institution. It was to this system that the well known statement of Bishop Agobardus referred when he said: "It often occurs that five men walking or sitting together are each under a different law." [8]

**The Statutes of the Italian Cities.** The rise of free municipal commonwealths in Italy from the tenth century onward brought a check to the system of personal laws. A very flourishing trade grew up between the cities after the wreck of the Roman civilization, for the regulation of which the rules of personal law, which dealt principally with family life, were ill adapted. Furthermore, the greater precision of the Roman law promulgated by Justinian in its codified form from the Byzantian center in the East, lent itself much more readily to the needs of the times. A gradual disappearance of the reign of race law then set in in favor of the Roman as the common law. The nobles were being attracted to city life. The cities enjoyed wide legislative autonomy. Their municipal laws, called *statuta,* differed materially one from another, and numerous conflicts of law arose between the various *statuta.* By the twelfth century, we find the whole people subject to Roman law, with the variants from that law contained in the statutes of the cities. Jurisdiction was based on domicil.

Here, for the first time, we are face to face with conflicts of law comparable to those of the modern world. For they arose, as now, from conflicts of positive law having a limited territorial application before courts of restricted territorial authority. Here was a new condition not envisaged by the Roman law of either the republican or the imperial era. As the known texts of the Roman law were the only sources acknowledged as common to all the cities, it was natural that the glossators of that law should seek some analogy from within, to

[8] See Savigny, *Geschichte des römischen Rechts im Mittelalter,* i, p. 115.

solve the conflicts which the variants from it, namely the statutes, were producing. This analogy they seemed to find in the relation of the citizen to the *peregrinus* in the Roman state. Westlake intimates that the glossators might have been able to develop such an analogy had they possessed the fragments of the pre-Justinian law in which the position of the citizen is marked so much more clearly than by anything in the Digest or the Code.[9]

It is difficult to see how the most detailed knowledge of the relative status of the Roman citizen and the *peregrinus* could change our opinion of the underlying cause for the differentiation. The intent of the Roman lawgiver was to create a *political* privilege whereas the conflicts of the Italian city-states arose from the assumption of an equality of *legislative* authority. This was never conceded to the provinces of the Roman world.

**The Trinitarian Doctrine and the Statutes.** Whatever the basis for the analogy, all agree that the text selected for determining the application of statutes could never have been adopted with a view to anything like the situation to which they were now to be applied. This text was the first law of the Code by which Gratian, Valentinian and Theodosius enjoined upon "the peoples joined together" under the imperial authority, to profess the Trinitarian doctrine.[10]

As the religious dogma accepted by the ruler did not extend beyond the peoples subject to his rule, it was concluded by the commentator that the application of all positive laws was likewise determined by political subjection. Accordingly, the Justinian codes were interpreted as applicable only to the parts of the empire in which the Trinitarian doctrine had been accepted. The scope of application of the Roman law was thus limited by the words *"cunctos populos quos."* Later jurists, especially from the time of Bartolus (1314–1355), continued to discuss the local application of the laws in connection with this *lex* of the Code and it thus became the focal point of that branch of the legal science of the times known as the "statutory theory," or the "theory of the conflict of statutes." It must be remembered that the term "statute" was applied to all positive laws of the cities, whether derived from usages and custom or from direct executive or legislative enactment. The authority of the *lex* not only limited the application of

[9] Westlake, Private International Law, 7th ed., (1925) p. 11.

[10] *Lex 1, C., de summa trinitate et fide catholica et ut nemo de ea publice contendere audeat; 1, 1: "Cunctos populos quos clementiae nostrae regit imperium in tali volumus religione versari quam divinum Petrum apostolum tradidisse Romanis."*

the Roman law to cities in which the Roman imperial authority was accepted, but also gave a local application to the laws of the cities when in conflict *inter sese*.

**The Effect of the Feudal System.** It can readily be seen that even with the most minute analysis, the *lex* gave no clue to the solution of conflict. At most, it was the source of legal reasoning with reference to such conflicts; but in order to understand the trend of doctrine it is necessary to take account of what had been happening north of the Alps, in the principalities and kingdoms in process of consolidation in England, France and Germany. As the Frankish kings demanded an oath of allegiance from those who occupied land under their authority, the great landlords and municipalities in turn demanded it of their own tenants. The relationship of service, proceeding out of the personal obligation of military service, was later (about the tenth century) applied in a more general way to private rights. Expressed more definitely, subordinance to the law of the overlord was presumed from residence within his territory. Speaking of the later Carlovingian period, Huebner says that the principle of personal (or race) law gradually disappeared and the territorial principle took its place in ever increasing degree. "A man was no longer born into the law of his forefathers, but into the law of his home." [11] Territorial law laid hold of legal relationships within a given territory and as the great provinces split up into increasingly small and numerous districts, every court followed the legal customs of its particular district. The feudal basis of law was summed up in the doctrine *omnes consuetudines sunt reales* and thus codification of provincial laws such as by the Book of Customs of the various provinces in France, and the "Mirrors" of the Saxons (Sachsenspiegel, 1215–1235) and Suabians (Schwabenspiegel, 1273–1276) in Germany, accentuated the overthrow of what Sir Henry Maine called "tribe sovereignty" in favor of the territorial application of law.[12]

With the multiplication of fiefs and municipalities and the lack of any strong central control in Italy, in southern France, or northern Spain, a need for modification of the strictly territorial application of law became imperative. This the jurists supplied by the application of "principles of justice to be determined by reasoning," while at the same time citing numerous irrelevant texts from the Digest and Code

[11] Huebner, A History of Germanic Private Law, (Philbrick's trans., 1918, Continental Legal History Series) p. 3.

[12] *Cf.* Brissaud, History of French Public Law (Garner's trans., 1915), §210.

and basing the whole framework on the Law *"cunctos populos quos."* [13] Laurent appropriately exclaims: "What relation is there between an incomprehensible dogma and a question of jurisprudence and what connection is there between the words *'cunctos populos quos'* and the statutes?" [14]

We may say that there were two competing theories in the territories formerly within the old Western Empire. One sought to apply the law of the particular jurisdiction to every controversy determined within it, the other to apply even an external system, if the demands of justice and the particular nature of the transaction so required. It is to the triumph of the latter principle that we owe the development of a true science of the conflict of laws. Legal treatises or comments on particular texts began to make their appearance from this period onward through the activities of scholars in the law schools and universities of France and Italy. Among the most famous of these commentators, or "post-glossators," were Bartolus (1314–1355) and Baldus (1327–1400).

**Bartolus.** Bartolus was not the first but certainly the most distinguished of the so-called post-glossators who sought to develop a true science of the application of law. Phillimore speaks of his work as "the fountain of private international jurisprudence. Without a careful study of this commentary, nobody can be thoroughly versed in the history of the progress of the principles of private international law." [15] In his work entitled, *"In primam codicis partem commentaria,"* Bartolus attacked the problem under two heads which, in great measure, he kept separate, *viz.,* (1) whether a particular statute applied to non-subjects outside the territory of the jurisdiction; (2) what effect a statute may have beyond the territory of the jurisdiction. Under the first heading he maintained that the capacity of persons was not dependent on the law of the place in which an obligation was entered into. We have already pointed out that the jurists of this period frequently sought in sections of the Justinian codes, authority for propositions only tenuously analogous. In this way Bartolus relied

[13] Westlake, (1925) pp. 15–17; Lainé in Clunet, 1886, pp. 149–154.

[14] Laurent, *Droit Civil International* (1881) i, p. 633; Phillimore, Commentaries upon Int. Law (1889) iv, p. 19n., remarks: "Who would have expected such a treatise in a gloss on the words *'cunctos populos quos'* in a chapter *De summa trinitate?"*

[15] Phillimore, Commentaries, (1899) iv, p. 19. *Cf.* also Lainé, *Introduction au droit int. privé,* i, p. 128. Meili in *Zeitschift für int. Privat. u. Strafrecht,* iv, 258, 340; ix, 24.

upon the law of the Digest restricting the right of a provincial president to appoint tutors only for persons domiciled within the province.[16] Similarly Bartolus developed the rule that contracts are governed as to their effects by the law of the place of contracting; that the form is governed by the law of the place of the transaction; that the law of the forum determines whether a cause of action is barred by limitation, but if a particular place of performance has been indicated, the law of that place must decide; that the *lex sitae* determines the transfer of property.[17]

Under the second heading, Bartolus made the test of the extraterritorial effect of a law depend upon whether or not it was ordained *for the benefit of* the person upon whom it operated. Thus, the incapacity of a minor created in one city-state should continue even beyond the territory because created for his benefit (*statutum favorabile*). But the incapacity of a woman to inherit should not apply to property outside the jurisdiction because this is a statute created against her interest (*statutum odiosum*). Where the deceased, a subject of an Italian city, left property in England, the English law of primogeniture was, according to Bartolus, dependent upon whether the law provided: "the first-born shall succeed" or whether it provided: "immovables fall to the first-born."

**The Statutory Theory.** Originally the *statuta* had a significance not very different from statute law of today used in contradistinction to the common or unwritten law. The enactment of local statutes by the Italian municipalities in the twelfth and thirteenth centuries compelled the judges to decide whether to apply Roman (*i.e.*, the common) law, or the statutes, to citizens not of local allegiance. Originally conflicts arose only as between the interpretations given in the various municipalities to the Roman law. This was a conflict of *consuetudines* or customs, similar to the conflicts which exist today between various English and American jurisdictions in their interpretation of the unwritten English common law. With the increase of local statutes, the importance of the "customs" diminished, so that eventually the jurists of the period gave their attention only to the conflict of statutes. To resolve these conflicts, resort was had again to the Justinian texts which were not at all appropriate for giving a solution in questions of conflict between the laws of two independent municipalities. Thus it was that unconsciously the jurists arrived at conclusions which the-

[16] Lainé in Clunet, 1886, p. 158.

[17] Bartolus on the *Lex "cunctos populos,"* Nos. 16, 27, 29, 32.

oretically reproduced or extended Roman rules, while in reality they were following their own judgment in adapting Roman principles to the needs of their times. It is for this reason that a large part of these rules, though formulated under the theory of the statutes, maintained their authority long after the Roman law as such had ceased to remain in force.[18]

**The Successors of Bartolus.** During the succeeding two centuries the science did not greatly advance because the method remained unchanged. The attempt to formulate new rules in the old moulds became increasingly difficult. One of the primal Roman principles of succession, for example, was to dispose of the estate of the deceased as a unit, irrespective of the situation of the property of which it was composed. In order to retain this unity various devices were set up. Baldus (1327–1400) insisted upon the application of personal law to testamentary succession. Rosate (died 1354) and Saliceto (1363–1412), through various interpretations, came to the conclusion that all succession should be governed by the law of origin of the deceased, thus anticipating the modern Italian school of Mancini.[19]

Many of these devices lead to involved scholastic interpretations. It is obviously impossible to determine whether a given statute dealing with the rights of persons in property is more concerned with persons or with things. Again, the "favorable" character of a law is largely dependent upon insignificant differences of terminology. It is therefore not purposeful to follow the variances given to the statutory theory by the Italian successors of Bartolus.

**Dumoulin.** A new approach to the problem was presented by the discussions of Charles Dumoulin (Molinaeus), a French advocate and teacher (1500–1566). Westlake refers to him as "one of the greatest legal geniuses who have worked on it," [20] while Meili views him as "an internationalist of modern character." [21] Dumoulin gave much weight to the intent of the parties in determining the application of laws. It is true, he continued to discuss the subject by way of commentary to the Law *"cunctos populos"* but, in his celebrated *Consilium 53,* he broke new ground. Where a marriage is celebrated in a certain state without express contract regulating property relations, the husband being domiciled there, the particular regime of property relations which

[18] Meijers, *Académie de Droit Int., Recueil des Cours,* 1934, iii, pp. 592–593.
[19] *Ibid.,* p. 610.
[20] Westlake (1925) p. 17.
[21] Meili (Kuhn's trans.) p. 74.

the law there recognizes was held by Dumoulin to apply even to property situated abroad. In other words, the provisions of the local law were given extraterritorial effect through tacit consent of the parties. Dumoulin applied similar principles to certain kinds of contracts, especially sales of personal property. On the other hand he recognized that certain statutes did not depend for their effect upon the will of the parties, but only upon the power of the law. In this way he arrived at a local application of laws affecting personal capacity.[22]

These doctrines exerted a notable influence even down to modern times. In France private international law relating to matrimonial property is still influenced by the theory of tacit consent. The doctrine of the autonomy of the parties in ordinary contracts has long been recognized in England and the United States, and only recently has it been seriously questioned.

**D'Argentré.** The Italian doctrines in the form adopted in France by Dumoulin received a setback through the vigorous opposition of a contemporary French authority, D'Argentré (Argentraeus), a renowned historian and jurist of Brittany (died 1590). True to the ancient tradition of this principality, D'Argentré warmly supported the autonomy of the provinces. He took direct issue with the earlier Italian authors, especially Bartolus, and by way of reproach, referred to others as "scholastic." Out of their "false principles" came "still falser consequences." D'Argentré insisted upon the supreme authority of the territory over all who enter into legal transactions within its boundaries. The sway of personal law was recognized only by way of exception. This led to a recognition of the *lex rei sitae* for the modes of acquiring, transferring and asserting ownership to property.[23]

A similar clash between the doctrines of Dumoulin and D'Argentré is to be noticed with respect to the dotal system to be applied to foreign immovables where there has been no matrimonial contract. Dumoulin maintained that the law of the matrimonial domicil should apply everywhere, because of the implied consent of the parties.[24] D'Argentré preferred the law of the situs.[25]

We refer to this clash of opinion not only for historical reasons but also to emphasize the source of much of the difference of doctrine and

[22] *Ibid.*, p. 75.

[23] See Story, Conflict of Laws, §371a.

[24] *Commentarii ad Cod., lib.* 1, *tit.* 1, (1); see Story, §450.

[25] *Commentarii ad Briton. Leg.*, Art. 218, Gloss 6, No. 46 of the Coûtumes of Brittany; Story, §451.

legislation existing between various jurisdictions even at the present time. It must not be forgotten that the doctrines of D'Argentré were the result of his political views in the interest of the provincial rights of Brittany which survived the feudal system. But these rights were destined soon to disappear. As Meili expresses it: "Territorial independence was approaching its end, and the reign of Louis XIV was in sight."

**The Netherlands School.** In the Netherlands, the insistence upon the authority of the territorial law over transactions taking place within the territory or concerning property located there, received new impetus in the seventeenth century. Meili asserts that the political situation of the Netherlands at this period was as though especially prepared for the reception of the doctrines of D'Argentré.[26] International intercourse was increasing. The independence of the United Netherlands did not greatly disturb the independence of their separate provinces. It is not surprising therefore that the Netherlands writers of this period derived their solutions through reference to the public law of their provinces, which they deemed to be sovereign. Even Grotius makes reference to the significance of sovereignty in regard to civil transactions. In discussing the effect of the acts of minors and wards he remarks that while determined by municipal laws and not by the law of nature or of nations, yet if a foreigner (presumably a minor) makes an agreement with a citizen in the local state, "he will be bound by the laws of the latter's country, for the reason that a person who makes a contract in any place is under the law of the place as a temporary subject."[27]

**Huber and J. Voet.** The doctrines of Ulric Huber (1636–1694) and of John Voet (1647–1714) were particularly characteristic of the Netherlands school. These authors viewed the conflict of laws as a collision between statutes or customs of equal authority although not of equal value or applicability. Both writers exercised very great influence upon the development of the law in England and the United States because of the weight and authority given them by Story. Huber was of Swiss descent. He had the advantage of both academic training and practical experience, having been Professor at the University of Franeker and also Senator of the Supreme Court of Frisia. The clearness and brevity with which Huber presented his views gave

[26] *Op. cit.*, p. 76.

[27] Grotius, *De Jure Belli ac Pacis,* (Classics of International Law, Trans., Kelsey and others) Bk. ii, chap. xi, no. v.

to his work a notable advantage in extending its influence abroad. In a short treatise entitled, *De conflictu legum diversarum in diversis imperiis,* constituting Part II of his *Praelectiones juris Romani et hodierni,* he advanced the following principles: The laws of a state have no force outside of the territory of that state but are good there for all persons found within it. The strictness of this axiom is only modified by the friendly intercourse existing among different states and the *comitas* which they observe. In consequence, the application of foreign laws is permitted in so far as it is not repugnant to the sovereign power or the rights of its subjects. It is obvious, however, that these rules, neat as they may seem, do not supply solutions for individual problems and Huber himself did not apply them strictly, for he favored the domiciliary law to determine the status or quality of the person, even where the domicil was foreign.

In this respect John Voet (1647–1714) supported a more logical adherence to the idea of exclusive sovereignty. According to his views, no foreign domiciliary law can be permitted to vary the capacity of a person as determined by local statute or custom, though, by way of exception, Voet maintained that the transfer of movables is determined by the laws of the owner's domicil.[28]

**French School of the XVIII Century.** The doctrines of the Netherlands jurists had strong repercussions in France and elsewhere on the Continent. Jurists, such as Froland (died 1746), Bouhier (1673–1746) and Boullenois (1680–1762), although holding to the theory of statutes, were yet induced to vary the old applications because of two influences, both perhaps traceable to ideas received from the north. These were (1) that certain laws were intended to apply only within the local state and (2) that the various countries should grant concessions as a matter of self-interest in the application of each other's laws. The statutory theory had entered a new phase, which was reflected by the fragmentary rules contained in the French Civil Code. Art. 3 provides:

> Laws of police and public order are binding upon all persons within the territory.
>
> Immovables, even though possessed by aliens, are governed by French law.
>
> Laws relating to the status and capacity of persons apply to French persons, even though in a foreign country.

[28] Lainé considered John Voet to be the true founder of the Netherlands school. *Introduction au droit int. privé,* ii, (1892) pp. 99, 172, 388.

**German School of Natural Law.** The next progressive step must be sought east of the Rhine. Political antipathies seem to have had their influence in the development of opposition to the Napoleonic codifiers. However, leaving this consideration aside, German jurists of the first half of the nineteenth century earnestly rebelled against the formalism of the statutory theory and sought to establish rules of conflict on the basis of justice and natural law. At first this progress was made unconsciously, as in the discussions of Wächter. This author maintained that in the case of conflicts, the court must first determine whether the positive law of the forum contains a rule of application; if no positive law is to be found, the court must examine "the spirit and tendency" of local laws to determine whether a foreign system of law may be applied.[29] To this Meili makes the following appropriate comment:[30] "The substantive law which shall be applied to an international dispute is not to be determined through the spirit and tendency of the domestic private law, but through the spirit and tendency of the domestic rules of conflict." When the judge is in doubt, Wächter favored the application of the *lex fori.*

Thöl[31] represents a slight variant of doctrine. Primarily the *lex fori* is applicable; but the court should examine all the competing systems in the particular issue to determine whether they do not yield *inter sese.*

**Savigny.** The commanding figure of Friedrich Carl von Savigny, significant in so many fields of history and jurisprudence, represented a new approach to problems of private international law. Opposed as he was to the *a priori* method and applying new thought to old problems, he worked out new formulae also for the choice of law. This he did in the sequence which is his *System des heutigen römischen Rechts,* published between 1840 and 1849. In the eighth and final volume[32] he assumes the existence of an international community of law which tends toward wider recognition under the influence of a common Christian morality and because of the real advantage which is derived by all concerned.[33] If there are conflicts,

[29] Wächter, *"Ueber die Collision der Privatgesetze"* in *Archiv für civilistische Praxis.* (1841) vol. xxiv, pp. 239–240, 261–262.

[30] Meili, *op. cit.,* p. 91.

[31] Thöl, *Einleitung in das deutsche Privatrecht* (1851), pp. 168–190.

[32] Translated by William Guthrie, a Scotch advocate, under the title: A Treatise on the Conflict of Laws and the Limits of Their Operation in Respect of Time and Space. (1869; 2nd ed. 1880.)

[33] *Ibid.,* 2nd ed., p. 70.

it is necessary to determine the law of the jurisdiction to which the issue properly belongs, or to which it is subject according to its peculiar nature. Savigny recognized four possible points to be taken into consideration in order to determine the "natural seat" of an issue, *viz.*, (1) the domicil of persons; (2) the place where the thing is situated in respect to which interests are to be determined; (3) the place where an act-in-the-law occurs or ought to occur; (4) the seat of the court which will decide the issue which results from the particular legal relationship in question. From among these elements it is necessary to choose which is the most intimately bound up with the legal relationship in question. To these rules must be added the exception that where the issue is controlled by a law of a coercive character or where the rules would otherwise lead to the application of legal concepts not recognized in the local state, the law of the local state must prevail.[34]

A distinguished countryman of Savigny rightly points out that the Achilles' heel of the doctrine consists in the exceptions which place the community of law at the mercy of any state which decides to adopt legislation of a nationalistic trend.[35]

Savigny's doctrines influenced both the theory and the legislation of the German states as well as of other Continental jurisdictions. His principal disciple, Von Bar, was a fervent partisan of the theory of the seat of legal transactions, relying more than his master, however, upon the idea of natural law. As a result, Von Bar deduces an obligation in the law of nations to limit national legislation to a certain degree, so that natural law may operate. Dr. Simons remarks that Von Bar did not succeed in answering the question in detail as to the limits which may properly be placed upon national legislation in this respect. He contented himself with having formulated the problem.[36]

**Mancini.** The development of private international law received a new impetus in the middle of the nineteenth century through the doctrines of Pasquale Mancini. Through his insistence upon the application of national law in the determination of personal and family relations of Italians abroad and of aliens in Italy, he became the founder of the modern Italian school. After having taken refuge

[34] *Ibid.*, p. 77.
[35] W. Simons, (formerly President of the *Reichsgericht*), *Académie de Droit Int., Recueil des Cours,* 1926, vol. 5, p. 468.
[36] *Ibid.*, p. 469.

in Piedmont from the political measures of the Bourbons in Naples, he was appointed professor of the first chair of international law at the University of Turin. In his inaugural address on January 22, 1851, he insisted that nationality was or ought to be the focal point for determining individual rights and obligations, not only in the law of nations, but also in private international law.

Mancini's doctrines were announced before Italy had won her independence or established unity. It is not surprising therefore that the idea of the personality of law as determined by political allegiance should have taken on an almost religious significance. Mancini maintained that "Climate, temperature, geographic situation, whether mountainous or maritime, the nature and fertility of the soil, the diversity of needs and morals determine almost inevitably among all peoples the system of their legal rights and obligations." [37]

When Italy had established her independence, the Italian parliament undertook a national codification of civil law and procedure. Mancini became a member of the legislative commission. The draft submitted by him substantially incorporated his principles on the application of law and they were finally adopted with certain modifications as part of the *Disposizioni,* or preliminary title of the Civil Code of 1865.

**The School of National Law.** In 1874 Mancini presented a report to the Institute of International Law at its Geneva session which best illustrates the foundations underlying his doctrines.[38] While he accepted Savigny's theory of an international community of law, Mancini tempered the undenied power of sovereign states with the duty not to enact laws which are unjust and injure the community of law. This is a veritable international *duty* and not a mere *regard* growing out of good will. He pointed out the difficulty of discovering the seat of obligations under Savigny's theory and substituted for it a compromise between individual liberty and the exercise of the social power of the state. Upon this is based the application of national law to personal status, the regulation of family relations, intestate succession and the intrinsic requisites for testamentary dispositions. On the other hand, liberty is granted to

[37] Mancini, quoted by the Belgian jurist Laurent in *Droit Civil Int.,* (1881) i, p. 633. Laurent dedicated his eight-volume treatise to Mancini and was one of his most devoted followers.

[38] *Cf.* Diena, *Académie de Droit Int., Recueil des Cours,* 1927, ii, pp. 350–360.

the individual in the application of law in matters of property rights and contracts.

We shall see that the *lex patriae* or national law is the governing principle in the field of personal and family law in many civil-law countries. It has been widely adopted in some of the modern codifications such as in the Spanish Civil Code of 1889, the Japanese Statute of 1898, the German Introductory Statute of 1900 and the Polish Statute of August 2, 1926.

**Development in England.** England did not participate in the struggle between territorial sovereignty and personal law. Her geographic isolation caused a divergence of historical experience. Frequent warfare with the countries of continental Europe resulted in practical non-intercourse over centuries. Overseas possessions were not regarded as integral parts of the kingdom. Moreover, the Norman conquest was final and complete and was followed, first by a strong kingship, later by a parliament with real legislative powers. Though there was some need for adjustment between Anglo-Saxon and Norman customs, the two systems rapidly blended, as did also the two races themselves. The *curia regis* early developed "unexampled centralization of the administration of law." [39] All these elements united to constitute a uniform system of law, powerfully territorial and exclusive, without the slightest demand for that finesse of logic required by jurists in France, Germany, Italy and the Netherlands in solving the conflicts of statutes and customs.

Of course, conflicts must have occurred even in England. We know that they did occur, but so infrequently that they were disregarded in the ruthless application of the territorial principle. We are astounded as we read in the ancient Year Books, of a case decided in 1308, wherein a writ of debt was brought upon a document drawn and executed at Berwick in Scotland. And the court said, with greater simplicity than justice: "because it [the instrument] was made at Berwick, where this court has not cognizance, it was awarded that John took nothing by his writ." [40]

The maintenance of any foreign commerce whatever under such extreme territorialism would have been difficult indeed had it not been for the existence of a law merchant, and special commercial courts and jurisdiction to which foreign merchants could appeal during the three centuries preceding the English Revolution. "Some-

[39] Brunner-Hastie, Sources of the Law of England, pp. 12–13.
[40] Year Book, 2 Edward II; Selden Society Publications, i, p. 111.

times they came before the specially erected courts of the Staple; and sometimes they sought speedy redress from the Chancellor or the Council . . .; but seldom, if at all, did they come before the local courts, which were thus deprived of the most important and most progressive source of business." [41] It is a mistake to believe that the English common law was developing in a manner fundamentally different from the law of the Continent. The historian emphasizes that "the general similarity of the English institutions to those of the Continent is striking and fundamental, and renders a careful study of the latter necessary in order not only to grasp the essential meaning and import of the former, but also to place the English law in its proper perspective amidst a great international setting of European commercial law, of which it formed a part." [42]

When jurists of continental Europe or Latin America speak of territorial law in connection with the choice of law, they refer to something quite different from the territorial law of common-law jurisdictions. It is, therefore, necessary to clarify this ambiguity. Dicey points out that when we speak of the law of a given country it may mean every rule enforced by the courts of that country. It may also mean that part of the rules enforced by the courts of a given country excluding rules for the choice of law. It is said that every case which comes before an English court must be decided in accordance with the law of England. But the law of England, or of any other country, includes also its rules or directions for the choice of law. If a certain transaction is properly governed by French law in an English court, and the judge actually applies French law, it is because English law wills it so.[43] To mark the distinction from the entire law of England (including rules for the choice of law) the English lawyer often uses the term "territorial law of England" in order to indicate the exclusion of rules for the choice of law. Territorial law in this sense applies to transactions without any foreign element, *i.e.*, cases in which no foreigner is a party, or which are not connected with any transaction taking place wholly or in part beyond the limits of the jurisdiction.[44] Continental-European and Latin-American jurists use the term "territorial law" to indicate a choice of law in favor of the local law in a case in which there is

[41] Sanborn, Origins of the Early English Maritime and Commercial Law (An American Historical Assoc. Publication, 1930) p. 347.

[42] *Ibid.*, p. 399.

[43] *Cf.* Dicey, Conflict of Laws, (1932) pp. 2–4.

[44] *Ibid.*, p. 3.

some foreign element. In other words, the term "territorial" is used by them in contradistinction to such terms as "domiciliary law" or "national law" or "law of the place of contracting."[45]

**Early Development in the United States.** Problems arising out of the conflict of laws assumed great importance in the United States almost from the beginning because the Constitution created a Federal or central government of delegated powers. All powers not enumerated are therefore reserved to the separate states. The Tenth Amendment ratified in 1790 specifically declared that: "The powers not delegated to the United States by the Constitution, nor prohibited by it to the States, are reserved to the States respectively, or to the people."

The States surrendered their sovereignty only with respect to their public relations with other nations and to the restricted number of other matters named in the Constitution. In all other matters they remained sovereign, having exclusive jurisdiction over persons and things within their several territories and over the subject matter of law and legislation upon private relations in general. The Constitution at the same time decreed the greatest freedom of commerce between the States by prohibiting any tax or duty on articles exported from any State or any preference by any regulation of commerce or revenue to the ports of one State over those of another.[46] Conflicts of law and jurisdiction were therefore inevitable between the several States, as well as between state law and federal law and between States of the Union and foreign countries.

**Livermore.** These considerations weighed with the earliest writers in the United States to endeavor to create a system which might make the administration of justice work smoothly under the new federal system. The first writer to undertake the task was Samuel Livermore (1786–1833), a distinguished advocate of New Orleans, where the Roman law as derived from Spanish and French sources was, to a very great degree, retained in 1812 when Louisiana was admitted as a State. Accordingly, as might have been expected, Livermore was deeply influenced by the doctrines of French and other European writers. His book[47] follows the old statutory theory in seeking the determination of the category to which any particular

[45] *Cf.* Meili (Kuhn's trans.) §§19, 37, 47. Bustamante, *Projet de Code de droit int. privé* (1925) p. 37.

[46] Constitution, Art. I, par. ix (5).

[47] Dissertations on the Questions which arise from the Contrariety of the Positive Laws of Different States and Nations. New Orleans 1828.

foreign law belongs. Doubtless these doctrines had acquired some measure of acceptance by the courts of Louisiana through French precedents of the eighteenth century. But as has been well said: "His doctrines could not be applied in a country where both commercial and social intercourse between all parts of it are constant and continuous." [48] Curiously enough, the influence of Livermore's writings has almost entirely disappeared and his work is seldom referred to by the courts or by modern authors. We shall see later that some of his comments are most clarifying and might well be studied as a corrective of errors due to extreme applications of the territorial principle.

**Chancellor Kent.** While Livermore was the earliest American author to treat the subject as a complete system, others had already considered conflicts of law in the particular cases which occupied their attention. James Kent, Chancellor of the State of New York, in his celebrated "Commentaries on American Law," published 1826–1830, dealt with the conflict of laws and jurisdictions in connection with foreign suits and judgments, marriage and divorce, minority, succession and bankruptcy. He remarked that such problems were almost unknown in the English courts prior to the time of Lord Hardwicke (1690–1764) and Lord Mansfield (1705–1793). When the courts in the first half of the eighteenth century were confronted with conflicts of law, the work to which their attention was drawn was the brief tract in Huber entitled *"De Conflictu Legum"* in his voluminous Prelections on the Roman law. Kent observed that the main discussion in continental European countries centered about the division of laws, written or unwritten, into personal statutes and real statutes. To an American lawyer, then as now, a "statute" is an express act of legislature. Kent drew attention to this difference and protested against allowing a perversion of terms to be introduced into American jurisprudence. He observed moreover that Continental jurists had found it difficult to draw "a clear, precise and practical line of distinction, and one worthy of insertion in the code of international jurisprudence, between the real and personal statutes." [49] Indeed he found the discussions of the civil law jurists "involved in perplexity and confusion." Where Livermore had followed the old method of the statutory theory, Kent refused to consider it authoritative for Ameri-

[48] Beale, A Treatise on the Conflict of Laws, (1935) iii, p. 1911.
[49] Kent, Commentaries on American Law, iv, pp. 456–457 (14th ed. 1896).

can conditions and it is probably to him we owe the repudiation of conceptions which already had proved sterile on European soil. However, Kent accepted the views of the statutists at least to the extent of giving recognition everywhere to personal status. He said that as a personal quality, such as infancy, was fixed by the law of the domicil, it was to the interest of all nations mutually to respect and to sustain that law. The same applied to coverture, a civil relation of a universal nature.[50]

According to Kent's view, the conflict of laws forms a secondary branch of the law of nations, a view shared by some even to the present time.[51]

**Story.** In 1834, the year after Livermore's death, Joseph Story, a Justice of the United States Supreme Court and Professor of Law at Harvard University, published his Commentaries on the Conflict of Laws.[52] The enormous importance of the work of Story follows not only from his having occupied the bench of the Supreme Court in a formative period, but because of his great learning and the cogency of his arguments. He fashioned the law anew to the needs of the times. He called attention to the fact that the subject had never been systematically treated by writers on the common law of England and, like Chancellor Kent, was of the opinion that English lawyers seem generally to have been strangers to the discussions on the effect given to foreign law by the celebrated jurists of continental Europe.[53] Story, therefore, entered upon a most exhaustive review of the principles supported by Continental authors, after quoting their texts at great length under each of the classifications into which he divided his discussions. He then reviewed the English and American cases and concluded each topic with elucidations of his own, based upon the preponderance of authority, the demands of justice, convenience and domestic policy. The foreign authors most frequently relied upon by Story are the French writers, Bouhier, Boullenois, Merlin, and Pothier; the German author Hertius; and particularly the Netherlanders, Ulric Huber and the two Voets, Paul and John. Story expressed great respect for the writings of his

[50] Kent, *op. cit.*, ii, p. 419.

[51] See Ehrlich in *Rev. de dr. int. privé*, iv, (1908) 902; trans. in Beale (1935) iii, 1914–1915.

[52] Commentaries on the Conflict of Laws Foreign and Domestic, in regard to Contracts, Rights and Remedies, and especially in regard to Marriages, Divorces, Wills, Successions and Judgments. Boston, 1834.

[53] Story, §10n.

distinguished contemporary Chancellor Kent, but did not hesitate to dissent from his views, especially when opposing Kent's tendency to ascribe exaggerated importance to personal law.

**Later Writers.** The treatise of Francis Wharton,[54] which first appeared in 1872, was notable because of the attention given to the laws of various countries constituting the sources of particular conflicts. Wharton opposed the doctrine that comity is the basis for the application of foreign law.

The work of Raleigh C. Minor,[55] of the University of Virginia, is a well-reasoned treatise in which *situs* is regarded "the foundation and basic principle" for the application of law.

The Handbook of Herbert F. Goodrich of the University of Pennsylvania, published in 1927, gives a concise and logical statement of the American law with a careful analysis of many new problems that had reached the courts in the preceding two decades.

The recent treatise of Joseph H. Beale[56] of Harvard University, published in 1935, is an exhaustive work in the form of a commentary on the Restatement of the Law of Conflict of Laws promulgated by the American Law Institute. We shall have occasion to refer to the Restatement throughout the present work. Beale assumes to set forth "the positive common law of England and America,"[57] but it is difficult to understand the term "positive" except as referring to the various rules followed by courts in the so-called "common-law jurisdictions," diverse as these may be. The origin of any systematic formulation of law in this field in England did not precede the eighteenth century; even at that time, English judges were obliged to refer to Continental authors, as there were few precedents in the English law books. Story's work, which exercised the greatest influence in the formative period of the nineteenth century in both England and America, is practically a work of the comparative principles of private international law. He constantly refers to the discussions of authorities of various national origin, although there is no segregation of doctrine by countries.

[54] A Treatise on the Conflict of Laws, or Private International Law, including a Comparative View of Anglo-American, Roman, German and French Jurisprudence. Phila. 1872; 3rd ed. by Parmele, 1905.

[55] Conflict of Laws; or Private International Law. Boston, 1901.

[56] A Treatise on the Conflict of Laws, 3 vols., New York, 1935. An introductory portion appeared in 1916 under the title: "A Treatise on the Conflict of Laws or Private International Law." The completed work has omitted certain historical matter contained in the earlier publication.

[57] Beale (1935) i, p. 12.

In addition to these general treatises, there have been a number of works dealing with special fields, such as Lorenzen's excellent treatment of the conflict of laws relating to negotiable instruments,[58] to which must be added numerous monographs and articles by many others in legal periodicals, some of which will be referred to in the course of our discussions.

[58] E. G. Lorenzen, The Conflict of Laws relating to Bills and Notes, New Haven 1919.

## Chapter II

# GENERAL NATURE AND SCOPE

### 1. The Sanction of Private International Law

The problem presented by the conflict of sovereign jurisdictions in the application of law to private rights has provoked much thought as to the theoretical basis for applying any law but that of the forum. Does a conflict of law or jurisdiction affect the relations of the states whose laws have thus come into conflict? In other words, is private international law part of the law of nations? Beale in his preliminary work (1916) classified the theories upon this subject into three main groups which he called the statutory, the international and the territorial systems. The first of these (the statutory) supposes two independent laws effective at the same time and place, and subject to a possible choice. The second (the international) supposes a single set of principles, binding on all nations, by which the need of any choice between two independent nations is avoided. The third (the territorial) asserts that no law can have value as such, except the law of the land; but that it is a principle of every civilized society that vested rights be protected. Therefore each country should recognize rights wherever created and enforce them if in other respects not repugnant to the law of the land.[1]

While a classification thus expressed is valuable for the purpose of analysis, it must not be supposed that the three principles are necessarily exclusive. The statement may seem bizarre, but all three principles have been adopted for one purpose or another in the United States. The capacity of a person restricted at his domicil abroad, to do certain acts in the local state, inevitably requires a statutory choice.[2] So far as concerns our subject, viewed as an international system, Mr. Justice Gray, writing the majority opinion

[1] Beale, Conflict of Laws or Private International Law (1916), p. 63.
[2] Woodward *v.* Woodward, (1889) 87 Tenn. 644.

of the Supreme Court in Hilton *v.* Guyot, said: "International law, in its widest and most comprehensive sense—including not only questions of right between nations, governed by what has been appropriately called the 'law of nations,' but also questions arising under what is usually called 'private international law' or the 'conflict of laws,' and concerning the rights of persons within the territory and dominion of one nation, by reason of acts, private or public, done within the dominion of another nation—is part of our law, and must be ascertained and administered by the courts of justice as often as such questions are presented in litigation between man and man, duly submitted to their determination."[3] Justice Gray said that the most certain guide would be a treaty or a statute but in the absence of any such written law, a duty rests upon the judicial tribunals to determine the rights of the parties and obtain "such aid as they can from judicial decisions, from the works of jurists and commentators and from *the acts and usages of civilized nations*."[4] [Italics supplied.] When we say that the recognition of the supremacy of the territorial law is consistent with the view that there is an international system of law for solving conflicts of law, we mean that the territorial law includes *within itself* the duty of applying foreign law or local law, as the case may be, according to a system which is international in its principles, philosophy and purpose. It is the *ideal* which is international, not the source of the law by which this ideal is expressed, nor its sanction, both of which remain territorial. This is by no means a metaphysical conception. It is peculiarly well adapted for an unwritten and elastic system like the English common law. As Story has said: "The common law of both countries (England and the United States) has been expanded to meet the exigencies of the times, as they have arisen; and, so far as the practice of nations, or the '*jus gentium privatum*,' has been supposed to furnish any general principle, it has been followed out with a wise and manly liberality."[5]

With these considerations from the highest American sources, it seems unnecessary to become immersed in the otherwise interesting discussions of the various European schools of thought upon private international law. The fertile and thoughtful discussions of Pillet and Zittelmann, on the one hand, and Weiss, Laurent and Jitta, on the other, to mention only a few, have become known to American

[3] Hilton *v.* Guyot, (1895) 159 U.S. 113 at p. 163.
[4] *Ibid.*, citing decisions from Federal and State courts.
[5] Story, §24.

scholars, and are highly respected. But the contradictions in the results reached by them, would indicate that there is no agreement among jurists as to what such a single international system ought to be.

The basis of any legal system must ultimately rest upon the sanctions provided for its enforcement. We are on sure ground when we recognize that the sanction of private rights rests with the national tribunals, whether such rights are claims by foreigners or by citizens, and whether such rights arose abroad or entirely within the national state. This is inherent in the nature of territorial sovereignty. To this extent therefore, private international law results from sovereign functions as recognized by the general principles of international law. The extent to which the national state exercises this function is, as Story says, "a matter purely of municipal arrangement and policy." [6]

It is in the *content* of this arrangement and policy that an international system and method of solving conflicts may be found; not in the manner in which such conflicts arise or in the sanction by which their solution is enforced. It is only in this sense that we understand Pillet's statement: "All conflicts of law are conflicts of sovereignty." [7] Of course, the manner in which law is applied by one state to the rights or obligations of a citizen of another state may always give rise to a true international dispute. When the Permanent Court of International Justice consented to hear the claims of Mavrommatis against the British Government, it was because the Greek Government had adopted these essentially private rights as its own under Art. 26 of the Mandate for Palestine. In this connection the Court had occasion to say: "By taking up the case of one of its subjects and by resorting to diplomatic action or international judicial proceedings on his behalf, a State is in reality asserting its own rights—its right to ensure, in the person of its subjects, respect for the rules of international law. The question, therefore, whether the present dispute originates in an injury to a private interest, which in point of fact is the case in many international disputes, is irrelevant from this standpoint." [8]

It is upon this foundation that a right exists by one state against another state to claim that there has been a denial of justice as to the

[6] Story, §541.

[7] Pillet, *Traité Pratique de Droit Int. Privé*, (1923) i, p. 20.

[8] Publications of the Permanent Court of Int. Justice, Judgments, (1924) Series A, No. 2, p. 12.

private right of one of the citizens of the complaining state. It is a well known rule that when such denial has been made by the judicial tribunals of a state, resort must first be had to the court of final appeal; and even then, there is no cause for diplomatic intervention so long as civilized standards of justice have been maintained. A state is otherwise unfettered in its choice of the forms of procedure or in the adoption of a particular system of law.[9]

It follows therefore that the sanction of private international law lies not in the law of nations but in national law. Notwithstanding this, the national law may, and to a large extent in practice actually does regard private international law as a system which may some day tend to become internationally uniform. Even the law of nations has no superstate to enforce its decrees and is therefore no more law in the strict sense of Austin than is private international law, except in the aforementioned national sense. Aubry's sarcasm appears to be much too biting when he says: "In spite of the arbitrary or fantastic solutions which the conflicts of laws may have received, they have never provoked even the slightest frown upon the brow of a diplomat."[10] Especially do we not follow him where the violation of a well-recognized principle of private international law results in a conflict *of jurisdiction*. Although the sanction be national, the juridical principles are international and therefore tend toward, though they may in practice be far from, uniformity. The action of the American Law Institute in selecting the Conflict of Laws as one of the first subjects for a nation-wide Restatement, is evidence that this conception has gained recognition in the United States.

**How Part of the Common Law?** The principle reiterated by Beale that the Conflict of Laws is part of the common law is, of course, quite correct. We believe that his further statement is quite misleading, *viz.* that the principles of this subject "have grown up as a part of the common law and that the doctrines of foreign law have influenced them only as they have been considered by the authors of some of the treatises on the subject, notably Story and Westlake."[11] One would suppose there had been an indigenous body of English common law upon this subject, whereas one will search in vain in Bracton or Coke for the most elementary principles of

[9] Moore, Digest of International Law, (1906), ii, 88; Hyde, International Law chiefly as interpreted and applied by the United States, (1922) i, 386–387.

[10] Clunet, 1901, p. 651.

[11] Beale (1935) §5.1.

such a science. It was precisely because of the lack of prior authority that Story was obliged to seek foreign sources and the English courts, after his time, in turn to lean upon Story. The sanction of any dispute involving private rights remained then as now with the local courts. The law is the law of the forum, but the courts, then as now, recognize that these problems affect international intercourse. Beale's example of *renvoi* as "a doctrine foreign to the common law" and therefore eliminated by the courts within a comparatively short time is not fortunate. The doctrine has been repudiated by some American courts, and by the Restatement, not because it is foreign but because it is erroneous, besides being illogical and impractical. Even the Restatement has retained *renvoi* in regard to "all questions of title to land" and "all questions concerning the validity of a decree of divorce." In both cases, the governing law includes also its conflict-of-laws rules.[12] English courts still employ *renvoi* in a modified form to determine the status of an English person domiciled abroad.[13] So that the doctrine of *renvoi* cannot be said to be repugnant to common-law jurisprudence; nor is its origin as a subject of legal discussion to be considered essentially foreign.[14]

In contrast to what might well be called an "isolationist" view of the conflict of laws we refer to Beale's earlier view of the practical necessity for this branch of law. "International commerce created the necessity for some principle of law which should protect the interests and give effect to the undertakings of the foreigner. As foreign commerce has increased, this necessity has increased with it; and now that our whole manner of life is based upon exchange of products between nations, a body of legal principles to regulate international juridical relations is as supremely needed as a similar body of principles to give effect to ordinary contracts or protect ordinary property."[15]

The comparative method was adopted by Kent and Story because it was necessary in fields in which the English common law gave few if any precedents. As Dean Pound has so well pointed out, both Kent and Story made creative use of comparative law

[12] Restatement, §8.

[13] See *post*, pp. 51–52.

[14] See Pawley-Bate's enlightening monograph published in 1904, "Notes on the Doctrine of Renvoi." The correct view is indicated at p. 78. Keith (of Edinburgh) with much force refers to *renvoi* as "rather a misnomer." Am. Bar Assoc. Jour., 1935, p. 237.

[15] Beale, (1916) p. 5.

throughout our formative era. These authors paid particular respect to the rules of the Roman law as accepted in the modern Continental systems and in the writings of foreign jurists as declaratory of reason and yet substantially similar to those to be found in English decisions and law books. "We must not forget that reception of English law as the law of post-Revolutionary America was not a foregone conclusion: nor did it take place without some struggle. . . . Many would have rejected English law, which suffered from the odium then attaching to all things English, and would have received French law. Not the least of the means by which Kent and Story overcame these prejudices and made secure and permanent our reception of the English common law was a skillful use of comparative law. They strove to show and they made plausibly apparent the identity of an ideal form of the common-law rule on all the disputed points of the day with an ideal form of the rule to be found in the Roman texts or in the civilian treatises."[16]

## 2. The Doctrine of Comity

**Its Origin and Significance in the United States.** No discussion of the conception of private international law in the United States can leave out of account the theory of comity (*comitas gentium*) which we owe to jurists of the Netherlands. Writers and the courts are continually referring to it. What, therefore, is its precise significance?

One of the axioms of the law of nations respecting territorial sovereignty is that no law is effective *ex proprio vigore* outside the territory of the state. Story expressed it in a very trenchant manner by saying that if this were not true, "it would be equivalent to a declaration that the sovereignty over a territory was never exclusive in any nation, but only concurrent with that of all nations."[17] But this axiom is accompanied by, and we may also say that it is complicated by another axiom of the modern state, namely that of allegiance between the sovereign and the subject. Blackstone said that an Englishman owed allegiance in France and in China as well as at home, and distinguished natural allegiance from local allegiance.[18] Allegiance is a term used to denote the sum of the obliga-

[16] Roscoe Pound in Amer. Bar Assoc. Jour., (1936) p. 57.
[17] Story, §20.
[18] Commentaries on the Laws of England, Bk. I, ch. 10, pp. 369–370.

tions of a natural person to the state to which he belongs. The territorial sovereign may and frequently does assume to bind the person and the property of domiciled foreigners as well as nationals. Thus we have a clash between territorial sovereignty and personal allegiance.

It was not until after the English Revolution (1688) that any extensive mercantile relations were developed between England and the Continent of Europe. By this time the Netherlands were enjoying a commercial prestige which had stimulated the science and the practice of law in all its branches. Grotius, Rodenburg, the two Voets, Stockmans and Huber were known in England through the intimate political and commercial relations with the Low Countries. It is said that English and Scottish advocates attended universities in the Netherlands. As each of the states of the Low Countries was independent in regard to private legislation and was, indeed, jealous of the others, the doctrine of comity, derived from the public relations of states, seemed ideal to modify and temper the rigorous application of territorial law and to accord recognition to foreign law on local territory. The courtesy which each sovereign owes to every other was theoretically supposed to allow recognition of foreign law in proper cases provided no sovereign right was surrendered nor the rights of native subjects injured. Lainé has pointed out that the doctrine is so vague that the widest discretion must be left to the judge.[19] Yet the doctrine of comity as developed by Huber, because of its neatness and conciseness and its ready application to a federal system, gained Story's acceptance.[20]

Livermore, our earliest writer upon the subject, had already pointed out the correct view: "It having been at last conceded that foreign laws must be in some instances respected, it has been fashionable, in this country and in England, to impute this to the comity of nations; a phrase which is grating to the ear, when it proceeds from a court of justice. Comity between nations is to be exercised by those who administer the supreme power. The duty of judges is to administer justice according to law, and to decide between parties litigant according to their rights. When an action is brought upon a foreign contract, it is not from comity that they receive evidence of the laws

[19] Lainé in Clunet, 1896, p. 485.

[20] *Cf.* Beale, (1935) 1, p. 53. Even in England the "old woman's fable," as Lorimer pronounced it, often reappears. In Chancellor Halsbury's compendium, Laws of England (1909) vol. 6, p. 81, the application of foreign law, even in appropriate circumstances, is declared to be *ex gratia!*

of the country where such contract was made, but in order to ascertain in what manner and to what extent the parties have obligated themselves."[21]

Notwithstanding this remarkably clear presentation by a pioneer, the authority of Story fixed the concept of comity as part at least of the phraseology and ideology of private international law in the United States, and through Story, in England as well. However, although this result may be traced to the maxims of Huber, Story's adaptation was not a mere paraphrase of Huber, as Lainé claims;[22] because Story recognized "a sort of moral necessity to do justice, in order that justice may be done to us in return."[23] On the other hand, he completely ignored the fact that the local state does not resign any of its sovereign prerogatives, even voluntarily, in applying foreign law in a proper case, because the local system *includes* the application of the foreign system to an issue properly controlled by it. If comity and not the demands of justice were the basis of the application of law, there would be continued uncertainty concerning it. Later American authorities, especially Wharton, recognized this and remarked that "when a foreign law binds a particular case, then it becomes part of our common law, and the parties are entitled of right to have it applied."[24]

**Applied Comity.** The recurrence to comity in decisions of the courts sometimes produces strange results. As late as 1895, the Federal Supreme Court (four of the nine judges dissenting) introduced the prerequisite of reciprocity as a condition of executing a foreign judgment. Action was brought for the execution of a French money-judgment in a United States court. Because the law of France was understood to permit a French court to re-examine a foreign judgment upon the merits of the case (*au fond*), it was held that a French judgment would not be executed in the Federal tribunals of the United States except upon the same terms. The Supreme Court was "satisfied that the comity of our nation does not require us to give conclusive effect to the judgments of the courts of France" in the absence of reciprocity.[25]

Although this rule is undoubtedly binding for the Federal courts

[21] Livermore, pp. 26–28.
[22] Lainé in Clunet, 1896, p. 486.
[23] Story, §35.
[24] Wharton, 3rd ed., §1½.
[25] Hilton *v.* Guyot, (1895) 159 U.S. 113.

until reversed, it does not represent the prevailing rule of State courts. We refer to it here as an illustration of the results sometimes reached by a recurrence to the doctrine of comity, without the more wholesome limitations to which the idea has been subjected in practice. What we believe to be the correct view, and perhaps also the one which has the best current of opinion behind it, was expressed by Chief Justice Fuller in his dissenting opinion: "Now the rule is universal in this country that private rights acquired under the laws of foreign states will be respected and enforced in our courts unless contrary to the policy or prejudicial to the interests of the state where this is sought to be done; and although the source of this rule may have been the comity characterizing the intercourse between nations, it prevails today by its own strength, and *the right to the application of the law to which the particular transaction is subject is a juridical right.*" [26]

About thirty years after the decision in Hilton *v.* Guyot, an American firm sued the Compagnie Générale Transatlantique in the French courts for the loss of a shipment of merchandise to France during the World War, upon a bill of lading issued in New York, non-negotiable by its terms. The bill of lading was presented by a person not entitled to receive the goods, though one of the copies of the bill of lading was by some oversight sent to him endorsed in blank. The French court gave judgment for the defendant. When action was again brought in New York, the defendant set up the French judgment in defense, and the plaintiff relied upon Hilton *v.* Guyot. Judge (later Chief Judge) Pound said: "When the whole of the facts appear to have been inquired into by the French courts, judicially, honestly and with full jurisdiction, and with the intention to arrive at the right conclusion, and when they have heard the facts and come to a conclusion, it should no longer be open to the party invoking the foreign court against a resident of France to ask the American court to sit as a court of appeal from that which gave the judgment. I reach the conclusion that this court is not bound to follow the Hilton case and reverse its previous rulings." [27] Thus we have a reversion to the original common-law rule, which,

[26] Hilton *v.* Guyot, *ut cit.* Dissenting opinion at p. 233, (italics supplied).

[27] Johnston *v.* Compagnie Générale Transatlantique, (1926) 242 N.Y. 381, 387. (All concurred.) This ruling was again confirmed in an action brought in New York upon a money judgment obtained in Quebec. Cowans *v.* Ticonderoga Pulp & Paper Co., (1927) 219 N.Y.S. 284. Affd. (1927) 246 N.Y. 603.

in this respect, is much more liberal than the rules recognized in countries of the Continent of Europe for the execution of foreign judgments.[28]

About one hundred years ago, the Supreme Court was called upon to decide the power of a corporation of one State of the Union to enter into binding contracts in another. Although a corporation is a fictitious person deriving its powers from the law of its creation, it was decided that it could have extraterritorial existence by comity. The court adopted Story's doctrine but declared that it was the comity of the nation or state, not the comity of the courts, and must be ascertained by the same reasoning as other principles of municipal law.[29]

In a case involving the validity of a contract by a married woman, incapable according to the *lex loci contractus et domicilii* but good by the *lex solutionis,* it was held by the Supreme Court of Massachusetts that the contract was good on the ground of comity; but comity to be determined by fixed and consistent rules.[30]

Comity has therefore come to be more of a connotation than a principle. Perhaps comparison with another legal concept may be illuminating. Under French law, foreigners do not possess the civil rights of citizens; and yet their rights and privileges on the basis of natural rights have become well established in French jurisprudence. The term has come to possess a certain definite signification although the term "natural right" would of itself indicate only the theoretical origin of the right. So comity, vague and flexible though the term may be, refers to the theoretical origin of certain fixed principles which jurisprudence has developed. It does not of itself determine the rule of law. Thus understood, the doctrine of comity has undoubtedly become part of our system.

Before leaving this question, we wish to give a recent exposition of the doctrine by the highest court of the State of New York. The issue involved the right of the Russian Soviet Republic, a government which had received no diplomatic recognition by the United States, to begin an action in our courts. A recognized government has the right to sue in its own name "as a body analogous to one possessing corporate rights, but solely because of comity." The

[28] *Cf.* Pillet, (1923) i, pp. 94–95.
[29] Bank of Augusta *v.* Earle, (1839) 13 Pet. 519.
[30] Milliken *v.* Pratt, (1878) 125 Mass. 374.

court proceeded to define the term as fellows: "Comity may be defined as that reciprocal courtesy which one member of the family of nations owes to the others. It presupposes friendship. It assumes the prevalence of equity and justice. Experience points to the expediency of recognizing the legislative, executive and judicial acts of other powers. We do justice that justice may be done in return. . . . Rules of comity are a portion of the law that they [the courts] enforce. Both in England and in the United States so universally and for such a length of time have actions by alien corporations and individuals been allowed, that the right to bring them in a proper case has become fixed. Unless restrained by legislative fiat no court may now deny it. . . . The use of the word 'comity' as expressing the basis of *jurisdiction* has been criticized. It is, however, a mere question of definition. The principles lying behind the words are recognized. Whether or not we sum them up in one expression or another, the truth remains that jurisdiction depends upon the law of the forum and this law in turn depends upon the public policy disclosed by the acts and declarations of the political departments of the government." It was therefore decided that as the Soviet government was not recognized by the United States, it was not entitled to sue in our courts.[31]

### 3. Public Policy in Private International Law

**General Limitations upon the Recognition of Foreign Law.** The earlier American writers, notably Story, endeavored to set bounds to the force of comity in the recognition of foreign law. "No nation can be justly required to yield up its own fundamental policy and institutions, in favor of those of another nation. Much less can any nation be required to sacrifice its own interests in favor of those of another; or to enforce doctrines, which, in a moral or political view, are incompatible with its own safety, or happiness, or conscientious regard to justice and duty."[32] Story then proceeded to give examples of possible laws which might exist in some "heathen nation" justifying polygamy, incest, or contracts involving moral turpitude. He also referred to the paternal power recognized by ancient Roman law giving a life-and-death power over the children.

[31] Russian Socialist Federated Soviet Republic *v.* Cibrario, (1923) 235 N.Y. 255, 258–260. Opinion by Andrews, J.

[32] Story, §25.

"In these, and in many other cases, which may easily be put, without any extravagance of supposition, there would be extreme difficulty in saying that other nations were bound to enforce laws, institutions, or customs of that nation, which were subversive of their own morals, justice, or polity."[33] The doctrine of public policy was described by Story as one of self-defense, because to recognize foreign laws prejudicial to the rights of the nation or its subject would "annihilate the sovereignty and equality of every nation, which should be called upon to recognize and enforce them; or compel it to desert its own proper interest and duty to its own subjects in favor of strangers, who were regardless of both."[34]

It will be observed that the principle is thus stated in very general terms. It is a principle in derogation of the extension of comity; and like comity, it does not in itself decide anything because it does not give us any definite standards from which to determine what is against public policy and what is not. If the legislation of the local state declared certain transactions to be illegal and void no matter where they take place, the problem would be simple. But the legislator seldom proceeds in this manner, especially in states restrained within territorial limits by a federal constitution. Certain it is that public policy cannot be measured in each case by the discretion of the judge. It becomes necessary, therefore, to classify the cases according to their individual nature.

**Where the Application of the Foreign Law would Contravene the Morals of Civilized Society.** Whatever classification be adopted, it is clear that there are certain rules of morality which are recognized by nearly all civilized countries, East or West. Contracts violating these rules are to be considered void no matter where they were entered into, such as "contracts made in a foreign country for future illicit cohabitation and prostitution; contracts for the printing or circulation of irreligious and obscene publications; contracts to promote or reward the commission of crimes; . . . in short, all contracts, which in their own nature are founded in moral turpitude, and are inconsistent with the good order and solid interests of society."[35]

To the same category may be added contracts of marriage between brother and sister. When, however, we speak of marriages between

[33] *Ibid.*
[34] *Ibid.*, §32.
[35] Story, §258.

uncle and niece or aunt and nephew, or between first cousins, we find there is no common opinion even among Western nations. Some states prohibit such marriages while others do not and it cannot be said that when performed abroad and valid there, local public policy will refuse to give recognition, even though invalid in the local state.[36] A Massachusetts court has said: "it is not to be inferred from a toleration of marriages which are prohibited merely on account of political expediency that others, which would tend to outrage the principles and feelings of all civilized nations, would be countenanced." [37]

Thus we see that what is sometimes called a general law of morality, applicable in theory everywhere, is often only a question of degree. It also shows that there are two kinds of public policy, one which operates no matter where the transaction takes place, and another which is not offended if the transaction is completed abroad. Such an institution as slavery, abhorred in territory in which it did not prevail, was not considered in the free states of the Union as preventing an action upon a negotiable instrument given in payment of a completed sale of a slave, though the status of the slave itself would not be recognized.[38] Although this was the rule when slavery existed in the Southern States, it would perhaps be different today since the abolition of slavery has been made an international obligation. In other words, the conception of what is *contra bonos mores* in the universal sense is just as little static as ideas of morality in the national sense. Certainly, the courts of the United States have not taken a narrow view in applying moral standards. The Federal Supreme Court, for example, has refused to enforce a contract which involved improper influence exercised upon officers of a foreign country to induce them to purchase munitions from an American firm, even on the presumption that it might be enforceable there. It was held so repugnant to all notions of right and morality that it could have no recognition in the courts of the United States.[39]

[36] See Minor, §9.

[37] Medway *v.* Needham, (1819) 16 Mass. 157. *Accord:* Com. *v.* Lane, (1873) 113 Mass. 458; Pennegar *v.* State, (1889) 87 Tenn. 244.

[38] Greenwood *v.* Curtis, (1810) 6 Mass., 358; Roundtree *v.* Baker, (1869) 52 Ill. 241.

[39] Oscanyon *v.* Winchester Repeating Arms Co., (1880) 103 U.S. 277. The moral lesson would have been stronger, however, if the American firm had not been thus relieved of paying an inconvenient commission.

**Where the Application of the Foreign Law would Contravene Certain Prohibitory Statutes of the Forum.** A contract entered into in a foreign state may be legal there but illegal at the place where action is brought to recover damages for its breach. It does not necessarily follow that such contract cannot be enforced in a state in which it could not have legally been made in the first instance. If, however, the contract is deemed to contravene a strong public policy of the forum, it will not be given effect. What is to determine the difference between ordinary illegality and the contravention of a strong public policy? The dividing line is indeed difficult to define. Where the enforcement in the local state would tend to give effect to moral iniquity or disturb "good order and solid interests of society," it would be too much to expect the local court to grant a remedy even though a different standard prevailed in the foreign state where the transaction was entered into. The difficulty arises where the act complained of is merely *malum prohibitum.*

Let us illustrate: The defendant, a common carrier, undertook to carry, under a through bill of lading, a quantity of silk from Shanghai via Vancouver to New York. Part of the silk was stolen on the voyage to Vancouver. The jury found that the theft occurred because of the defendant's negligence and that it was committed by its servants. The bill of lading made in Shanghai provided that the contract should be construed according to the law of Great Britain. The bill of lading limited the liability of the carrier from liability for the negligence of its servants and from theft of whatever kind. This clause was valid under British law but illegal under the law of New York. The court held that the will of the legislature had been clearly expressed to the effect that contracts which purport totally to exempt a carrier from liability for negligence are against public policy.[40] The reasoning of the court is not convincing. It was fully recognized that public policy is necessarily variable. Indeed, the public policy of the state was formerly quite different and such contracts were recognized.[41] Does it not therefore follow that the court failed to recognize rights established by free agreement of the parties in a foreign jurisdiction? If the plaintiff had been suing for the enforcement of a contract deemed legal at the place of the contract but illegal in the forum, the case might have been

[40] F. A. Straus & Co. Inc., *v.* Canadian Pacific Ry. Co., (1930) 254 N.Y. 407.
[41] See opinion by Hubbe, J., at p. 413.

stronger because the court might very well have said that the procedure of the forum would not lend its aid to a contract prohibited by the local legislature. In the instant case, however, the plaintiff is asking for redress *against* its own free undertaking to exempt the carrier, made under the laws of a foreign country where such undertaking was valid. Public policy should be deemed something stronger than the law or legislation of a particular state. If this be not so, there is grave danger of requiring all contracts consummated abroad to conform to the law of the forum. Beale has remarked with much force that, "There is, moreover, in the law of every jurisdiction a strong policy in favor of recognizing and enforcing rights and duties validly created by the foreign law." [42]

The Restatement provides: "No action can be maintained upon a cause of action created in another state the enforcement of which is contrary to the strong public policy of the forum." [43]

The decision in the Straus case seems to be opposed on principle to the liberal doctrine established in the Loucks case,[44] in which it was said that "we are not so provincial as to say that every solution of a problem is wrong because we deal with it otherwise at home."

**Where the Foreign Law Contravenes some Established and Important Policy of the Forum.** There is a class of cases in which the foreign law otherwise applicable will not be applied because the local state finds such application to be objectionable in view of some important and established policy of the local state, or because it would disturb its public order. It may very well be that no such objection would be found in the particular foreign state, or in most other states, or indeed in no other but the local state. The true test here is not the widespread acceptance of some particular moral standard such as we have already mentioned, but the importance attached to it by the local state. Of course not all the laws of a state, even those relating to public tranquility or to the maintenance of moral standards, are necessarily applicable to transactions which take place abroad. If such were the case, each jurisdiction would be engaged in a futile struggle to maintain such standards over every other. The result would lessen its influence even as to transactions within its proper scope, because such transactions often require the co-operation of a foreign jurisdiction to make them effective.

[42] Beale, (1935), iii, p. 1651.
[43] Restatement, §612.
[44] Loucks *v.* Standard Oil Co., (1918) 224 N.Y. 99.

Let us illustrate: Laws against usury are generally considered laws of morality; indeed originally they had a religious sanction. Yet if a contract is made abroad with a rate of interest valid there, but usurious in the state of the suit, it will nevertheless be enforced.[45] Suppose, however, the foreign contract was based upon a wager. Even though it was made by parties residing outside the state, and intended to be performed there, the local state will say that it will lend no aid whatever for its enforcement because wagering is against the public policy of the forum. As a court in New Jersey said: "a plain distinction at once presents itself between a usury law and a law against gaming. One affects only the parties to the contract, and is framed for the protection of the borrower. The other relates to the public or classes of the public who are interested therein and affected thereby. . . . The vice aimed at is not only injurious to the person who games, but wastes his property, to the injury of those dependent on him, or who are to succeed him. It has its more public aspect for if it be announced that a trustee has been false to his trust, or a public officer has embezzled public funds, by common consent the first inquiry is whether the defaulter has been wasting his property in gambling." [46]

It will be observed that the rule as thus expounded leaves considerable ground for difference of opinion. Courts in various countries will consider certain laws to be "coercive" (to use a phrase of Savigny) while courts of another will not. Morals are greatly influenced by history and environment and no uniform rule can be expected. We know that acts considered harmless in one country are made the subject of the strictest taboo in others. In democratic states, public opinion makes public policy. Under a dictatorship, acts elsewhere considered most innocent may be pronounced void and visited with penalties. The concept of public policy is therefore variable both in space and time.

**Where the Repugnant Foreign Law Constitutes a Defense not recognized in the Forum.** Ordinarily, public policy operates as a prohibition against a recovery in the local state; but a foreign law which may be repugnant to principles of justice of the local state, may constitute a defense in the foreign state. Let us illustrate: The plaintiff was the general manager of a corporation in Germany con-

[45] Campion *v.* Kille, (1862) 14 N.J. Eq. 229.

[46] Flagg *v.* Baldwin, (1884) 38 N.J. Eq. 219. *Accord:* Nonotuck Silk Co. *v.* Adams E. Co., (1912) 256 Ill. 66.

nected with the German government railways. He was discharged solely upon the ground of racial origin pursuant to laws enacted in Germany after the making of the contract. He sued in New York for wrongful discharge and the German statutes were pleaded as a defense. A motion to strike out the defense as repugnant to American public policy was granted by a court of first instance.[47]

The Conflict of Laws Restatement[48] provides: "No action can be maintained upon a cause of action in another state the enforcement of which is contrary to the strong public policy of the forum." No provision is made for cases permitting a defense not recognized at the forum but there are many cases in which affirmative relief has been denied because the foreign law ordinarily applicable has been considered repugnant upon the ground of public policy.[49]

**Comparative Principles relating to Public Policy.** We may assume that all systems of law refuse to give effect to transactions, wherever consummated, where the peace and order of the local state would be disturbed. The difficulty is in determining what transactions are of such a character and what particular laws of the local state must be exclusively observed in order that peace and order may be maintained. The difference of approach is indicated somewhat by the difference of legal phraseology. Where English law speaks of public policy, countries of the Continent speak of public order (French: *"ordre public"*; Italian: *"ordine pubblico"*); or of law against good morals (German: *"gegen die guten Sitten"*).

The early systems of law in Europe, both before and during the development of the statutory theory, did not recognize any parallel principle of public order because the application of law was based either upon personality or territoriality, as these terms were then understood. Valery points out that these principles were in themselves rules of public order, territoriality being derived from sovereign control over a particular territory, and personality representing a qualified variance.[50]

The German jurist, Savigny, seems to have exercised an enormous influence on the jurisprudence of his own and other countries of the Continent in his concept of coercive laws which he defined as

[47] Holzer *v.* Deutsche Reichsbahn., (June 22, 1936) N.Y. Law Jour. p. 3171.
[48] §612.
[49] See F. A. Straus & Co. Inc., *v.* Canadian Pacific Ry. Co., (1930) 254 N.Y. 407 referred to *supra,* and cases cited by S. Sichel in Yale Law Jour., 1936, p. 1469, n.27 and comment thereon.
[50] Valery, (1914) *Manuel de dr. int. privé,* p. 571.

an exception to the recognition of an international community of law. According to his formula, where the application of foreign law would violate the basic tendencies of the law of the local state, recognition cannot be given to it.[51] The classification of local laws which are coercive, so that a foreign law of different content cannot be applied, has been attempted by many jurists. Thus, Laurent maintains that so much of the local law as relates to the social order within the local state must have absolute preference over the foreign rules. Brocher attempts to separate laws which relate to "internal public order" from those which relate to "international public order." The former restrict individual freedom; the latter, the extraterritorial force of foreign laws.[52] This is based upon the idea that certain laws are necessarily to be observed, as opposed to any foreign law, because their purpose affects public order everywhere, whereas laws designed only to maintain the local public order become coercive only if the effects are noticeable in the local state. The Italian school relies upon the difference between public law and private law, the result of which would be that foreign public law could never be applied by the local state. This formula is manifestly unsatisfactory.

One may say that there are almost as many theories upon this question as there are writers and we are upon safer ground in dealing with it as a matter of legislation and jurisprudence.

The *French* Civil Code declares that: Laws of police and public order are binding upon all those who inhabit the territory.[53] This is not a rule of private international law but one of internal public order. The distinction made by Brocher between internal public order and international public order is so widely made by French jurists as well as by the courts that it is well to clarify it by the illustration given by Arminjon. An Egyptian Moslem of 18 years will be considered of age in France by virtue of his national law although a Frenchman will not be of age until his 21st year. No act or agreement upon his part can change this situation. The law which regulates this matter is one of internal public order but does not apply internationally. On the other hand, the Egyptian Moslem will not be allowed to marry a second wife in France, although his national law permits, because the law of France against

[51] Savigny, (Guthrie's trans., 1880) §35.
[52] Brocher, *Nouveau traité de dr. int. privé* (1876) p. 367.
[53] Art. 3 (1).

polygamy is one of international public order.[54] Arminjon is not opposed to the concept of public order but to the fact that it is left to the judge to decide whether or not a French law should be applied although the foreign law would ordinarily be applied by the rule of conflicts. It is the *legislative* and not a judicial intent which is to be determined. Thus the Law of June 15, 1872, makes inalienable under certain conditions securities to bearer which have been lost or stolen. Even though such securities have been negotiated abroad, French law must apply because otherwise the whole purpose of the legislator could be thwarted. This is the test which Arminjon supports and recommends the phrase "rules of purely national attachment" rather than "rules of public order."[55] However, the result is not very different because the interpretation of such legislative intent still remains a judicial function. Furthermore, a great body of French law lies outside of statute. We cannot lay down any fixed rule but French courts have applied local law in cases where the rule of conflict would point to a foreign law and no coercive principle would seem apparent upon grounds of morals or the social order, and to this Niboyet enters an energetic protest.[56]

The Introductory Statute to the *German* Civil Code[57] provides that the application of a foreign law is prohibited if such application is opposed to good morals or the purpose of a German law. An analogous provision is found in the Code of Civil Procedure with reference to the recognition of foreign judgments.[58] Thus we have the principle declared by statute but in terms no less ambiguous and indefinite. Indeed, Art. 30 taken literally, would permit the court to refuse to apply a foreign law which differed from the parallel German rule even though the foreign rule were applicable by the ordinary rule of conflict. However, the *Reichsgericht* has declared that the application of the foreign law is to be excluded under Art. 30 only in the event that "the difference between the political and social

[54] Arminjon, *Précis de droit int. privé* (1927) i, p. 192.

[55] *Ibid.*, p. 203.

[56] Niboyet, *Manuel de dr. int. pr.* (1928) §§441–443.

[57] Art. 30.

[58] German Code Civ. Proc. §328. The draft of the Civil Code by Gebhard originally contained the phrase "*öffentliche Ordnung*" in both sections, the exact equivalent of the French terminology, but Lewald is of the opinion that the statutory intent as finally expressed leads to the same result. Lewald (1931) pp. 23–24. The Swiss Code of Obligations, §20, also uses the phrase "against good morals."

policies, upon which rest respectively the foreign and the competing German law, is so substantial that the application of the foreign law would directly threaten the bases of German political or economic life."[59] While the formula is effective in curbing too wide an exercise of discretion by the judge in favor of German law, it fails to fix any definite standard. It can be said perhaps that the statute as interpreted by the formula is not so destructive of ordinary rules of conflict as is the wide discretion exercised in France. However, as Lewald points out, there are no fixed boundaries and the application of Art. 30 depends upon empirical rules for each particular case.[60] By way of illustration we may cite the refusal to apply German law on the ground of public order or policy in measuring the period of prescription;[61] the application of the article so as to make the revaluation of obligations payable in German marks compulsory under the German statute, even though the proper law of the contract is not German law;[62] the application of the article so as to refuse recognition to a maritime mortgage completed in Russia because publication of the pledge under Russian law was not equivalent or nearly equivalent to the German provisions for publicity.[63] The last mentioned case is rightly criticized by Lewald and others.[64] The right of inheritance having been abolished by decree of the Soviet government, German courts have allowed Russian nationals in Germany to inherit pursuant to German law because of the rule of public policy.[65]

The *Italian Disposizioni* or preliminary rules of the Civil Code provide that "laws of police and of public security are binding upon all who are situated within the territory of the kingdom."[66] Further, the *Disposizioni* provide that notwithstanding the articles of the statute, the acts and judgments of a foreign country and provisions and agreements of a private nature shall in no case be in derogation of the prohibitive laws of the kingdom concerning persons, things, or acts, nor of the laws which relate in any manner to public order

[59] Mar. 21, 1905, 60 *Reichsger.* Civ. cases 296; Feb. 9, 1925, 110 *Ibid.*, 173; Dec. 14, 1927, 119 *Ibid.*, p. 259.

[60] Lewald (1931), p. 28.

[61] See *Reichsger.*, Mar. 20, 1936.

[62] *Reichsger.*, Mar. 5, 1928, 120 *Reichsger.*, Civ. cas. p. 277.

[63] *Reichsger.*, Feb. 10, 1912, 80 *Reichsger.*, Civ. cas. p. 129.

[64] Lewald (1931) pp. 31–32.

[65] H. Freund in Clunet, 1924, p. 58 *et seq.* The matter is now regulated by treaty.

[66] Art. 11.

or good morals.[67] Italian authorities are accustomed to make a strict classification of laws into public and private and to make the local laws applicable to all constitutional, administrative, penal and procedural laws.[68] It would be very difficult in practice to make any such sharp distinction. Questions of personal status and of family relations are partly of a public character and the Italian doctrine would perhaps be the last to apply local law in preference to the *lex patriae* in all such matters. Udina rightly points out that Italian legislation is not to be interpreted in this sense, but only to exclude the application of foreign law where the local is "rigorously coercive." [69] This phrase may be compared with that of the American Restatement which speaks of "the strong public policy of the forum." [70] Here again, we are unable to lay down any fixed boundaries but Italian courts have been influenced by the distinction made by Brocher between laws contrary to international public order and those contrary to internal public order.[71]

The Bustamante Code adopted by a large number of *Latin-American* countries also accepts this distinction although with a seemingly different application. The code speaks of laws "applying to persons by reason of their domicil or their nationality and following them even when they go to another country"; and these laws are termed "personal or of an internal public order." [72] Here the designation is internal *qua* the state of domicil or nationality and not *qua* the territorial state or state of sojourn. Probably the same result would be recognized especially as each state is to apply its own definition to the juridical institutions or relationships corresponding to the groups of laws of internal or international public order, as the case may be, unless specifically provided for in the Code.[73] Among those specifically provided for as of an international public order are constitutional precepts and all rules of individual and collective protection established by political and administrative law.[74] We shall have occasion to observe that the Code also designates laws

[67] Art. 12.
[68] Udina, *Droit int. privé d'Italie,* (1930) p. 98.
[69] *Ibid.,* p. 92.
[70] §612.
[71] Court of Cassation, Florence, Dec. 5, 1895, *Annali della Giurisprud. Ital.,* 1895, i, p. 575.
[72] Bustamante Code, Art. 3 (1). Int. Conference of American States, (1931) p. 327.
[73] *Ibid.,* Art. 6.
[74] *Ibid.,* Arts. 4–5.

relating to certain other categories as of an international public order. Accordingly, the judge has a more restricted field within which to exercise a discretion to apply local law because outside of these categories, the application of law follows the regular rules which the Code lays down.

The principle that certain laws of the local state are coercive, by whatever terminology or ideology may be current in the particular jurisdiction, is recognized in countries of the civil as well as of the common law. We shall have occasion to observe particular applications under each topic.

### 4. Penal and Revenue Laws

Under the common law, crimes are local and punishable exclusively in the jurisdiction in which they are committed. No other jurisdiction is under any obligation to enforce penal judgments rendered by the tribunals of the state where the crime was committed.[75] We are not here considering the principles of jurisdiction which govern tribunals seeking to punish a crime, even where two or more states seek to punish an offender for the same offense. Such questions are within the field of public law. The question which here concerns us is to determine what effect shall be given in one state to the law of another state which provides a penalty against a violator of that law.

Crime and punishment in the modern state are matters of public concern. They involve public policy in the wider sense and according to the common law the definition of the offense as well as the place of punishment should be in the state in which the act was committed. "No society takes concern in any crime but what is hurtful to itself."[76] Expressed in the language commonly used by the courts, the penal laws of one state will have no extraterritorial effect in another state; or as expressed by Chief Justice Marshall early in the jurisprudence of the Supreme Court: "The courts of no country execute the penal laws of another."[77]

The doctrine thus simply expressed has gained uniform acceptance in the United States but there has been considerable difficulty in determining just what laws are penal. Let us proceed from the

[75] *Cf.* Story, §619.
[76] Kames on Equity, quoted by Story, §622.
[77] The Antelope, (1825) 10 Wheat., 66, 123.

general to the particular. A law of Wisconsin imposed a penalty upon any insurance company which should do business in that state without having deposited with the proper officer a full statement of its property and business during the previous year. Action was brought against a Louisiana company for such penalty in Wisconsin and a judgment was obtained. The State of Wisconsin sought to enforce the judgment by action commenced in the United States Supreme Court, complaining that full faith and credit was denied to one of its judgments under the Constitution. The Supreme Court decided that Wisconsin was not entitled to enforce the judgment because the judgment was obtained under a penal law; that the rule applied not only to prosecutions and sentences for crimes but to all suits in favor of the state for the recovery of pecuniary penalties for any violation of statutes for the protection of its revenue, or other municipal laws and to all judgments for such penalties. The cause of action was not for a private injury, but solely for the offense committed against the state by reason of the violation. The prosecution was in the name of the state and the whole penalty would accrue to the state.[78]

Suppose now that the penalty is to be recovered by an injured private party. A law of New York made any director who knowingly should sign and record a false certificate of the amount of its capital stock liable for all its debts. An officer of a corporation did make such a false statement to the effect that all of its capital was paid up. One of the unpaid creditors of the corporation recovered a judgment in New York against the officer and sought to enforce it in Maryland. The Maryland court refused to execute the judgment on the ground that the law was penal and the plaintiff appealed to the Supreme Court. About the same time, the plaintiff sought to enforce the same judgment in Canada. Curiously enough, the Canadian court rested upon the view of New York State itself that the action was penal, and dismissed the action. But on appeal to the British Privy Council, it was held that the international test was whether the action is in favor of the state whose law had been violated. Here it was in favor of the individual. The Supreme Court followed substantially the rule thus laid down by the Privy Council and decided for the plaintiff. The Court said: "The test is not by what name the statute is called by the legislature or the courts of the state in which it was passed but whether it appears to the

[78] Wisconsin *v.* Pelican Insurance Co., (1887) 127 U.S. 265, 290, 299.

tribunal which is called upon to enforce it, to be, in its essential character and effect, a punishment of an offense against the public, or a grant of a civil right to a private person." [79]

While agreeing that the particular law in this case is not a penal law, Minor has criticized the decision because it follows a test that is not international. It distinguishes between crime and civil wrong according to whether the penalty inures to the state or to the party, irrespective of whether the damages are compensatory or punitive. This, Minor claims, should not be the test, because the international rule should seek only to do justice, not to inflict punishment, even though a private party is to benefit: "Where he [a private individual] seeks to enforce his claim in another state, what right has he to ask this of the forum whose policy may be entirely different?" [80] Doubtless the criticism is just to the extent that it points out the real test, which is whether the law seeks punishment or to provide some form of remedy to the person injured to compensate him for his injury. We shall see, however, that when the foreign law permits recovery in favor of a private person in the form of a penalty to an extent not measured by the amount of his injury, we are confronted with a different problem. The courts have not agreed upon the test in such cases.

**Foreign Tax Laws.** A similar principle is involved in the attempt to make tax and revenue laws of one state effective also in a foreign state. The State of Colorado sought to recover an inheritance tax upon the estate of one of its domiciled citizens who died in the State of New York while temporarily there, leaving certain testamentary trusts of personal property all of which was located in New York. The Colorado statute provided that the tax should be a lien on the property transferred and that all legatees and executors should be liable for such taxes. The State of Colorado sued the legatees and trustees in New York for a judgment for the amount of the transfer taxes assessed in Colorado. Leaving aside the questions of jurisdiction and of due process, the court said: "The attempt to give such a statutory provision extraterritorial effect would conflict with another well-settled principle of private international law which precludes one state from acting as a collector of taxes for a sister state and from enforcing its penal or revenue laws as such. The

[79] Huntington *v.* Attrill, (1892) 146 U.S. 657. In the Privy Council: Huntington *v.* Attrill, [1893] A.C. 150.

[80] Minor, (1901) §10, n. 3.

rule is universally recognized that the revenue laws of one state have no force in another."[81] A similar result was reached in England where action was brought by the Netherlands Government to recover succession dues from personalty located in England belonging to a domiciled subject of the Netherlands.[82]

**Remedial Laws in the Form of Penalties.** The statutes of some states create a pecuniary liability for the intentional or negligent killing of a person fixing the liability in favor of his family, in accordance with the degree of wrongdoing and not in accordance with the damage sustained. These laws are in a sense penal and some courts refuse to give them extraterritorial effect.[83] The preponderant view however is to regard such a law as penal in form though remedial in the international sense. A law of this nature exists in the State of Massachusetts. A resident of New York was run over and killed in Massachusetts by the negligence of a servant of the defendant. Under the law of Massachusetts an action can be brought by the estate of the deceased for the benefit of the widow and children and allows damages between certain fixed limits, according to *culpability*. In an action brought in New York, Judge Cardozo pointed out that the common law originally did not give a cause of action to surviving relatives: "In the light of modern legislation its rule is an anachronism. Nearly everywhere, the principle is now embodied in statute that the next of kin are wronged by the killing of their kinsmen. The family becomes a legal unit, invested with rights of its own, invested with an interest in the continued life of its members, much as it was in primitive law. The damages may be compensatory or punitive according to the statutory scheme. In either case the plaintiffs have a grievance above and beyond any that belongs to them as members of the body politic. They sue to redress an outrage peculiar to themselves." He concluded therefore that though the damages are punitive, the law is not penal in the international sense.[84]

The Restatement[85] provides that: "No action can be maintained

[81] State of Colorado *v.* Harbeck, (1921) 232 N.Y. 71. Pound, J., at p. 85.

[82] *In re* Visser, [1928] 1 Ch. 877.

[83] Cristilly *v.* Warner, (1913) 87 Conn. 461.

[84] Loucks *v.* Standard Oil Co., (1918) 224 N.Y. 99. At p. 106: "The executor or administrator who sues under this statute is not the champion of the peace and order and public justice of the commonwealth of Massachusetts. He is the representative of the outraged family. He vindicates a private right."

[85] Restatement of the Law of Conflict of Laws (1934) §§610–611.

on a right created by the law of a foreign state as a method of furthering its own governmental interests. No action can be maintained to recover a penalty the right of which is given by the law of another state."

**Comparative Principles with respect to Penal and Revenue Laws.** Substantial agreement with the principles of common-law jurisdictions is to be found in the countries of continental Europe although the approach is somewhat different. The French jurist, Valery, points out that the right to punish and the right to tax are exclusive attributes of sovereignty and similar to royal prerogatives. He adds, however, that sometimes a penal court will award a judgment in favor of the victim of a punishable act and in such a case the judgment partakes of a civil character.[86] It is to be remembered that countries of the civil law frequently follow a procedure under which punishment and civil compensation may be awarded in the same proceeding, with the victim as a proper party. A passenger on a Belgian railroad continued to make use of a commutation ticket after it had expired. The Belgian Government, owner of the railroad, prosecuted the passenger in a police court. A fine was imposed and judgment obtained for the equivalent of the fare. The Belgian Government then sought to execute the judgment, but not the fine, in France. The court confirmed the principle that foreign penal laws would not be executed but added that the judgment was a civil reparation although rendered by a repressive tribunal.[87]

Fiscal laws are not entitled to extraterritorial effect because, by their very nature, they are *intended* to be restricted to the territory, according to Franz Kahn, a German jurist.[88] Niboyet seems to express it more realistically when he maintains that there are no vested rights, internationally speaking, in fiscal claims "because the existing concept of states is not in this sense." He believes that some day this may be changed by treaty, especially between neighboring countries.[89]

In some countries, a criminal penalty will have the effect of working a loss of civil rights with consequent influence upon the capacity to act. Where the disability is created in the country of the of-

[86] Valery, *Manuel de dr. int. privé* (1914) §570.
[87] Clunet, 1925, p. 128.
[88] Kahn, *Abhandlungen zum Int. Privatrecht* (1928) i, p. 24.
[89] Niboyet, *Manuel de dr. int. privé* (1928) §369 ter.

fender's personal law, national or domiciliary as the case may be, it is sometimes regarded as having extraterritorial effect, at least if the local state recognizes a similar effect.[90]

The prohibition against actions brought for the recovery of taxes due to a foreign government is sometimes effected by procedural laws which give to local courts jurisdiction to hear only *civil* causes of action. This is the case in Germany so that the prohibition results from a "qualification" or interpretation of the terms of a positive statute.[91]

## 5. The Doctrine of Renvoi

Where a court is presented with the problem of determining which of two or more possible systems of law are applicable to a pending issue, it is obliged, of course, to seek the rule of the forum for resolving the conflict. Ordinarily, that rule consists in indicating not the law of State A or State B as such, but the law of some place indicated by description, as *e.g.*, the law of the domicil of a certain person, or his national law, or the law of the situs of certain property, or of the place where a certain instrument was executed. Now if a parallel case were to be decided in a court of the foreign state thus indicated, that court might be obliged to apply not its own law but the law of quite another state. To illustrate: A citizen of New York died domiciled at Nice, France, leaving a large estate of personal property in New York. By his will he disposed of his residuary estate in favor of two persons, only one of whom survived him. Under New York law the bequest of one-half the residuary estate would have lapsed so that the next of kin of the testator would receive it. Under French law, in the case of a domiciled French testator, the surviving joint legatee would receive it. Under New York law, the succession to personal property is determined by the law of the testator's domicil, which was, in this case, French. But under the French law, the devolution of the estate of a foreigner is determined by his national law, in this case, New York law. Shall the New York court therefore say: "French law is to be applied and a French court would refer to New York law; therefore New York law shall finally apply"? If it does so decide, it

[90] Weiss (1898) iii, pp. 376–378; Meili (Kuhn's trans. 1905) pp. 176–177. The disability created under a foreign law by entering into religious orders will not be recognized in France. *Ibid.*, pp. 380–382.

[91] Nussbaum, *Deutsches Int. Privatrecht* (1932) p. 385.

would be applying not only the French law of wills but also the French private international law. In other words, the New York court would be accepting a "reference" or "remission" back to its own law (French: *"renvoi"*; German: *"Verweisung"*; Italian: *"rinvio"*).

A case involving the problems thus briefly described came before the New York courts in 1919,[92] and was characterized by the referee as entirely new in New York. Indeed, so far as any clear formulation of the problem was concerned, it was new to American courts generally. The early writers had not discussed it but it had received considerable attention during the preceding two decades by Pawley-Bate, Bentwich and others in England, and later, by Beale, Lorenzen and Schreiber in the United States. Just one year before the Tallmadge case, Lorenzen had pointed out the herculean task laid upon a judge compelled to apply the foreign law in its totality, *i.e.*, including the foreign private international law, because it would be necessary for him to decide the issue as though he were sitting in the foreign jurisdiction.[93]

In the Tallmadge case, the referee reviewed the doctrines which had been advanced in the various countries with learning and ability and summed up the result as follows: (1) If *renvoi* be part of the New York law, and not that of France, a New York court must apply New York internal or territorial law. (2) If *renvoi* be part of the laws of both New York and France, an endless oscillation between the conflict-of-laws rules of the two countries will be instituted, or a New York court must apply French internal or territorial law. (3) If *renvoi* be no part of the New York law, even though it be part of the law of France, a New York court will apply French internal law according to the provisions of the New York Decedent Estates Law.[94]

The referee therefore came to the conclusion, both upon principle and the meager jurisprudence to be found upon the question in American courts, that *renvoi* is no part of New York law and that a New York court must apply the internal or territorial law of France, which was, in the instant case, the law of the domicil.

A Minnesota court seems to have deemed itself bound to adopt *renvoi*. Two domiciled citizens of Minnesota entered into marriage

[92] *In re* Tallmadge, (1919) 181 N.Y. Supp. 336.
[93] Lorenzen in Yale Law Jour., 1918, p. 527.
[94] §47.

in Hamburg without complying with the formalities of German law but observing the simpler forms of Minnesota law. In a proceeding for dower after the husband's death, her claim was opposed on the ground of the illegality of the marriage. The parties submitted the cause by a stipulation in which the effect of the German conflict-of-laws provision was included. Under this law the *lex patriae* is made the test of the formal validity of a marriage between foreigners. The Minnesota court applied the *lex loci celebrationis* or German law and then, by *renvoi*, the *lex patriae* or Minnesota law. But it could scarcely have done otherwise in view of the general equity rule in favor of recognizing the validity of a marriage entered into in good faith, followed by years of cohabitation.[95]

We believe the doctrine enunciated in the Tallmadge case to be sound from the viewpoint of principle as well as of convenience. *Renvoi* does not resolve the conflict. As Lainé trenchantly remarks: "When the lawmaker has designated a foreign system of law for the solution of a question, the judge has no longer to demand the will of the foreign legislature as to what system of law is applicable. He knows it." [96]

In an unwritten system like the common law it ought to be clear enough that the only conflict-of-laws rule which is authoritative is the rule of the forum. The foreign law is referred to in order to settle the issue; not to select the governing law. This has been fully recognized by the Restatement of the American Law Institute.[97]

**Renvoi in England.** In England, however, a series of recent decisions leads to the conclusion that irrespective of whether or not the doctrine of *renvoi* is part of English law, English courts in referring to a foreign domiciliary law will apply that law as the foreign court would apply it. If the foreign court uses a *renvoi*, the English court will follow it. If it does not, it will do likewise. To illustrate: X, a British subject, died domiciled *de facto* in France leaving a will of movables, the validity of which came before the English court. The court held that its validity must be determined by French law because English law applies the domiciliary law, *viz.*, French law. France refers to the national law of the testator, *viz.*,

[95] Lando's Estate, (1910) 112 Minn. 257.

[96] Lainé in Clunet, 1885, p. 16. To the same effect is the resolution of the Institute of International Law. *Annuaire*, 1900, p. 3.

[97] Restatement of the Law of Conflict of Laws, 1934, §7 (b). *Cf.* also Schreiber (1928) 31 Harvard Law R. 523; Beale, A Treatise on the Conflict of Laws (1935) i, §7.3.

English law, but accepts a *renvoi* back to the law of the domicil, *viz.,* French law.[98] Had the domicil been in Italy, English law would have been applied, because Italy recognizes the national law of the testator as authoritative, but does not accept *renvoi.*[99] In the Annesley case, Russell, J., cited the Tallmadge case in New York and approved its reasoning. In the later case of *In re* Askew,[100] the court, per Maugham, J., again appeared sympathetic to the American rule, "the simple and rational solution" suggested by Justice Russell. After a review of the English authorities, however, the conclusion adopted was that an English court is bound to apply the foreign law "in the wide sense," *i.e.,* as a court sitting in the country of the domicil would apply it, which would demand the application of that country's own private international law.

An English marriage settlement gave a power of appointment to the husband in favor of any wife who might survive him, or of any child of that marriage. The husband separated from the wife and acquired a German domicil. The marriage was thereafter dissolved in Germany and the husband then married a woman by whom he already had a child born subsequent to his acquiring a domicil in Germany. The question arose as to the legitimacy of the child. By English municipal law, the child would not be legitimate; by German law, legitimation by subsequent marriage is recognized. English law looks to the domiciliary law, and this (the German) law in turn refers to the national law of the father. The court nominally repudiated the doctrine of *renvoi* and yet it made use of a *renvoi* because it was part of the German law "in the wide sense." English courts prevent the deadlock, however, by putting the question thus: "What rights have been acquired in Utopia by the parties to the English suit by reason of the *de facto* domicil of John Doe in Utopia?"[101]

We believe the result to be unfortunate both on principle and from the view of the practical administration of justice. Obtaining an opinion of foreign experts on the private international law of a foreign country is costly and often results in a sharp conflict of expert testimony. We believe the English view is due in the last analysis to a confusion of law and jurisdiction. The court remains

[98] *In re* Annesley, [1926] Ch. 692. Cf. comment by Cheshire, Private Int. Law, (1935) pp. 138–140.

[99] *In re* Ross, Ross *v.* Waterfield, [1930] 1 Ch. 377.

[100] [1930] 2 Ch. 259.

[101] *Ibid.,* at p. 267.

seized of the issue even though it looks to a foreign law for the determination of a particular point involved in the case. In doing so, it does not decide that point as though it were seized of the issue abroad. As Lindell Bates has said: "If one were to consult the whole foreign law, foreign procedure and public policy should logically be applied, but in actual practice foreign procedure is nearly if not always excluded in a reference to foreign law and foreign public policy is rarely taken into account." [102]

**Renvoi in France. The Forgo Case.** The celebrated Forgo Case may be said to have firmly introduced *renvoi* as an accepted principle of French jurisprudence. Indeed its influence spread rapidly in other countries of the Continent of Europe although in France itself the error and inconvenience of the doctrine was promptly exposed by legal analysts such as Labbé [103] and Bartin.[104] Forgo was an illegitimate child of Bavarian national origin who had been taken to France by his mother at the age of five. He died in France after long years of residence, leaving a considerable estate but no will and no legitimate heirs. Under Bavarian law, natural collateral relatives would have succeeded to his estate, but under French law, he would have been considered without heirs and the estate would have escheated to the French fisc. The Tribunal and the Court of Appeal of Pau applied French law as the law of the last domicil, but the Court of Cassation held that this was applicable only to foreigners "authorized" to acquire a French domicil within the meaning of Art. 13 of the Civil Code. As to foreigners with only a *de facto* French domicil, the law of the domicil of origin must apply.[105] Accordingly, the cause was remanded. The French authorities were ordered to restore the succession in accordance with Bavarian law. At this point, reference was made to the Bavarian law itself and the discovery was made that in the case of Bavarians domiciled abroad, the devolution of estates followed the law of the decedent's last domicil. The appeal of the French administrative authorities for cassation of the decree of restitution was thereupon sustained by the Court of Cassation in a new opinion in which the *renvoi* of the Bavarian law was accepted.[106]

[102] L. T. Bates in 16 Cornell Law Quar., (1931) 313.

[103] J. E. Labbé in Clunet, 1885, pp. 5–19.

[104] Bartin in 30 *Revue de dr. int.* (1898) pp. 129–187; 272–310.

[105] *Cour de Cassation,* May 5, 1875; Clunet, 1875, p. 358.

[106] *Cour de Cassation,* June 24, 1878; same case, February 22, 1882, Clunet, 1883, p. 64.

Lewald remarks that through the decision in the Forgo case, the *renvoi* doctrine was elevated to a position of the highest importance in private international law.[107] While recognizing the general acceptance of the doctrine by the courts, Pillet characterized it as "absolute error," to be persistently combatted.[108] National law is applied to the succession of French persons in France whereas domiciliary law applies to foreigners in most cases. This Pillet characterized as completely "*antijuridique.*"[109] But *renvoi* is by no means restricted to succession. It is applied in France also to status, marriage and divorce, legitimation and to other questions of personal and family law. This results from a sort of juristic nationalism, as evidenced by the fact that *renvoi* is not accepted where the foreign conflict-of-laws rule refers to a third system or "*renvoi* in the second degree," and not to French law.[110]

**Renvoi in Germany.** German law has carried still further the application of *renvoi* (*Verweisung*). By reason of the interpretation given to Article 27 of the Introductory Statute to the Civil Code, wherever a foreign law is made applicable under other specified articles of the statute (*viz.*, Art. 7, par. 1: Capacity; Art. 13, par. 1: Contract of Marriage; Art. 15, par. 2: Matrimonial Property; Art. 17, par. 1: Divorce; and Art. 25: Succession), and the foreign law makes German law applicable, German law is applied. Expressed in other words, national law having been made applicable to these questions by German law, the Introductory Statute then provides that if the national law refers to the German (domiciliary) law, German law shall prevail. But does this apply also to other questions not specifically referred to in Art. 27, or is it to be taken as the establishment of a general rule of *renvoi?* Ordinary rules of statutory interpretation would indicate the former: *expressio unis exclusio alterius.* Not so the interpretation given by the courts which approve *renvoi* even as to the validity of contracts.[111] The courts also carry out the doctrine to the second degree of reference (*Weiterverweisung*) although this is not expressly demanded by Art. 27. For example, the succession to lands situated in Russia owned by a Belgian domiciled there, was

[107] H. Lewald, *La Theorie du Renvoi, Recueil de l'Académie de dr. int.*, 1929, p. 539.

[108] A. Pillet, *Traité pratique de dr. int. privé* (1923) i, p. 530.

[109] *Ibid.*, p. 531.

[110] *Ibid.*, p. 543.

[111] *Ibid.*, p. 548; Melchior in *Juristische Wochenschrift*, 1925, p. 1571.

determined by the *Reichsgericht* under Russian law because the national (Belgian) law made applicable by German law, in turn refers the question to the *lex rei sitae* or the Russian law.[112]

A Swiss citizen marries his niece in Russia where both were domiciled. Russian law permits such a marriage but the Swiss Civil Code (Art. 100) does not. However, the Swiss Civil Code does not assume to regulate conflicts of law. These are governed by the Swiss Federal Statute of 1891 concerning the civil legal relations of persons domiciled or sojourning. Under Art. 7, the law of the domicil is applicable to the marriage of Swiss citizens abroad. The marriage would therefore be regarded as valid also in Switzerland. Suppose, however, that the couple go to Germany where one of them begins an action for nullity before a German court. Art. 13 of the Introductory Statute of the German Civil Code refers the question of the validity of marriage to the national law of the parties, *viz.*, Swiss law. Under the doctrine of *renvoi* adopted by Art. 27 of the same statute, however, where the national law itself refers to another system of law, that law (in this instance the Russian law) shall apply. Accordingly, the marriage was good also by German law. We have here an example of two states, each with a different principle of private international law, arriving at the same result through the adoption of *renvoi* by one of the states.[113]

**Renvoi by Convention.** Where the application of the proper system of law is established by international convention, the parties contemplate the exclusion of any possibility of a conflict of laws. The very purpose of such conventions is to *fix* the law by international consent. Sometimes, however, "the meeting of the minds" of the contracting states is not complete. This is particularly true where state policy intervenes. National law and domiciliary law are strongly competitive legislative principles for determining personal and family relationships. The groups of states following these respective principles have had great difficulty in arriving at any real compromise. In the Hague Convention of 1904 on Private International Law with reference to Marriage (Art. 1), a compromise was effected by designating as the test of the right of contracting marriage "the national law of each of the parties intending to be married, unless such national law refers expressly to some other law." This was un-

[112] (1917) 91 *Reichsger.* Civil Cases, p. 139.
[113] *Cf.* Raape, *Recueil de l'Acad. de dr. int.*, 1934, iv, p. 413.

doubtedly accepted to conciliate those nations which follow the law of the domicil on this point. Thus a citizen of Norway or Switzerland might contract a valid marriage in Germany by conforming to German law notwithstanding the general rule of national law established by the convention. However, the *renvoi* which the convention adopts is a compromise only as to nationals of such countries domiciled abroad and not as to foreigners domiciled in such countries.[114]

The Convention for the Settlement of Certain Conflicts of Laws in connection with Bills of Exchange and Promissory Notes, signed at Geneva on June 7, 1930, adopts a similar *renvoi* in determining the capacity of a person to bind himself by bill or note. The national law applies, unless the national law itself refers to another law. A person who lacks capacity according to these rules will still be bound if the *lex loci actus* recognizes such capacity, saving the right of any nation to refuse such validity to an obligation upon a bill or note by one of its nationals which would not be deemed valid in the territory of the other signatory states, were it not for this provision of the convention.[115] This represents a partial compromise between the systems of national law and domiciliary law.

On the other hand, a convention may also specifically agree in the negative sense, leaving each state full power to apply the system of law which its domestic legislation may have prescribed, or may hereafter prescribe. This in substance is the effect of Article 7 of the Bustamante Code adopted by certain Latin-American states through multipartite convention.[116]

Where under a convention such as the Hague Convention relating to Marriage (Art. 1) *renvoi* is expressly permitted and only one of two given states, parties to the convention, follows the *renvoi* doctrine, the other state cannot claim a failure of reciprocity under the convention, because such state has the *privilege* of also adopting *renvoi*. As Niboyet expresses it, such treaties are not based upon a balance of consideration but upon a theoretical identity of rights.[117]

[114] Lewald, *ut cit.* p. 580.

[115] Art. 2. For the text of the Convention see "Publications of the League of Nations," 1930, ii, 20.

[116] Art. 7, Code of Private International Law. International Conferences of American States, 1889–1928. Ed. by James Brown Scott, 1931, p. 327. Philolenko observes that the only agreement here is that there is no agreement! Clunet, 1928, p. 327.

[117] Niboyet, *Recueil de l'Acad. de dr. int.*, 1935, ii, p. 345.

## 6. Movements toward Uniformity in Private International Law

Although many parts of the English common law have been codified during the past half century in various jurisdictions, it still retains its characteristic to a very great extent as a law residing in judicial precedent. Civil-law countries have maintained the ancient Roman tradition of codification ever since the Roman law was restated with imperial authority in the Justinian period. Even in modern times, the authority of judicial precedent as a source of law in civil-law countries is a controversial question. Gray says, "While on the Continent of Europe, jurists have insisted and still insist that a decision by a court has, apart from its intrinsic merit, no binding force on a judicial tribunal even on a tribunal from which an appeal lies to the court rendering the decision, it is law in England and in the United States that, apart from its intrinsic merits, the decision of a court is of great weight in that court and all co-ordinate courts in the same jurisdiction, and that it is absolutely binding on all inferior courts." [118] And he adds that the cause of this distinction between the English and the Continental law is one of the unsolved problems of comparative jurisprudence.

The rigidity of the rule of *stare decisis* as understood in English and American jurisdictions can be corrected by progressive tendencies in judicial decisions. Some writers believe that in the United States, by reason of the multiplicity of jurisdictions and the consideration given to the decisions rendered in other states, a proposition supported by only a single decision has a better chance of being overruled if the court can be convinced of its unsoundness. In this respect American courts are believed by some to reach a condition more nearly like that prevailing in France, Germany and Italy.[119] Even if this were true, private international law in the United States remains, as it is in England, not a complete or logical system, well-balanced in all its parts. Its principles have not been codified to any great extent, except in eliminating conflicts of competence by laws of procedure. The increasing diversity between the states of the Union in both legislation and judicial decisions in matters of private law has grown apace with reference to the conflict of laws. It is of the

[118] John Chipman Gray, The Nature and Sources of the Law, (1900) pp. 199–200.

[119] Beale, (1935) §4.6.

greatest importance that at least the rules for the application of law tend toward uniformity everywhere, particularly between jurisdictions derived from a common system.

**Uniform State Legislation.** During the past half century, an earnest attempt has been made to eliminate conflicts of law between the various states of the Union through the work of the official Commissioners on Uniform State Laws. Draft statutes have been elaborated upon more than fifty subjects for uniform enactment. Unfortunately, the legislatures of the states have been dilatory in acting upon these statutes. The ideal of unanimity has never been achieved except with regard to the Negotiable Instrument Law, the Warehouse Receipts Law, and, to a less extent, the Sales Law. A considerable number of states have adopted the drafts on other subjects, but this movement is only palliative because incomplete. Conflicts of law will of course disappear to the extent that uniformity of substantive law is accomplished.[120]

**The Restatement of the Law of Conflict of Laws.** A second movement toward uniformity is more comprehensive. It is nothing less than the Restatement of the common law in all its various branches under the auspices of the American Law Institute which was organized in 1923 upon the invitation of a voluntary committee under the leadership of Elihu Root as a permanent organization for the improvement of the law. The Conflict of Laws was one of the three subjects to be taken up in the first year of the establishment of the Institute. After eleven years of drafting and discussion by the members of the Institute and by the Bar generally, the Restatement was finally accepted at its session in Washington on May 11, 1934.

The Restatement, complete in 625 sections, has for its object an orderly system of the general common law of the United States relating to the Conflict of Laws, including not only the law developed through judicial decision but also as the result of statutes that have been in force for many years. It is not intended that the Restatement itself should be enacted into law by statute. There was an ever increasing volume of decisions of the State and Federal courts, many of which showed irreconcilable differences of principle in solving conflicts of law between two states of the Union, or between a state and a foreign country. Some step was essential in the direction of promoting certainty and clarity in this field. Differences in principle for

[120] *Cf.* Amer. Bar Assoc. Proceedings, 1936, p. 1051, for list of states which have adopted the various uniform statutes.

applying one system of the law rather than another are particularly unfortunate. Such differences permit a litigant to deliberately change the system of law to be applied by selecting a favorable forum. Differences between the substantive law of any two of our states, or *a fortiori,* between a state and a foreign country, are to be assumed. It is precisely such differences which make necessary a science of private international law. But discordance in the very principles which are designed to *solve* such conflicts is a negation of the science viewed as an international or universal system.

The acceptance by the courts of the authority of the Restatement as persuasive evidence of the common law upon this subject will not eliminate the need for continued research. Systematic training in the law schools will be required to understand the spirit and the significance of its principles. Nor will its proper application to specific questions of fact be understood by lawyers or judges without a knowledge of the judicial reasoning from which its rules were derived. We shall have occasion to search for the principles not only in the Restatement but by constant reference to the underlying cases and with a background of foreign jurisprudence as well. The comparative method has especial value in a branch of legal science which, if viewed with functional approach, will tend to resolve conflicts of law not in one jurisdiction alone but everywhere. A nationalist view is quite possible in private as in public international law. We venture to believe that it is not the progressive view, nor does it respond to the facts of modern life.

**Movements toward Uniformity in Continental Europe.** Negotiations were undertaken as early as 1867 by Italy, and in 1870 by France and Spain, for the elaboration of a convention upon Private International Law. Again in 1874, the Netherlands sought to convene a diplomatic congress for the elaboration of a convention for the execution of judgments. None of these plans materialized. The Netherlands again opened negotiations for the consideration of a wider range of topics, with the result that 13 European nations were represented at The Hague at the first conference of 1893. A second conference followed in 1894, with 15 nations, a third in 1900, a fourth in 1904 in which Japan participated and a fifth in 1925.

As a result of the first two conferences, a convention was signed November 14, 1896, concerning certain matters of private international law relating to civil procedure. It was ratified by a sufficient number of countries so as to bring it into effect on May 25, 1899, and taking account of subsequent adherences and denunciations, it is still effective between more than 15 European nations.[121] This convention covers only a small number of questions of civil procedure principally with regard to judicial assistance relating to the service of documents, the furnishing of security for costs and the execution of judgments for costs. As questions of procedure are not assumed to be dealt with in detail in the present work, we shall not have further occasion to refer to this convention.

On June 1, 1904, ratifications were exchanged making effective a Convention to regulate the Conflict of Laws in regard to Marriage, a Convention to regulate the Conflict of Laws and Jurisdictions in regard to Divorce and Separation and a Convention to regulate the Conflict of Laws and Jurisdictions in regard to Guardianship of Minors. Projets were elaborated also in regard to Succession and Wills, Bankruptcy, and other topics upon which further action was taken at the Conferences of 1925 and 1928. We shall have occasion to refer to the provisions of some of these in dealing with the specific topics.

In view of the extreme complexity of the subject-matter and the difficulty of arriving at acceptable compromises in the field of private international law, the accomplishments of the Hague conventions must be considered notable. Some writers are inclined to belittle these accomplishments because some of the treaties, after having become effective for a time, were denounced by certain of the parties. It is of interest to observe that political considerations had a great part in this result. A German writer explains the denunciation by France and Belgium, of the conventions relating to marriage and divorce, which took place in 1912, as having been caused by the interpretation given to the conventions by Germany with respect to the prohibition against the marriage of persons in the military service without official consent. (German Civil Code, §1315.) As deserters still retain their military character, the German Government refused to recognize the marriage of German soldiers in Alsace and Lorraine who had married in France or Belgium. The recognition of this position would have signified a permanent prohibition against marriage by these persons. Belgium and France thereupon denounced the conventions.[122]

[121] Nussbaum, *Deutsches Int. Privatrecht* (1932), p. 140. See also Art. 287 of the Treaty of Versailles.

[122] Nussbaum, *Deutsches Int. Privatrecht* (1932), pp. 139–140.

In addition to the Hague conventions relating to certain questions of civil procedure and to the fields of family law to which reference has already been made, the Netherlands Government also laid a foundation for the unification of the law of negotiable instruments through conferences held at The Hague in 1910 and 1912, in which 37 nations participated. Great Britain and the United States were also officially represented. The protocol was never ratified and with the consent of the Netherlands Government, the work was continued in 1930 under the auspices of the League of Nations. Three conventions were signed at a conference at Geneva on June 7, 1930, relating to the unification of the law of bills of exchange and promissory notes, and three further conventions were signed on March 19, 1931, relating to cheques. Later ratifications have made all of these effective between certain European countries. The conventions deal separately with the general substantive law and the conflict of laws because the unification does not extend to every subject-matter and a margin is left for domestic legislation. Accordingly, one of the conventions of 1930 deals with the conflict of laws relating to bills and notes, and one of the conventions of 1931 relates to the conflict of laws upon cheques.[123]

**In Latin-American Countries.** An effort to codify the rules of private international law in the form of a multilateral treaty was made as early as 1878 at Lima. A more serious effort was again undertaken at the Conference of Montevideo in 1889, in which 7 nations participated. Separate conventions were elaborated, dealing with conflicts in Civil Law, Commercial Law, the Law of Procedure and Penal Law. Later in the same year a Congress of the North, South and Central American Republics convened at Washington, continuing into 1890, at which the conventions upon the first three subjects were recommended for study and report in the form adopted at Montevideo.[124] The conventions were ratified by only a few South American states.

**The Bustamante Code of Private International Law.** A new impetus was given to the work of codification by the Third Inter-American Conference which met at Rio de Janeiro in 1906, at which an international committee of jurists was appointed to prepare projets for the codification of international law, public and private. The

[123] Amer. Jour. of Int. Law, 1931, pp. 318, 730.

[124] Report of the International American Congress (Washington, 1890). An English translation of the conventions is to be found at pp. 876–933.

committee was reconstituted somewhat at the conference held at Santiago in 1923. In co-operation with the purpose of this committee, a committee of four experts was appointed by the American Institute of International Law in 1924, of which the distinguished Cuban jurist, Antonio S. de Bustamante, was the most active member. Having had long and varied experience, both as a teacher and in practice, in dealing with problems of private international law, he was unusually well qualified to prepare a draft which would serve as a compromise between the various systems recognized in the American Republics. In 1925 he published his *Projet de Code de Droit International Privé*. This was presented to the Sixth International Conference of American States held at Havana in January and February, 1928, and was, with certain modifications, finally adopted as a part of the Final Act of the Conference. It has been ratified by 15 Latin-American nations.[125]

It is important to observe that the Bustamante Code was drafted with a view to its acceptance not only by Latin-American nations but, in part at least, by the United States.[126] Doubtless many of its provisions are better suited to countries of the civil law than to common-law jurisdictions. The distinguished author of the Code has endeavored to prove its acceptability, at least in part, by the United States and other common-law jurisdictions.[127] The declared inability of the United States delegation to accept its provisions in view of the Constitution and the relations of the States to the Federal Government has been criticized by some as being unfounded.[128] The delegation did indeed promise to study the Code with a view to later adherence to at least a large portion; but this seems to have remained only a pious wish. The opportunity seems to have passed with the final adoption of the Restatement by the American Law Institute.[129]

[125] The countries which have ratified prior to May 1, 1937, as reported by the Pan American Union, are as follows: Bolivia, Brazil, Chile, Costa Rica, Cuba, Dominican Republic, Ecuador, El Salvador, Guatemala, Haiti, Honduras, Nicaragua, Panama, Peru and Venezuela.

[126] An English translation of the Code is to be found in: The International Conferences of American States, 1889–1928. Edited by James Brown Scott, 1931, at pp. 327–370. The Declaration of the United States Delegation at the Havana Conference with respect to the Code is given on p. 371.

[127] Bustamante, "The American Systems on the Conflict of Laws and their Reconciliation," (1931) 5 Tulane Law Review, p. 537.

[128] Proceedings, Amer. Soc. Int. Law, 1929, pp. 36–43.

[129] See the remarks by Manley O. Hudson upon this point. *Ibid.*, pp. 41–42.

## Chapter III

# NATIONALITY AND DOMICIL

In reviewing the historical development of private international law we have observed that the earliest conflicts of law comparable to those with which we have to deal in the modern world arose in the Italian cities of the Middle Ages. Although governed by a common (Roman) law, a certain independence was enjoyed in matters legislative. Differences of nationality in the modern sense did not exist, and yet persons domiciled in the cities claimed the right to be governed by the law of their particular city in personal matters even outside the city's territorial limits. The law of the domicil was the regulatory principle for personal law as opposed to the territorial law applicable in a forum foreign to the domicil. The feudal system with its emphasis upon territorial sovereignty increased the diversity of law. However, even after the formation of political unity in France and Italy, domicil continued to be the determinant of personal law. As De Magalhaes points out, conflicts of law arose between individuals subject to different laws within their own state, conflicts which were determined by the law of their domicil. Once unity of law was established and intercourse became more and more international instead of merely interprovincial, a new standard of personal law entered the arena, that of nationality.[1] Thus a battle ensued between the two standards for the determination of personal law which has continued to the present day.

The principle of national law celebrated a significant victory in the adoption of the Civil Code of France which provides in Art. 3 (3): "The laws concerning the status and the capacity of persons govern Frenchmen even residing in foreign countries." The analogous principle was soon applied by the courts to the status of aliens residing in France.[2] The spirit of nationalism which pervaded the French

[1] De Magalhaes, *Acad. de droit int., Recueil des Cours,* 1928, iii, p. 10.
[2] Weiss, *Traité* (1899) iii, pp. 298–299. Clunet, 1878, p. 502.

Revolution was characterized not only by a fervid attempt to protect the citizen in the possession of his newly acquired rights but also to place the foreigner at a disadvantage in his private relations with the citizen. Provisions for a national forum for French citizens even with respect to transactions entered into abroad with foreigners, the privileges accorded to French citizens in matters of succession, the distinction made between the authorized domicil of foreigners and *de facto* domicil are all evidence of this policy, although there have been important relaxations since the adoption of the codes both by statute and the jurisprudence of the courts.

The second triumph of the national law principle was celebrated through the efforts of Mancini to fortify the cause of Italian unity to which reference has already been made.[3] It is therefore manifest that the doctrine is political and based upon political motives though not without certain justifications of a private-law nature to which we shall presently refer. Living as we do in an age of extreme nationalism, it is not surprising that a publicist so impartial as De Magalhaes should view the principle of national law as gaining progressively more and more ground among the nations, both in theory and in legislative practice.[4]

**National Law and Domiciliary Law as Determinants.** Even though we leave aside considerations of a political nature, it may be said that national law represents a more permanent standard for governing personal and family relations because it cannot be readily changed by the mere will of the party. Objection to national law lies in the fact that there are serious conflicts of laws in regard to nationality itself. Nationality is not regulated by international law, and each state is as yet free to determine by its own internal legislation what shall be the requisites for acquiring or losing the nationality of that state. As a result, persons may be and, under modern conditions, frequently are without any nationality, or they may possess double or multiple nationality. Where such conflicts occur, it becomes necessary either to adopt another standard of personal law, such as the law of the domicil, or to make an arbitrary legislative choice of the particular nationality which shall be authoritative.

The acceptance of the law of the domicil avoids some of these objections. The concept of legal domicil in contradistinction to the mere domicil *de facto* may differ somewhat from state to state, but

[3] See *ante*, p. 14.
[4] De Magalhaes, *ut cit.* p. 11.

the concept itself is a unitary one; so that a person must be recognized as having his legal domicil in one and not in several places.[5] Accordingly, the standard of law may be established by proof of the relevant facts relating to domicil. A further argument in favor of domicil as a standard of personal law is that in federal states, there is frequently great diversity of law and legislation within the territory of the national state. It therefore becomes necessary even in jurisdictions which apply the national law to look to the domicil in order to determine the particular subdivision of the federal union to which the subject belongs. An Italian court endeavoring to find the proper personal law of an American citizen would have to determine his domicil in order to apply the law of that State of the Union which constitutes the *lex patriae* from the viewpoint of Italian law.

An important objection to the law of the domicil has already been indicated, *viz.*, that domicil may be acquired by voluntary acts on the part of the individual, which may have the effect of changing his domicil after a short period of time. Accordingly, the temptation is presented of making a change of domicil in order to effectuate a change of law.

Efforts have been made to compromise the two competing systems of national and domiciliary law by treaty applicable to specific problems. Such a compromise was adopted in the Hague Convention to regulate the Conflict of Laws in regard to Marriage, and the Hague Convention in Regard to Divorce and Separation.[6] A similar effort at compromise is to be found in the Geneva Conventions relating to the Conflict of Laws in respect to Bills, Notes and Checks.[7]

A further compromise was incorporated in the Bustamante Code of Private International Law by permitting each state full liberty of action relating to the standard of personal law, while fixing the application of laws in all other matters. In the reservations jointly made by Colombia and Costa Rica in signing the protocol to the Code, the delegations of these states called attention to the objection of the national standard for countries of immigration. While accepting the compromise, they assert that it should be considered transitory

[5] Dicey, Conflict of Laws (1932) pp. 75–77, declares this to be the rule although a possible modification is suggested that no person can, *for the same purpose,* have at the same time more than one domicil. The Restatement of Conflict of Laws (1934) §11, provides: "Every person has at all times one domicil, and no person has more than one domicil at a time."

[6] See *post,* p. 187.

[7] See *ante,* p. 61.

because the law of the domicil is the only one which is suitable to the peoples of America. Immigration countries should be opposed to the acceptance of national law because, as they believe, it amounts to creating a state within a state to allow so many immigrants from various European countries the right to invoke in the country of their permanent domicil, laws of their origin to determine their civil status. Accordingly, the two delegations expressed the earnest hope that there would soon disappear from legislation of all American countries the "traces of theories (more political than legal) favored by Europe in order to preserve her jurisdiction over her nationals, who have established themselves in these free lands of America. . . ."[8]

The regulation of nationality being within the control of each sovereign state under international law, efforts have been made to eliminate by treaty the conflicts of nationality laws. The diplomatic conference held at The Hague in 1930 endeavored to elaborate such a convention. The subject is, however, not within the limitations of the present work.[9]

**Common-Law Principles for Ascertaining Domicil.** The Anglo-American concept of domicil is the place or country which is in fact a person's permanent home, or which is so regarded by a rule of law. A person's home as defined by Dicey is that country "either (i) in which he in fact resides, with the intention of residence (*animus manendi*), or (ii) in which having so resided, he continues actually to reside, though no longer retaining the intention of residence (*animus manendi*), or (iii) with regard to which, having so resided there, he retains the intention of residence (*animus manendi*) though he in fact no longer resides there."[10] In this definition it is important to observe that "residence" is employed to denote the physical fact included in the word "home." This is not its general use in the United States where it is frequently used as synonymous with domicil both by the legislature and by the courts. Furthermore, Dicey's definition is intended to apply only to persons having freedom of choice. It does not apply to persons who for one reason or another are not free to choose their home and to which the law *attributes* a domicil. Thus an infant actually residing with his father partakes of his domicil. A married woman is by English law invariably domiciled

[8] Int. Conferences of American States (1931) p. 373.

[9] *Cf.* Flournoy and Hudson, Nationality Laws of Various Countries, (1929). See also the Draft Convention on Nationality elaborated by the Harvard Research in International Law (1929).

[10] Dicey, Conflict of Laws (1932) p. 66.

with her husband in the eyes of the law,[11] though this is not the case in the United States and in other systems.[12] In other words, "domicil" is a legal concept while "home" is a factual one from which the legal is in greater or less measure derived. Where domicil results from the acts and intent of a person free to act and intend, it may be denominated a "domicil of choice." Where the domicil is attributed, it is often spoken of as a domicil by "operation of law." Mr. Justice Holmes has said: "what the law means by domicil is one technically pre-eminent headquarters, which as a result either of fact or of fiction every person is compelled to have in order that by aid of it certain rights and duties which have been attached to it by the law may be determined." [13]

The principal example of an attributed domicil by operation of law is, of course, that which every person receives at birth, and which is called the "domicil of origin." This is, in the case of a legitimate child born during his father's lifetime, the domicil of the father at the time of birth. In the case of an illegitimate, a posthumous or a legitimated child, the domicil of the mother at the time of birth.[14]

In Udny *v.* Udny the question involved the legitimation of a child born out of wedlock in England of parents who were afterwards married in Scotland. The subsequent marriage of parents has the effect of legitimation by Scotch law but did not have that effect under English law then prevailing, the status of the child being determined by the domicil of the father at the time of the birth of the child. Colonel Udny, the father, was born in Italy of domiciled Scotch parents. He became an officer in the Scots Guards before he came of age, but later married, retired from the army and settled with his wife in London where he resided for thirty-two years. He then gave up his establishment in London and moved to Boulogne in France where, after his wife's death, he formed a connection with the mother of the child, later marrying her in Scotland. The court found that the father had no intention of settling permanently in France and also that having given up his domicil in London, his domicil of origin at

[11] Lord Advocate *v.* Jaffrey, [1921] 1 A.C. 146; H. *v.* H. [1928] p. 206.

[12] See *post*, pp. 73, 162.

[13] Bergner & Engel Brewing Co. *v.* Dreyfus, (1898) 172 Mass. 154, at p. 157. The court was considering the domicil of a corporation. Justice Holmes held that domicil, at least for any given purpose was "single by its essence" and that a corporation does not differ from a natural person in this respect.

[14] Dicey, (1932) p. 80; Udny v. Udny, (1869) L.R. 1 H.L (Sc. App.) 441; Goulder *v.* Goulder, [1892] p. 240; *In re* Wright's Trusts, (1856) 2 K. & J. 595; 25 L.J. Ch. 621.

once revived and the child had become legitimate by that law.[15]

The doctrine of a presumed reversion to the domicil of origin after abandonment of a domicil of choice has not been generally followed in the United States. It is not a doctrine suited to the conditions of a country of immigration where the domicil of origin has ordinarily been abandoned with no intent of returning and where the domicil is frequently changed in search of new opportunity.[16] The reverter theory has not found favor in New York. When a new domicil is acquired, it does not revert "unless intention and residence unite again." [17] Dicta are indeed sometimes to be found to the effect that "the native domicil easily reverts, and fewer circumstances are necessary to establish it than to establish foreign domicil"; [18] also that "less evidence is required to establish a change of domicil from one state to another than from one nation to another." [19] But these are all factual circumstances which must be taken into consideration along with others, the relative values of which were well discussed in a recent House of Lords decision. The deceased, born in Germany, had resided for many years in England and obtained naturalization there. However, he returned frequently to Germany, and although he maintained an establishment in England for his wife, and occupied another house in England after her death, he was held to have retained his domicil of origin in Germany. The effect of these important facts was negatived by the continued close personal and business relations retained in Germany by the deceased. Even the declaration made in applying for naturalization, of his intention to reside permanently in the United Kingdom, was held not conclusive. "It is important to remember that naturalization is one thing, change of

[15] (1869) L.R. 1 H.L. (Sc. App.) 441. It has been said that this case contains the whole of the law of England relating to a change of domicil when taken together with Bell *v.* Kennedy, (1868) L.R. 1 H.L. (Sc. App.) 307. In the latter case, the domicil of origin was Jamaica and although the husband had left Jamaica and remained for a considerable period in Scotland it was held that the Jamaican domicil of origin was retained in the absence of definite proof of a different intent.

[16] Beale, Treatise (1935) i, 184, remarks: "In America the British loyalty to one's place of birth is little felt." We believe the American, native or naturalized, has the same loyalty, which is, indeed, of biologic character; but the English cases are more frequently those in which political allegiance has not changed with the change of residence.

[17] Matter of Newcomb, (1908) 192 N.Y. 238, 251. *Accord: In re* Jones Est., (1921) 192 Ia. 78.

[18] *In re* Lachenmeyer's Estate, (1928) 258 N.Y. Supp. 641, 644.

[19] Vann, J. in Matter of Newcomb, *ut cit.* at p. 250.

domicil is another: and that it is not the law either that a change of domicil is a condition of naturalization, or that naturalization involves necessarily a change of domicil."[20]

**The Restatement Rules for Ascertaining Domicil.** The Restatement has not changed the general concept of domicil established by the English common law but it has given effect to certain changes because certain presumptions drawn by the leading cases in England are not favored by the preponderance of authority in the United States.

The domicil of origin is described as "the domicil assigned to every child at his birth."[21] A domicil of choice is described as one acquired "through the exercise of his own will, by a person who is legally capable of changing his domicil." To acquire a domicil of choice, a person must establish a dwelling place with the intention of making it his home and if the fact of physical presence concurs with the intention to make the dwelling place a home at the moment, the change of domicil takes place.[22]

"A domicil once established continues until it is superseded by a new domicil."[23] This rule applies whether the last domicil was a domicil of origin, a domicil of choice, or an attributed domicil. The point at which the Restatement draws away from the English doctrine is in the case of an abandonment of a domicil of choice without acquiring a new domicil of choice. The domicil of origin is not thereby revived but the last domicil of choice continues.[24]

The Restatement employs the term "home" rather than "residence" because of the frequent confusion of terms as used in statutes. There is a hopeless lack of distinction both in statutes and the decided cases between the term "residence" when used to indicate a home and when having the legal significance of domicil. It follows as a corollary from the continuing nature of domicil that when a person able to make a choice has more than one home, his domicil is in the earlier home unless he regards the second as his principal home.[25]

One of the most difficult questions of domicil is that which determines the right of a wife living apart from the husband to acquire

[20] Wahl *v.* Attorney General, (1932) 147 L.T. 382. Opinion of Lord Atkin at p. 385.

[21] Restatement, §14.

[22] Restatement, §§15, 20.

[23] Restatement, §23.

[24] *Ibid.*, comment and illustrations.

[25] Restatement, §24.

a separate domicil. The Restatement first accepts the principle that a wife has the same domicil as that of her husband.[26] This, however, is subject to the qualification that if the wife lives apart without being guilty of desertion according to the law of the state which was their domicil at the time of separation, she can have a separate domicil.[27] The Restatement, however, does not express any opinion as to whether a wife guilty of desertion according to the law of the husband's domicil at the time of separation, may acquire a domicil in another state. There is much confusion of authority and, indeed, as the question of domicil itself is determined by the law of the forum, the principles applicable are dependent upon the underlying rule for accepting jurisdiction. This leads to a vicious circle for the reason that jurisdiction itself is predicated upon domicil. The solution lies only in the arbitrement of a supreme court in a federated state, or of the judgment ultimately given in a foreign country upon the question of jurisdiction. This is fully discussed in the chapter relating to divorce.[28]

The Restatement confirms the common-law rules of attributed domicil of a minor child already mentioned and adds the case of divorce or judicial separation of the parents, in which event the minor child's domicil is attributed to the parent to whose custody it has been legally given or with whom it lives.[29]

An illegitimate child has the same domicil as that of its mother except that it is governed by the rules relating to emancipation, abandoned children or adopted children.[30] A child abandoned by one parent has the domicil of the other; and if abandoned by both parents, has the domicil of the parent who last abandoned it; or if abandoned by both at the same time, it has the domicil of the father at the time of abandonment.[31] A person who is mentally deficient or of unsound mind can acquire a domicil as if he had normal mental capacity if he is able to choose a home.[32] These rules are, of course, subject to the power of a guardian of a minor child or of an incompetent to change the domicil.[33]

26 Restatement, §27.
27 Restatement, §28.
28 See *post*, pp. 155–174.
29 Restatement, §§14 (2), 30, 32.
30 Restatement, §34.
31 Restatement, §33 (1).
32 Restatement, §40.
33 See Restatement, §§37, 38, 39.

**Comparative Principles for Ascertainment of Domicil. France.** Under the policy and the legislation of the revolutionary period, every foreigner who desired to establish a domicil in France required the authorization of the government.[34] This authorization was good only for five years and was a preliminary step to naturalization. In the meantime, the foreigner enjoyed all the citizen's civil rights as that term is understood in France. While some authorities interpreted the rule as preventing a mere factual residence from being the source of private rights, others pointed out that this article of the Code appeared under the heading "Concerning the enjoyment of civil rights"; therefore its object was to assure to every foreigner admitted to domicil by authorization the enjoyment of all civil rights, whereas other foreigners enjoy only those civil rights "which are or shall be accorded to French persons by the treaties of the nations to which such foreigners belong."[35] Other articles of the Code[36] indicate that the domicil is located at the situs of a person's "principal establishment." Although speaking only of French persons, these articles were interpreted by the courts as applicable by analogy also to foreigners.[37]

The French statute of August 10, 1927, relating to nationality repealed the provision of the Civil Code relating to authorized domicil[38] without substituting any other system. Art. 11 was allowed to remain so that the distinction between *de jure* and *de facto* domicil has become unimportant so far as concerns domicil as a determinant of private law. The rules of French law relating to domicil vary from common-law principles not so much because of fundamental differences but because of statutory definition and statutory procedure. A married woman has no other domicil than that of her husband.[39] A minor, not emancipated, is domiciled with his father, mother or guardian. An adult under guardianship is domiciled with his guardian.[40] Adults who work for another person while living in the same house are considered as having their domicil there.[41] A woman separated from bed and board ceases to have the husband's domicil

[34] French Civil Code, Art. 13 (repealed Aug. 10, 1927).
[35] Art. 11.
[36] Arts. 102–103.
[37] André Weiss, *Traité,* (1899) ii, 377 and note citing cases, *e.g.,* Sirey, 1873, vol. 2, p. 265; Clunet, 1887, p. 479. *Accord:* Belgium, Clunet, 1889, p. 713.
[38] Law of Aug. 10, 1927, Art. 13. Clunet, 1927, p. 1213.
[39] French Civil Code, Art. 108.
[40] *Ibid.*
[41] Art. 109.

and is assigned a domicil by the court. However, an agreement between husband and wife to assign a separate domicil to the wife would be deemed void.[42] The Code thus lays down certain principles of domicil fixed by law. A change of domicil may be presumed (where the individual has freedom of choice) by reason of an actual residence in another place coupled with the intention of the person to make it his "principal establishment."[43] The Civil Code provides a formal method of expressing intention to change by means of a declaration to be made at the place of the old as well as of the new domicil;[44] but the formal declaration is not mandatory and if not filed, proof will depend upon circumstances.[45] While no fixed rule can be predicated, it may be said that French courts are more liberal than courts in English or American jurisdictions in assuming that a change of domicil was intended. This can only be tested by an examination of the facts of decided cases. Greater stress seems to be laid upon the fact of actual change than upon psychological forces from which particular intent may be inferred. Pillet intimates that this attitude of French courts may be explained by the fact that domicil in England plays a much more important role from an international point of view than it does in France and therefore English judges pay more particular care to the determination of domicil.[46]

Just as in England and the United States a domicil may exist for certain purposes, such as for taxation, so French law speaks of an "elected domicil" for special purposes, commercial, jurisdictional, electoral, fiscal and the like.[47] This is not to be confused with domicil as a determinant of law in the international sense. An example of an election of this nature is furnished by Art. 111 of the Civil Code by which a forensic domicil may be established by written instrument at a place other than the "real domicil." An "elected domicil" in this sense is, furthermore, not to be confused with the "domicil of choice" under the common law. The French conception is strictly one of attributed domicil for a special purpose whereas the English concept is that of an actual domicil established by free will and the act of the party.

[42] Arts. 214, 1388.

[43] Art. 103.

[44] Art. 104, but the declaration must refer to a particular and not to a general locality. Lebaudy's notice of removal to "The Sahara" was held ineffective. Clunet, 1906, p. 396.

[45] Art. 105.

[46] Pillet, *Traité* (1923) i, p. 300.

[47] Arminjon, *Précis,* (1934) ii, p. 18.

**Germany.** The Civil Code provides that domicil is established by permanent settlement at a given place.[48] A domicil may be had simultaneously at several places.[49] Accordingly, the concept differs essentially from that of the common law at least so far as concerns the determination of a particular domiciliary law. While not specifically providing that a person may be without a domicil, this would seem to follow from the provision of the Code by which the domicil ceases when the place of residence is discontinued with the intention of abandoning it.[50] Schuster draws this conclusion and remarks that German law does not make the distinction between domicil of origin and domicil of choice.[51] This results from the difference of approach where a codified law assumes to fix the domicil for particular relationships. Thus the domicil of the father determines that of the legitimate child; the domicil of the mother that of her illegitimate child. As the child retains its residence until it abandons it in some legally recognized manner, elements of the domicil of origin are present without, however, any principle for a resumption of a prior domicil by surrender of a later one.[52]

In a similar manner, a separate domicil for a married woman is provided in the event that the husband has no domicil, or when he establishes a domicil in a foreign country to which the wife does not follow him and is not legally compelled to follow him.[53]

**Switzerland.** In contrast with the German provision, Swiss law specifically provides that no one may have a domicil at more than one place; but this is not inconsistent with the establishment of a commercial domicil at more than one place.[54] Also contrasting with German law, a domicil of a person once established remains fixed until the acquirement of a new domicil.[55] To provide for the difficulty of proving a prior domicil, Swiss law seems to allow a presumption in favor of the place of actual sojourn where the former domicil cannot be proved, or if a domicil abroad has been abandoned and no new domicil is established in Switzerland.[56]

**Italy.** The Civil Code draws a distinction between civil domicil and residence. The former is declared to be at the principal seat

[48] German Civil Code, §7 (1).
[49] *Ibid.*, §7 (2).
[50] *Ibid.*, §7 (3).
[51] Schuster, The Principles of German Civil Law (1907) pp. 27–28.
[52] *Ibid.*, §11.
[53] *Ibid.*, §10.
[54] Swiss Civil Code, Art. 23.
[55] Art. 24.
[56] *Ibid.*, 24 (2).

of a person's affairs and interests, whereas the latter is described as at his place of principal abode (Art. 16).

**Latin-American Countries.** The Bustamante Code does not provide any general principles but lays down rules for the conflict of laws relating to domicil. In this it is unique. The principle that the concept of domicil must be determined by the law of the forum is specifically accepted in the Code; the law of the forum must also determine the loss and recovery of domicil.[57] This seems to be subject to an exception in the event that the question relates to the domicil of a person alleged to be domiciled in one of the interested states adhering to the Code. If, however, the question relates to a change of domicil from a place not within the territory of any of these states, it must be determined by the law of the place alleged to be that of the last domicil.

For persons having no domicil, the place of their residence or, in the absence of residence, the place where they happen to be, shall be considered as the domicil.[58] This solution is similar to the provision of the Brazilian Civil Code.[59]

**Proposed International Regulation of the Conflict of Laws relating to Domicil.** The review which we have given of law and legislation in various countries relating to domicil would seem to point to three major sources of conflict, *viz.*, (1) the recognition of the possibility of multiple domicil by some systems and not by others; (2) a person may have a domicil of choice in one country under the laws of that country and yet he may be considered as having his domicil by operation of law under the laws of another country; (3) a person may have a domicil by operation of law in one country and in a different country by operation of the law prevailing there.

The conflict of laws relating to domicil was one of the subjects considered by the Committee of Jurists of the League of Nations for the Progressive Codification of International Law with a view to possible codification by convention. A learned report was presented by De Magalhaes and Brierly in June, 1928.[60] De Magalhaes proposed to fix the competent system for the determination of a domicil by operation of law. He also proposed that a domicil of choice should give way to a domicil by operation of law where the

[57] Bustamante Code, Art. 22.
[58] *Ibid.*, Art. 26.
[59] Brazilian Civil Code, Art. 33.
[60] Publications of the League of Nations, Legal, 1928, V. 3.

two were in conflict. The fixation of conflicting domicils by operation of law should be accomplished by accepting the domicil of that country in which the person was actually residing. This solution seems reasonable at first glance but it may not be so easy of accomplishment by convention. A married woman living apart from her husband is regarded in some countries as still having her domicil with her husband whereas in another country in which she is in fact residing, she may be regarded as domiciled there. The solution would tend to upset a principle regarded in some countries to be upon a point of fundamental social importance and would therefore undoubtedly encounter much opposition.

De Magalhaes proposed also that a domicil of choice should be more easily proved and provided for a certificate to be issued by the proper public authorities of the place to which a person removes. The certificate should follow upon a declaration that the person intends to establish his domicil at the place of registration. A certain length of residence would be necessary before registration.

The *lex fori* was accepted as the proper system of determining conflicts of law resulting from different conceptions of domicil. This is in accordance not only with the prevailing rule in Europe but also with the Restatement of the American Law Institute. The important question is raised as to whether the *lex fori* should determine even when the person in question is not alleged to be domiciled in the forum at all. Thus for example, would a French court decide in accordance with French law as to whether a Russian is domiciled in China or in Japan? De Magalhaes implies that the *lex fori* should not govern and proposes a somewhat complicated rule. It is not wise to attempt to find solutions by mere *a priori* reasoning. Brierly supposes a case in which an English court is called upon to administer the movable estate of a person who died intestate in France under circumstances by which he would be regarded as domiciled in Portugal under English law. Under Portuguese law he would not be considered domiciled there. The important question is not as to whether a Portuguese court would consider the person domiciled in Portugal by Portuguese law but how Portugal would distribute his property if he *had* been domiciled in Portugal. We believe that the choice of law remains in the forum even though the domicil can by no interpretation be regarded as located in the country of the forum. The *lex fori* is therefore indicated as the proper law to determine the place of domicil.

## Chapter IV

# JURISDICTION AND PROCEDURE

### 1. Conflicts of Jurisdiction

The administration of justice in civilized states is entrusted to courts of law under definition or limitation of powers. Where the facts and conditions upon which judicial action is founded in a particular case may properly be the subject of action also by the courts of another state, a conflict of jurisdiction is presented, to be regulated by rules of private international law. Such conflicts may result where one of the parties is domiciled within or a national of a foreign state; or where the transaction took place in whole or in part within a foreign state; or where judicial action is sought in the local state with reference to rights or interests in property in a foreign state.

Beale assumes to draw a distinction between "jurisdiction" and "power." The former he describes as "the power of a state to create rights that will be recognized abroad" and the latter as "its power to act as it pleases within its own territory."[1] There are, however, no generally accepted rules by which a state can create rights that are sure to be recognized everywhere abroad. There are certain rules accepted in some states but repudiated in others. Furthermore, there exists no supranational authority which can compel a state to recognize rights created by exercise of the power of a foreign state. We can arrive at an approximation of the rules which states generally accept with reference to the powers of their own courts to deal with controversies in which there is a foreign element and, conversely, an approximation of the rules which states accept with regard to powers of the courts of a foreign state to create rights which the local state will recognize. The fixation of jurisdic-

[1] Beale, Treatise, (1935) p. 275.

tion applicable to two or more states may be accomplished by treaty. There are also certain principles of public international law which limit the jurisdiction of states, such as the immunity granted to the person of a foreign sovereign and diplomatic representatives, and the immunity from process of the property of foreign states. The violation of these rules may give rise to diplomatic claims under international law and are not within the limitations of our subject.

**Historical Precedents.** The establishment of the Roman Empire found its territory divided into a number of urban communities each with its own magistrates, its own jurisdiction and, to some extent, its own system of positive law. Italy, beside the capital city, contained a large number of towns, *municipia* or *civitates,* while the rest of the Empire was divided into separate provinces, the constitutions of which gradually approximated the municipal system of Italy.[2] Originally, the cities of the provinces did not have original jurisdiction. The forum of origin was the forum to which every Italian belonged by municipal citizenship, although he might be domiciled in another *civitas* or in a province, and if so, he was subject also to the jurisdiction of his domicil. Westlake suggests that after the edict of Caracalla (A.D. 212) extending Roman citizenship to all free subjects of the Empire, it is likely that by some express provision, now lost, the plaintiff was precluded from choosing the forum of his origin except when the defendant was to be found within its territory.[3]

The strictness with which the rules of jurisdiction were applied is intimated in the well known extract from the Digest by which it is said that a judge could not be obeyed with impunity if he exercised jurisdiction outside his territorial limits: *Extra territorium jus dicenti impune non paretur. Idem est, et si supra jurisdictionem suam velit jus dicere.*[4]

Besides the rules of jurisdiction indicated by the origin or domicil of the defendant, the Roman law allowed jurisdiction in the place fixed by the facts and conditions of the litigation itself, as for example, the forum for the performance of certain contracts, or under certain circumstances, the place in which an obligation arose.[5]

Medieval jurists did not work out a system of international civil

[2] *Cf.* Savigny, Conflict of Laws, (Guthrie's trans., 1880) §351.
[3] Westlake, Private Int. Law (1925) p. 236.
[4] Digest, ii, 1, 20.
[5] *Cf.* Savigny, *op. cit.,* §370.

procedure, but contented themselves with a classification of laws into two divisions, *viz.*, those which had to do with the *ordinatio litis* and those which regulated the *decisio litis*. This division was recognized in the days of Bartolus in the 14th century and received only slightly different definition in the days of Boullenois in the 18th century. Boullenois described the former group as relating to the form and ceremonies of the judicial process preceding the judgment, whereas the latter includes all laws and regulations which define and determine the substance of the principal issue.[6]

It will be observed that this classification in itself does not determine the application of the law. It merely decides that questions of procedure are determined by the law of the forum whereas questions of substance may or may not be so determined. In its scientific results the division was very similar to the classification of substantive laws under the statutory theory, and in fact the division may be taken as a corollary.

The early jurisdiction of the English courts was co-extensive with the realm. Differing from the rules derived from Roman practice, the domicil of the parties did not determine jurisdiction for a particular English court. At common law, it was necessary that the action should be begun by service upon the defendant personally within the realm. If the writ was so served, a judgment could be obtained against the defendant even though his domicil and national allegiance were foreign. Originally courts did not take cognizance of all cases which occurred abroad even if the defendant was served within the realm. The plaintiff was in danger of being nonsuited upon that ground alone. This is well shown by a case in Year Book, 2 Edward II (1308), wherein the plaintiff was nonsuited because the cause of action arose in Scotland.[7] Although all actions were originally considered local, the place where the facts in issue arose was required to be alleged and the venue of the action correctly laid. It is said that the rule arose out of the early practice which required a case to be tried before a jury of men of the vicinage, who were presumed to have knowledge of the facts and of the parties.[8]

The jurisdiction recognized by English courts over foreign land was laid down by equity courts in the days of Lord Hardwicke

[6] Boullenois, *Traité de la personnalité et de la réalité des loix* I, title 2, chap. 3, obs. 23.

[7] Selden Society Publications, i, pp. 110–111.

[8] See Mitchell, J., in Little *v.* Chicago & St. Paul Ry. Co., (1896) 65 Minn. 48.

through the authority which the chancellor exercised over the person of a defendant found in England. In the well known action of Penn *v.* Lord Baltimore,[9] which concerned a dispute over a contract affecting the boundaries of the provinces of Pennsylvania and Maryland, objection was made that the court lacked jurisdiction because it was unable to enforce its decree *in rem.* Although the case was decided upon the reservation of dominion and property in the king and council, Lord Hardwicke, by way of dictum, reasserted the power of the court to act *in personam* even though the *res* was without the territory. This power was early recognized by the United States Supreme Court in an action brought by a citizen of Kentucky in a Federal court against a citizen of Virginia, to compel conveyance of land in Ohio which the defendant had obtained through a fraudulent survey. Both upon the English authorities and upon principle, the court held that "in case of fraud, of trust, or of contract, the jurisdiction of a court of chancery is sustainable wherever the person be found, although lands not within the jurisdiction of that court may be affected by the decree." [10]

The jurisdiction of the court is, of course, a fundamental requisite in every action. It is an issue frequently underlying cases in private international law because it is likely to be raised where one or more of the parties are domiciled abroad, or of foreign nationality, or where the subject-matter of the action is located abroad. The validity of a foreign judgment always involves the jurisdiction of the foreign court. We shall, therefore, be discussing jurisdictional questions under each division of our subject, omitting the details here.

## 2. Local Jurisdiction and Extraterritorial Recognition

The fact that a judgment has been obtained in a foreign country under conditions giving the foreign court jurisdiction under the law of that country, is not sufficient to give the judgment the quality of having been rendered by a court having jurisdiction from the viewpoint of private international law. To illustrate: The defendant and his wife left Germany in 1901 to take up permanent residence in New York. In 1906 he declared his intention of becoming a citizen

[9] (1750) 1 Ves. R. 444.

[10] Marshall, C. J., in Massie *v.* Watts, (1810) 6 Cranch 148. For the later cases, see *post*, p. 225.

of the United States. The plaintiff, domiciled in and a subject of Germany, obtained a judgment against the defendant in 1907 by publication at a time in which the defendant was not in Germany. The judgment was not accorded recognition in New York because not obtained on personal service, although it was recognized that jurisdiction was complete under German law.[11]

The nub of the problem is that not all judgments obtained on proper grounds of jurisdiction will be accorded extraterritorial recognition. The Restatement[12] recognizes that a state has jurisdiction over its nationals although not present within the territorial limits. But this in itself is sufficient only to recognize the validity of the judgment within the state in which it was recovered. The court (per Cullen, C. J.) quoted the celebrated case of Pennoyer *v.* Neff,[13] to the effect that process sent out of the state and process published within it are equally unavailing in proceedings to establish a personal judgment which will be recognized from one state of the Union to another; and then concludes that it is unreasonable to give greater respect to judgments recovered in a foreign country than to one recovered in a sister state. This is another way of saying that the question involved is not strictly one of jurisdiction but of the particular *kind* of jurisdiction which will entitle it to recognition in the local state.

An illustration of these principles is given in a Privy Council case which involved the validity of a judgment obtained in Faridkote, a native state of India, by its Rajah, against one of his employés. The defendant was served with process in Jhind, another Indian state, in which he was then domiciled and judgment entered against him by default. Upon seeking to enforce the judgment before a British Indian Court, it was held that the judgment was void for lack of jurisdiction. The plaintiff "must sue in the court to which the defendant is subject at the time of suit (*'Actor sequitur forum rei'*); which is rightly stated by Sir Robert Phillimore (International Law, vol. 4, s. 891) to 'lie at the root of all international, and of most domestic, jurisprudence on this matter.' All jurisdiction is properly territorial and *extra territorium jus dicenti, impune non paretur.*"[14]

[11] Grubel *v.* Nassauer, (1913) 210 N.Y. 149.
[12] Restatement, §47 (2).
[13] (1877) 95 U.S. 714, 727.
[14] Sirdar Gurdyal Singh *v.* Rajah of Faridkote, [1894] 1 A.C. 670. Lord Selborne at p. 683, with references to both Kent and Story.

**Jurisdiction over Foreign Corporations.** Where jurisdiction is founded upon personal service, it is of great importance to determine the conditions under which a foreign corporation may be subjected to process within the state. A corporation being the creature of the state in which it is organized, personality can be ascribed only by the consent of other states when a foreign corporation seeks to do business therein. In England, a corporation is regarded as "residing" in the country if it does business at some fixed place, even though temporarily. Thus, service of process has been effectually recognized upon a foreign company although it had only rented a stand for offering its goods for sale at a bicycle show.[15] Residence in this sense is not synonymous with domicil but rather with mere presence within the jurisdiction.

The American doctrine is not the same because jurisdiction is not recognized without a statute providing for service of process upon a foreign corporation.[16] Statutes of this kind are now to be found in practically all the states, although the provisions of such statutes vary with reference to the conditions required for doing business within the state. Assuming, however, that the foreign corporation does not comply with the statute and nevertheless does business within the state, what shall be the justification for service upon the corporation through its officers or agents? Has the foreign corporation consented to the exercise of jurisdiction by merely doing business? Mr. Justice Holmes maintains that the consent thus implied is a mere fiction.[17] Mr. Justice Cardozo maintains that the corporation is estopped from denying that it has done what it ought to have done, in order to do business within the state.[18] To this result Beale remarks: "It is surely unfortunate to deal with a question of jurisdiction on the basis of a fiction." [19] He, therefore, offers the theory of submission, by which a corporation submits itself to the jurisdiction of the state by doing business therein as to all actions arising out of the business done.[20] This seems to be substituting one fiction for another because there is no intent to submit to the jurisdiction in either case. The truth would seem to be that, as legal personality is itself ascribed to corporations by a fiction,

[15] Dunlop Pneumatic Tire Co., *v.* A. G. Cudell & Co., [1902] 1 K.B. 342.
[16] U.S. *v.* American Bell Tel. Co., (1886) 29 F. 17.
[17] Flexner *v.* Farson, (1919) 248 U.S. 289.
[18] Bagdon *v.* Phila. & Reading C. & I. Co., (1916) 217 N.Y. 432.
[19] Beale, Treatise (1935) i, p. 388.
[20] *Ibid.*, p. 390.

justice requires that jurisdiction be recognized upon the basis of doing business, this being an essential corollary of their legal personality.[21]

**Jurisdiction and Public Policy. Recognition of the Effects of Soviet Decrees.** The principle which determines whether a local court will give effect to the acts of a foreign government through legislation or judicial determination is sometimes said to rest upon the basis of public policy. Doubtless the term may be extended in this way but it will not ordinarily be construed to be against public policy to recognize acts completed within the foreign state even though similar acts at home would not be given effect. On the other hand, where a decision involves rights of property of which the situs is properly placed within the local state, the acts of the foreign state through legislation or judicial decision may be considered as without jurisdiction.

A railroad corporation organized under the old regime in Russia had a deposit in a New York bank. After the revolution and the nationalization decrees of the Soviet, it sought to withdraw funds through surviving directors residing in France. The bank endeavored to defend on the ground that the directors had no authority and that the corporation had ceased to exist. It was decided that the nationalization decree affecting the corporation in Russia was not a defense to the action for the deposit.[22] The court in referring to the prior decisions held that although the corporation was extinguished in its homeland, it continued its existence as a juristic person with capacity to sue in the local state. "The confiscation of its assets and the repudiation of its obligations by decrees, is contrary to our public policy and shocking to our sense of justice and equity."[23] Moreover, the local court having jurisdiction over the fund in question, could effectively deny the extraterritorial force of these decrees over funds situated in the local state.

The Court of Appeals had already passed upon the power of such decrees to confiscate property and pass title under them. In Salimoff *v.* The Standard Oil Co.,[24] it was contended that such decrees should have no more effect than the forceful taking by bandits. However, the property confiscated was taken in Russia from Russian nationals and the court held that title to the property

[21] *Cf.* Restatement, §§87–93.
[22] Vladikavkazsky Ry. *v.* N.Y. Trust Co., (1934) 263 N.Y. 371.
[23] *Ibid.*, at p. 378.
[24] (1933) 262 N.Y. 220.

had passed and no cause of action in tort would be recognized in favor of Russian nationals against American corporations who were purchasers for value from the Soviet government in Russia in accordance with Soviet law. "The government may be objectionable in a political sense. It is not unrecognizable as a real governmental power which can give title to property within its limits." [25] The court thus decided the question irrespective of diplomatic recognition. Both this case, in which the acts occurred before recognition, and the later case above referred to, decided after recognition, may be distinguished and confirmed upon the principles of jurisdiction. Could the Soviet government exercise an effective control over the subject matter of the action? If it could, then jurisdiction was present. If it could not, then its acts were not entitled to extraterritorial recognition, whatever the public policy of the local state.

Under policies of an American life insurance company doing business in Russia before the Revolution of 1917, it was provided "that all disputes which may arise in connection with the assurance operations carried on by the Society in Russia shall be settled according to Russian laws and in Russian courts of justice." The court said: "Wherever sued that obligation is to be determined by Russian law, for such is the contract, and no court of this State has power to make a new contract for the parties." [26] Accordingly, the nationalization of all insurance companies, the appropriation of their assets and the cancellation of their policies by Soviet law was held to be cancellation of the obligation. The Soviet Union had been recognized as a government by the United States at the time of the decision but not at the time of the beginning of the action. Under the well-recognized rule such recognition was retroactive in effect,[27] at least with reference to contracts made in Russia to be performed there.

The majority of the court laid preponderant weight upon the recognition of the Soviet government by the United States. In a concurring opinion by Lehman, J., this consideration is declared to carry no practical consequences in this case because under previous decisions the Court of Appeals had refused to give extraterritorial effect to Soviet decrees of confiscation. It was thought that the basis of the previous decisions was not the lack of recognition,

[25] *Ibid.*, per Pound, C. J., at page 227.

[26] Crane, J., in Dougherty *v.* Equitable Life Assurance Soc., (1934) 266 N.Y. 71 at p. 81.

[27] See Oetjen *v.* Central Leather Co., (1917) 246 U.S. 297.

but the fact that confiscatory decrees offended our own public policy.[28] Distinction is made between a decree regulating performance and one which annuls the agreement. There is much force in the argument that the agreement could not be discharged by confiscation of the obligation, even under the principle that the place of performance regulated the contract, because under the policy, the assured had pledged its assets everywhere, *i.e.,* in New York as well as in Russia, in "exact fulfillment" of the terms of the policy. The case, therefore, rests upon principles of jurisdiction; the difference between the majority and the minority of the court was upon the question whether or not the obligation of the insurer was intangible property located within Russia. The majority thought that it was, and if so, the Russian government had dominion over it. The practical result reached by both opinions, however, was the same, because all the judges were agreed that the currency in which the policies were payable was the old ruble, which had become practically valueless.

### 3. Procedure Distinguished from Substantive Law

The principle that the procedure by which rights and interests are judicially determined, is governed by the law of the forum, has been referred to as universal.[29] But there remains the problem of distinguishing procedure, *i.e.,* the mode of the proceedings, from elements of substantive right. Story speaks of "merits and rights involved in actions" and "forms of remedies and the order of judicial proceedings."[30] The decisions are not uniform although it is assumed that a line may be drawn somewhere. Lorenzen says: "the fact is, that no line can be found between 'substance' and 'procedure' by analysis but must be drawn arbitrarily with reference to the purpose in view. The mere fact that a particular matter is regarded by the law of the forum as 'procedural' for some purpose does not prove that it should be so regarded also in the Conflict of Laws."[31]

**Burden of Proof.** Thus, for example, a statute which shifts the burden of proving contributory negligence from plaintiff to defendant is held procedural when the question is as to its retroactive effect

[28] Dougherty *v.* Equitable Life Assurance Soc., (1934) 266 N.Y. at p. 106.
[29] Story, §558.
[30] *Ibid.*
[31] Amer. Bar Assoc. Jour., 1935, p. 374.

and its constitutionality; but where the problem concerns a conflict of laws the result is not the same. In the federal courts the plaintiff must prove contributory negligence where the defendant, a carrier, has shown the loss to have occurred by an act of God. In New York, the carrier must show both the act of God and his own freedom from contributory negligence. A New York court decided that in an action for a loss of an interstate shipment, the burden of proof would be regarded as a rule of substance, following the decision to this effect of the United States Supreme Court.[32] It is important to observe, however, that the Supreme Court does not arrive at this conclusion by directly placing the burden of proof in the category of substance. The question which required a reference to substantive law was whether the contract had been discharged.[33] Thus indirectly rather than directly, the burden of proof may enter into determination of "substantial" questions to be referred to the system of law under which the cause of action arose.

**Parties to Actions.** The determination of the necessary and proper parties is of the essence of procedure. In civil-law countries, a partnership is a legal entity having rights and obligations including the right to sue and be sued in its own name separate and apart from its members. A creditor must sue the firm or all partners jointly before proceeding against one of the partners. In an action against the executors of a deceased member of a Spanish firm, without joining the other partners, the civil-law rule was pleaded before an English court. The court held that the right to sue the partners severally was a rule of procedure, a mode of administering the partnership estate, of which a creditor could avail himself in England.[34] In an action brought against the defendant as a shareholder and acting-director of a French company for negligence in the operation of a ship belonging to the company, application of French law was admitted. The judges were divided as to whether the law absolutely absolved the defendant or whether it imposed a joint liability.[35] Thus there was really no question of procedure involved but the existence of a liability *ab initio*.[36]

[32] Barnet *v.* N.Y. Central & H.R. RR., (1918) 222 N.Y. 195, following Southern Ry. Co. *v.* Prescott, (1915) 240 U.S. 632. See comment by W. W. Cook in (1932) 42 Yale Law Jour. 345.

[33] Southern Ry. Co. *v.* Prescott, *ut cit.*, at p. 639.

[34] *In re* Doetsch, [1896] 2 Ch. 836.

[35] General Steam Navigation Co. *v.* Guillou, (1843) 11 M. & W. 877.

[36] See Cheshire (1935) p. 544.

In a recent case, in which a married woman endeavored to sue her husband in New York for damages due to the negligent operation of an automobile in Connecticut, the Court of Appeals decided that the reciprocal disability between spouses to sue for personal injuries precluded the suit. "No other state can, outside its own territorial limits, remove that disability or provide by its law a remedy available in our courts which our law denies to other suitors." [37]

**Set-off and Counterclaim.** The claim of a defendant to present a set-off or counterclaim in the action brought against him is a matter of procedure because even if denied, it does not affect the defendant's right to proceed independently upon his cause of action. The contract of the plaintiff may preclude the defense of set-off, as, for example, in an action on a negotiable instrument. But here the defendant is precluded under a right which, though it may have been created abroad, is recognized by the local laws according to local as well as foreign procedural rules.[38]

**Measure of Damages.** A cause of action which has arisen under a foreign system and recognized at the forum should be measured as to its extent by the foreign law and redressed accordingly,[39] provided the local procedure is capable of doing so. In a case before the United States Supreme Court, the widow and children of the deceased brought action in Texas for damages for his death by negligence in Mexico. The remedy allowed by Mexican law contemplated annuities not provided for by Texas law and continuing only upon contingencies which the Texas law was not designed to control. The court held that the measure of damages must follow the cause of action but relegated the parties to the courts of Mexico because of the impossibility of executing the law of Mexico in Texas.[40]

The principle referring the measure of damages to the foreign law of the cause by action is complicated by the peculiar English doctrine that for a foreign tort to be actionable in England it must be recognized as actionable by English law.[41]

[37] Mertz *v.* Mertz, (1936) 271 N.Y. 466 at p. 473.

[38] See Stevens *v.* Gregg, (1890) 89 Ky. 461. Restatement, §593 and Comment.

[39] Restatement, §412.

[40] Slater *v.* Mexican Nat. Ry. Co., (1904) 194 U.S. 120. Dissenting opinion by Fuller, C. J., held that the means of redressing the wrong appertain to procedure and should be regulated by the *lex fori.* See also *post,* p. 307.

[41] Phillips *v.* Eyre, (1869) L.R. 4 Q.B. 225; (1870) 6 Q.B. 1. Cheshire (1935) p. 552, admits that Machado *v.* Fontes, [1897] 2 Q.B. 231, is inconsistent with the principle stated in the text.

**Damages for Breach of Contract.** As damages are awarded in compensation of the breach of performance, the quality and measure of such compensation should be governed by the same law by which performance is regulated.[42] The obligation is violated at the place where it should have been performed.[43] It may be taken that this rule is merely a corollary of the broader principle that a contract is governed by its proper law. Chancellor Kent applied the Chinese law relating to interest for the breach of a contract distinctively subject to that law.[44] The New York courts reject the forum where the basis for application of the foreign law has been properly laid,[45] but where there is no proof that the rate of interest under the foreign law differs from that of the forum, the court cannot apply a different rate.[46] On the other hand, Massachusetts and some other jurisdictions, at times prior to the Restatement, have viewed interest granted by way of damages as remedial and therefore to be determined solely by the *lex fori*.[47]

**Evidence.** The rules of evidence are intimately bound up with the mode of conducting trials. The competency of a witness to testify concerning transactions which took place abroad cannot be referred to the law of the place where the acts occurred because the mode of ascertaining the truth is determined by the tribunal upon which falls the duty of inquiry.[48] Does this apply also to the kind of evidence by which the witness is allowed to testify as to the acts? Rules of the common law as to the admissibility of hearsay or of the variance of a written instrument by parol evidence do not exist in all countries. According to Lord Brougham's dictum,[49] whether a certain matter requires to be proved by writing or not, whether certain evidence proves a certain fact or not, are determined by foral law. It is said, however, that "according to the modern and better view, the rule which prohibits the modification of a written contract by parol is a rule, not of evidence, but of substantive law. Parol proof is excluded, not because it is lacking in evidentiary value, but because the law for some substantive reason declares that

[42] Restatement, §§413–415.

[43] Beale, Treatise (1935) p. 1334.

[44] Consequa *v.* Fanning, (1818) 3 Johns. Ch. (N.Y.) 587, at p. 607.

[45] Sirie *v.* Godfrey, (1921) 196 A.D. 529.

[46] See Parker *v.* Hoppe, (1931) 257 N.Y. 333, 343, referring to the Restatement before final numbering of the sections.

[47] Ayer *v.* Tilden, (1860) 15 Gray 178. Beale (1935) p. 1335 n.6.

[48] Restatement, §596.

[49] Bain *v.* Whitehaven & Furness R. Co., (1850) 3 H.L. Cas 1, 19.

what is sought to be proved by it (being outside the writing by which the parties have undertaken to be bound) shall not be shown."[50] Conversely, where the writing sought to be varied by parol, was executed abroad where such variance is permitted, it has been held that the testimony bears upon the nature and validity of the contract, and should be allowed. Specifically, the writing was an indorsement upon a note limited by an oral agreement with the indorsee, made simultaneously.[51]

The question is discussed more fully in connection with the Statute of Frauds.[52]

### 4. Statute of Limitations

The Restatement of the American Law Institute gives expression to two principles which may be accepted as authoritative for English and American jurisdictions. "If action is barred by the statute of limitations of the forum, no action can be maintained though action is not barred in the state where the cause of action arose."[53] To this must be added the converse principle: "If action is not barred by the statute of limitations of the forum, an action can be maintained, though action is barred in the state where the cause of action arose."[54]

The principle that the prescription or limitation of the right of action is procedural and relates to the remedy may be traced to the jurists of the Netherlands school, particularly to Huber and Paul Voet, and to the French jurist, Boullenois.[55] There is, on the other hand, much to be said in favor of the view that an element inhering in the cause of action itself, such as the period over which the cause of action continues to exist, should be considered part of its essential nature and outside of remedial law. In favor of the common-law viewpoint, Lord Brougham insisted that a party does not bind himself for a particular period when he agrees to do something on

[50] Archbald, D. J. in Pitcairn *v.* Phillip Hiss Co., (1903) 125 Fed. 110, 113. Lorenzen, Cases (1924) p. 179n.

[51] Baxter Nat. Bank *v.* Talbot, (1891) 154 Mass. 213. The Restatement provides, §598, that the law of the forum determines whether a certain fact can be proved by oral evidence but (§599) where a contract is integrated in a writing by the law of the place of contracting, no variation by parol will be allowed in another state.

[52] See *post*, p. 273.

[53] Restatement, §603.

[54] Restatement, §604.

[55] Story, §577.

a certain day. "The argument that the limitation is of the nature of contract, supposes that the parties look only to the breach of the agreement."[56] To which it may be answered that a right without a remedy is a right only in name. Moreover, a cause of action which arises out of foreign transactions such as the making of a contract abroad or the causing of damage in a foreign state to person or property through negligence or willful intent, is completed in the foreign state by virtue of its laws. The period during which the cause of action continues, should be, theoretically speaking, as much a part of the cause of action as any other. It is true that the local state may determine whether or not to give redress for a cause of action completed in the foreign state; but having once decided to recognize the cause of action, the court should recognize it according to its tenor as already completed in the foreign state. However, as Dicey points out, even though logic may be on the side of regarding the limitation of actions as part of their substance and not of the remedy, the rule is now firmly established.[57] We shall presently see the important modifications that have been made to the rule which would seem to indicate that both legislatures and courts are desirous of adopting a different principle with reference to causes of action specially created by statute or by agreement.

It should be stated in justification of the English and American rule that after a certain period of time it is difficult to establish a cause of action by the necessary evidence. Witnesses die; document are lost or destroyed. What that period should be is, in large measure, a matter of legislative policy. The system of administering justice in the local state is of course a matter strictly within the power of the local legislature and statutes of limitation may therefore be subjected to a uniform practice, whether the cause of action arises at home or abroad. The result of this reasoning would seem to justify the application of the local statute where the period is shorter than the foreign; but not where it is longer. Indeed it is precisely this result which we find reached in some jurisdictions by statute or by some judicial modification of the general rule in certain cases.

**Application of a Period of Limitation Shorter than that of State in which Cause of Action Arose.** In a number of states, legislatures have provided that where a cause of action arises outside

[56] Lord Brougham in Don *v.* Lippmann, (1837) 5 C. & F. at p. 16.
[57] Dicey, 1st ed., (1896) p. 21.

the state, the remedy will be limited to the time provided by the laws of the state or country where the cause of action arose, except where it accrued in favor of a resident of the state.[58] The obvious purpose is to prevent a non-resident coming into the state and prosecuting a claim against a resident or non-resident which has already been barred by a less favorable statute in the foreign state where the cause of action arose. This provision is not intended to overrule the general principle by which the running of the statute is stopped as against a defendant who is absent from the local state and could not be sued there on that account. Accordingly it has been held that the cause of action is not barred where the defendant was a non-resident of the local state and absent both when the cause of action accrued and continuously thereafter.[59] The import of this decision would seem to render nugatory what Beale regards as the purpose of the enactment of the statutes, *viz.*, "the practical desirability of conclusively fixing the rights of the parties after a single specified period has elapsed."[60]

Another instance in which a statute of limitation may become a substantive part of the claim, arises in cases where a foreign statute creating a right of action prescribes also the time within which the action must be brought. At least Minor argues that it must be so regarded because the time is a condition essential to prosecuting the action at all. He holds that if the period is not prescribed by the same statute, but is found in a general statute, it is a law relating to the remedy.[61] The principle seems to be accepted on the theory that the foreign statute extinguishes the right rather than bars the remedy.[62] It is difficult however to perceive why a statute partakes of substance rather than remedy simply because it creates both right and remedy in the same enactment. On the other hand, where the limitation is by terms and intendment a condition of the right, action will be barred in the local state when it has been extinguished in the state of origin. This has been applied to statutes to recover a penalty or forfeiture against directors or stockholders within a given period (longer, indeed, than the general statute) but which take away the usual exception made in case of absence of the plain-

[58] N.Y. Civil Practice Act (ed. 1934) §13; Mass. Gen. L., 1932, ch. 260, §9.
[59] National Surety Co. *v.* Ruffin, (1926) 242 N.Y. 413.
[60] Beale, Treatise (1935) iii, §604.2.
[61] Minor, Conflict of Laws (1901) p. 524, citing Canadian Pacific R.R. Co. *v.* Johnson, (1894) 61 Fed. 738 and other cases.
[62] Pulsifer *v.* Greene, (1902) 96 Me. 438 adopts this view.

tiff from the state.[63] Mr. Justice Holmes has appositely remarked that the circumstance that the limitation is contained in the same statute is material only as bearing on construction.[64]

**Foreign Theory and Practice Respecting Limitation of Actions.** A survey of the principles recognized in civil-law countries with regard to the application of law to determine the limitation of actions discloses a wide discrepancy in theory though the practice of courts is in substantial agreement. Arminjon, a recent French commentator, remarks that the limitation of actions (*prescription extinctive* or *libératoire*) presents one of the most uncertain and controversial questions of private international law.[65] He points out that Pothier, in the time before the codes, favored the law of the creditor's domicil because the debt extinguished by the statute must be regarded as located there. Other writers had favored the law of the domicil of the debtor because they localized the obligation at that place and the position of full liberty which the statute of limitation grants to the debtor is enjoyed at the debtor's domicil.[66] At a later period, Pillet favored the national law of the debtor because the statute was for his protection. Some authors favor the law of the place of performance because an obligation becomes outlawed through the laches of the creditor and his laches may be located at the place where he should receive performance.[67] There is also support for the doctrine of English and American jurisprudence, the *lex fori,* and some cases have been decided upon the theory that the limitation is part of the remedy, though this is not the recognized rule in Europe.[68]

The preponderant view both in France and other Continental countries rests upon the proposition that the duration of a right of action is part of its substantive character and that the limitation of actions is not part of the regulatory process of administering justice. It should be deemed fixed at the time the obligation is created and therefore should be determined by the proper law of

[63] Davis *v.* Mills, (1904) 194 U.S. 451.

[64] *Ibid.,* at p. 454. The Restatement, §605, adopts the principle that where the right of action is conditioned upon its expiration after a certain period, no action after the period can be maintained in any state; the comment particularly refers to statutory actions for wrongful death.

[65] Arminjon, *Précis de Droit int. Privé* (1934) ii, §157.

[66] *Ibid.,* §159, citing earlier authors as well as the modern writer, Vareilles-Sommières.

[67] *Ibid.,* §160, referring to Troplong and Lehr.

[68] *Trib. de la Seine.* Oct. 27, 1911, Clunet, 1912, p. 1195.

the obligation. This view was expounded in detail by Savigny and has been widely adopted in Germany and elsewhere.[69] The Swiss jurist, Meili,[70] was so strongly in favor of the rule expounded by Savigny that he expressed the hope that English and American jurisprudence might some day be brought to see the light. Arminjon favors it, particularly because interested parties, including assignees of the creditor's right, should know the duration of the obligation at the time of creation.[71] Recent German authors are also strongly in favor of it upon principle and refer to it as being the Continental legal doctrine.[72] Decisions in Belgium, France, Germany and Italy follow it as the prevailing principle.[73]

Assuming that the proper law of the obligation also determines the period of limitation, should intention of the parties, expressed or presumed, be respected in regard to limitation of action? There has been much confusion of thought upon this matter wherever the tendency prevails to allow a wide latitude in the choice of law. The German *Reichsgericht* inferentially concluded that the judge must follow the will of the parties even in the matter of limitations. It recognized however that this applies only to contracts and does not apply either to quasi-contracts or torts, because there the obligation is *ex lege*.[74] Arminjon rightly points out that the autonomy of the parties must be measured by the very law by which the contract comes into existence and the limitation of actions there prevailing must be regarded as limiting their freedom of choice.[75]

The French jurist, Weiss, though favoring what we have called the generally accepted principle of civil-law countries, believes that where the local state has a longer period of limitations than the foreign state in which the cause of action arose, the rule of the forum must prevail as a matter of public policy. This is the rule of the Argentine Civil Code.[76] Of course there is nothing to prevent

[69] Savigny, Treatise (Guthrie's trans., 1880) §374.

[70] Meili, (Kuhn's trans., 1905) §56.

[71] Arminjon (1934) ii, §162.

[72] Lewald, *Das deutsche int. Privatr.* (1931) §97.

[73] Belgium: Clunet, 1907, p. 1148; Clunet, 1908, p. 569, in which the foreign statute provided a longer term than in the forum; France: Clunet, 1916, p. 1225; Clunet, 1927, p. 462; Germany: Clunet, 1912, p. 249; *Reichsger.*, Dec. 19, 1922, *Revue Darras,* 1926, p. 278. The rule was followed long before the enactment of the German Civil Code: *Reichsger.* Civil cases, 1879, vol 1, p. 126.

[74] *Zeitschrift für int. Recht.* (1911) v. 21, p. 64 and note on p. 66.

[75] Arminjon (1934) ii, §161.

[76] §2281.

the legislature from enacting a rule of this kind. We have seen that the statutes of some American states, including New York, have limited the *lex fori* principle in this manner. In the absence of statute, it seems a negation of the principle that the limitation of action is part of the underlying obligation. For this reason German courts have refused to accept this modification.[77]

Notwithstanding the acceptance of the principle that the prescription of actions is a part of the substantive right of action, German courts have adopted a peculiar doctrine where the right of action is subject to the law of an English or American jurisdiction. Let us illustrate: Certain drafts were drawn in London in English form on a Polish firm and accepted in Poland by one of the defendants and endorsed by the payee in Poland. The drafts were negotiated in London where they were made payable. Upon presentation in London, they were dishonored and the usual notice given. Action was brought against the acceptor and the endorser in Berlin and the defense interposed that the action was barred by the three-year prescription of German law (§78, *Wechsel Ordnung*). The English statute of six years had not yet run. The German *Reichsgericht* decided that English law was applicable to the acceptance and endorsement and that the same law should also govern the statute of limitations. The action was therefore held to be maintainable.[78] The earlier decisions to this effect were criticized by Melchior, who rightly emphasizes the point that the result leads to a *renvoi* from the law of the obligation to the *lex fori* and back again to the law of the obligation.[79] To which Philolenko adds the further striking observation that by attributing the character of a substantive prescription to the English statute of limitations, the court gives an extraterritorial character to a statute, which the English legislator never intended.[80] Philolenko proposes that under the principle recognized in Continental countries, there should be a distinction between limi-

[77] Lewald (1931) p. 29. The *Reichsgericht,* in a decision of Dec. 19, 1922, refused to recognize a foreign law making a claim incapable of being outlawed. *Rev. Darras,* 1926, p. 278.

[78] *Reichsger.* 2nd Civil Senate, July 6, 1934, vol. 145, p. 121. Clunet, 1935, p. 1190. The *Reichsgericht* relied upon certain earlier decisions of the Court, especially of Apr. 8, 1880, vol. 2, p. 13; Jan. 14, 1882, vol. 7, p. 21; and May 18, 1889, vol. 24, p. 383, but also took occasion to point out that by the provisions of the Civil Code in effect since 1900, the German law of prescription had also in part become a procedural law.

[79] Melchior, (1932) p. 216.

[80] Philolenko in Clunet, 1936, p. 542.

tations of the long period which are applicable to causes of action in general, and the shorter limitations (*prescriptions*) applicable by statute to specific causes of action. The former should be governed by the rule prevailing at the forum because appertaining to local powers of police and security, whereas the latter should be governed by the same system of law which applies to the particular cause of action itself.[81]

In *Italy* a tendency is noticeable to refuse the application of a longer statute of limitations than that which prevails in Italy, even though the courts recognize the principle that the prescription of actions is referable to the substantive law of the obligation. To illustrate: The plaintiff, an Italian, met the defendant, a German, in London and there entered into an agreement to form a limited partnership with its place of business in Italy. An action growing out of the agreement would have been maintainable under English law but would have been regarded as outlawed in Italy. The Court of Appeal of Milan decided that the will of the parties as to the application of law would ordinarily be respected and that the parties must have contemplated Italian law because the place of contract was merely accidental. The court, therefore, applied the Italian statute of prescription and, by way of dictum, remarked that in any event, an agreement, express or tacit, to apply a longer period of limitation would be considered against public policy.[82]

The Bustamante Code of Private International Law in force in certain Latin-American countries has adopted the prevailing European principle: "Extinctive prescription of personal actions is governed by the law to which the obligation which is to be extinguished is subject." (Art. 229.)

**Principles of Foreign Systems Relating to Procedure.** The principle that the local judge is bound by the local rules of procedure is accepted generally in foreign systems but the same difficulty is found there in distinguishing between substance and procedure. It may be said that not the same results are reached, although the general principles are comparable. French writers and courts are accustomed to refer to laws of procedure as having public-law significance. Thus, a court will say "that the laws of French procedure constitute laws of public order, the observation of which is imposed upon all persons in an issue before a French court, to the exclusion

[81] *Ibid.*, p. 545.
[82] Clunet, 1917, p. 737.

of all foreign laws."[83] When, however, French authorities are confronted with a question of proof, the difference between the Anglo-American and the French point of view becomes immediately noticeable. The proof of a fact is not necessarily a part of judicial procedure. French authors draw a distinction between a question of the admissibility of proof and a question of the administration of the proof. Pillet asserts that this distinction is as old as Bartolus. The question whether a certain kind of proof is admissible depends upon the law of the place where the right in issue has been created which it is desired to establish. On the other hand, the mode of proof is governed by the law of the place where it is offered, that law being most often, but not always, the *lex fori.*[84] A French court has decided that the law of the place where the contract is created determines the means of proof.[85] Arminjon maintains that this is a confusion of ideas and that it is necessary to distinguish the act of consent from the creation of the contract, the act of consent being only one of the elements essential to the creation of the obligation. The mode of proof of a foreign country may be applicable to show consent but the mode of proving the obligation itself should be governed by a different law.[86] Arminjon also maintains that the weight of authority as well as of the decisions is to apply the rule of *locus regit actum* rather than the *lex fori.* The question arises most frequently under the rule of the French Civil Code (Art. 1317) which provides "that an authentic instrument is one which has been made by public officers having the right to draw up instruments in the place where the instrument has been prepared and with the formalities required." The rule would give authority to follow the foreign requirements of an authenticated instrument rather than the law of the forum. Arminjon insists that French law desires only to have the instrument authenticated in a manner giving the same faith to its contents as French law gives to French documents; and, therefore, the foreign form of proof should suffice.[87]

The same principle is applied with respect to the provision of the Civil Code (Art. 1341) requiring an instrument to be drawn up in the presence of notaries or under private signature for matters involving more than a certain sum. The admission of oral testimony

[83] Clunet, 1897, p. 1036. Pillet, *Traité,* (1924) ii, p. 497.
[84] *Ibid.,* p. 500.
[85] Clunet, 1904, p. 457. *Accord:* Civil Court of Geneva, Clunet, 1905, p. 452.
[86] Arminjon, (1931) iii, p. 415.
[87] Arminjon, *ibid.,* iii, p. 426.

is allowed, provided such testimony is permitted in the place where the transaction occurred.[88] From the point of view of French law, Arminjon appropriately remarks that the legal provisions necessary to the security of transactions in one country may not be so in another. The point of approach is similar to cases under the Statute of Frauds wherever the statute makes the contract invalid unless incorporated in written proof.[89]

In *Italy* the statute provides that the modes of proof of obligations are governed by the laws of the place in which the legal transaction was completed.[90] The extent to which the concept represented by this statute differs from Anglo-American views is strikingly summed up in the phrase of Fiore: "The proof is an integral element of the obligation." [91]

The Introductory Statute to the *German* Code of Civil Procedure (Art. 14) refers to provisions excluding certain kinds of proof for particular legal transactions as being exclusively of a procedural character. Under the law of Soviet Russia, oral testimony is excluded for the proof of contracts involving more than 500 rubles. The question arose whether the Soviet rule was binding on a German court in the matter of proof. An oral contract made in Soviet Russia was sued upon in Germany. The German court took the Russian viewpoint that the statute was passed in order to assure the use of the written form and, therefore, was a rule of substantive law.[92] The decision has been severely criticized by Melchior. He rightly points out that the duty of the court was to determine whether the requirement of the statute was procedural or substantive according to German law; and this is answered specifically by the statute referred to.[93]

In contradistinction to the admissibility of proof, Continental authorities are practically agreed that the burden of proof is not a question of form of procedure but one of substantive law.[94]

[88] Clunet, 1880, p. 480.
[89] See Wharton, Conflict of Laws, (1905) ii, §690b.
[90] *Disposizioni* of Italian Civil Code, Art. 10 (2).
[91] Fiore, *Dir. Int. Privato,* (1888–1893) i, §184.
[92] *Kammerger.,* Oct. 25, 1927, *Jur. Wochenschrift,* 1929, p. 448.
[93] Melchior, (1932) *Die Grundlagen des deutschen int. Privatrechts,* p. 156.
[94] German *Reichsger.* (1882) vol. 6, p. 413; Swiss *Bundesger.* (1890) A.E. vol. 16, p. 790. The same court bases its view to this effect in a later decision upon the ground that the substantive private law of the foreign country in which the transaction took place must alone determine whether the facts have given rise to a cause of action or have terminated a right of action. A.E. (1898) vol. 24, part 2, p. 357.

## 5. Proof of Foreign Law

The trial of a case under common-law procedure involves an oral hearing of witnesses in the presence of the judge and jury. All matters of which the court cannot take judicial notice must be proved as facts are proved. It is sometimes said that foreign law is a matter of "fact"; but this is a confusion of the substance of proof with the manner of proof. When Lord Eldon said that the law of Scotland "should be given in evidence to me as a fact," he indicated that this affirmative proof was part of the case.[95] Story was careful to point out that foreign law was to be proved not for the jury but for the court to enable it to instruct the jury what in point of law is the result of such proof.[96] The English Supreme Court of Judicature Act, 1925, has enacted the principle by statute, so that the effect of the evidence must be decided by the judge alone. Pearson, J. in Hooper *v.* Moore [97] said that "What is the law of another state or of a foreign country, is as much a 'question of law' as what is the law of our own state." Yet the foreign law must be pleaded and proved like any other fact in the case.[98] In the absence of such proof, it is presumed that the foreign law is the same as that of the forum, and if the foreign system is derived from the English common law, the presumption is sometimes made that the foreign law is the same as the common law as understood at the forum.[99] This may well lead to absurdities. It is difficult to see how a New Jersey judge writing in the year 1912, can seriously announce that since the New York law of negotiable instruments has not been put in evidence, it must be presumed that the common law is there in vogue; and can offer as a statement of the existent New York law a case from the Term Reports of 1791.[100] Several states have corrected this archaism of procedure by statutes which provide that their courts shall take judicial notice of the laws of other states in the same manner as of the law of the forum.[101]

[95] Male *v.* Roberts, (1800) 3 Esp. 163.
[96] Story, Conflict of Law, §§637–638.
[97] (1857) 5 Jones (N.C.) 130.
[98] Hanley *v.* Donoghue, (1885) 116 U.S. 1.
[99] *Cf.* Kales, Presumption of the Foreign Law, (1906) 19 Harvard Law Rev. 401 and cases cited.
[100] Case note in (1920) 20 Columbia Law Rev. 476, citing Bodine *v.* Berg, (1912) 82 N.J. Law 662.
[101] See Wigmore, The Anglo-American System of Evidence (1923) v. 5, §2573.

The Restatement [102] limits the presumption to "the common law of another common-law state" and makes the comment that the court will take judicial notice that the law of another state is or is not based on the common law; and if the foreign state does not base its law on the common law, the presumption will not be made that the foreign law is like that of the forum. This distinction may be logical on principle but if carried to extremes, it may give rise to gross injustice. Even though a foreign law may be based upon a different system, it should not be presumed that the nature of that law does not recognize certain fundamental rights and wrongs such as the right to have contracts observed and the right to be compensated for their breach. In Parrot *v.* Mexican Central Railway Co.,[103] a contract was made in Mexico between the plaintiffs and the general passenger agent and the general traffic manager of the defendant to contribute toward the expenses of the plaintiffs in publishing a guide. The defendants denied the authority of the agents to make such a contract and the obligation of the defendant under it, in the absence of proof of the Mexican law. The court held for the plaintiffs. "We treat this," said Chief Justice Knowlton, "not as a presumption that the law of the foreign country is the same as the law of the forum, but as a presumption that all countries, in their courts of justice, will give effect to universally recognized fundamental principles of right and wrong in deciding between contending parties." [104] On the other hand, in Riley *v.* Pierce Oil Corp.,[105] the plaintiff sued to recover certain oil belonging to him in Mexico, which he alleged was converted by the defendant. A contract was made between the plaintiff and a subsidiary of the defendant, of which all the stock was held by the defendant. The defendant's officers were officers of the subsidiary which, in fact, was a mere shell organization. The plaintiff failed to prove the Mexican law as to the title in or right of possession to the oil and also as to the liability of a corporation holding all the stock in a subsidiary. For this failure, judgment for the defendant was affirmed by the Court of Appeals in a *per curiam* opinion. Mr. Justice (afterwards Chief Judge) Crane, in a dissenting opinion, quoting at length from the Parrot case, said that on such a fundamental proposition as a liability to pay for property

[102] §622.

[103] (1911) 207 Mass. 184.

[104] At p. 194, *Accord:* E. Gerli & Co. Inc., *v.* Cunard Steam Ship Co. Ltd., (1931) 48 Fed. 115.

[105] (1927) 245 N.Y. 152.

taken or purchased, he could not imagine the law of Mexico to be different from the common law of our own country and referred to prior decisions of New York and of the United States Supreme Court, not in terms of the presumption of similarity, but of the necessity that the local court will administer the law of its own jurisdiction in the absence of any proof of the foreign law.[106]

The Restatement declares that it is not to be presumed that the *statutory* law of another state is the same as that of the forum.[107] With regard to the various presumptions acted upon by separate States of the Union, there seems to be hopeless confusion, some holding (1) that the law of a sister state will be presumed to be similar to the common law of the forum as it existed prior to the statute; some (2) that the law of the sister state will be presumed to be the same as the law of the forum; and (3) that the court will apply the law of the forum unless the foreign state was formed from territory once under the political control of England, in which event it is presumed that the law there is the unmodified common law.[108] The solution of the problem by means of presumption is most unsatisfactory. Beale quotes from a case in Pennsylvania: "There is no state where the common law prevails that it has not been more or less modified by statute; and if so, what foundation is there for the presumption that it exists in any state without modification?"[109] Beale remarks quite properly that the solution to the dilemma would be a statute giving the courts broad and comprehensive powers of judicial notice.

A more fortunate turn has been given to recent jurisprudence in the United States. The real point turns upon whether foreign law is to be regarded as a question of fact for the jury. We have already pointed out the error of this older view. As was said in Rood *v.* Horton:[101] "Where proof of foreign laws is necessary to be introduced, such proof should be addressed to the court, and not to the jury, and the court should interpret the foreign laws for the

[106] At pp. 155–156, citing Hynes *v.* McDermott, (1880) 82 N.Y. 41. The Scotland, (1881) 105 U.S. 24, 29, 30. In cases subsequent to the Riley case, *supra,* New York law, whether statutory or common, has been substituted for the unproved foreign law. Matter of Masocco *v.* Schaaf, (1931) 234 A.D. 181; Matter of Dumarest, (1933) 262 N.Y.S. 450.

[107] Restatement, §623.

[108] Beale, Treatise, (1935) vol. 3, pp. 1682–1685, where the various authorities are collated.

[109] Bennett *v.* Caldwell's Executor, (1871) 70 Pa. 253.

[110] (1924) 132 Wash. 82.

jury, and instruct the jury thereon." So too we find the direct statement made that where a question of foreign law involves the construction and effect of a statute or judicial decision, such questions are for the court "and not questions of fact at all."[111] The Massachusetts doctrine is in accord where the evidence is a single statute or decision; not, however, where the law is to be determined from numerous decisions more or less conflicting.[112] Accordingly, the highest courts will examine into the construction given to the foreign law by inferior courts and reverse for error.

In England the Supreme Court of Judicature Act, 1925, provides[113] that "Where it is necessary to ascertain the law of any other country which is applicable to the facts of the case, any question as to the effect of the evidence given with respect to that law shall, instead of being submitted to the jury, be decided by the judge alone."

**Principles in Civil-Law Countries as to the Proof of Foreign Law.** The Swiss jurist, Meili, combats the principle that foreign private law is *res facti* and therefore should be proved as facts are proved. He recognizes this as the prevailing theory and practice not only in common-law countries but in civil-law countries as well. He particularly opposes the doctrine that in the absence of proof, the foreign law will be presumed to be the same as that at the forum. Meili maintains that private law does not lose its character as such merely because it is foreign and for that reason the judge should apply foreign law *ex officio* to an issue properly governed by it. He believes that the doctrine should be rectified in view of the fact that the application of foreign law is now recognized to be no longer dependent upon mere comity.[114] Meili does not stand alone in this belief. Gierke in Germany and Fiore in Italy were of the same opinion.[115] So too the Institute of International Law at its Session of 1891 resolved that proof of foreign laws should not be a question of fact left to the initiative of the parties.[116]

There is a noteworthy disagreement between the views of authoritative text writers in France and Italy and the decisions of the

[111] Bank of China *v.* Morse, (1901) 168 N.Y. 458 at p. 470.

[112] Wylie *v.* Cotter, (1898) 170 Mass. 356, 357.

[113] §102.

[114] *Int. Civilprozessrecht* (1906) pp. 134–140.

[115] Gierke, *Deutsches Privatrecht,* i, p. 216; Fiore, *Diritto Int. Privato,* i, 268.

[116] Clunet, 1892, p. 315.

courts in respect to the proof of foreign law. French and Italian tribunals approach the problem in a spirit comparable to that of courts of common-law jurisdictions. The proof of foreign law is considered to be incumbent upon the party who relies upon it, just as the complainant has the burden of proving all other facts necessary to his case.[117] French writers, such as Weiss, Pillet and others, combat this view as a manifest error, and maintain that it is no more a mere question of fact than the national law itself and that it is the duty of the judge to seek out and apply the foreign law when properly applicable, even though the parties do not prove it.[118]

In Germany, the latter view has found confirmation by express legislation. The German Code of Civil Procedure provides that the customary law or the statutes of a foreign state require to be proved only if not known to the court. In carrying out this provision the court is not limited to the evidence produced by the parties; it may employ other sources of information and may take the necessary steps to carry out this purpose.[119]

The high courts have encouraged the judges to take the initiative in learning the foreign law involved in controversy. The higher the conception of the duties of his office, the more energetically will the judge carry out this privilege.[120]

While the rules of Austrian, German and Swiss procedure are more liberal in regard to the proof of foreign law inasmuch as they allow the judge to seek such proof on his own initiative, they seem to be curiously narrow in the review permitted of findings of foreign law when a case is on appeal. Courts of last appeal in Germany and Switzerland refuse to review determinations of the lower courts where the error assigned is on the interpretation of foreign as distinguished from the local law. This result is reached by reason of the interpretation given to statutes giving such courts jurisdiction to review only where an imperial or federal law has been violated.[121] In Italy there is some difference of opinion. Some courts do not allow revision of foreign-law findings on procedure for cassation;[122]

[117] France: Clunet, 1892, p. 681; 1899, p. 794; 1901, p. 975; Italy: Clunet, 1896, p. 907; 1899, p. 191.

[118] Weiss, *Traité* (1898) iii, p. 167; Pillet, *Traité* (1923) i, p. 140.

[119] German *Civil Prozess-Ordnung,* §293.

[120] *Reichs Oberhandelsger.* (1879) xxv, 53. Clunet, 1904, p. 195.

[121] German *Civil Prozess-Ordnung,* §549, Meili, *ut cit.* pp. 145–156.

[122] Clunet, 1886, p. 746. It is otherwise if the judge is specifically directed to apply the foreign law. Cass. Naples, Jan. 26, 1897, *Monitore,* 1897, p. 466.

while other authorities maintain the contrary.[123] In France the opinion of authors is in favor of revision on appeal;[124] but the decisions of the courts seem to be to the contrary.[125] Belgium courts adopt a similar rule.[126]

It would certainly seem that when, for example, a German statute requires the application of a foreign law, the German law is violated if the judge does not properly apply the foreign law.

The Bustamante Code has made a noticeable advance in respect to the methods recognized for the proof of foreign laws. The principle of applying a foreign law *ex officio* whenever applicable is specifically adopted so far as concerns the laws of the states adhering to the Convention.[127] In order to effectuate the proof of foreign law a party may show the text and its significance by means of a certificate of two practicing lawyers of the country in question.[128] What is more important is the provision that in carrying out the *ex officio* duty of the judge or court in deciding the content and significance of the foreign law, a procedure is provided through the diplomatic channel. The foreign state may be requested to furnish a report on the text, force and sense of the law applicable. Each state binds itself to furnish to the others, as soon as possible, this information, either from its supreme court or from the State Attorney, or the Department or Ministry of Justice.[129] Furthermore, appeal for annulment of a judgment in which a foreign law has been wrongly interpreted or applied is allowed upon the same conditions and in the same case as in respect to the national law; and the appeal of the appellate tribunal may make use of the same methods for informing itself upon the content and interpretation of the foreign law as were open to the lower court under the provisions already referred to.[130]

We here have a progressive system which may very well serve as a model for international co-operation in the administration of

[123] Fiore, *Diritto int. pr.* (1888–93) i, §273.

[124] A. Colin in Clunet, 1890, pp. 406–414, 794–807. Pillet (1923) i, p. 141.

[125] Clunet, 1916, p. 1603; 1918, p. 707. Pillet, i, p. 141, points out that very few provisions of French law specifically provide for the application of foreign law.

[126] *Pasicrisie Belge,* 1909, i, p. 25.

[127] Code of Private Int. Law, Art. 408. Int. Conferences of American States (1931) p. 366.

[128] *Ibid.,* Art. 409.

[129] *Ibid.,* Arts. 410–411.

[130] *Ibid.,* Arts. 412–413.

private justice. The system may seem somewhat strained to those familiar only with the methods of English and American judicial tribunals. Co-operation between the judicial and administrative branches of government has not progressed to the extent reached in civil-law countries. However, this is not an insuperable barrier to the adoption of some system of certification through reciprocal certificates issued by ministers of justice, provided the proper basis has been established by conventional agreement. Such certification would of course not have the effect of finality but of *prima facie* proof. The progress already made by statute away from the early common-law rule of dealing with the foreign law as though it were a question of fact points the way to the further progress which many Latin-American countries have thus already accepted as part of their legal system.

## 6. Foreign Judgments

The judgment of the court of a foreign country is frequently the basis of an assertion of rights in the local state. A party may wish to enforce the judgment in the local state according to its tenor, whether by way of money compensation or otherwise, so as to have another judgment parallel to that which he obtained abroad. Or he may wish to enforce the judgment as a defense against a claim made against him in the local state. Assuming that the foreign court had jurisdiction of the parties and of the subject-matter of the action and that the proceedings were regular, what effect should be given the foreign judgment?

It is reasonable to say that as a court will recognize rights duly acquired by acts of the parties in a foreign jurisdiction, it should *a fortiori* recognize rights acquired there by the judgment of a competent court after a trial of the issues. This follows both from a proper respect for the sovereignty of the state having jurisdiction of the parties and of the subject-matter of the action, but also because a proper administration of justice requires that the local state shall not assume to be competent to decide issues which have properly come before a tribunal abroad and have been finally there determined.

Under the English common law a judgment created a legal obligation which might be enforced by an action of debt. Accordingly, competent foreign judgments are conclusive upon the merits. Story said that it is difficult to perceive what could be done if all the evidence and merits were opened anew. The witnesses might not be available; the proof lost or destroyed.[131] In an action brought in England upon a French judgment it appeared that the French court in rendering judgment had been mistaken as to the English law applicable to the original cause of action. The court nevertheless held the judgment to be conclusive.[132]

The procedure for obtaining an affirmative enforcement of the foreign judgment is by a new action upon the judgment in the local state. The forms of action developed under the common law did not permit of recognition of the foreign judgment to the extent of rendering it *per se* executory in the local state. Even as between the several states of the United States, it was early decided under the full-faith-and-credit clause of the Constitution, that a new action in the forum was necessary.[133] This has found expression as to all judgments in the Restatement where it is declared that "A foreign judgment will not be enforced by issuing execution on it."[134] In order that a new action may be brought upon it, it must be final, certain in amount, unconditional, not vacated and execution thereon not superseded in the state where rendered.[135] We have previously pointed out that reciprocity of treatment in the foreign state of the judgment is not on principle a requisite of recognition, although demanded by the rule of the Federal courts and some of the States of the Union.[136]

**"Extension" of Foreign Judgments in Great Britain.** Quite different, however, is the approach of recent British legislation. Emphasis has there been laid not so much upon the recognition of foreign judgments but upon the more practical step of making them executory under proper limitations within the local state. The Foreign Judgments (Reciprocal Enforcement) Act of 1933 permits a

[131] Story, §607.

[132] Godard *v.* Gray, (1870) L.R. 6 Q.B. 139. *Accord:* Dunstan *v.* Higgins, (1893) 138 N.Y. 70.

[133] McElmoyle *v.* Cohen, (1839) 13 Pet. (38 U.S.) 312. This was an action brought in Georgia upon a judgment obtained in South Carolina where there was no statute limiting suits upon judgments. The defendant pleaded the Georgia statute. The court held that the South Carolina judgment had no executory force in Georgia under the Constitution and that the *lex fori* applied to the limitation of judgments as to other causes of action. "Prescription is a thing of policy" . . . per Wayne, J.

[134] Restatement (1934) §433.

[135] *Ibid.*, §§434–439.

[136] See *ante*, pp. 30, 31.

foreign judgment, if final and conclusive, to be registered in Great Britain so as to place the registered judgment upon the same basis as an original judgment of the registering court in respect to execution, proceedings upon the judgment, the sum upon which interest accrues and judicial control over execution. It is quite proper that here reciprocity of treatment should be required both in return for the facilities afforded and as an inducement to other nations to enlarge the scope of British judgments upon an equally favorable basis. The statute not only consolidates a fundamental reform of the common-law procedure but, as we shall presently observe, in effect brings the English practice fairly close to that of countries of Continental Europe.[137]

**A Foreign Judgment as Res Judicata.** Quite apart from the recognition to be accorded a foreign judgment for the purpose of affirmative enforcement in the local state, is the question of its recognition as settling the controverted issues which were raised in the action. Kent, when Chief Justice of New York, pointed out the distinction between seeking the aid of local courts to carry a foreign judgment into effect, and reliance upon a foreign judgment under the *exceptio rei judicatae*. In the latter case, it should be received as conclusive.[138] Let us illustrate. An action was brought in Canada against a carrier for the value of goods shipped under a bill of lading. Judgment was rendered for defendant. A new action was then brought for the same cause in New Hampshire and the Canadian judgment was set up in bar. The court held that the plaintiff having suffered defeat, without fraud or mistake, by the judicial determination which he himself invoked, is estopped from presenting the same issue elsewhere. The right of defendant to rely upon the Canadian judgment depends not upon its extraterritorial force but upon a "universal law of justice."[139]

**Foreign Systems in respect to the Execution of Foreign Judgments.** Comparing systems derived from the Roman civil law with common-law countries, we may emphasize the distinction made in both groups between enforcement of judgments by affirmative

[137] *Cf.* H. E. Yntema in (1935) 33 Mich. Law Rev. 1129.

[138] Smith *v.* Lewis, (1803) 3 Johns. 157, 169.

[139] MacDonald *v.* Grand Trunk Ry. Co., (1902) 71 N.H. 448, 452. *Accord:* Johnston *v.* Cie. Gen. Transatlantique, (1926) 242 N.Y. 381. It is insisted that the same principle should prevail with regard to a foreign equity decree, such as with regard to the possession of land or the custody of a child. *Cf.* Goodrich (1927) p. 483.

action and recognition accorded as *res judicata.* A Belgian jurist refers to the former as an arm of attack, the latter as an instrument of defense; the one a sword, the other a shield.[140] Some countries like the Netherlands and the Scandinavian group do not accord any recognition to foreign judgments for the former purpose in the absence of treaty. A new action must be brought in which the foreign judgment can at best be proved by way of corroboration.[141] Where affirmative action is sought other civil-law countries do not regard the foreign judgment as a cause of action in itself but provide for a separate proceeding by which the foreign judgment is made executory in the local state. This is known as the proceeding for *exequatur* and while it seems on principle to accord greater power to the foreign judgment than the common-law practice requiring a new action, it is nevertheless so hedged about with conditions in some countries that in reality less weight is accorded the foreign judgment than under the common law. These conditions are so diverse that no general statement can safely be made as to any two countries. The question is not strictly one of conflict of laws. It will suffice to reflect the general outlines of some of the principal Continental systems.

**France.** Art. 546 of the Code of Civil Procedure provides that judgments rendered by foreign tribunals and instruments drawn by foreign officials cannot be executed in France except in the manner and in the cases provided for by Arts. 2123 and 2128 of the Civil Code. These articles are not specific but are negative insofar as they provide that no lien results from judgments rendered in foreign countries or from contracts entered into abroad unless they have been declared to be executory by a French tribunal (without prejudice to provisions to the contrary in political laws or in treaties). Accordingly, the matter is left for judicial determination by proceedings resulting in a judgment of *exequatur.*

Pillet[142] tells us that the courts early adopted a system of revision of foreign judgments by which the main circumstances of the judgment were examined in order to determine whether it was justly rendered. Doubtless the French system is one of re-examination but, although the contrary is sometimes stated, it is not a re-examination

[140] De Cock in *Acad. de Droit Int., Recueil de Cours,* 1925, V, p. 438. See also decision of Court of Cassation of Turin, Clunet, 1910, p. 671.

[141] De Cock, *ut cit.,* pp. 446–447. Netherlands Code of Civ. Pro., Art. 436. Sweden; see Clunet, 1906, p. 581.

[142] Clunet, 1914, p. 753.

of the merits of the original cause of action. What then are the matters to which the re-examination is directed? It must, of course, be assumed that the foreign court had jurisdiction of the persons and parties. In this respect French law is peculiar because it requires jurisdiction to be observed not in accordance with the rules of private international law but in accordance with French law, at least insofar as to require action to be brought before a French tribunal and not a foreign tribunal on a cause of action upon obligations contracted abroad with a French citizen.[143] The French citizen may waive the national forum provided for his benefit, and a judgment rendered abroad would then be eligible for execution in France; but the waiver will be strictly construed and a mere appearance or even the joinder of issue in a foreign court will not be sufficient to renounce the benefit of Arts. 14–15 of the Civil Code. It must be a free and voluntary choice and if the French citizen sues in a foreign country upon obligations contracted by him there with a foreigner, it may be shown that he had no other redress because the defendant had no assets in France.[144] These jurisdictional rules are considered to be a matter of public policy in France and are not readily defensible upon principle. They must be regarded as a peculiarity of French law though widely criticized by jurists abroad as well as in France.[145]

The re-examination to which a foreign judgment may be subject in France upon the ground of public policy has resulted in refusing recognition to Soviet nationalization decrees. Control over a Russian company owning a fleet of merchant ships was claimed by the Soviet Government by virtue of these decrees. Officers and directors provisionally appointed in France were alleged to be without authority. The French court decided that these decrees were in effect confiscatory and against the public policy of French law and would therefore not be given effect in France. The provisional officers appointed in France were therefore confirmed in their control of the company.[146]

[143] Civil Code, Arts. 14–15, Court of Paris, June 22, 1843; Sirey, 1843, p. 346; Seine, Mar. 20, 1897, Clunet, 1897, p. 546.

[144] Clunet, 1902, p. 812; Clunet, 1924, p. 114 and note; Clunet, 1926, p. 953.

[145] Arminjon, *Précis de dr. int. pr.* (1931) iii, p. 209, remarks that the nationality of a party, taken by itself, should not be considered a proper circumstance to make a tribunal competent or incompetent. See also Meili, *Int. Civilprozessrecht* (1906) p. 207.

[146] Clunet, 1926, p. 667.

The foregoing result is similar to that reached in other countries and is in harmony with the concept of public policy as generally interpreted. However, French courts sometimes go beyond the generally accepted tests of public policy. Thus a divorce was sought to be rendered executory in France on the application of a French woman who had been divorced by her German husband in Germany where the parties were domiciled. The divorce was granted by reason of alleged remarks insulting to the husband's feelings of patriotism toward Germany and replies called forth on the part of the husband similarly insulting to the wife as a person of French origin. These remarks, taken with other circumstances, were accepted by the German court because they were deemed inconsistent with the permanence of the marriage relation. The French court decided that it was against French public policy to recognize the allegations as grounds for divorce and refused *exequatur*. The result is curiously paradoxical because the sentiments of French patriotism or loyalty on the part of the wife were the very cause of her not being able to remarry again in her country of origin.[147] The case illustrates the difficulty of defining public policy. The acceptance of such evidence in support of grounds for the severance of the marriage tie should not be considered opposed to public policy provided the grounds are reasonable according to standards recognized by civilized countries. The continuance of the marital relation may very well be permanently destroyed by differences of patriotic sentiment, especially in times of grave national crisis. The case is illustrative of the effect of emphasizing mere differences of law or legislation instead of restricting the matters of policy to fundamental principles of justice and the social order.

The rule that the public order or policy of the executing state shall not be violated is common to all jurisdictions. In France its application goes beyond fundamentals and judgments are sometimes refused with a general statement that the foreign judgment was "against the principles of justice and equity."

To illustrate: A bill of exchange was drawn by a French firm on a person residing in Barcelona where it was accepted and made payable in a city in France. It was sued upon at Barcelona after being dishonored. The acceptor claimed that a Spanish revenue stamp should have been placed upon the bill and the Spanish court sustained the defense and awarded a judgment of costs and dis-

[147] Clunet, 1923, p. 295.

bursements. This judgment was refused execution in France upon the ground that it was "against the principles of justice and equity" to hold that a Spanish stamp was required upon a bill drawn in France, payable in France, even though it had been accepted in Spain.[148]

A judgment of an Arkansas court was refused execution because not motivated, although rendered by default, this being held to be against French public policy.[149]

The French Civil Code (Art. 340) provides that proof of paternal descent is prohibited. The rule against filiation decrees obtained upon allegations of paternity outside of marriage is fundamental in French law. Accordingly, no decree of this nature obtained abroad, even where no French citizen is a party, will be accorded recognition in France. However, a judgment for damages caused by seduction will be granted *exequatur* provided no finding of paternity is involved.[150] A judgment rendered upon a contract of indemnity entered into after the breach of a promise to marry was also granted *exequatur* although the action for unliquidated damages for breach of promise to marry is not known to French law.[151] A judgment for damages obtained in England by an investor against one of the promoters of an English company was based upon the violation of a duty prescribed by the Directors Liability Act of 1890. A French court granted *exequatur* upon the judgment because the statute did not violate French public policy, although no such provision was contained in French legislation.[152] Similarly, although French law does not grant a right to French barristers of suing for their fees, a judgment fixing compensation for an Italian barrister was granted *exequatur* in France as not being against public policy.[153]

The foregoing analysis of French jurisprudence illustrates the difficulty of laying down any rigid rule. Courts will re-examine both the facts and the law underlying a foreign judgment but the

[148] Montpellier, August 14, 1896, Clunet, 1897, p. 550.

[149] Clunet, 1935, p. 1188. Although *exequatur* was refused, action was entertained upon the original cause.

[150] Clunet, 1907, p. 400. *Exequatur* refused upon a judgment in Clunet, 1931, p. 1143, because equivalent to a filiation decree.

[151] Clunet, 1891, p. 1208.

[152] Clunet, 1907, p. 745. The defendant was considered to have waived his right to a French forum under Art. 14 of the Civil Code because he appeared in the English action without objection and there entered upon the merits of his defense.

[153] Clunet, 1935, p. 369.

phrase *au fond* by which this re-examination is described does not signify that the French court is re-trying the cause of action anew upon the merits but that it is exercising a wide judicial discretion.

**Germany.** The principles to be observed in Germany for the recognition of foreign judgments have not been left so much to judicial determination as they have been in France. The Code of Civil Procedure contains a series of conditions to be observed. Conforming to what we have declared to be the general practice of civil-law countries, execution is granted upon the foreign judgment itself, provided a judgment of execution (*Vollstreckungsurteil*) is obtained.[154] The foreign judgment, if final, will not be examined upon the merits.[155] The seemingly liberal provisions of this part of the code are, however, subject to the almost prohibitive requirements set up in another part. Recognition must be refused if (1) the courts of the state in which the judgment has been rendered are not competent according to German laws; (2) the defendant is a German and was not served in person in the state of the judgment through the means of German legal process; (3) the foreign judgment prejudiced the rights of a German party to the cause by failure to observe certain named provisions of the Introductory Statute to the Civil Code relating to rules of the conflict of laws and jurisdiction in regard to marriage, divorce, legitimacy and legitimation; (4) the judgment violates good morals or the purpose of a German statute; (5) reciprocity is not accorded.[156] The requirement of reciprocity as interpreted by German courts would alone prevent recognition from all but a small number of countries. Countries which are deemed to grant reciprocity are Austria, Brazil, Bulgaria, Denmark, Italy, Roumania and Spain; but the requirement that the competence of the court rendering the judgment shall be tested according to German law, would necessarily exclude even some of these countries.[157]

It remains only to add that the requirement of reciprocity applies

[154] Code of Civ. Pro. §722.

[155] *Ibid.*, §723.

[156] *Ibid.*, §328.

[157] *Cf.* de Cock, *ut cit.*, p. 466. A statute of California of February 17, 1907, attempted to meet the requirement of reciprocity by giving to judgments of a foreign country "the same effect as in the country where rendered and also the same effect as final judgment rendered in this state." But the *Reichsgericht* refused to recognize a judgment of California, though obtained after the enactment of the statute, because the test of jurisdiction in California differs from that of German law and reciprocity was therefore lacking. *Reichsger.* Civ. cases, Mar. 26, 1909, vol. 70, p. 434.

only to money judgments and those affecting title to property and not to judgments affecting only the status of persons, and of family rights in general.[158] A judgment of divorce will also be granted recognition without the requirement of reciprocity provided there is no forum open to the parties in Germany; but we shall see that this represents a reservation which greatly limits the recognition of foreign divorces of German subjects.[159]

**Italy.** The Italian system for the execution of foreign judgments was a very liberal one down to the close of the World War. Art. 10 of the Preliminary Title of the Civil Code declares that judgments pronounced in civil matters by foreign tribunals will receive execution provided they are declared executory pursuant to the forms prescribed by the Code of Civil Procedure. These provisions are contained in Arts. 941–950 of the Code. After the World War, German citizens who had been disadvantaged by war legislation, obtained judgments in Germany which they sought to execute in Italy under the liberal provisions of the codes. Accordingly, legislation was passed, first by the Decree Law of July 20, 1919, and afterwards by the Law of May 28, 1925, by which Art. 941 was considerably modified. The judgment of *exequatur* (*giudizio di delibatione*) must find that the foreign court had jurisdiction according to an international standard, though not necessarily the same standard as Italian law provides. Precisely what this international standard of jurisdiction consists of is not quite clear and seems to allow a wide discretion in the courts. It has, however, been declared that the fact that the procedure followed in the foreign court, *e.g.*, in England, differs from that of an Italian tribunal in a similar case, is not an objection to a judgment of execution in Italy.[160]

The foreign judgment must be irrevocable and have executory force according to the law of the place where it was rendered and must not have been contrary to any judgment rendered by an Italian tribunal nor shall there be any suit pending before an Italian tribunal for the same cause and between the same parties at the time when demand for execution is served.

Where there is a judgment for default or where the defendant alleges fraud or presents new evidence of a decisive nature that was not considered in the original judgment or where the judgment re-

[158] German Code of Civ. Pro. §328 (2), 606 (2–3), 642.
[159] See *post*, p. 173.
[160] Milan, Mar. 6, 1923, Clunet, 1924, p. 254.

sults from an error of fact deduced from records and documents in the case, the Italian court may examine the merits of these allegations and decide whether the foreign judgment shall have executory force or not.[161] A further condition for enforcement is that the foreign judgment shall not contain dispositions contrary to the public policy or public law of Italy.

It will be observed that these changes have profoundly affected the former liberal system of Italy and, as Udina remarks, make it possible practically to destroy the institution of *exequatur*.[162]

The new legislation is also not without influence upon foreign judgments sought to be executed in Italy not for affirmative action but for their probative force as *res judicata*. Formerly no *exequatur* was required. Thus, for example, a foreign adjudication in bankruptcy was formerly recognized if no sequestration of assets or other affirmative act was sought.[163] Now, however, the matter seems to be in considerable doubt.[164]

A judgment of divorce between Italians domiciled abroad, of a marriage celebrated in Italy, will not be granted *exequatur* because, under the Concordat of 1929 between the Holy See and Italy, the ecclesiastic authorities are alone competent.[165]

**Switzerland.** The cantons of Switzerland have legislative independence with regard to their judicial organization, procedure and the adminstration of justice, except with regard to matters of federal competence.[166] Accordingly, unless federal legislation or federal treaties intervene, recognition of foreign judgments is a matter of cantonal law. There is only a single provision of federal legislation relative to the recognition of foreign judgments. This provides that the divorce of Swiss spouses residing abroad will be recognized in Switzerland when decreed by a judge competent according to the terms of their domiciliary law, even if this does not agree with the demands of (Swiss) federal legislation.[167]

As the Federal Supreme Court has the power to review any matter in which the Confederation has legislative competence, a judg-

[161] Art. 941 as amended, referring to Art. 494, pars. 1–4.
[162] Udina, *Droit int. privé d'Italie* (1930) p. 182.
[163] Clunet, 1911, p. 670.
[164] Udina, *op. cit.* p. 182, referring to discordant decisions of the courts.
[165] Court of Cassation, June 11, 1934, Clunet, 1934, p. 1073.
[166] Constitution, Art. 64.
[167] Art. 7 g (3), Fed. Stat. of June 25, 1891; Art. 59 of the final title of the Swiss Civ. Code.

ment of *exequatur* granted in one canton in a matter of a foreign divorce will be considered effective in all the other cantons. On the other hand the judgment of one canton according or refusing *exequatur* to a foreign judgment *not of divorce* is binding only within the canton in which such decision was rendered.[168]

**Latin-American States.** The Bustamante Code of Private International Law, ratified by 15 Latin-American countries, presents a well-rounded and reasonable system for the execution of foreign judgments applicable in civil matters both to judgments of courts and of administrative tribunals where there has been a dispute between parties litigant. The conditions for execution are that the judge or court shall have had jurisdiction in accordance with the rules elsewhere fixed by the code. In this respect the code is a vast improvement upon some of the systems we have been discussing where jurisdiction is subjected to examination upon basis of unwritten rules, neither constant nor certain.[169] The parties must have been summoned for trial either personally or through their legal representative; the judgment must not conflict with the public policy or the public laws of the country of execution; it must be final; it must be accompanied by an official translation and authenticated according to the requirements of the state of judgment as well as of the state of execution.[170]

The code also provides that final judgments have the effect of *res judicata* if they fulfill the conditions provided for that purpose by the code, except those relating to their execution.[171]

**Treaties.** The reciprocal execution of foreign judgments has been a subject of treaty provision between countries over a long period. The treaties are usually bilateral and are more frequently to be found between neighboring countries.[172]

A multipartite treaty was signed after the Hague Conference on Private International Law held in 1894, with the title "Convention to Establish Common Rules Concerning Certain Matters of Private International Law in Regard to Civil Procedure." The treaty came

[168] Petitpierre, *La Reconnaissance et l'Execution des Jugements Civils étrangers en Suisse* (1924) pp. 19–22.

[169] Bustamante Code of Private International Law, Art. 423 (1). The rules of jurisdiction are contained in Arts. 318–339. International Conferences of American States (1931) pp. 357–359.

[170] *Ibid.*, Art. 423 (2–6).

[171] *Ibid.*, Art. 431. See also Arts. 174, 396.

[172] See Meili, *Das int. Civilprozessrecht* (1906) pp. 456–469.

into effect May 25, 1899, and among other things provides that judgments for processual costs obtained in any of the states of the treaty union may be executed in any other state. For this limited purpose, the state of execution must recognize the judgment and may examine the judgment only in respect to its conformity with the laws of the state of the judgment with respect to authentication and legal force.[173]

The Bustamante Code represents, of course, the basis of a model statute upon the subjects which it treats and constitutes a multipartite convention upon these subjects.

The difficulty of arriving at the basis for a multipartite convention between countries having divergent legal institutions, as for example, between jurisdictions of the common law and civil law, respectively, has led to statutes such as the British statute of 1933 specifying the conditions upon which execution will be accorded on the basis of reciprocity. It establishes a relationship comparable to that of a multipartite convention except that an alleged breach of any provision could not be the foundation of a claim for the breach of an international agreement. The British statute is also an inducement to countries not according reciprocity, to enter into a treaty by which reciprocity may be established. A treaty of this kind was signed between France and Great Britain on January 18, 1934.[174]

[173] *Ibid.*, p. 106; Arts. 12–13 of the Convention.
[174] *Cf.* Audinet in Clunet, 1935, p. 52.

## Chapter V

# STATUS AND CAPACITY OF PERSONS

## 1. Capacity to Act in General

**Definition of Terms.** In the sense in which the term "status" is used in the Restatement of the American Law Institute, it is "a legal personal relationship, not temporary in its nature nor terminable at the mere will of the parties, with which third persons and the state are concerned."[1] This is a restricted definition which may serve the purpose of the Restatement. However, if restricted to this sense, "status" no longer imports "state" or "condition," but "relation." Indeed, Beale[2] would exclude majority and minority as examples of status though they are almost invariably so considered in civil-law countries and the very term "infancy," as known to the common law, imports a status. Without the concept of status, infancy as a source of rights or as a defense, would seem unintelligible. The fact that the status of minority or infancy acquired in one state does not necessarily have an extraterritorial effect, does not detract from its character as a status. As Westlake says: "But what is status except the sum of the particulars in which a person's condition differs from that of the normal person?" Westlake points out that in the opinion of some, a partial limitation of capacity ought not to be classified as a status, to which he replies that it is around capacity, and status in no other sense, that the problems turn which concern us here.[3] On the other hand, Beale seems to define status wholly from the viewpoint of one system. He maintains that "the effects of

[1] Restatement, §119.

[2] Beale (1935) §120. 12.

[3] Westlake, (1925) p. 49. Westlake was considering the English cases in which French citizens domiciled in France were placed under the guardianship of a *conseil judiciaire* in France, and afterwards sought to sue in the courts, or to receive funds in England. Worms *v.* De Valdor, 1880, 49 L.J. Ch. 261; *Re* Selot's Trust [1902] 1 Ch. 488.

minority are not so uniform or clearly fixed by the common law as to be described as the incidents of a status." By this mode of reasoning, the use of the term "status" becomes useless in solving conflicts of law, because the very question in issue is the extent to which capacity or incapacity attributed to a person by one state is to be recognized in another. As Cheshire rightly puts it: "A rule which regulates the capacity or incapacity of a person is part of the law of his status." [4]

We therefore shall use the term both in its absolute and in its relative significance as circumstances may require, keeping in mind always that the specific cases require us to determine the validity of the acts or the scope of the rights of persons whose status is under consideration. The importance of such a viewpoint in any work devoted to a comparative study of the conflict of laws is manifest. Legislation in many countries, of which the French Civil Code [5] may be taken as an outstanding example, indicates the proper law by reference to status. "The laws concerning the status and the capacity of persons are controlling upon Frenchmen even though residing in foreign countries." Thus the law to be applied is derived from the status. If a certain quality of the person is to be interpreted as a status according as it is or is not given extraterritorial effect, then legislation such as we have referred to becomes meaningless.

**Historical Development of Personal Law.** The common law does not recognize an ubiquitous personal law applicable to all questions of the capacity of persons, but it does recognize a normal personal law controlled by the law of the domicil. The question to which the norm applies must be considered with reference to the particular act or transaction. No understanding of the scope of personal law in common-law or civil-law countries can be properly understood without some realization of the historical development of the concept of personal law.

The conflict of the personal law with the law of the territory was a concomitant of the development of territorial sovereignty in Europe. This conflict persisted long after the jurisdiction of the state over all persons and things within its territory was acknowledged. Yet the influence to be granted to personal law still remains

[4] Cheshire (1935) p. 143.
[5] Art. 3, par. 3.

as a problem of the *rightful* exercise of jurisdiction, even though the *power* of such jurisdiction is conceded. In other words, it is a problem of the *exact administration of justice.*

We have already observed the immense influence of the so-called statutory theory in the attempt to solve the conflict between the personal and the territorial law and the sterility of the statutory theory except as a convenient though unnecessary method of classification.

The conflict between the personal and the territorial law was no less perplexing in the early legal experience of the United States, especially by reason of the independent jurisdiction reserved to the separate states. Story, in his usual scholarly manner, analyzed the discussions of the eighteenth century jurists of France, Germany, Italy and the Netherlands. Under their system of methodology, all laws which have for their object the regulation of the status and capacity of persons could be divided into (1) universal laws, or those which regulate the status generally, such as general laws with reference to minors, married women, mental incompetents; and (2) special laws which create a disability to do particular acts.[6] When Story came to apply the classification to concrete cases, however, he found no uniformity of opinion as to which laws should belong to the first category and which to the second.

**The Principle of an Ubiquitous Personal Law.** Only seven years before Story's work was published, the "very learned opinion," as he termed it, of Justice Porter in *Saul* v. *His Creditors*[7] was rendered in the Supreme Court of Louisiana. Saul, formerly domiciled in Virginia where he had married, removed to Louisiana with his wife and minor children. After the death of the wife, insolvency proceedings were brought against the husband in Louisiana and the children claimed the property which had been acquired during the period of the marriage, as against the creditors. Under the law of Virginia, there was no community of property in the acquests, the entire property going to the husband. The case brought up a wide number of collateral questions discussed as *dicta,* from which Story observed that the court was willing to recognize the law of the domicil, as the personal law, to govern the capacity of a minor if he were capable by it, even though not capable by the local law. But

[6] Story, §51.
[7] (1827) 17 Martin 596.

where the situation was reversed and he was incapable by the foreign domiciliary law though capable by the local law, the opinion demanded that he should nevertheless be held to be capable. Thus the domiciliary law was applied where the domiciliary law recognized capacity though the local law did not; and local law was applied where the local law recognized capacity but the foreign (domiciliary) law did not. Story found this result to be objectionable and insisted that by general reasoning and by logic, the test of capacity should be either the domicil, or the place of the contract, not both; "otherwise it would seem to stand upon mere arbitrary legislation and positive law, and not upon principle." [8]

The real objection to the recognition of one fixed rule is that it tends to upset transactions completed by non-residents in the local state with resident citizens who were unaware of the disability created by the law of the foreign state. *Qui cum alio contrahit, vel est, vel esse debet, non ignarus conditionis ejus.* He who contracts with another ought not to be ignorant of his condition. But this rule was not intended to apply to contracts made with a person whose status has been created under some foreign law. Story seemed in the end to be undecided and adds: "Even courts of justice do not assume to know what the laws of a foreign country are; but require them to be proved. How then shall private persons be presumed to have better means of knowledge?" Curiously enough, the dictum of Justice Porter did not become the law of Louisiana, which still shows its adherence to the earlier precedents of France and Spain by recognizing the universality of a capacity or incapacity created by the domiciliary law.[9] On the other hand, the general American rule is to apply the *lex celebrationis* of the contract.[10]

Both the earlier discussions and the later jurisprudence give effect to a rule of public policy for the greater security of commercial transactions. It is not because (as Wharton thought) it is a part of our public order and public morals that young men of twenty-one should be capable of making contracts that will bind them to others and bind others to them.[11] The public policy is not against the extension of the period of infancy, but in favor of credit and the facility of commercial intercourse in the local state. Infancy does not

[8] Story, §76.

[9] Baer *v.* Terry, (1901) 105 La. 479, 483; Marks *v.* Germania Savings Bank, (1903) 110 La. 659.

[10] Amer. Law Institute, Restatement, §333.

[11] Wharton, (1905) §8.

create an absolute incapacity to act under the comman law. It is a privilege granted to the minor to take advantage of his "infancy," thus rendering a contract voidable and not void. This privilege is determined by the law of the place of contracting because it is there and at the moment of contracting that the privilege attaches.[12]

By analogous reasoning, the capacity of a married woman to make a guaranty is recognized if capable in the local state where the contract is made, even though she would be incapable by the law of her domicil.[13] The converse is also true. A married woman domiciled in Iowa, where she was capable, was temporarily visiting in Indiana, where she was incapable of entering into a guaranty. She executed the contract in Indiana and was sued upon it in Iowa. In holding the guaranty void, the court affords an insight into the motive of the policy which underlies the great weight of American authority: "We do not think the Continental rule applicable to our situation and condition . . . and in this country, where travel is so common, and business has so little regard for state lines, it is more just, as well as more convenient, to have regard to the laws of the place of contract, as a uniform rule operating on all contracts . . ."[14]

This illustrates graphically the repugnance of our courts to accept any fixed classification for determining the choice of law. It was precisely the urge to follow such a classification which led the English law into some confusion. Lord Eldon had held to the place of the contract as early as 1800.[15] Lord Stowell raised doubts about the correctness of this ruling some twenty years later.[16] Then came the sweeping dictum of Lord Westbury in Udny *v.* Undy,[17] which seems to have led the courts of England into a morass from which

[12] Thompson *v.* Ketchum (1811) 8 Johns. N.Y. 192. See Minor, §72 n 8. *Accord:* Philpott *v.* Mo. Pac. RR. (1884) 85 Mo. 164.

[13] Milliken *v.* Pratt, (1878) 125 Mass. 374.

[14] Nichols & Shepard Co. *v.* Marshall, (1899) 108 Ia. 518. Of course, public policy may be absolutely opposed to the enforcement of such contracts against married women even though made in a state wherein they are capable. Armstrong *v.* Best, (1893) 112 N.C. 59. But the tendency toward the emancipation of married women is leading away from earlier drastic concepts. See Poole *v.* Perkins, (1919) 126 Va. 331.

[15] Male *v.* Roberts, (1800) 3 Esp. 163. This was an action for necessaries supplied to an infant in Scotland. The defendant was assumed to be English, but as no evidence was given as to the law of Scotland, the law was therefore assumed to be the same as English law, and judgment was given for the defendant. The reference to the *lex loci contractus* was therefore dictum.

[16] Ruding *v.* Smith, (1821) 2 Hagg. Cons. 371.

[17] (1869) L.R. 1 Sc. App. 441, 457.

they have never fully escaped. Lord Westbury's dictum was substantially to the effect that capacity to enter into any contract is governed by the law of the domicil. This was applied in Sottomayor *v.* De Barros.[18] The case involved the validity of a marriage entered into in England between first cousins prohibited from intermarrying by their domiciliary (foreign) law. But the capacity to enter into a marriage contract is quite distinct from the general capacity to contract because it gives rise to a continuing status in which the community and the state are deeply interested. Marriage is the foundation of the family and the conditions under which it may or may not be entered into and the persons which may assume to engage themselves by the contract of marriage are elements which essentially concern both the law of their domicil and the law of their nationality as distinguished from the law of the place in which the marriage was celebrated. We do not wish at this time to discuss which of these three possible systems should govern. We shall see that all three govern respectively in various countries.[19] We desire to accentuate that the criterion of capacity to marry is not and should not be the same as the criterion of capacity to contract in general, and the failure to distinguish adequately between the two concepts has led the English courts to pronounce *dicta* concerning the general capacity to act, in cases in which only the capacity to contract marriage was directly involved.[20]

We shall give attention later to the peculiarities inherent in the capacity of persons to enter into the marriage relation requiring the application of different principles.[21] The peculiarities of capacity for entering into marriage lead not to a wider recognition of the personal (foreign) law but to the recognition of incapacities both of the personal and of the local law (*lex celebrationis*) because, as Westlake pointed out, "without a lawful celebration the tie cannot arise." [22] But so far as concerns capacity to enter into ordinary mercantile contracts, the sweeping dicta tending toward the recognition of an ubiquitous personal law has been much criticized in later years.[23]

[18] (1879) 37 L.T. 415; 5 P.D. 94.

[19] See *post,* p. 127.

[20] See for example the comprehensive terms of Lord Westbury in Udny *v.* Udny, 1869, L.R. 1 Se. Ap. 457; by Sterling, J., in Re Cooke's Trusts, 1887, 56 L.J., N.S., Ch. 637; and by Lord Halsbury in Cooper *v.* Cooper, 1888, 13 A.C. 99.

[21] See *post,* p. 125.

[22] Westlake, (1925) p. 42.

[23] See Ogden *v.* Ogden [1908] P. 46 and Chetti *v.* Chetti [1908] P. 67, although both of these were marriage cases.

**Comparative Study of Foreign Systems relating to Capacity to Act.** When we compare the law of other countries with that of England and the American States in this matter, we are at once struck with the different manner of approach. The existence of a codified norm for determining capacity to act, to be found in many systems, at once leads to inquiry as to the scope of the norm. Does it or does it not apply by its terms to the particular capacity involved in an issue before the court?

**German Law.** Let us consider a provision like that of the German Civil Code. The *Einführungs Gesetz* (Introductory Act) Article 7 (1) provides: "A person's capacity to transact business (*Geschäftsfähigkeit*) is judged by the laws of the state to which he belongs." At once the commentator determines that this is intended to be a complete rule for the solution of conflicts irrespective of where the act occurs, and applicable to Germans and aliens alike.[24] It is limited, however, by a provision which would approach what we have seen to be the prevailing American rule. For if an alien enters into a legal transaction in Germany for which he is incapable or of restricted capacity, he is to be regarded as capable to the extent that he would be so regarded under German law; but this provision does not apply to transactions disposing of foreign realty or relating to family law or the law of succession.[25] What is most significant is the difference in the method of approach which such statutory regulation requires. A German court or jurisconsult must immediately analyze the scope of the terms "capacity to transact business," "transactions relating to family law" and "transactions relating to the law of succession." These general terms must be made specific by reference to other parts of the code. Thus the article does not apply to a restriction upon the capacity to deal with certain kinds of property, such as the incapacity of a bankrupt to deal with the bankrupt estate, or the incapacity of the heir to deal with property within the control of an executor.[26]

The application of the German law as the *lex loci actus* is demanded except in regard to the three categories mentioned and this likewise demands analysis of the scope of the terms employed. The court has no legislative discretion such as American courts have exercised

[24] Nussbaum, *Deutsches int. Privatrecht* (1932) pp. 118–119. See Gustav Walker, *Int. Privatrecht* (1924) p. 97. The provision is modified under Art. 27, Introductory Act, so as to recognize any *renvoi* to German law.

[25] Introductory Act, German Civil Code, Art. 7 (3).

[26] Walker, *ut cit.*

through recourse to the principle of public policy. Undoubtedly, this legislative method makes for greater certainty. If the alien has entered into a transaction in Germany, it is immaterial whether the particular transaction is otherwise governed by German or foreign law, whether the transaction was entered into with a German or with another alien, or whether the other party was ignorant of his nationality or not. As Nussbaum points out, the practical scope of the exception is likely to be greater in actual practice than that of the rule itself.[27]

The *Swiss* law is to the same effect although expressed somewhat differently. A foreigner not having capacity to act, who enters into a legal transaction in Switzerland, cannot take advantage of his disability if he possessed capacity according to Swiss law at the time of the transaction.[28]

The law of *France* represents an older variant in this respect. The French Civil Code adopts the national law for determining the status and capacity of persons. Although it speaks only of "French persons even residing in a foreign country" [29] the rule is applied to aliens in France.[30] When the transaction is entered into in France between an incapable foreigner and a French citizen, it becomes material to inquire whether the French citizen in good faith believed the foreigner to be capable without himself being guilty of negligence in not making proper inquiry.[31]

Some writers criticize the result because they insist that the law was intended to protect incapables and that the interpretation violates the very purpose of the law. However, recent writers are inclined to agree that the matter of protecting public credit must be the superior consideration and therefore approve of this example of judicial legislation which serves to bring the law of France into harmony with that of its neighbors and with the preponderating rule of the United States.[32]

**Latin-American Law.** The principles recognized in Latin-American countries may to some extent be discussed collectively as to these countries, owing to the adoption by convention of the so-called

[27] Nussbaum, *op. cit.* p. 120.

[28] Fed. Stat. of June 25, 1891, 7 (b), now incorporated in Art. 61, Final Title, Swiss Civ. Code.

[29] French Civ. Code, Art. 3 (3).

[30] Arminjon, *Droit int. privé* (1934) ii, pp. 95–96.

[31] Ct. of Cassation, Jan. 16, 1861, Lizardi case, Sirey, 1861, vol i, p. 305. See also Clunet, 1899, pp. 364–367; 1906, p. 1119; 1908, p. 46.

[32] Arminjon, (1934) ii, *op. cit.* pp. 96–97; Pillet, *Traité* (1923) i, pp. 509–511.

Bustamante Code by a large number of states and the pending ratification of the code by others. We have already discussed the general principles of the code.[33] We shall refer to its specific provisions, keeping in mind that there is no fixed standard or determinant of the personal law laid down in the code. Each state is free to apply as personal law that of the domicil or that of the nationality, or any other determinant prescribed by its domestic legislation.[34] But in accordance with the rule of modern civil law, a "personal law" governing status is recognized as a continuity of governing law controlled by domicil or nationality as the case may be, in respect to the capacity of individual persons, except where it is otherwise restricted by the code or by local laws.[35] Now the extent of restrictions upon the status by such conditions as minority, insanity, or prodigality, or civil interdiction, *i.e.* whether they restrict in whole or only in part, leaving certain rights and obligations intact, is a question left to local legislation.[36] This is evidently not a *renvoi* but rather a surrender on the part of the code regulation in favor of the autonomy of each state; accordingly, if the law of the state itself prefers to refer the question of the extent or effect of the restriction or disability to some other system of law, there appears to be nothing in the code which prohibits such reference. The personal law yields to the local law. This intention may be derived also from other parts of the code which apply the rule specifically. Thus a decree of prodigality made in one of the contracting states, with its attendant restriction on capacity, has extraterritorial force in respect to the others *in so far as the local law may permit it*.[37] Again, the capacity to engage in commerce and to become party to commercial acts and contracts is regulated by the personal law, but every disability to so engage resulting from local law shall be respected.[38]

The distinguished author of the Bustamante Code sheds some light upon its underlying principles by his classifications of all laws into a threefold division, *viz.*, (1) personal laws, or those of an internal public "order" or character; (2) territorial or local laws, or those

[33] *Cf. ante*, pp. 43, 61, 102, 113.
[34] Bustamante Code, Art 7.
[35] *Ibid.*, Art. 27.
[36] *Ibid.*, Art. 30. The general rule is again stated in Art. 176 referring the capacity or incapacity to give consent to contracts, to the personal law of each party.
[37] *Ibid.*, Art. 100.
[38] *Ibid.*, Arts. 232, 236.

of an international public "order" or character; and (3) voluntary laws, or those of a private "order."[39] But the classification does not of itself give a definite clew to the character of particular laws though it does furnish a general guide upon which may be based the reasoning by which a law is to be ascribed to one category or another. It also furnishes a general guide to the interpretation of these terms when used in the code itself. But the express provision of the code gives the preference to local law because in all cases not provided, "each one of the contracting states shall apply its own definition to the juridical institutions or relationships corresponding to the groups of laws" mentioned.[40] Accordingly, we must still look to national legislation to see whether there is a provision limiting the uniform but restricted application of the Bustamante Code.

**Law of Argentine.** The Argentine law requires particular mention for two reasons. Argentine has not ratified the Havana Convention of 1928 and thus the Bustamante Code is not there in force. Argentine is one of the few Latin-American states which holds to the domicil as the determinant of personal law. We have a direct statement that "the capacity or incapacity of persons domiciled in the territory of the Republic, whether nationals or aliens, will be judged by the laws of this Code, even in a case of acts performed or goods existent abroad."[41] The converse rule applies to persons domiciled abroad. The domiciliary law controls "even in a case of acts performed or property existent in the Republic."[42]

The principle thus consistently applied has the advantage of simplicity, to be sure; it is also readily to be understood in a country like the Argentine, so largely a country of immigration. But the result, viewed internationally, is far from satisfying when conflicts occur with countries applying national law for personal capacity. An Argentinian of 21½ years (majority at 22), domiciled in Germany, would be considered a minor in respect to a contract entered into in Germany (majority at 21), whereas in the Argentine he would be considered of full capacity. A German writer has, with much force, termed this legal result bizarre.[43]

[39] *Ibid.*, Art. 3; Bustamante in Tulane Law Review, 1931, p. 541; see also his "*Projet de Code de Droit int. privé*" (Paris, 1925) pp. 29–33.

[40] Bustamante Code, Art. 6.

[41] Argentine Civil Code, Art. 6.

[42] *Ibid.*, Art. 7.

[43] Dernburg, *Das bürgerliche Recht des deutschen Reiches und Preussens* (1902) i, §36.

## 2. Capacity to Marry

We have already remarked that the capacity to enter into the marriage contract is not necessarily controlled by the same rule which governs the capacity to enter into ordinary contracts. The contract of marriage not only establishes rights and obligations between the parties but also creates a continuing status in which the community and the state have a deep interest. We are dealing here with capacity to marry and not with the rights and obligations arising out of the marital relation.[44]

One of the earliest recorded English cases to present a conflict in private international law involved the capacity of two British subjects, temporarily in France, both being minors, to contract a marriage there without the consent of their parents as provided by French law. This was Scrimshire *v.* Scrimshire decided in 1753.[45] The court examined very fully into the Continental authorities as to the scope of the personal law and arrived at the conclusion that endless confusion would result if the domiciliary law of the parties were recognized; for then the marriage might be deemed good in one country and null in another, with consequent injury to the innocent children of the marriage. The court, therefore, applied the *lex celebrationis, i.e.,* French law, as a rule of convenience and as part of the *jus gentium.* It may be remarked parenthetically that Sir Edward Simpson, the judge of the Consistory Court, was horrified at the mere thought of not conforming to a uniform rule valid in all countries under international law. "If that principle is not to govern such cases, what is to be the rule, where one party is domiciled, and the other not? The *jus gentium* is the law of every country, and is obligatory on the subjects of every country." The insistence of the judge that there should be one uniform rule of the conflict of laws prevailing everywhere under international law with regard to the validity of a marriage is remarkable, even though under present conditions it appears now to be almost naïve. For if it is a good rule as to capacity, it should apply to other conditions affecting the validity of marriages.

The rule of Scrimshire *v.* Scrimshire was recognized as fully authoritative by Story and its doctrine was adopted as the common law of the American States, especially as it antedated American in-

[44] *Cf. post,* p. 143.
[45] Haggerty's Consistory Rep. 395.

dependence. The requirement of consent should ordinarily be deemed a part of the ceremony, though it will depend upon the construction of the law of the place of celebration whether it is a formality or an absolute prohibition.

**Prohibitions by the Personal Law.** The Restatement of the American Law Institute recognizes [46] that a marriage is valid everywhere if the requirements of the law of the state or country of marriage are complied with, except in the case of particular prohibitions. These are prohibitions resulting from a prior divorce, which need not be discussed here; and particular prohibitions of the domiciliary law which may be considered coercive in character, such as against marriages which are considered polygamous or incestuous, or otherwise considered odious in the domiciliary state.

In the House of Lord's case of Brook *v.* Brook,[47] the question at issue was the validity of a marriage in Denmark between a domiciled Englishman and his deceased wife's sister, also domiciled in England, against the prohibition of the English law, though valid by Danish law. The marriage was held void in England because of the English statute prohibiting such marriages. Lord Campbell appears to have accepted the view that the validity of the contract depends upon the law of the domicil, while the other judges concurred in holding the marriage void, not because the parties were incapable but because of the coercive prohibition of English law and because the marriage was in fraud of that law. The case has been followed down to a comparatively recent date,[48] and is perhaps supportable on the principle that England was the place of contemplated conjugal residence and not because of the domicil of the parties at the time of marriage.[49]

The Restatement of the American Law Institute recognizes the law of the place of celebration,[50] but makes exceptions not only of polygamous and incestuous marriages,[51] but also of marriages between persons of different races, "where such marriages are at the domicil regarded odious." [52] It also embraces the doctrine of Brook *v.* Brook by a general exception [53] of "marriage of a domiciliary which a statute

[46] §§121, 131, 132.
[47] (1861) 9 H.L.C. 193.
[48] *In re* Bozélli, [1902] 1 Ch. 751.
[49] Cheshire (1935) p. 160.
[50] §§121–122.
[51] §132 (a) and (b).
[52] 132 (e).
[53] 132 (d).

at the domicil makes void even though celebrated in another state."

In New York a statute forbids marriage with a female under 18 years without parental consent. Two domiciled citizens of New York entered into marriage in New Jersey in violation of the statute but in accordance with New Jersey law. The courts of New York, differing from the House of Lords, recognized the original validity of the marriage but granted annulment on the ground that New York had power to control a continuing status between two of its own domiciled subjects.[54]

**Comparative Study of Foreign Systems relating to Capacity to Marry.** The underlying difference between the common law and the civil law of European countries in the conception of personal capacity, according to Beale, is that the natural facts and powers of human life are accepted under the common law, whereas under modern civil law "until the law gives a man any capacity, he is not regarded as possessing it. Civil capacity, in short, is altogether a creature of the law, and is dependent, therefore, upon some law having conferred it."[55] Whether or not the contrast may be stated thus broadly is open to question, but it would lead us too deeply into the philosophical concepts of man's natural and attributed rights and powers to be here adequately discussed. The important difference, as it seems to us, is that the civil-law countries predicate a capacity for an unlimited, at least an indefinite, number of acts or legal relationships and also regard such capacity as a continuity following the person wherever he goes. Of course, the concept is subject to many exceptions both by legislation and in its application in litigated cases.

The French Civil Code, as we have seen, refers the status and capacity of French persons to French law even when domiciled abroad.[56] It goes beyond this, however, in recognizing a marriage contracted in a foreign country between French persons or between a French person and an alien, only if preceded by the publication required by the Code, and provided the person has not violated the provisions of the Code concerning the qualifications and conditions required to contract marriage.[57] The legislation of Belgium, Germany, Italy, Japan, the Netherlands, Spain and Switzerland is in sub-

[54] Cunningham *v.* Cunningham, (1912) 206 N.Y. 301.

[55] Beale, "The Law of Capacity in International Marriage," (1902) 15 Harvard Law Rev. 382.

[56] French Civil Code, Art. 3.

[57] *Ibid.*, Art. 170.

stantial accord with these provisions, with this difference: the French code does not provide specifically as to the status and capacity of aliens in France but only as to French citizens abroad. The courts have, however, applied the national law by analogy. In Belgium, Germany, Italy, Japan and Switzerland, national law is applicable by specific legislation.[58]

The Italian law adopts the national law of the parties as a general principle applicable to the capacity to marry, and yet it subjects aliens marrying in Italy to the same disabilities as those provided by the code for Italian citizens.[59] Italian law contains certain prohibitions which may be considered so fundamental as to be a part of international public order, such as those against polygamous marriages, marriages within the immediate family, whether of legitimate, illegitimate, or adoptive members. We may say that these represent a proper reservation of the application of the personal law. Marriages of this class may be compared to those which Bishop denominates as "marriages which by the common voice of civilized nations are vicious past toleration."[60] But the Italian law goes further and makes the Italian law coercive even in respect to the age of consent. Even Italian writers agree that to this extent the provisions are "excessive and irrational."[61]

Legislation in Latin America dealing with capacity to marry may be divided into two groups. Some countries have adopted the rule of *lex loci celebrationis*.[62] Countries of another group demand that national law be applicable to citizens, while the capacity of aliens is referred to the *lex celebrationis*.[63]

[58] Moselli *v.* Moselli, Clunet 1918, p. 1192. Pillet, *Traité* (1923) i, 507, citing cases. Belgium, Act of July 12, 1931, in connection with Civil Code, Art. 170 *ter*. Germany, Introductory Statute, Art. 13, together with Art. 27 enacting the recognition of a *renvoi* in favor of German law. Japan, Act of January 15, 1898, Art. 13; Netherlands, Civil Code, Art. 138; Spain, Act of June 18, 1871, Art. 41; Switzerland, Civil Code, Final Title, Art. 61 adopting Art. 7c of the Act of June 25, 1891 (referred to as the statute "N & A").

[59] Italian Civil Code, Arts. 100–102 referring to Arts. 53–59.

[60] Bishop, Marriage, Divorce and Separation, (1891) i, §857.

[61] Udina, *Droit int. privé de l'Italie,* (1930) p. 131. See Weiss, *Traité de droit int. privé,* iii (1898) p. 409, based upon opinions of Pic and Rollin.

[62] Argentine, Act of November 2, 1888, Art. 2, at least in the absence of the impediments mentioned in Art. 9 of the Act. These relate principally to rules of consanguinity. The Act modifies the Civil Code, Arts. 159 *et seq.* Mexico, Civil Code, Arts. 174 *et seq.*

[63] Chile, Civil Code, Art. 119; Uruguay, Civil Code, Art. 101, Act of May 22, 1885; Venezuela, Civil Code, Art. 124 *et seq.*

By accepting a diversity of standards for determining the capacity of parties to a marriage, we manifestly encounter dangers of considerable importance. If we accept the power of the state to legislate with reference to the marriage of its subjects, domiciled abroad, as well as at home, we are presented with conflicting principles, both by the domiciliary rule and that of the law of the place of celebration. A marriage considered valid where celebrated may be void or voidable in the country of the personal law. On the other hand, while reference to the *lex celebrationis* has the advantage of simplicity, it permits the avoidance of inconvenient disabilities by resort to Gretna Green.

The conflict in systems which our discussion has brought to light and the attack on the sanctity of the marriage tie which this conflict, with others which we shall presently consider, makes possible, have led various groups of countries to regulate the governing law by treaty.[64]

## 3. Capacity to Transfer Property

In making one of his customary inventories of the opinion of foreign jurists before stating a conflict-of-laws rule, Story comments upon the great difference of opinion prevailing upon the question whether the *lex situs* determines the capacity to transfer property, movable or immovable, or whether the personal law prevails. There was no doubt in his mind that under the common law, the law of the situs was controlling; and he ascribed the difference of opinion in countries of the Roman law to the desire of the civilians "to carry into effect their favorite system of the division of laws into real and personal." [65] In other words, capacity being a quality of the person, some jurists were inclined to ascribe to the personal law the capacity to transfer title in property. However, capacity to convey is inextricably tied up with the validity of title of the transferee. Therefore, it cannot escape the test of the same law which determines title, namely the *lex situs.*

To illustrate: A note is made by a man and his wife domiciled in Louisiana to secure the debt of the husband. This was void in Louisiana because of incapacity of the wife to make such a contract. At the time of the making of the note, the wife had a separate estate of lands in Mississippi which she intended to charge and which she

[64] *Ante,* p. 55.
[65] Story, §§463; 431–435.

could validly charge by the law of the latter state. It was held that the note was good as a valid charge upon the property because she was capable by the *lex situs*.[66] If the note had been valid as a personal obligation in the state where made but void for incapacity of the wife to alienate or to charge her land for this purpose by mortgage or otherwise in the state where the land was located, the note would be deemed invalid.[67]

In Polson *v.* Stewart[68] a covenant was entered into by the husband in North Carolina surrendering all marital rights in his wife's lands located in Massachusetts. She had been made a "free trader" by statute in the former state, their domicil, by a procedure not known in Massachusetts. The opinion of the court (by O. W. Holmes, J.) recognized the exclusive power of Massachusetts in regard to a conveyance of land within its borders because of control over the *res*. "But the same reason inverted establishes that the *lex rei sitae* cannot control personal covenants not purporting to be conveyances, between persons outside the jurisdiction, although concerning a thing within it." Accordingly the release of the husband's marital property rights was considered good because the wife's capacity *to receive the covenant* was valid by the *lex contractus et domicilii*.

An illustration of the controlling effect of the *lex rei sitae* in respect to capacity is afforded also by the capacity of a foreign corporation to acquire property in the state in which the land is situated. Even if it has such capacity at the place of creation, it will avail nothing if it has not the capacity in the state where the property is located.[69]

## 4. Capacity of Corporations

In the famous Dartmouth College Case it was said: "A corporation is an artificial being, invisible, intangible, and existing only in contemplation of law. Being a mere creature of the law, it possesses only those properties which the charter of its creation confers upon

[66] Frierson *v.* Williams, (1879) 57 Miss. 451. *Accord:* Thomson *v.* Kyle, (1892) 39 Fla. 503.

[67] Swank *v.* Hufnagle (1887) 111 Ind. 453. *Accord:* Bank of Africa Ltd. *v.* Cohen [1909] 2 Ch. 129.

[68] (1897) 167 Mass. 211.

[69] American and Foreign Christian Union *v.* Yount, (1879) 101 U.S. 352. So too, a mortgage to a corporation which has not been authorized to do business in the state of the land will not be upheld. Mutual Life Ins. Co. *v.* Overhold, (1878) 4 Dill. 287.

it, either expressly, or as incidental to its very existence." [70] What, therefore, are its powers outside the territory of the state in which it was created? If its charter permits it to act abroad as well as at home, what recognition will be accorded in the foreign state in which it assumes to act? A bank chartered in Georgia discounted and purchased a bill of exchange payable in Alabama through an agent acting in Alabama with funds of the bank. The maker and indorser defended upon the ground that the bank could not lawfully exercise its powers in Alabama. Interpreting its Georgia charter as permitting it to engage in such transactions abroad, the United States Supreme Court proceeded to determine its capacity from the viewpoint of Alabama law and decided that though a mere artificial being, a corporation is a person for certain purposes in contemplation of law and, by analogy to the powers of a natural person, may lawfully engage in transactions in a state in which it does not reside provided the act is not unlawful there.[71] It is not surprising that the court should have based its reasoning upon the comity of nations in a decision rendered only five years after the first edition of Story's work. The court quotes from Story the passage in which he points out that it is not the comity of the courts but the comity of nations which is administered. The reference to comity would seem to have been quite unnecessary as the court itself recognizes that nothing more is involved than the admission of the existence of an artificial person created by the law of another state clothed with the power of making certain contracts. The right of a foreign corporation to sue in English courts had long been recognized without reference to the doctrine of comity.[72]

"A foreign corporation can legally perform any act within its corporate powers under the law of the state of incorporation unless the act is prohibited by the law of the state where it is to be performed." [73] If the corporation has ceased to exist in the state where it was created, it will also cease to exist abroad. The decrees of the Soviet government "nationalizing" industrial enterprises were held in New York not to have effectually terminated the existence of a Russian corporation so as to prevent it from suing for a deposit made subsequent to the decree. The opinion of Crane, J., that even if the

[70] Dartmouth College *v.* Woodward, (1819) 4 Wheat. U.S. 518 at p. 636.
[71] Bank of Augusta *v.* Earle (1839) 13 Pet. U.S. 519.
[72] Henriques *v.* Dutch West India Co., (1729) 2 L. Raymond 1532.
[73] Restatement, §165.

corporate existence had terminated, it should not be recognized in an action at law, may be taken as dictum.[74]

Although the capacity of a foreign corporation is limited by its charter, it does not follow that it is limited by the general laws of the state of its incorporation. Where the general laws of New York prohibited corporations to take land by devise unless expressly authorized by charter, a Connecticut court permitted a New York corporation to receive a devise of Connecticut land.[75]

The law of the state in which a foreign corporation performs an act must of course be respected. The effect of the act is governed by the law of the state where it is performed.[76] The question is one of statutory interpretation. The act of a foreign corporation cannot be expected to receive any higher degree of recognition than a similar act performed by a natural person not domiciled within the state. On the other hand, where the prohibition applies to domestic corporations, the exercise of a similar power by a foreign corporation does not necessarily contravene state policy. Thus a foreign corporation was allowed to make an assignment to creditors in contemplation of insolvency despite a prohibitory statute interpreted as applicable only to domestic corporations.[77]

A state may prohibit "doing business" within its territory by foreign corporations or may make such privilege subject to the compliance with certain formal and substantial provisions contained in local statutes. This is now the almost universal practice because the competition of foreign aggregations of capital represented by the corporate form are thus brought under local regulation and control. The conditions imposed are often fiscal as well as legal. The complex problems to which legislation of this character gives rise are largely within the domain of public law and are not here dealt with.

**Principles of Foreign Systems with reference to Capacity of Foreign Corporations.** Legal personality is ascribed to a wide group of unincorporated organizations including partnerships and limited partnerships not recognized as separate entities in England or the United States. In contrast with the comity theory, Continental authors ascribe the recognition of civil personality for foreign group-types by referring to the respect which the local state owes to private

[74] Joint Stock Co., of Volgakama O. and C. F. *v.* National City Bank, (1925) 240 N.Y. 368, 377.

[75] White *v.* Howard, (1871) 38 Conn. 342.

[76] Restatement, §166. Dicey (1932) Rule 126 and Comment.

[77] Vanderpoel *v.* Gorman, (1894) 140 N.Y. 563.

rights,[78] or to the necessity of commercial international intercourse.[79] In France recognition was afforded formerly as a matter of right, but when the courts came to regard the personality of group-forms to be the result of a legal fiction, recognition was refused upon the ground that the fiction could have no extraterritorial effect.[80] Since the Law of 1857, associations with capital stock are recognized only on condition of the issuance of a decree by the Council of State or by treaty. A decree is not required for each particular corporation but is issued for the particular country. If it has not been issued, corporations organized in that country cannot sue in French courts.[81]

In some countries, such as Belgium and Italy, recognition rests upon the basis of reciprocity, in which event the foreign corporation is permitted to exercise such civil rights as it derives from the foreign law of its creation, subject to the same conditions and restrictions as are imposed upon organizations of the same type in the local state.[82]

Foreign group-forms composed of natural persons, such as partnerships, limited partnerships and the like, enjoy the same capacity in the local state. In France this is accorded as a matter of right because these group-forms have a personality not ascribable to a fiction of law.[83] In Germany, a similar result is reached *ipse jure,* the statute prescribing the specific types which are subject to recognition by executive decree. The statute provides that societies belonging to a foreign state with capacity to have rights according to its laws, but which can acquire such capacity in Germany only after complying with the provisions of §§21–22 of the Civil Code, are recognized as having such capacity by a decree of the *Bundesrat* (now *Reichsrat*).[84]

The practical result is to subject foreign commercial corporations to the necessity of obtaining an executive decree for each organization.

[78] Pillet, *Traité* (1924) ii, p. 803.

[79] Von Bar (Gillespie's trans. 1892) p. 228; Walker, (1924) *Int. Privatrecht,* p. 128.

[80] Dalloz, 1860, i, 444.

[81] Clunet, 1911, p. 242. This was an action brought against the celebrated actress, Sarah Bernhardt, for breach of a contract with a Danish corporation. The court held that the requirement for the decree of recognition could not be waived by the individual. A decree in favor of the recognition of corporations organized in the United States was issued in 1882. The matter was covered by treaty with Great Britain, April 30, 1862.

[82] Van Berchem in *Rev. de dr. int.* (1889) xxi, 1. Italian Commercial Code, §§230–232. Fedozzi, *Recueil de l'Académie de dr. int.,* 1929, p. 195.

[83] Pillet, (1924) ii, p. 803.

[84] Art. 10, Introductory Stat. to German Civ. Code.

If the decree is not obtained, all persons who engage in transactions in Germany in behalf of the corporation become liable personally.[85]

The Bustamante Code (Art. 32) adopted in certain Latin-American states provides that: "the concept and recognition of juristic persons should be governed by territorial law." However, it would seem that unless the territorial (local) law has affirmatively acted to restrict such recognition, the civil capacity of corporations is referred to the law which has "created or recognized them" (Art. 33). This text seems somewhat ambiguous, the intent being doubtless to refer to the law of the state to which the corporation owes its organic existence, unless the local state has provided specific legislation.

**Right to Carry on Business.** The capacity to have rights and to be recognized as a legal personality in the local state is to be sharply distinguished in foreign systems, as well as under English and American practice, from the right to carry on business in the local state. An isolated transaction may not constitute the carrying on of a business but the establishment of an office or the regular conduct of a business is subjected to specific requisites. This is a matter of statutory detail in each country which is not within the limitations of our subject. These statutes relate to a franchise within the territory, not to the mere recognition of capacity.

[85] German Civ. Code, §54 (2) and comment of Lewald, (1931) *Das deutsche int. Privatrecht,* p. 52.

## Chapter VI

# THE CONTRACT AND THE STATUS OF MARRIAGE

### 1. The Nature of the Contract

Marriage is often spoken of as a contract but it is also something more, because when once entered into, it constitutes a continuing relationship or status which cannot be discontinued at the will of the parties alone. If it can be so dissolved, or if it be polygamous, it ceases to be marriage according to the civilization of the Western World. Its effects in conferring the status of legitimacy upon the children born in wedlock and the relations of consanguinity and affinity to which it gives rise, make of it an institution deeply bound up with the system of civil society as a whole. As Story has said, "It is the parent and not the child of society."[1]

The term frequently used to designate the institution is "a Christian marriage" although the concept did not originate with Christianity nor is it by any means restricted to that faith. Indeed under the law of some of the pre-Christian peoples, the equality of the parties in marriage obtained a recognition which was not realized until a very recent period. Wigmore gives us verbatim an Egyptian marriage contract from the fourth century before Christ, illustrating "the independence and equality of women with men in all legal relations.[2] We wish to emphasize that the institution requires certain essential elements to be regarded as a marriage, although there are many variations in the conceptions of marriage entertained in the different countries of Christendom. Thus in some countries it is regarded in no other light than as a civil contract whereas in others it requires religious sanction. There are im-

[1] Story, §108.

[2] Wigmore, A Panorama of the World's Legal Systems, (1928) i, p. 26.

portant variations in the legal capacity demanded of the parties and in the formal requisites for the creation of the marriage status which give rise to the very conflicts we are discussing. The pervading identity and universal basis of the marriage relation as demanded by law has been described as "the voluntary union for life of one man and one woman, to the exclusion of all others."[3] But the incidents of Christian marriage have undergone and are still undergoing profound changes due to the emancipation of women and the results which the modern industrial system has introduced into family life.

Marriage at its inception is brought about by the voluntary act of competent parties; but once the contract has been consummated in the marriage ceremony, a status has been created which is beyond the powers of the parties to alter. However, in a free state of society, the parties have the liberty of emigration and settlement and may in numerous ways affect the character of the status by residing or becoming naturalized in another state. A state has a direct interest in maintaining and controlling the relationship between the parties, though it was entered into elsewhere, because, as we have said, marriage constitutes the basis of society. Society is not unthinkable without marriage, or with a radically different conception of marriage from that which now preponderates; but as the conception of marriage changes, so society will likewise change.

## 2. The Form of the Celebration

We have seen that the capacity to marry is governed by the law of the place of celebration, under the prevailing law of the American States, while in certain other countries the personal law prevails.[4] Even stronger reasons prevail for the application of the law of the place of celebration to determine the form of the ceremony, because of the principle of convenience, the rule of *locus regit actum,* and also because the contract of marriage is a voluntary act of the parties. The celebration relates to the *making* of the contract, not its continuation, and should be governed by the situs of the making. In discussing the principles applicable to contracts in general, Minor points out that the law of the place of performance is immaterial

[3] Lord Penzance in Hyde *v.* Hyde, (1866) L.R. 1 Pro. & Div. 130. It has been recently held that a Soviet Russian marriage satisfied these requirements. Nachimson *v.* Nachimson (1930) p. 85 and 217; (C.A.) 46 T.L.R. 166 and 444. *Cf.* British Year Book of Int. Law, 1931, p. 187.

[4] *Cf. ante,* pp. 126–128.

because that law applies only to contracts made there; "to hold otherwise would be to suppose its legislature intent upon usurping the authority of other states over acts done within their limits."[5] Now when we apply this reasoning to the celebration of marriage, it illustrates admirably the difference of approach which the law-making authorities of different countries have assumed. The American, and, to a more limited extent, the British courts, in laying down the common law, do not wish to usurp the authority of foreign states in respect to marriages performed abroad.[6] The rule of *locus regit actum* is adopted by the Restatement, with exceptions in favor of certain prohibitions against remarriage after a divorce,[7] and certain marriages declared void by the law of the domicil, which we shall presently consider.[8] This may be ascribed partly to the greater authority of the family tie and partly to the historic role of matrimony as a sacrament of the church. Wharton thought that so far as the rule in the United States is concerned, it is a matter of national policy to encourage matrimony and early marriages. "They are peculiarly suitable to the conditions of a country such as ours, which needs that young, active, and adventurous element, which in the Old World is often looked on with such distrust."[9]

The practical difficulty is to determine what elements affect the form of the marriage contract and what may be considered part of its essential validity. Where one or both of the parties require the consent of parents under the personal law (domiciliary or national as the case may be), will this be deemed a formal requirement when the marriage is entered into abroad, or is it an essential requisite, voiding the marriage even though the local law does not require it? Under the prevailing American rule, it is assumed that the requirement is part of the forms of solemnization. Even if the requirement is viewed as creating an incapacity, the same result would be reached under the American prevailing doctrine because capacity is also referred to the local law. It is to be noted, however, that the lack of consent does not invalidate the marriage though the parties went into another state merely to avoid the necessity of obtaining such consent.[10]

[5] Minor, §172.
[6] *Cf.* Restatement §121; Cheshire (1935) p. 240.
[7] Restatement §§121, 129, 131.
[8] Restatement §132. See *post*, pp. 142–143.
[9] Wharton, §127.
[10] Levy *v.* Downing (1913) 213 Mass. 334.

In England a confused situation confronts us based upon the *quaestio famosissima* as to whether there is a "personal law" governing status, a continuity of governing law, which an English court will recognize. Westlake and Dicey are protagonists for the affirmative view, which as we have seen, was strongly criticized by Story. The first attempt at general recognition by the courts was made, however, in regard to consanguinity and not in regard to lack of parental consent.[11] The question of the effect of such consent arose squarely in Ogden *v.* Ogden where a marriage in England between a domiciled Englishwoman and a Frenchman domiciled in France was declared good notwithstanding the lack of parental consent demanded by the husband's domiciliary law.[12] The court treated the consent as being a matter of form though disclaiming the application of the *lex loci* if both parties had been French domiciled subjects, this on the authority of Sottomayor *v.* De Barros distinguishing Simonin *v.* Mallac.[13] Ogden *v.* Ogden was severely criticized by Westlake, as might have been expected.[14] The situation has been further complicated by certain dicta in Salvesen *v.* Administrator of Austrian Property, decided by the House of Lords.[15] In that case, the appellant, a British woman domiciled in Scotland, had entered into a marriage in Paris with an Austrian subject, the pair becoming domiciled at Wiesbaden, Germany. When the World War broke out, the plaintiff removed to Switzerland. The respondent, as administrator of Austrian property, claimed her movable property located in Scotland as being the property of an enemy alien, the marriage having made her an Austrian national. The appellant, however, relied upon a decree of nullity of the marriage pronounced by the court of Wiesbaden, based upon the failure to observe certain formalities at the time of the marriage relating to residence and publication, thus leaving her British status intact. The House of Lords held that the decree of annulment was binding before a British tribunal even though the respondent was not a party to the proceedings before the German court and was now alleging collusion. The real basis of the decision was not so much upon the proper law of the parties in the matter of determining formal re-

[11] Sottomayor *v.* De Barros, (1877) 3 P.D. 1.

[12] Ogden *v.* Ogden [1908] p. 46.

[13] Simonin *v.* Mallac (1860) 2 S. & T. 67.

[14] Westlake §25.

[15] Salvesen *v.* Ad'or of Austrian Property [1927] A.C. 641. *Cf.* British Year Book on Int. Law, 1928, pp. 106, 182.

quirements but whether the domiciliary court has jurisdiction to annul a marriage performed elsewhere, to the same effect as in an action for divorce. Ogden *v.* Ogden is indeed distinguished on the ground that in that case the woman never acquired a French domicil if she were not legally married, because she did not follow the man to France.[16] But both Lord Dunedin and Lord Phillimore go farther and intimate doubts upon the authority of Ogden *v.* Ogden at least to the extent of insisting that the determination of the original validity of a marriage is a question affecting the status of the parties just as much as is the dissolution of a valid marriage; and that "for the purpose of pronouncing upon the status of parties as well as for the purpose of affecting that status, the court of the law which regulates or determines the personal status of the parties, if they are both subject to the same law, decides conclusively."[17] In its narrowest application, the foreign decree is a judgment *in rem* determining status, if the ground of nullity is informality.[18]

**Comparative Study of Foreign Systems relating to the Form of the Celebration.** Under French law, nullity will be decreed for a marriage celebrated without the consent of parents as provided by law; but only if the parents raise objection within a reasonable time. This would lead to the conclusion that the marriage was voidable or "putative," rather than void. It remains in full force until annulled by judicial decree at the suit of a party to the marriage who needed such consent, or of the ascendants, or of the family council.[19] Where a Frenchman marries a foreigner abroad who was ignorant of the requirements of parental consent under the French law, it has been held that the children would be deemed legitimate, although the marriage had not been published in France, as required by Art. 63 of the Civil Code.[20]

The celebration of marriage is regarded by the law of certain countries as wholly within the function of the ministers of religion of the parties. Under the former regimes of Russia and Spain, respectively, and the present systems of Austria, Bulgaria, Greece and Jugoslavia, marriage is regarded as essentially a religious ceremony and recognition is refused to the marriages of subjects per-

[16] Lord Phillimore's opinion at p. 670.
[17] *Ibid.*, p. 670.
[18] See comment of Latey, (1932) 17 Transactions of the Grotius Society 127.
[19] Civil Code, Art. 182.
[20] Clunet, 1902, p. 1050. *Cf.* Pillet, *Traité* (1923) i, p. 550; Clunet, 1920, p. 205.

formed without the formal sanction of the church.[21] Under such a system, the nature of the ceremony, whether civil or religious, cannot be deemed a mere formality. At least it is an essential form. But what should be the attitude of courts in countries recognizing marriage solely as a civil contract, when nationals of countries where marriage is under the control of the religious authorities seek to enter into marriage under the local forms? France prohibits a religious marriage unless it has been preceded by a civil marriage as provided by French laws.[22] And yet the French courts have sometimes declared a mere civil marriage null when entered into between persons whose personal (national) law demands a religious marriage. Conversely, French courts have annulled marriages celebrated in France between such persons in accordance with the requirements of their national law, because not conforming to the local law. This result has been criticized by some French writers.[23] The rigorous application of personal law in regard to celebration of marriages should not be taken as an established rule, however, as the courts seem to exercise some discretion where the parties were acting without fraudulent intent.[24]

The German Introductory Statute to the Civil Code provides (Art. 13, 3) that the form of a marriage celebrated in Germany is determined exclusively according to German law. We have seen that the same result has been reached in France by judicial decision and has been criticized by some French authors as inconsistent with the general rule of national law. In Germany there seems to be no doubt that the rule is one of strict public policy. Accordingly, a marriage entered into in Germany according to German forms will be considered valid in Germany even though the national law of the parties would consider it invalid as to form.[25] Conversely, a German marriage of foreigners valid by the national law of the parties but invalid as to form in Germany will be considered invalid. Lewald mentions the case of the marriage in Germany of a Greek with a Serbian woman celebrated only according to the religious form of the Greek Church. Such a marriage would be valid

[21] Buzzati, *Trattato di Diritto int. priv. secondo le Convenzioni dell'Aja* (1907) i, 282–287.

[22] French Penal Code, Art. 199.

[23] Arminjon, *Précis de Droit Int. Privé*, ii, (1934) §60, p. 202, citing recent cases.

[24] Clunet, 1922, p. 135; Clunet, 1924, p. 117.

[25] *Reichsger.*, Dec. 17, 1908; Clunet, 1910, p. 1254; Clunet, 1927, p. 161.

by the national law of both parties though invalid in Germany.[26]

On the other hand the marriage of Germans or other foreigners in a foreign country may be celebrated according to either the forms of the place of celebration or that of the national law of the parties so far as German law is concerned. This follows from Art. 11 of the Introductory Statute to the Civil Code which enacts the rule of *locus regit actum* as a general principle and in its facultative form.

Italy has avoided some unfortunate complications by expressly adopting the principle of *locus regit actum*.[27] While the coercive provision of the French Penal Code prevents the celebration of religious marriage before the civil ceremony on French soil, it would seem that religious marriages of foreign persons (*e.g.*, Catholics of the Greek Church) may be validly celebrated in Italy.[28]

**Marriages Deemed Incestuous. Miscegenation.** Prohibitions growing out of the blood relationship of the parties to an intended marriage, or out of divergence of race or color, present problems requiring special consideration. Under certain systems, these prohibitions are regarded as affecting personal capacity to marry. Clearly a prohibition of this nature does not affect the general incapacity of the parties but only their *relative* incapacity. Ordinarily such prohibitions are not considered applicable to marriages contracted by persons not domiciled within the state at the time of marriage.[29] Of course, a court of the forum is obliged to apply the local law if a statute compels it to apply local prohibitions to marriages even though celebrated abroad. It must therefore be regarded as part of the essential requisites of the marriage itself to the extent that certain systems will not recognize as being a marriage a union attempted in defiance of the prohibitions even though solemnly entered into abroad according to the law there in force. A Tennessee tribunal having to consider a criminal prosecution for violating a prohibition against remarriage after divorce said: "It is not always easy to determine what is a positive state policy. It will not do to say that every provision of a statute prohibiting marriage, under certain circumstances, or between certain parties, is indicative of a state policy in the sense in

[26] Lewald, *Das Deutsche int. Privatrecht* (1931) p. 84, citing *Reichsger.* Dec. 10, 1912; Feb. 16, 1914.

[27] *Disposizioni*, Art. 9 (1).

[28] *Cf.* Dienna, *Diritto int. priv.*, ii, p. 132 and note.

[29] Garcia *v.* Garcia, (1910) 25 S.D. 645; Whittington *v.* McCaskill (1913) 65 Fla. 162, where the prohibition was contained in the Constitution; Medway *v.* Needham (1819) 16 Mass. 157.

which it is used in this connection. To so hold would be to overturn this most solemn relation, involving legitimacy of offspring, homestead dower, and the rights of property, in the face of the conclusions of approved text writers, and the concurrence of the adjudications in numerous cases, relating not only to forms or ceremonies and qualifications of the parties, but also to prohibited degrees of relationship, not incestuous in the common opinion of Christian countries, and relating to marriages between persons of different race or color." [30]

Minor points out that the struggle is one between the general policy of upholding the sanctity of the marriage tie entered into abroad in good faith and the application of the domestic policy of the domicil and forum, a balancing of evils.[31] In this struggle we would expect to see the application of domiciliary law to marriages performed abroad in states where the problem is acutely social as for example in the southern states of the United States in respect to marriages between whites and blacks.[32]

An interesting illustration of the differing viewpoints of the American and the Continental principles of private international law is suggested by the discussions of a recent writer. Wigny [33] presupposes a case arising in Belgium involving the validity of a common-law marriage between a white person and a negro, both British subjects, in an American state in which common-law marriages are recognized.[34] So far as form is concerned, the marriage would be good, but a Belgian court would not consider the *lex loci* but the law proper for determining capacity, which by Belgian law is the *lex patriae,* or English law.

**Marriages in fraudem legis.** Does the entrance into marriage in a foreign state in order to overcome the prohibition of the domiciliary state constitute bad faith to the extent of rendering the domiciliary law applicable? Undoubtedly special legislation may make it so,

[30] Folkes, J., in Pennegar *v.* State, (1889) 87 Tenn. 244. Notwithstanding the dictum on prohibitions of the nature mentioned, the court interpreted the statute against remarriage as coercive in respect to a person domiciled within the state at the time of the remarriage.

[31] Minor, §73.

[32] Kinney *v.* Com., (1878) 30 Gratt. Va. 858; Eggers *v.* Olson, (1924) 104 Okla. 397.

[33] *"La théorie des droits aquis"* in *Revue du droit int. et de legislation comparée,* 1931, p. 362–3.

[34] New York: Laws of 1907, c. 742 repealing Laws of 1901, c. 339, §6, again made common law marriages recognizable. *In re* Hinman, 131 N.Y.S. 861, aff'd (1912) 206 N.Y. 653.

although it thereby violates the international rule which the law otherwise recognizes. The uniform Marriage Evasion Act drafted by the National Conference of Commissioners on Uniform State Laws has been adopted in five States.[35] It provides (§1) that the recognition of a foreign marriage is prohibited for all purposes when the parties though domiciled and "intending to continue to reside" in the state, yet enter into a marriage prohibited by its laws. Even where the validity of such marriage is considered in a third state, the court will give effect to the statute if a similar statute exists there.[36]

In the absence of statute, however, the common law rule applies. This is the rule which Bishop conceived to be "the international law of marriage," according to which the element of intent to evade the domiciliary law becomes immaterial.[37]

The Restatement [38] goes beyond the international rule. "A marriage which is against the law of the state of domicil of either party, though the requirements of the law of the state of celebration have been complied with, will be invalid everywhere in the following cases: (a) polygamous marriage, (b) incestuous marriage between persons so closely related that their marriage is contrary to a strong public policy of the domicil, (c) marriage between persons of different races where such marriages are at the domicil regarded as odious, (d) marriage of a domiciliary which a statute at the domicil makes void even though celebrated in another state."

The very terms of the Restatement indicate that the rule is a rule of policy, rather than a solution of the conflict of laws. In common-law countries where the personal law is determined by domicil rather than by nationality, foreign unions deemed odious at the domicil are less likely to be tolerated because of the "affront" to the domiciliary community in which the parties live.

## 3. The Marriage Status. Its Continuance and its Incidents

As we have seen, the conception of marriage in the United States is that of a civil contract which gives rise to a continuing status. The

[35] See Amer. Bar Assoc. Annual Reports, 1934, p. 745.

[36] Hall *v.* Industrial Commission, (1917) 165 Wis. 364. In Meisenhelder *v.* Chic. & N.W.R.R., (1927) 170 Minn. 317, a Kentucky marriage between first cousins, where such a marriage is not prohibited, was held void in Minnesota because of the evasion-statute of Illinois where the parties were domiciled.

[37] Bishop, Marriage, Divorce and Separation (1891) i, §843.

[38] §132.

beginning of this status is by contract but its continuance is governed by operation of law, and hence the place of celebration loses its significance as the governing law. It has been succinctly expressed as follows: "The marriage status is essentially a mode of life, and it is peculiarly appropriate therefore that it should be governed in all particulars by the law of the place where the parties live, that is, by the law of their domicil, and that when their domicil changes, the law governing their status should change with it." [39]

As the measurement and enforcement of strictly personal rights of husband and wife deeply affect the order of the community in which the parties live, the law of their residence will determine, and not that of the domicil, if these places be different. Sir Robert Phillimore says: "The question of whether any, and if any, what amount of force, control or chastisement may be exercised by a husband to a wife, must be under the cognizance of the law of the place of residence. So, too, it would seem, must be complaints as to the violation of the conditions of the marriage bond. For instance, if the husband deserts his wife, refuses her maintenance, or ill-treats her by violence, she has a right *jure gentium* to redress in the tribunals of the place where they reside." [40] Phillimore is here undoubtedly referring to a wife of foreign nationality which indeed suggests the principle. Her status may very well be referred to a foreign domiciliary law for determination but it is in her capacity as a resident, or indeed a mere sojourner, whether foreign or native, that she applies to local courts for the protection of her individual liberty and safety. As expressed for the United States in the Restatement: "If any effect of a marriage created by the law of one state is deemed by the courts of another state sufficiently offensive to the policy of the latter state, the latter state will refuse to give that effect to the marriage." [41] But with this exception, "a state will give the same effect to a marriage created by the law of another state that it gives to a marriage created by its own law." [42]

Alimony is an incident of the marriage relation. It is usually a concomitant of a decree of divorce and as such will be later considered.[43] But it may be granted independently and will be so granted

[39] Minor, §79.

[40] Phillimore, International Law (1889) iv, 320; quoted with approval by Wharton, Conflict of Laws (1905) i, p. 365.

[41] Restatement §134.

[42] *Ibid.*, §133.

[43] See *post*, p. 190.

even against a husband not domiciled within the state in a case in which jurisdiction for process against his property must be founded upon the existence of property within the state.[44]

**Analysis of Foreign Systems relating to Personal Relations of the Spouses.** The sharp contrast between the Anglo-American view of personal relations between husband and wife and that of certain European countries is best illustrated by so modern a code as the German. The Introductory Statute (Art. 14) provides: "The personal legal relations of German spouses to each other are adjudged according to German law, even though the spouses have their domicil in a foreign country. The German laws are also applicable if the husband has lost German nationality and the wife has retained it." While the code does not speak of foreign spouses in Germany, the practice of the courts has applied the principle in the converse case as well.[45]

The acceptance of the national law as the determinant in this matter seems particularly ill advised in view of the tendency in many countries to permit the wife to retain her citizenship upon marriage. This creates a problem only too well realized in international law in respect of political rights and obligations. Here we are presented with the problem in an application to purely private and personal rights and obligations with the possibility of a conflict between the personal law of each of the parties where their nationality is not the same. A rule to solve conflicts thus itself becomes the source of conflict. Theoretically this state of the law would be one of much confusion because the conception of alimony as a concomitant of the equitable remedy of divorce does not prevail in Germany. It is indeed granted as an incidental remedy but it exists independently and it is not restricted to the wife. While the husband's duty is the primary one, the wife must accord maintenance corresponding to his station in life, if he is unable to maintain himself.[46] Is this applicable then to an alien spouse in Germany? There is considerable authority to the effect that the national law must govern, but Lewald believes the prevailing rule to be that German law will apply because it requires the application of a procedural remedy and therefore German substantive law should

[44] Rhodes *v.* Rhodes, (1907) 78 Neb. 495. However, where the wife seeks alimony in the forum, after a divorce which she does not contest has been granted without alimony in a foreign state, the status upon which alimony is founded has ceased to exist and she must fail McCoy *v.* McCoy, (1921) 191 Ia. 973.

[45] Lewald, *Das deutsche int. Privatrecht* (1931) p. 88.

[46] German Civil Code, §1360.

be the measure of it; and he adds: "The latter view should be given the preference for practical reasons." [47] Thus the prevailing rule in Germany, though theoretically sharply in contrast with the Anglo-American view, arrives by what would appear to be the sheer force of necessity at an approach to that system in applying the law of the forum to foreign spouses domiciled in Germany. Moreover, a German court would, in the nature of things, rarely have the opportunity of passing upon questions of support as between Germans domiciled abroad, and if it did, it would find it difficult to enforce its decrees over a continuing period of time.

The French courts classify the duty of support and maintenance as coming within the laws of "police and security" and therefore aliens will be subjected to French law in this matter when jurisdiction is obtained over them. The Court of Cassation has approved an order of this kind in an action brought jointly against the husband and the husband's parent as allowed by French law.[48] Pillet criticizes this result, finding it difficult "to sustain the view that the maintenance of order in France is bound up with the application of our laws on this point," but indicating that it might be defensible if applied only to direct ascendants or descendants.[49]

The Bustamante Code of Latin-American States leaves to the local or territorial law the specific "obligation of the spouses to live together and be faithful to and help each other." [50] The duties of protection and obedience, the obligation or non-obligation of the wife to follow the husband when he changes his residence, the disposal and administration of their joint property and all other special effects of the marriage relation are referred to the personal law of the spouses. If their personal law is different, that of the husband prevails.[51] This must be taken in connection with the underlying rule that the personal law may be either that of the nationality or of the domicil, according to the particular domestic legislation of the contracting state in which the issue may arise.

[47] Lewald, *ut cit.* p. 92, citing recent cases.

[48] Clunet, 1922, p. 115.

[49] Pillet, *Traité* (1923) i, 598. *Cf. post,* p. 196, as to the duty of support between parent and child.

[50] Code of Private Int. Law. Art. 45. Int. Conferences of Amer. States, 1889–1928, (1931) p. 332.

[51] *Ibid.,* Art. 43.

### 4. Marital Property Rights

As one of the most important incidents of the matrimonial status, the law of most if not of all countries creates a series of rights in the spouses with reference to one another's property. The nature and scope of these rights vary greatly from country to country. The mobility of domicil as well as the mobility of personal property will be the frequent cause of conflicts of law between the law of the place where the rights were acquired and the law of the place to which the property has been removed, or to which the parties have removed their domicil.

The political and social emancipation of woman since the middle of the nineteenth century has exercised an enormous influence on the property relations of the spouses. Under the English common law, the husband took as his own, all the movables of the wife except paraphernalia, and also the *choses in action* which he was able to reduce to possession. Consider the astounding contrast with the situation of the present day where, in some of the American States, there is an approach to a complete separation of property, both movable and immovable, with abolition of both curtesy and dower.[52] But this movement has progressed faster in some states than in others, and so conflicts of law between the states as well as with foreign countries are still frequent.

A similar change may be observed in other countries. A Latin-American writer viewing the later legislation in countries influenced by the Napoleonic codes remarks: "The authority of the husband as the head of the family and manager of the community property has been tempered more and more in the wife's interest." He also observes "the tendency to enlarge the participation by the wife in the management of the community and even to effect a more or less complete separation of the respective estates of the two." [53]

Where the parties have entered into a contract with each other with reference to their property by antenuptial agreement, and such contract is valid at the place where it was made, and not inconsistent with any rights acquired at the domicil, the contract, so far as it relates to movables, will be construed and enforced according to the law

[52] *E.g.*, New York, Real Prop. Law, §§189–190 as amended by L. 1929, ch. 229, in effect Sept. 1, 1930.

[53] Alvarez in Continental Legal History Series, vol. xi, (1918) p. 62.

of the place where it was made, even though the parties move to a place where the contract would not have been valid.[54]

With respect to the transfer of property rights or interests by virtue of the marriage, the same separation of rules according to the nature of the property, whether real or personal, applies here as in all other transactions or relationships effecting a transfer of property rights. The law of the state of the situs of land will determine the effect of the marriage upon rights or title in it, whether the property be acquired before or after coverture. As to this, there seems to be general agreement.[55]

With regard to movables, however, there has been much difference of opinion among jurists, reflected today in a great divergence of law and legislation. Story analyzed the discussions of the eighteenth-century authorities and came to the conclusion that the place of celebration or the *lex loci contractus* of the marriage governed as to the acquisition of movable property in the absence of a nuptial contract and where there has been no change of domicil. Where the parties have made a change during coverture, the question admits of a double aspect, first, in respect to property already acquired and second, in respect to property acquired after the change of domicil. It is in the closely reasoned analysis of this more complicated problem that Story sympathizes with the exclamation of Mr. Justice Porter in Saul *v.* His Creditors that questions upon the conflict of the laws of the different states are the most embarrassing and difficult of decision of any that can occupy the attention of courts of justice; and Story adds "that the vast mass of learning which the researches of counsel can furnish, leaves the subject as much enveloped in obscurity and doubt, as it would be if one were called upon to decide without the knowledge of what others had thought and written upon it."[56] Unfortunately the discussion of Story was weighted down somewhat with reverberations of the statutory theory, like the old man of the sea holding on to impede a vigorous effort to make progress toward a better goal. Is the law relating to the matrimonial regime of property more real than personal? If so, it could have no force, in case of a change of domicil, upon property acquired after the change. Fortunately, Story proceeded to his conclusions without the meta-

[54] Richardson *v.* De Giverville, (1891) 107 Mo. 422.

[55] Restatement, §§237–238; 248.

[56] Story, §173. *Cf. ante,* pp. 117–118, as to Saul *v.* His Creditors, (1827) 17 Martin (La.) 571.

physical reasoning of the statutory theory. He arrived at the result by adopting D'Argentré's theory of a tacit consent supposed to exist between the parties to a marriage that the law of their first matrimonial domicil shall govern their property in the absence of agreement; and that this tacit consent remains good even in the event of a change of domicil *unless* the law of the new domicil prohibits the particular matrimonial regime, *e.g.*, community as to property there, in which event the law of the new domicil must govern.[57]

These conclusions have been substantially approved by subsequent practice. Thus where the law of the matrimonial domicil gives to the wife a continuing lien upon her property administered by the husband during coverture, the lien will be recognized in a state to which the husband has removed and in which such a lien does not exist.[58]

An interesting question arises where the parties marry under a system like the French where, under §1400 of the Civil Code, they are presumed to adopt a particular statutory regime of property (referred to as *communauté légale*) in the absence of a written agreement. The parties then move to New York where separation of property and full rights are accorded the wife to acquire and manage her property as a separate estate. Has the wife a community interest in the husband's property? It was held that she has not, so far as property acquired in New York is concerned. Under the New York law, every agreement made in consideration of marriage is void unless it be in writing, except a mutual promise to marry. This would seem to be decisive of property acquired in New York but not as to property lawfully acquired in France under the French law when the parties were domiciled there. As to this, the court was not called upon to decide.[59]

In Harral *v.* Harral,[60] the property was located in New Jersey while the marriage took place in France without an express contract. The parties were found to have been domiciled in France after the marriage and the property was distributed in accordance with the French

[57] Story, §174, 184–187. In discussing the meaning of the term "matrimonial domicil," some insist that notwithstanding Story's verbal deference to a wider meaning it seems safe to say that matrimonial domicil, as the term is actually applied, means the domicil of the husband at the time of marriage. Goodrich, Conflict of Laws. (1927) p. 277.

[58] Bonati *v.* Welsch, (1861) 24 N.Y. 157. See also Gleitsmann *v.* Gleitsmann, (1901) 60 N.Y. App. Div. 371.

[59] *In re* Majot's Estate, (1910) 199 N.Y. 29, citing §31 N.Y. Personal Property Law.

[60] (1884) 39 N.J. Eq. 279.

law of marital property. Curiously enough, the court reached this conclusion, quite logical and sound in itself, by a reference or *renvoi* to the French law inclusive of its doctrine of the conflict of laws in respect to marital property rights. The conflict-of-laws rules of the forum would have indicated French law, without a gratuitous search of the French law relative to conflict of laws.[61]

In the case last discussed, the property was acquired prior to the change of domicil. If its acquisition had been subsequent, the community regime of the French law would not have applied to it. Thus by the law of the State of Washington, property acquired by either spouse during coverture becomes community property, with survivorship in the other spouse. The parties were domiciled in New York where separation of estates as to personalty prevailed, and while there, the husband made certain gains in his business which he invested in land in the State of Washington. The wife died first, leaving the plaintiffs her heirs; then the husband died disposing of the property to the defendants by will. It was decided that property acquired at the domicil in New York did not lose its separate character by being brought into another state. Rights thus acquired are vested rights.[62]

The Restatement[63] adopts in general form the principles applied in the cases considered. Interest in movables acquired by either spouse in one state continue into another state. Movables held by spouses in community, continue to be so held when taken into a state which does not create community interest, and conversely, interests in movables held separately, remain separate interest although the movables are taken into a state which creates community interests therein.

The English courts hold more strictly than do the American courts to a regime established between the spouses at the time of marriage, where the parties chose that place as their matrimonial domicil. This appears from the leading case of De Nicols *v.* Curlier.[64] A French marriage between two domiciled French citizens was entered into without express contract as to marital property. By French law this was equivalent to an acceptance of the community of movable property. After residing in France for some years, the parties moved to England where the husband amassed a fortune. He died domiciled in

[61] *Cf. ante*, pp. 50–52.

[62] Brookman *v.* Durkee, (1907) 47 Wash. 578. *Accord:* Bond *v.* Cummings, (1879) 70 Me. 125; Kraemer *v.* Kraemer, (1877) 52 Cal. 302.

[63] §§291–293.

[64] [1900] A.C. 21.

England and left a will disposing of his property without consideration of the community rights of the wife. The House of Lords gave judgment for the widow upon the basis of the system of property rights established by the French law at the time of marriage. Although the result has been criticized,[65] we see in it nothing illogical or unjust. It is primarily a question of intent. As between domiciled French citizens, a marriage without express agreement may be taken to comport an arrangement as well understood as though the arrangement had been express. "It is sufficient if the court arrives at the conclusion that the parties in fact contracted with reference to some law other than that of the matrimonial domicil." [66]

We have seen that the *Argentine Republic* recognizes a continuing and ubiquitous standard of personal capacity, governed by domiciliary law.[67] It is all the more surprising, therefore, to find that in respect to marital property, Argentine law dispenses with the idea of a continuing personal law and in some respects follows by express enactment the rule of the United States. While giving full liberty to the spouses to arrange their affairs by marriage contract, yet in the absence of such contract, the law of the place where the marriage was celebrated governs the movable property of the spouses wheresoever situated or acquired. With a change of the matrimonial domicil, the property acquired before the change is governed by the law of the old domicil while the law of the new governs property acquired after the change. Immovables are governed by the *lex rei sitae*.[68] As the Argentine Republic is a country of immigration with its centers of population away from its land frontiers, the place of celebration will most often be identical with the domicil of the parties.

The underlying principle of the *French law* relating to marital property is stated by the Civil Code.[69] "The law only regulates conjugal relations with respect to property when there is no special agreement, but the husband and wife may enter into any agreement they deem proper," not contrary to good morals or the provisions of the Code. The interpretation given by the courts to this principle gives free scope not only in respect to the particular property arrangements to be followed between the spouses but also with regard to the *system of law* which shall determine such arrangements.

[65] Beale, Treatise (1935) §290. 1.
[66] Cozens-Hardy, L. J., at p. 588.
[67] *Cf. ante*, p. 124.
[68] Argentine Civil Code, Arts. 162–163.
[69] Art. 1307.

So that where the spouses have not made any specific arrangements whatever, the system of law which they expressly or impliedly chose will make such arrangements for them.[70]

Thus the French rule adopts the principle of a "tacit consent" of the parties in the choice of law. The principle is carried out logically in regard to the substantive provisions of the French Code in respect to marital property where no conflict of law is involved, because it is expressly provided that if the parties do not enter into a special contract at the time of marriage regulating their property relations, a fixed statutory community regime will be taken to have been tacitly agreed to.[71] But does the assumption of a tacit agreement accord with the probable facts? It probably does so far as it concerns a property relationship between husband and wife fixed in detail by a statute of long standing and known to the people generally. On the other hand, so far as it refers to the choice of a *system of law* where there is a conflict between two or more possible systems, it probably does not. Only in rare cases will the parties have sufficient knowledge of the alternatives to think of any definite solution, especially at a period of life when the amount of their property may be very small. If they thought of the matter, it is not at all improbable that each would think of a different system, the one most familiar, or the one which was most favorable. This would be almost certain to be the case where the parties were domiciled in or nationals of different countries at the time of marriage. And yet the French courts accept the principle of autonomy in the choice of law for the regime of marital property and invoke reference to all the various circumstances throwing light on the system of law which the parties are presumed to have chosen, such as the nationality and domicil of the husband, the religion of the parties and the celebration of the marriage in a foreign country. As the establishment of the fictive choice often occurs in legal proceedings long after the time of the marriage, the practical difficulties are apparent.[72]

Whatever the disadvantages of the French system, it has at least insured itself against change of the governing law by a change of the domicil, which the Anglo-American principle permits. A choice of law for property relations once fixed between the parties under French law will continue even after a change of domicil.

[70] Arminjon (1931) iii, §95. Clunet, 1924, p. 419; 1925, p. 750; 1929, p. 439.
[71] Civil Code, Art. 1400.
[72] *Cf.* Arminjon (1931) iii, §95 citing the French cases.

The *Italian* law [73] adopts the national law of the parties for "family relations," which in the interpretation given by Italian law, includes marital property. The husband's nationality decides in the event of divergence of nationalities.[74] The national law applies equally to aliens in Italy and to Italians abroad. It also applies without distinction as to movables and immovables. Italian law, like the French, provides for a statutory system in the absence of nuptial contract at the time of marriage, but it is the system of separation of property and not community. Indeed community as to existing property is prohibited even by contract; it must be limited to acquests.[75] A change of domicil will not change the regime fixed by national law; neither will a change of nationality after marriage. To this extent the system is rigid; but the question arises whether a change of nationality may have this effect if the parties voluntarily agree to modify their property relations pursuant to a contract permitted by the law of their new allegiance. Anzilotti and Diena believe this to be allowable while Catellani and Olivi take the contrary view.[76]

To give effect to a voluntary change after a change in allegiance seems to be suggested by the law of *Switzerland* which permits the spouses to file a joint declaration approved by the competent officials for the purpose of changing the matrimonial regime after a change of the matrimonial domicil. Under Swiss law, the first matrimonial domicil governs the property relations of the spouses *inter se*. However, if the spouses are Swiss and have their first domicil abroad, Swiss law will govern, unless the foreign law assumes to apply by its own terms.[77] But the rigidity of their relations is maintained with the exceptions noted, even though they remove their domicil to Switzerland after the marriage.

The *German* law also adopts the principle of rigidity but it is that of the nationality of the husband at the time of marriage, so that even if the husband becomes German after marriage, or if aliens are domiciled in Germany, the national law at marriage will control both as to movables and immovables. An exception is made however in permitting the parties, in the two contingencies mentioned, to enter into a nuptial contract fixing their relations, even if the national law

[73] *Disposizioni*, Art. 6.

[74] Udina, *Droit int. privé d'Italie* (1930) p. 130.

[75] Italian Civil Code, Arts. 425, 1433.

[76] Udina, *ut cit.* p. 139.

[77] Swiss Federal Statute of June 25, 1891 (N. & A.) Arts. 20, 31, made part of the Civil Code.

does not so permit. Thus in the two contingencies mentioned, the national law may be modified by express contract, even after marriage.[78]

By this comparison of existing systems, two competing principles for regulating marital property are brought to light. One recognizes the immutability of the matrimonial regime, the other homologates the matrimonial regime to a change in the personal law. The rule of immutability justifies itself in so far as it tends to promote stability and harmony in marital property relations. It protects each against continual solicitation or even coercion of the other to improve his or her economic position at the expense of the other. It also prevents the husband from changing his domicil or his political allegiance with ulterior motives of property advantage at the expense of the wife. On the other hand, maintenance of a regime created by and perhaps peculiar to the laws of a foreign country after the parties have in fact severed their relations with it in other respects, may prove to be difficult in practical application and may be the cause of much confusion. The device by which the German and Swiss systems avoid the dangers of either rule by permitting the new personal law to govern provided the parties agree, is worthy of wider legislative consideration.

[78] Introductory Statute to the German Civil Code, §15. Walker, *Int. Privatrecht,* (1924) pp. 663–5. The provisions of §15 with regard to a change of nationality or in respect to married parties domiciled in Germany, are subject to a *renvoi* back to German law, if there be such a *renvoi* under the particular national law. Art. 27 Introductory Statute.

## Chapter VII

# DISSOLUTION OF THE MARRIAGE STATUS

### 1. Divorce

To the extent that the Roman Catholic Church was universal, the law which it administered through the bishop of the diocese was recognized throughout Christendom. After the Reformation, this unity ceased, and with the assumption of authority by the temporal power, conflicts of jurisdiction and law were bound to arise.

The problems of divorce in private international law are principally problems of jurisdiction; but even where the rule of jurisdiction is established, the grounds to be recognized may be those of another jurisdiction. Let us assume that the law of a certain country establishes a judicial proceeding leading to the dissolution of the tie of marriage. Must the parties be nationals, or will domicil be the test of jurisdiction? Will the place of the marriage and the place of occurrence of the act constituting the ground for divorce, be elements in determining jurisdiction for the institution of the proceedings? If the parties be aliens, how far must consideration be given to their national law? What recognition, if any, is to be granted to the decree of one state or country where it is brought into question in another state where, perhaps, other and different bases of jurisdiction or different grounds for divorce are recognized?

The importance of these questions has increased by reason of the profound changes of social law and custom with respect to the institution of marriage and family life. The principle of the equality of the sexes and the entrance of women into the field of economic activity have caused radical changes in the relations of husband and wife during the past half century. As the Chilean jurist, Alvarez, expresses it: "we find the wife's duty of obedience to her husband weakening, and a tendency arising to regard marriage as a bond which may be dissolved more and more easily by divorce."[1]

**Law of Various Countries relating to Divorce and Separation.** Social tendencies are only imperfectly reflected in the condition of the law. Divorce, though a recognized institution under the Roman law, was independent of the sanction or decree of a judicial officer or tribunal. It was regarded "as free as marriage" and within the power of the parties.[2] The marriage contract today, according to the principles still prevailing in most civilized countries, remains an indissoluble tie so far as action *by the parties* is concerned. So long as jurisdiction over the marriage relation was restricted to the priesthood of a common church, there was no opportunity for variance. The Reformation introduced variances in this matter even before jurisdiction became secular. These variances became more frequent when the ecclesiastical courts ceased to have control. Thus Reformation in Scotland led to the transfer of matrimonial causes to the crown and the establishment of judicial procedure for divorce *a vinculo* long before England reached this stage. The French Revolution introduced a similar diversity on the Continent of Europe. The legislation of the early years allowed divorce by mutual consent or upon slight causes; it found a place in the Civil Code upon a stronger foundation but disappeared after the downfall of Napoleon, reappearing again under fairly liberal conditions by the statute of 1884.[3] Spain introduced the institution of divorce after the recent Spanish revolution, by Law of December 4, 1931.

The Protestant law of divorce in the German States developed a sharp divergence from the Canon law. At one time it permitted self-divorce upon liberal grounds (though not by mutual consent); but the Protestant ecclesiastical law was replaced by that of the state after the French Revolution. The extreme diversity existing in the different jurisdictions with respect to the grounds for divorce disappeared in Germany only with the imperial statute of 1875. The German Civil Code has replaced this statute by enacting not only certain fixed grounds but by permitting the judge to dissolve a marriage on "relative" causes when the conduct of a party has effected "such a funda-

[1] Continental Legal History Series: "Progress of Continental Law in the 19th Century" (1918) p. 62.

[2] Muirhead, Historical Introduction to the Private Law of Rome (1899) p. 356.

[3] Brissaud, A History of French Private Law (1912) pp. 150–151.

mental derangement of conjugal relations" that the innocent party "cannot be expected to continue the marriage." [4]

Austria, Brazil, Italy and the part of Poland formerly belonging to Russia, still retain the ancient rule of granting no divorces to their Catholic subjects. The opposite extreme is represented by Soviet law where a marriage may be dissolved by mutual consent, or indeed by declaration of only one of the parties without the intervention of judicial authority.

**Judicial Separation.** In addition to the conflicts thus presented, there are likewise conflicts in respect to judicial separation or other proceedings abrogating the marriage status only in part, or for a temporary period. Here diversity arises because the statutes of the various countries create proceedings peculiar to their own institutions with different bases and purposes. The Canon law recognized only separation from board and bed (*a mensa et toro*), temporary or permanent according to the nature of the offense. Separation is thus permitted in countries like Austria and Italy which do not grant divorce, at least not to Catholics. The institution has been somewhat transformed by statute in England and the United States. It exists in some of the American States but not in others and the statutes vary greatly from jurisdiction to jurisdiction. It exists in France as *separation de corps*. It is by no means the same institution recognized in Germany under the title *Aufhebung der ehelichen Gemeinschaft,* or abrogation of the community of marriage, which in itself may be converted into a ground for divorce. As a further striking example of diversity it may be noted that in Denmark and Norway, separation cannot be asked of the courts but only of administrative authorities. Indeed divorce itself, though granted by the courts, may also, under certain circumstances, be obtained by administrative decree. Fedozzi says that the latter is preferred "because less shocking to the personal feelings of the parties." [5]

The second category of questions to which we have referred are those which relate to the effect to be given a foreign decree of divorce or separation. This involves an examination of the basis of jurisdiction both under the law of the foreign state as well as of the local state and implies an international conflict of a private legal nature. As the rules for the solution of such conflicts are various, it also follows that a different answer to the question of recognition

[4] §1568. *Cf.* Huebner, History of Germanic Private Law (1918) pp. 616–617.
[5] Fedozzi, *Académie de droit international, Recueil des Cours,* 1929, ii, p. 230.

may be and often is given to the same decree in different countries.

We must conclude from this brief general review that there is neither uniformity nor certainty in the many laws designed to establish the sanctity of the marriage relation. Where there is no adequate sanction, sanctity soon disappears. The divergence of law and legislation encourages a conscious search for the most favorable jurisdiction in which divorce proceedings may be instituted. Nor does it necessarily follow that the jurisdiction in which divorce is most difficult, is contributing the most to the maintenance of public morality and the purity of family relations. "The kind and number of causes for divorce," says Miraglia, "must be determined by principles of justice harmonized with social conditions. The number of causes should not be increased except upon a clearly shown necessity, in order to hinder, or at least not to hasten the destruction of custom, nor should it be so small as to exclude just and impelling causes";[6] and he adds that causes ordinarily recognized by wise legislation and reason are adultery, cruelty, indignities, life imprisonment or conviction for infamous crimes, and desertion.

**Divorce Legislation in the United States.** In the United States, the wide diversity of legislation relating to the jurisdiction of the courts in the matters of divorce and also relating to the grounds for divorce has long been recognized as creating a social problem of major importance. The geographic separation of the centers of population at the period of the adoption of the Constitution, when measured by the time factor, was so great as to maintain a commensurate separation of community custom. The diverse religious origins of the colonies, newly become states, also made for divergence in legislation affecting the family. Had the framers of the Constitution foreseen the tremendous increase of population through immigration and the new facilities of communication and transportation, they might conceivably have granted power to the central government to enact a federal law of marriage and divorce. Curiously enough, a sharp divergence in legislation exists today even between immediately adjoining states. Whereas the State of New York, for example, recognizes only one statutory ground, the State of Pennsylvania recognizes seven, including desertion, imprisonment for felonies, etc.[7] The general tendency in the United States is toward

[6] Miraglia, Comparative Legal Philosophy applied to Legal Institutions (Lisle's trans., 1912) p. 708.

[7] New York Civ. Prac. Act (1932 ed. §114); Penna., Purdon's Penna. Stats. (1930) "Divorce" §10.

liberality of divorce legislation. New York and South Carolina seem to be the only states which stand firmly against this policy. A competent observer in the field of comparative legislation emphasizes the fact that undue strictness "must have had an effect in the increasing hospitality offered by certain states to discontented spouses who either are not able to procure a decree in their own domicil or prefer the comparative secrecy of a distant tribunal." [8] The extreme cases of such "hospitality" are represented by recent legislation in Arkansas, Idaho and Nevada, the first two requiring residence for only ninety days, Nevada for six weeks.[9] The grounds for divorce recognized, for example, by the Nevada law include willful desertion for a period of one year, neglect of the husband for a like period to supply the wife with the common necessities of life, extreme cruelty, conviction of felony, habitual gross drunkenness and insanity.[10]

**Jurisdiction for Divorce.** We now approach the primary question. What court shall have competence to dissolve the status of marriage under the various circumstances which may arise? We have seen that marriage is regarded as a status as well as a mode of life. Therefore, it seems reasonable to accord to the state in which this mode of life is centralized, namely, the state of domicil, the power to dissolve it. It has been said: "The process of divorce is provided for because the lawmaking body deems it for the best interest of the parties and the state that, under certain conditions, which it sets out as grounds for divorce, individuals should no longer be compelled to maintain the relations of husband and wife." [11] It is in the nature of marriage that, though entered into under the local law of a particular country, it may be modified or dissolved by the sovereign power of any country wherein the parties may be domiciled.[12] Some early cases required domicil in the forum at the time of the delictum.[13]

Although originating in contract, marriage is a domestic relation in which the state has an immediate interest, and each state to which the parties remove has a similar interest; "and as every nation and state has an exclusive sovereignty and jurisdiction within its own

[8] Chamberlain in Amer. Bar Assoc. Journal (1932) xviii, p. 870.

[9] Laws of 1931: Ark., ch. 71; Ida., ch. 77; Nev., ch. 97 and ch. 169 (requiring corroborative proof of residence).

[10] Nevada, Compiled Laws (amended to 1934) §9460.

[11] Goodrich, (1927) p. 287.

[12] Bishop, Marriage, Divorce and Separation (1891) i, §174.

[13] *Cf.* Dorsey *v.* Dorsey (1838) 7 Watts (Pa.) 349, 32 Am. Dec. 767. Overruled by statute. Pa. Gen. Laws, Title 23, Divorce, §15.

territory, so it has exclusively the right to determine the domestic and social condition of the persons domiciled within that territory."[14] The place of the contract, therefore, should give way to the place where the relationship subsists, if the parties have removed from the former. This is true as an international or interstate rule of jurisdiction in the sense that a divorce is not entitled to recognition in another country or state unless the rule be observed. Even where local legislation permits action to be brought if the parties were married within the state, it is held that this does not dispense with the necessity of a domiciliary basis for jurisdiction.[15]

So long as personal and economic power was strongly centralized in the husband, the problem of jurisdiction for divorce remained simplified, if not entirely simple. "By marriage, the husband and wife are one person in law," said Blackstone, "that is, the very being or legal existence of the woman is suspended during the marriage, or at least is incorporated and consolidated into that of the husband."[16] Accordingly, the husband had the sole power to determine the domicil of the parties and to change it during marriage. Under the common law, therefore, the fact that the wife actually lives apart from the husband even with his consent, or that the husband has been guilty of misconduct, did not entitle the wife to acquire a separate domicil.[17] This still remains the rule in England even though the husband had contracted a bigamous marriage abroad after deserting the wife,[18] but, as we shall see, it is no longer the rule in the United States. It may be well, therefore, to consider certain phases of English law before proceeding to the complexities which the right of the wife under certain circumstances to acquire a separate domicil has imported into the law of the United States.

**Basis of Jurisdiction in England.** Originally no foreign court could under any circumstances pronounce a divorce of parties to an English marriage, which would be held valid in England. This followed from the conception of the indissolubility of the marriage tie

[14] Ames, C. J., in Ditson *v.* Ditson, (1856) 4 R.I. 87.

[15] N. Y. Civ. Prac. Act §1147 as interpreted by O'Brien, J., in Gray *v.* Gray, (1894) 143 N.Y. 354 at 357; followed and applied in Barber *v.* Barber, (1915) 151 N.Y.S. 1064, 89 Misc. 519. *Accord:* Wilson *v.* Wilson, (1872) L.R. 2 P. & D. 435.

[16] Commentaries on the Laws of England. Bk. i, ch. 15, §iii.

[17] Warrender *v.* Warrender, (1835) 2 Cl. & F. 488; Dolphin *v.* Robins, (1859) 7 H.L.C. 390.

[18] Lord Advocate *v.* Jaffrey [1921] 1 A.C. 146; Alberta *v.* Cook [1926] 1 A.C. 444.

together with the contractual theory by which the right to divorce depended upon the terms of the marriage contract.[19] When, however, English legislation itself recognized the dissolubility of the marriage tie, even as to marriages entered into prior to the statute, the contract theory fell to the ground and English courts recognized foreign divorces of English marriages pronounced by courts of the domicil.[20] Now where the wife is at fault, the fact that the domicil had been changed after the commission of the offense, to a country in which she had never in fact resided, becomes immaterial. The court is justified in imputing the domicil to the wife by the rule of law.[21] Suppose, however, the husband is at fault and assumes to change the domicil after the commission of an offense. James, L. J., in Harvey *v.* Farnie [22] suggests the case of an English husband going to a foreign country for the sole purpose of obtaining a divorce. This supposition is answered fully by Gorell Barnes, J., (afterwards Lord Gorell) in Armytage *v.* Armytage: [23] "without necessarily resorting to the American doctrine that in such circumstances a wife may acquire a domicil of her own in the country of the matrimonial home, it is considered that, in order to meet the injustice which might be done by compelling a wife to follow her husband from country to country, he cannot be allowed to assert for the purposes of the suit that he has ceased to be domiciled in this country." [24] Sir Samuel Evans, P., was likewise impressed by the cruelties of the rigid common law rule in a case in which an Englishwoman was married in England to a

[19] *Cf.* Dicey, A Digest of the Law of England with reference to the Conflict of Laws, (1896) Appendix, Note 9, citing the cases prior to the Matrimonial Causes Act of 1857. This statute did not allow divorce on equal terms when the wife was suing. Adultery was recognized as a ground only when coupled with desertion or cruelty. This law was changed by the Matrimonial Causes Act of 1923 allowing adultery as a ground on equal terms.

[20] Harvey *v.* Farnie, [1880], 5 P.D. 153; 6 P.D. (C.A.) 35; [1882], 8 A.C. 43. See dictum of Lord Penzance in Wilson *v.* Wilson, [1872], L.R. 2 P. & M. 435 at p. 442 quoted with approval in Le Mesurier *v.* Le Mesurier [1895] A.C. 517.

[21] Wilson *v.* Wilson, *ut cit.,* where the jurisdiction was English, although the marriage, the place of commission of the offense and the actual residence of the wife were in a foreign country. Warrender *v.* Warrender, (1835) 2 Cl. & F. 148., where the jurisdiction was Scottish.

[22] [1882] 6 P.D. at p. 47.

[23] [1898] P.D. 178 at p. 185.

[24] To the same effect are the remarks of Lord Gorell in Bater *v.* Bater [1906] P. 216; and Ogden *v.* Ogden [1908] P. 78. Westlake indicates (Treatise, 5th ed. p. 94) that Gorell Barnes, J., was influenced by the discussions of the third edition of his treatise.

Frenchman who afterwards deserted her and obtained a decree of nullity in France;[25] and Foote remarks that the learned judge thus "showed himself upon the side of common sense and equity, by refusing to adopt a too formal and rigid application of a legal theory."[26]

**Divorce Jurisdiction in the United States.** We have indicated that the complexities of divorce jurisdiction enter at the point where a separate domicil is permitted to the wife after the community life of the parties has in fact ceased through no fault of her own. This right followed, not only from the inherent cruelties of the old rigid rule of the common law, but also because it no longer squared with the emancipated state of woman in the home and out of it. This new view was taken by Bishop in his work on Marriage and Divorce and received judicial recognition in the United States in Ditson *v.* Ditson.[27] The opinion by Ames, C. J., is characterized by a clarity of reasoning and a philosophic outlook which has stood the test of time. The marriage took place in Massachusetts and after the husband's adultery, the plaintiff returned to the home of her parents in Rhode Island and three years later began the action. The husband had never been within the state and was given only constructive notice. It is interesting to observe that the opinion is almost entirely taken up with what may be termed the international question, *viz.,* how far has the court jurisdiction to dissolve a marriage by a judgment entitled to validity where only one of the parties is domiciled and no personal service has been obtained within the state? The court emphasized the peculiar nature of the marriage contract from which emerges a status recognized throughout the civilized world and which imposes social and moral duties and obligations of which every sovereign state is the judge so far as concerns its own citizens or subjects. A decree of divorce is therefore no mere personal judgment but operates directly upon the status and is likened to a proceeding *in rem* or *quasi in rem.* The court then referred to the so called "full faith and credit" clause of the United States Constitution which wisely provides against "the distressing consequences which otherwise might arise from the conflict of laws and decisions upon this interesting and important subject."[28]

[25] De Montaigu *v.* De Montaigu, [1913] P. 154.
[26] Foote, Private International Law (5th ed. by Bellot, 1925) p. 148.
[27] (1856) 4 R.I. 87.
[28] *Ibid.,* p. 107.

Unfortunately, the confidence of Chief Justice Ames that all would go well has never been realized and the consequences remain as distressing as ever they were. Let us follow the denouement of this drama of conflicts. Some courts followed Ditson *v.* Ditson to the extent of allowing the wife to acquire a separate domicil at the last common domicil of both.[29] Other courts however followed the rule to the extent of permitting her, for the purposes of divorce or separate maintenance, to establish a domicil in fact and in law at any place, after the husband was at fault.[30] Still other courts allow the wife to sue at the husband's domicil even after establishing a separate home.[31]

The first case to reach the Supreme Court which squarely involved the validity of a divorce granted to the wife upon the basis of separate domicil, but without personal jurisdiction over the husband, was Atherton *v.* Atherton, in which the divorce was granted in the "matrimonial" or last common domicil. The parties were married in New York and immediately settled in Kentucky, the domicil of the husband. The wife thereafter left her husband and returned to her old home in New York where, in an action of divorce from bed and board, she alleged cruel and abusive treatment as her ground for separation. The defendant denied the charge and set up a divorce granted in Kentucky upon the ground of abandonment after constructive service by mail in accordance with Kentucky statutes. Upon a writ of error to the Supreme Court the full faith and credit due the Kentucky decree was upheld practically upon the authority of Ditson *v.* Ditson. Judge Gray in writing the opinion of the court, however, emphasized that the Atherton case was stronger for recognition than the Ditson case, because Kentucky had been "the only matrimonial domicil of the husband and wife." [32]

**Haddock *v.* Haddock.** Five years later the case of Haddock *v.* Haddock reached the Supreme Court. The parties were married in New York where both had lived prior to the marriage but shortly after the marriage the husband left the wife and later obtained a divorce in Connecticut on the basis of his domicil there and con-

[29] Hunt *v.* Hunt, (1878) 72 N.Y. 217.

[30] White *v.* White, (1893) 18 R.I. 292. Cases collated by Beale for the American Law Institute; Treatise 1 (a) Conflict of Laws (1925); now to be found in his Treatise (1935) §28.2 note 3.

[31] Berger *v.* Berger, (1918) 89 N.J. Eq. 430.

[32] Atherton *v.* Atherton, (1901) 181 U.S. 155. *Accord:* Thompson *v.* Thompson, (1913) 226 U.S. 551.

structive service upon the wife. Eighteen years later the wife sued the husband for a separation and alimony in New York on the ground of abandonment. The husband set up the Connecticut decree and also averred that the marriage having been procured by fraud of the wife, the parties had separated by mutual consent immediately after the marriage. The court (four justices dissenting) held that the New York court was not bound to recognize the Connecticut decree because the matrimonial domicil had never been in Connecticut. The opinion of White, C. J., is based principally upon the reasoning that if the marriage relation is the *res* with which the Connecticut court assumed to deal, it could never have been present there because the husband had already abandoned the wife in New York; that if it be conceded that at least he took so much of the marital relation as concerned his individual status, he must have left in New York so much of the marital relation as concerned the wife's status, and therefore the *res* was divisible; therefore Connecticut had no power to affect the status of the wife in New York.[33] The court insisted that any other view would take away the power of the states over their own citizens and be equivalent to saying: "that to preserve the lawful authority of all the states over marriage it is essential to decide that all the states have such authority only at the sufferance of the other states." [34] But this argument has just as much logical force when applied to the lawful authority of the State of the decree (Connecticut) as of the State of the new proceedings (New York). The court deals with the decree as though it were a judgment *in personam*. The context indicates that the court was influenced by the quite laudable desire to prevent a race of diligence between the parties in seeking different fora in other states.[35] In the Haddock case, however, the wife had waited eighteen years before contesting the validity of the Connecticut decree and it is perhaps an open question whether the social evils which the court attempted to prevent are not matched by those which the decision permits. Mr. Justice Brown who dissented (with Harlan, Brewer and Holmes, JJ.) believed that the court had taken "a step backward in American jurisprudence in restoring the principle of comity which the constitutional provision was designed to supersede.[36] The danger of the decision lies in its

[33] Haddock *v.* Haddock, (1906) 201 U.S. 562, p. 577.
[34] White, C. J., at p. 574.
[35] *Ibid.*
[36] At pp. 627–628.

crystallization of a rule of law which is not a reflection of the actual facts of modern life. How can the marital relation be localized in only one place after it has once been recognized that the parties may have separate domicils? Moreover, the legal emancipation of woman has proceeded even further since the decision was rendered. Marriage in the United States, and in an increasing number of foreign countries, no longer effects a change in the citizenship of the wife. Women have been accorded the political franchise by the Seventeenth Amendment. There is judicial authority which accords power to the wife to establish her separate domicil whenever she is justified in living apart, even though she may not have cause for divorce, or indeed for any cause.[37] It is well known that the right to select a separate domicil on a perfect equality with the husband is part of the legislative program of the day,[38] and has already received some judicial recognition.[39] The result of the Haddock case permits a person to be legally married to another person in one state and legally married to still another person in another jurisdiction, or of a party being married in one state and unmarried in another; a situation which ought not to be tolerated as between the states of the same federal union. As Dean Goodrich expresses it: "The conception of a husband without a wife or a wife without a husband may be a metaphysical possibility, but it is a reproach to the common law whose courts and lawyers have always prided themselves upon freedom from mere theoretical speculation and boasted of actual contact with hard fact." [40]

[37] Shute *v.* Sargent, (1892) 67 N.H. 305; Bucholz *v.* Bucholz, (1911) 63 Wash. 213, at pp. 217–218.

[38] A separate domicil by mutual agreement even in the absence of any cessation of friendly relations has been recognized by United States authorities in the administration of the Tariff Act. Ganna Walska McCormick *v.* U.S., (1930) 78 Univ. of Penna. Law Rev., p. 780.

[39] "Since the law puts her upon an equality so that he (the husband) now has no more power and authority over her than she has over him, no reason would seem to remain why she may not acquire a separate domicil for every purpose known to the law." Blodgett, J. in Shute *v.* Sargent, (1892) 67 N.H. 305.

[40] *Ut cit.* p. 292. Beale, recanting his earlier criticism of the Haddock case, later acquiesced on the ground that jurisdiction should be dependent on the *fact* of blame. In other words if one spouse was at fault and leaves the jurisdiction, the other has in no way subjected his interest to a foreign court." *Cf.* "Haddock Revisited" in 39 Harvard Law Rev. (1926) at p. 417; Beale, Treatise (1935) §113.11. But as Holmes, J., points out in his dissenting opinion, if the finding of the second court, contrary to the first decree, that the husband was to blame destroys the jurisdiction of the first court, the same fact ought to destroy the jurisdiction in the matrimonial domicil if by such misconduct the wife has left the state.

The authority of Haddock *v.* Haddock cannot be questioned (except by the Supreme Court itself) as a rule of constitutional law. It is however not binding upon the State courts as a rule of private international law. Recognition of the decrees of another state cannot be *compelled* under like circumstances but the State courts may and in fact do accord recognition to divorces obtained in other states and in foreign countries upon the basis of the domicil of one of the parties.[41]

The Restatement[42] declares that a state can exercise divorce jurisdiction when both spouses are domiciled in the state, but it cannot, if neither is domiciled therein. It practically accepts the rule of the Atherton and Haddock cases by further declaring[43] that a state can exercise jurisdiction to dissolve the marriage where one of the spouses is domiciled within the state and the other outside the state if (*a*) the spouse not domiciled has consented that the other acquire a separate home; or by misconduct has ceased to have the right to object to the acquisition of such separate home; or is personally subject to the jurisdiction of the state which grants the divorce; or (*b*) the state is the last state in which the spouses were domiciled together as man and wife.

**Estoppel.** If domicil of both of the parties, or of one of them, *in the matrimonial domicil, is necessary to give jurisdiction* for a divorce which another state must recognize, the appearance of the defendant will not cure the defect of jurisdiction. If the parties did not have a *bona fide* domicil in the state of the decree, appearance or consent will not be adequate "to confer jurisdiction over a subject-matter not resting on consent."[44] It had been held, however, where the plaintiff (wife) alleged *bona fide* domicil at the forum, a finding of such domicil after appearance will not be disturbed "until overcome by adverse testimony."[45] This result is illogical if indeed

[41] Thus in Gildersleeve *v.* Gildersleeve, (1914) 88 Conn. 692 at p. 698 it is said: "For the present we may not have uniform divorce legislation, but we may contribute to a uniform treatment of divorced persons and their children, and property and property rights, by obeying the dictates of comity, and thus avoiding the unwholesome and harsh consequences which are the natural fruits of the opposite course." *Accord:* Howard *v.* Strode, (1912) 242 Mo. 210; Humphreys *v.* Strong, (1924) 139 Va. 146.

[42] §§110–111.

[43] §113.

[44] Andrews *v.* Andrews, (1903) 188 U.S. 14. *Accord:* German Savings Soc. *v.* Dormitzer, (1904) 192 U.S. 125.

[45] Cheever *v.* Wilson, (1869) 9 Wall. 108, 123, cited with seeming approval by White, C. J., in Haddock *v.* Haddock at p. 570.

domicil of both parties is the strict basis. The race for a favorable forum seems not to be objectionable if both parties join in the quest! In New York the court will not re-examine the question of domicil if the foreign court has found that the parties were domiciled within the meaning of the statute there in force and the defendant was served personally or appeared.[46] In New Jersey, even the complainant may attack the validity of the foreign decree on the ground of lack of domicil even though the respondent appeared, estoppel not being applicable where public policy is involved.[47] This seems directly opposed to the rule of the Restatement concerning estoppel.[48]

Of course it follows that if the foreign court had jurisdiction, the grounds of divorce and the method of procedure recognized at that place will control, even though not recognized at the forum.[49]

**Recognition of Foreign Divorce without Decree.** A striking example is furnished by a remarkable case in Massachusetts. A marriage between two Christians of Turkish nationality and domicil took place in Turkey. The husband came to the United States without his wife, intending to return to her later. The wife afterwards renounced the Christian religion and married a Mohammedan which, under the law of Turkey, constitutes a divorce without the necessity of legal proceedings. The husband thereupon married again in the United States. Later the second wife sought to annul the marriage on the ground of a previous subsisting marriage. It was decided that as the parties to the first marriage were domiciled in Turkey at the time of the act constituting a divorce, it would be recognized as valid in Massachusetts. The court said: "under the law of Turkey, a public and notorious fact, which constitutes a ground for divorce in most if not in all civilized countries allowing any divorce, is treated as of itself severing the marriage relation. There is nothing in this law so revolting to the moral sense of a Christian nation as to prevent recognition and enforcement by its courts."[50]

[46] Tiedemann *v.* Tiedemann, (1916) 172 A.D. 819; aff'd (1919) 225 N.Y. 709. The dictum of Hogan, J., in the later case of Gould *v.* Gould, (1923) 235 N.Y. 14, involving a French divorce, would seem to indicate that the question was still an open one where the ground for divorce was one not recognized in New York.

[47] So held: Hollingshead *v.* Hollingshead, (1920) 110 Atl. Rep. 19.

[48] §112. Estoppel is recognized as against the spouse who obtained the divorce or who has taken advantage of the decree by remarrying.

[49] Statutes sometimes modify the rule to protect evasion of the law of a former domicil. See *ante*, p. 142.

[50] Kapigian *v.* Der Minassian, (1912) 212 Mass. 412.

**Comparative Survey in Respect to Jurisdiction for Divorce.** The conception of Anglo-American jurisprudence that the marriage *res* is located at the domicil of the parties or domicil of either of the parties is not accepted by a preponderance of Continental systems. As the dissolution of the marriage tie affects the personal and family relations of the spouses and their relations with the children and the family generally, the courts of the national states are regarded as primarily competent. The rule of national jurisdiction prevails in France, Germany, Italy and Switzerland.[51] The same principle prevails according to the draft of a new civil code for Czechoslovakia[52] and also in Poland.[53] Whether the competence of the national courts is made exclusive and whether the law of the forum is applied to all questions arising with reference to the divorce when once the national state has assumed jurisdiction are questions which are answered differently in the different jurisdictions. We are here considering only the underlying principle of national jurisdiction which to the jurist unacquainted with the conceptions of civil-law countries seems at first to resemble the tribal laws of the Middle Ages. However, the award of jurisdiction to the national courts is defended by jurists of Continental countries with the same fervor that English and American jurists defend the domiciliary standard. Diena maintains that as the domicil has no influence in regulating the legal status of persons and family relations, there is no reason for applying a different rule as to divorce. Nor has the place of contracting the marriage such influence. He then continues: "It is evident that the regulation of marriage, particularly in regard to its dissolution, which has such importance in respect to the social order, cannot depend upon the autonomy of the parties and consequently not upon a law which the parties would have tacitly or expressly chosen. Furthermore, divorce concerns family rights and cannot be envisaged simply as the sanction of a civil tort so that there is no connection to be made here with the *lex loci delicti commissi*."[54]

It is in Italy that we find the purest expression of the influence of national law. Mancini as philosopher and statesman exercised an

[51] French Civ. Code Art. 14–15; German Code of Civ. Pro. §606; Italian *Disposizioni*, §6; Swiss Fed. Stat. June 25, 1895, Art. 7 g, Swiss Civ. Code, Final Title, Art. 61.

[52] §32.

[53] Poland, Stat. of Aug. 2, 1927, relating to Private International Law, §17.

[54] *Académie de Droit Int., Recueil de Cours.* 1927, ii, p. 418. Trans. by the author. Diena is of course speaking with particular reference to Italian law.

enormous influence upon the Italian Civil Code. His theories were based upon the importance of recognizing variances in climate, temperature, geographical situations, fertility of the soil and the physical development and diverse habits and needs of the various peoples of the world. From these he derived the right of the individual to have his national law respected even by the foreign jurisdictions in which he happened to be. Conversely the interest of the state required it to continue to regulate the personal and family relations of individuals while abroad in order to maintain the social order and national life of the state to which the individual belongs. This rule does not extend to voluntary transactions in which the social order does not play a part. It is also subject to the right of the foreign state to insist upon the application of its (territorial) law in matters of public policy.[55]

A logical application of national law would allow alien nationals of countries recognizing the institution of divorce to institute proceedings in the Italian courts. Several decisions to this effect were rendered toward the end of the last century but more recently the competence of Italian courts has been refused on the ground that the institution as such is against Italian public policy.[56]

The law of Italy recognizes the institution of separation from bed and board but does not recognize divorce. As Art. 6 of the Preliminary Title of the Civil Code (*Disposizioni*) makes the national law authoritative in matters of family relations, the admissability of divorce depends primarily on the national law of the spouses. Accordingly, the divorce of Italian citizens in a foreign country, even though they were domiciled there, and the marriage celebrated there, will not be recognized in Italy.[57]

Although from the authorities already referred to, we conclude that an original application for divorce on the part of aliens domiciled in Italy, will not be granted, there remains the question of the recognition of a judgment for divorce obtained by aliens before a court of their national jurisdiction. The question presents itself in practical form after one of the parties has married again and an Italian court is asked to recognize the validity of the second marriage, or the party endeavors to enter into a second marriage in Italy. Dienna states that

[55] *Ibid.*, pp. 354–355.

[56] *Ibid.*, p. 419, citing a decision of the Italian Court of Cassation of Nov. 14, 1900; *Annali della giurisprudenza italiana*, 1900, i, 600.

[57] *Ibid.*, pp. 417–418.

notwithstanding some hesitation on the part of the courts, the effects of a divorce legally pronounced in the foreign country according to the national law of the parties will be granted recognition because no rule of Italian public policy has been violated.[58]

A different legislative approach characterizes the *French law* because of the peculiar provisions of the Civil Code relative to jurisdiction in actions for the fulfilment of obligations in general. French venue is assured to French citizens as to obligations contracted toward aliens and citizens alike, whether at home or abroad.[59] As marriage is deemed a contract within the meaning of these articles, French courts will assume jurisdiction where one of the parties is French even though both are domiciled elsewhere. The rule of the national jurisdiction is supposed to be grounded in the necessity of protection against the national bias of foreign courts in favor of their own citizens and has been claimed to be promotive of international commerce. Judge André Weiss, whose impartiality may be assumed in a matter of French legislation, has strongly combatted the arguments in favor of the system, affirming that it rests upon no serious foundation and asserting that it calls loudly for legislative reform.[60] However, it is too strongly intrenched in French practice to expect an early change. The question confronts us here whether the national jurisdiction is compulsory as well as permissive. It seems this is not the case and a divorce obtained abroad by French persons is entitled to *exequatur* in France.[61] The French Courts have taken a reasonable view, however, with regard to foreigners domiciled in France. While Art. 3 of the Civil Code proclaims the national courts competent, the condition of foreigners unable to obtain relief in their own country because of their domicil in France has appealed to the equity of French jurisprudence and has induced the courts to grant the divorce if, under like circumstances, they could have obtained it in the home state, had they been domiciled there. This result has been reached not upon any mandatory rule of law or legislation, but as it were, *ex aequo et bono.* The courts are influenced by various circumstances such as the fact that the marriage was celebrated in France, that the complainant could

[58] *Ibid.*, p. 421.

[59] Arts. 14–15.

[60] Weiss, *Manuel de droit int. privé,* (1925) p. 621.

[61] Trib. of the Seine, April 6, 1922, Clunet, 1922, p. 674, relating to a divorce obtained in California. Pillet inclines to the opposite view. *Traité de dr. int. privé,* ii, p. 613, though he cites another case in which a divorce was recognized under such circumstances, ii, p. 622.

get no redress elsewhere or, that the respondent acquiesced in the jurisdiction. Domicil of the parties becomes then a necessary requisite as incidental to the foundation of jurisdiction. It is not sufficient in itself. The court is influenced by the denial of justice involved in refusing jurisdiction.[62]

Wherever jurisdiction is founded, however, the substantive law applicable is that of the personal law of the parties, *i.e.*, in France, the national law. This may be the *lex fori* or it may not. Arminjon points out that in a system like the Anglo-American, where domicil is the test of jurisdiction, the law of the forum will in most cases coincide with the personal law. This will not be the case in countries recognizing national jurisdiction. The grounds for divorce are wrapped up in the substantive law regulating the status and capacity of the parties and are not merely rules of procedure. Accordingly, the grounds must not only be recognized by the law of the forum but also by the national law of the parties. This is sometimes difficult of application where there is no strictly "national" law, as in the case of a federal union like the United States in which the state, not the union, is sovereign in matters of private law; but French courts do not hesitate in taking the law of the state in which the parties last had a domicil, or even in which they were married.[63]

Where the national law recognizes jurisdiction at the domicil of the parties, as in England and the American States, as well as in the Argentine and Germany,[64] French courts have accepted this as a *renvoi* to French law, where the parties are domiciled in France. We have already pointed out that this is an unwarranted confusion between the application of a foreign law and the application of the foreign rule of the conflict of laws. With respect to countries of the common law it is particularly unsound because these recognize the *jurisdiction* of the domicil, and not the law of the domicil as such. The law of the domicil is applied because it is also the law of the forum. However, French courts have frequently applied French law as to the grounds for divorce to American and British subjects domiciled in France and it is this practice which makes French courts hospitable to those seeking more liberal grounds of divorce.[65] The

[62] *Cf.* Bates, Divorce and Separation of Aliens in France (1929) pp. 62–78.
[63] *Ibid.*, p. 115.
[64] German Code of Civ. Pro., §606, by which domiciliary jurisdiction is made optional but not compulsory.
[65] Clunet, 1909, p. 474; *Gazette des Tribunaux*, Feb. 23, 1922. *Cf.* Bates, *ut cit.* pp. 112–114.

result has been sharply criticized by Pillet and indeed the decisions are by no means uniform, a recent case at Pau maintaining that a *renvoi* of this kind, though justifiable in matters of succession affecting property, should never be allowed in a proceeding of divorce which so profoundly affects the personal status.[66]

A curious anomaly results from these principles of French divorce jurisdiction. Where a civil marriage has been performed in France between two domiciled aliens whose personal law demands a religious marriage, the French courts will be free to exercise their discretion in favor of entertaining jurisdiction for divorce when no jurisdiction is available before the national courts, although neither the marriage nor their subsequent divorce would be recognized by the national law of either party.[67] A Spanish jurist confirms the fact that Spanish courts (of the old regime) would recognize neither the civil marriage nor the divorce of Spanish subjects domiciled in France.[68]

German law upon the subject of divorce and separation also proceeds upon the principle of the predominant control of the national law of the spouses. Whereas the French system had to be tediously developed out of a few general provisions of the Civil Code by decided cases and the learned discussions of well known jurisconsults, the German system has profited by being established as late as 1900. It has therefore not left so much for judicial interpretation and has attempted to anticipate conflicts by the enactment of solutions. A German forum is open to German spouses wherever they may be domiciled; likewise when the husband only is German, or if the wife has retained German nationality after the husband has lost it. But aliens may seek a German forum only if that forum be recognized by the national law of the husband.[69]

The application of the law of the husband's state at the time of the commencement of the action is made specifically applicable but the grounds for the divorce must be recognized not only by that law

[66] *Trib. Basses-Pyrénées,* May 28, 1930, Clunet, 1931, p. 1092. Pillet, *ut cit.* i, 625, citing Rouen, June 30, 1897, Dal. 1906, p. 511, in which it was said that the reference to any but the national (English) law is to be guilty of a veritable attack upon the sovereign powers of the interested state.

[67] Clunet, 1920, p. 128, relating to a divorce between a Russian and a Roumanian.

[68] M. Serins, *Les Conflits de Lois dans les Rapports Franco-Espagnol en Matière de Mariage, de Divorce et de Séparation de corps.* (1929) p. 205.

[69] German Code of Civil Procedure (*Zivilprozess Ordnung*) §606. *Cf.* Clunet, 1924, p. 214.

but also by German law.[70] This principle is subject to the exception of a *renvoi* to the German law to which we have already called attention. In this respect the prevailing rule of the French courts is accepted by direct legislation in Germany.[71]

We have observed that German spouses may resort to German courts in divorce proceedings, wherever be their domicil. The question remains whether they may also resort to a foreign court, *e.g.*, the court of their domicil. In this respect also German legislation does not leave the question to the determination of the courts. This results from the general rule applicable to the recognition of foreign judgments, which demands reciprocal treatment for German judgments.[72] The German forum is not made obligatory but as there *is* a German forum, reciprocity is demanded in the event of recourse to the forum of the domicil, or any other foreign forum.[73] It would seem that such reciprocity must be definite and not dependent upon the facts and circumstances of each case. Under the common law rule, the recognition of a foreign judgment itself depends upon a jurisdictional investigation in which a divorce judgment would be subjected to the scrutiny of the domicil of the parties as well as of the manner of obtaining jurisdiction over the defendant. It has often been held that American judgments of divorce are not entitled to recognition under the reciprocity rule.[74] As we have seen, the national law of the parties must be applied, whatever the forum; accordingly even if there be reciprocity, the judgment will not be accorded recognition if the substantive provisions of German law have not been applied.[75]

If a German obtains a divorce before the court of a foreign (domiciliary) jurisdiction upon grounds or in a manner not recognized by German law, and afterwards re-marries, the second marriage may be considered bigamous in Germany. The beginning of the

[70] German Civil Code, Introductory Stat. Art. 17. Similar rule in Chili, Civ. Code, Art. 120; Ecuador Civ. Code, Art, 116; Uruguay Civ. Code, Art. 103.

[71] *Ibid.*, Art 27. The *renvoi* to German courts and to German law is generally accepted for Americans domiciled in Germany though the proof of domicil proceeds according to German and not the American law. Clunet, 1922, p. 171. The *Reichsgericht* has held (Feb. 21, 1925) that though a divorce granted by religious authorities in the national state of the parties may be entitled to recognition in Germany, no such divorce granted to aliens in Germany by religious authorities there would be recognized. Clunet, 1925, p. 1055.

[72] German Code of Civil Proc. §328, par. 1 (5).

[73] *Ibid.*, §328, par. 2.

[74] Clunet, 1911, p. 286; Lewald, *Das deutsche int. Privatrecht* (1931) p. 127 citing cases.

[75] *Ibid.*

action in the foreign jurisdiction by one spouse may itself be considered a ground of divorce in an action brought by the other spouse in Germany.[76]

**Switzerland** has adopted a more liberal policy with respect to divorce jurisdiction. Although recognizing the national forum as primarily competent, Swiss citizens domiciled abroad may obtain a divorce at their foreign domicil even for causes not recognized by Swiss law.[77] Conversely, alien spouses domiciled in Switzerland may be divorced by the Swiss courts provided the national law of the parties, whether legislative or customary, recognizes the ground of divorce relied upon, as well as the jurisdiction of the Swiss court. A ground for divorce which arose at a time when the spouses had a different national law may be relied upon only if the ground is recognized also by the law of their former nationality.[78] If these conditions are observed, the divorce proceeding follows the Swiss law as to the effects of divorce, such as in respect to the parental control over the children, alimony, and the division of property between the spouses.[79]

## 2. Judicial Separation or Limited Divorce

The résumé which we have already given [80] of the law and legislation of different countries in respect to the judicial separation of the spouses and other forms of divorce limited as to time or effect, shows a divergence of basic concept and procedure too great to generalize into a single institution. This may be possible for divorce because

[76] Nussbaum, *Deutsches int. Privatrecht* (1932) p. 164 citing *Reichsger.* Feb. 5, 1906; Bavarian *Oberlandesger.* May 24, 1924. This result is comparable with that reached in some Anglo-American jurisdictions where a divorce obtained in a jurisdiction not considered domiliary by the foral court may be considered obtained *in fraudem legis.*

[77] Swiss Fed. Stat. of 1891, Art. 7 g (3) as incorporated in Final Title, Swiss Civ. Code Art. 61.

[78] *Ibid.,* Art. 7 h (1–2).

[79] Clunet, 1919, p. 431. In this case between French nationals, the Swiss Federal Supreme Court held that the mere fact that French administrative authorities would register the judgment in the registry of civil status did not satisfy the requirement of the statute, because the French courts would not recognize the jurisdiction of a Swiss court to divorce French spouses. In Clunet, 1920, p. 279, jurisdiction was accepted to dissolve the marriage of American spouses where the wife was alone domiciled in Switzerland, upon proof that the wife was entitled to acquire a separate domicil according to the law of the American state of which she was a citizen.

[80] *Ante,* p. 156.

it effects the one result of dissolving the marriage tie. Separation on the other hand, may be effected to a greater or less degree. It may be limited or unlimited as to time. Separation from board and bed was developed by the ecclesiastical courts at a time when marriage as a sacrament was regarded as indissoluble. But a separation by its terms and import does not sever the marriage tie. Often it is little more than authority for the spouses to live apart. It may or may not affect the marital property rights of the spouses according to the legislation in each jurisdiction. A reconciliation is not only possible at any time but is indeed, the very contemplation of the institution as such. As Chancellor Kent expresses it, the marriage relation thereby "undergoes a very inconvenient suspension and which is intended to operate as a continual invitation to the parties to return to their first love."[81] The parties remain man and wife; their marital status remains unchanged.

This has a profound importance in respect to the conflict of laws. While some American States require the same jurisdictional requirements as in an action for divorce, others do not.[82] The Privy Council, speaking by Lord Watson has said: "there are unquestionably other remedies for matrimonial misconduct, short of dissolution, which, according to the rules of the *jus gentium*, may be administered by the courts of the country in which spouses, domiciled elsewhere, are for the time resident."[83]

The Restatement[84] provides that "A state can exercise through its courts jurisdiction to grant judicial separation to any spouse petitioning therefor where both parties are subject to the jurisdiction of the courts of the state."

A distinction is made between (*a*) a separation proceeding which

[81] Barrere *v.* Barrere, (1819) 4 Johns. Ch. N.Y. 187. "An action for limited divorce is really an appeal to a court of equity by one of the parties to a marriage contract for a modification of the marriage relations, duties and obligations as they exist at common law." People *v.* Cullen, (1897) 153 N.Y. 629.

[82] Pa., Gen. Laws, Title 23, §15, requires the same jurisdictional facts for separation as for divorce. N.Y. Civ. Practice Act, §1162, provides for a residence of at least one year for actions of separation, whereas §1147 (4) requires strict domiciliary jurisdiction for divorce.

[83] Le Mesurier *v.* Le Mesurier [1895] A.C. 517 at p. 526; followed in Armytage *v.* Armytage [1898] P.D. 178, with the proviso that the parties were domiciled in England up to the time of the act which constitutes the jurisdiction for the separation. In the latter case, Gorell Barnes, J., at pp. 192–193, emphasizes the fact that an action for restitution of conjugal rights would be cognizable on the ground of mere residence. Westlake, *ut cit.* §48.

[84] §114.

protects a spouse against acts of the other spouse, for which any state may exercise jurisdiction and (*b*) a separation which does more than this and affects the marriage relation more profoundly. The question then arises: what recognition is to be given in another state or country to a judicial separation granted without the basis of domicil, or where only one of the parties was domiciled, especially when the other party has not been personally served with process within the jurisdiction? An interesting case arose in Connecticut where the husband was domiciled both before and after the marriage. The marriage took place in New York where the wife was domiciled before the marriage. About one year after the marriage the wife left her husband and returned to New York, where she obtained, on constructive notice, a judgment of separation with alimony, on the ground of cruelty. The husband thereafter brought an action in Connecticut for absolute divorce on the ground of desertion and the New York judgment was interposed as a defense. The court held that as New York was not the matrimonial domicil, the judgment was not entitled to compulsory full faith and credit, relying upon Haddock *v.* Haddock in which, curiously enough, a Connecticut divorce decree was denied recognition under like circumstances. The court then proceeded to consider whether the New York judgment should be recognized "as a matter of comity or of public policy." Now Connecticut is one of the states in which a divorce granted *ex parte* at the domicil of one of the parties will be given voluntary recognition on this basis.[85] But in a well-reasoned opinion in which the English decisions were analyzed and compared with the American legislation, the court held that there, as here, a judicial separation, "though it separates the parties and establishes separate interests between them" does not affect their marital status as such; and therefore the proceeding is *in personam* merely, and not entitled to extraterritorial effect.[86]

**Foreign Systems respecting Judicial Separation.** The same wide variances in the law of different countries outside the Anglo-American sphere observed in respect to divorce are found perhaps even to a greater degree in respect to judicial separation, limited divorce and other legally sanctioned interruptions of the common life of the spouses short of divorce. The variances apply not only

[85] See *ante*, p. 166, n. 41. See Gildersleeve *v.* Gildersleeve, (1914) 88 Conn. 692 at p. 698.

[86] Pettis *v.* Pettis, (1917) 90 Conn. 608.

as to the grounds for separation but also as to the systems of separation. A few countries, Italy, Netherlands, Norway and Sweden, permit separation by agreement of the parties.[87] This is in accordance with the rule of English law. In the United States a separation-agreement remains valid even after cause for divorce arises, and the property arrangements continue even after divorce is granted.[88] Countries such as Austria, Brazil, and Italy, which do not recognize the institution of divorce, allow separation on specific grounds and perpetual in time.[89]

*French* legislation establishes a separation from bed and board (*separation de corps*) which always carries with it a separation of property rights.[90] The judgment of separation may be changed after the lapse of three years on application of either party into a judgment of divorce.[91] A separation now also restores to the wife her full civil capacity entitling her to naturalization in a foreign country without her husband's consent. This results from legislation passed after the celebrated Bauffremont-Bibesco Affair.[92]

In *Germany* the Civil Code provides for a dissolution of the community of marriage (*Aufhebung der ehelichen Gemeinschaft*) which in itself constitutes a basis of divorce and which has the same effects as divorce upon the personal relations and the property of the spouses except that a new marriage is barred.[93]

**Foreign Rules of Conflict of Laws respecting Judicial Separation.** These variances give rise to conflicts the solutions of which often lead to unsatisfactory results. The control of national law, which we have seen to be the predominant rule in respect to divorce,

[87] Italy, Civil Code, Art. 158; Netherlands, Art. 291; Norway, Law of Aug. 20, 1909; Sweden, Law of Nov. 12, 1915.

[88] Galusha *v.* Galusha, (1889) 116 N.Y. 635, 643; Maryland, Laws of 1931, ch. 220.

[89] Austria, Civ. Code, §§107–108; Brazil, Civ. Code, §§315–324; Italy, Arts. 148–158.

[90] Civil Code, Arts. 306 adopting the same grounds as for divorce, Arts. 2229 *et seq.*, Art. 311 (2).

[91] Art. 310.

[92] Art. 311 as amended Feb. 6, 1893. Countess Caraman, a Belgian, married to the French Prince Bauffremont was separated by a French decree in 1874. Later she became naturalized in the Duchy of Saxe-Altenburg and under the law of her new allegiance obtained a divorce there. She then married Prince Bibesco of Roumania. The marriage was held void by the French courts because of the lack of consent by her French husband to the naturalization. The Belgian courts refused to recognize the penalties imposed by the French decree. Clunet, 1880, p. 215; 1882, p. 264.

[93] §§1575–1576, 1586.

is not relaxed in respect to judicial separation, even though it be recognized that the separation as such does not effect an absolute transformation of the status of the parties. However, as Audinet points out, "it profoundly modifies the relations of the spouses and the effects of their marriage."[94] He is, therefore, opposed to the contrary view which would permit the court of the domicil or residence to pronounce a separation where it would not have jurisdiction to decree a divorce. The question then arises how far the national law and the law of the forum must be in accord. Clearly the local law will not apply a foreign law requiring a procedure which the forum is unable to provide because of the variance in the legislation of the two countries. Thus difficulty has arisen in applications brought for separation before the German courts by foreign spouses domiciled in Germany. Art 17(4) of the Introductory Statute requires that the dissolution of the community of marriage on the ground of a foreign law can be adjudged only if the divorce is admissible by both the foreign and the German law. German courts have considered the dissolution of the community of marriage to be a remedy distinct and separate from that provided in other legislations, like the French, for example; hence, that a German tribunal is without power to grant such dissolution of the community of marriage to French spouses. This was the result reached by the joint chambers of the *Reichsgericht* after a single chamber had reached a result in favor of the decree.[95] The decision has been sharply criticized by Lewald both because French law (like the German) also provides for the conversion of separation into divorce after a lapse of time and because an absolute correspondence between the German and the foreign law is not contemplated by the statute. It ought to be sufficient that the foreign law recognizes the remedy of separation on like grounds. If the foreign law does not allow the separation to be converted into a divorce, that circumstance should only affect the eventual granting of the divorce in Germany, not the dissolution of the community.[96]

[94] *Académie de dr. int., Recueil des Cours.,* 1926, i, p. 246.

[95] Decision of Oct. 12, 1903, reversing Oct. 23, 1902. Clunet, 1904, pp. 193, 964.

[96] Lewald *ut cit.* (1931) pp. 122–124. A somewhat contrary view is held by Walker, *Int. Privatrecht,* (1924) p. 596 and note. He emphasizes the fact that only rarely is the national forum closed to the parties, and if it should be closed, it is upon the national law rather than upon German law that any charge of a denial of justice should fall. The decision of the *Reichsgericht* has been followed by the provincial courts. Lewald, p. 121.

Differences of procedure between the foreign law under which a separation is effected, and the local law, may be the basis for denying an application for divorce. A French woman married to an Italian and domiciled with her husband in Italy, was afterwards separated by mutual consent as permitted by Italian law, but not by French law. She then resumed residence in France and was reintegrated as a French citizen by decree. An application for conversion of the separation into divorce was denied upon the ground that the separation was not entitled to recognition as such in France, not being based upon a judgment of a contentious character or for a cause fixed by statute.[97]

The fact that husband and wife may have separate nationality greatly complicates the governing law for divorce and separation. A disturbance of the marriage relation equally affects both parties; therefore by recognizing the national law of only one of the parties, the sovereign right of the country of the other party to regulate the status of one of its citizens may be deemed to have been violated.

The Hague Convention relating to Divorce and Separation[98] provides that the system of law last common to each of the spouses shall be considered the national law. This is a rule which has found approval even in countries like France in which the convention no longer applies.[99] The spouses may have been of different nationality at the time of marriage and recent statutes in many countries have taken from marriage its former effect of changing the nationality of the woman.[100] German legislation in effect provides that in the case of separate nationality, the law of the husband shall determine nationality for the purpose of the application of laws.[101] This solution has received the approval on principle of some French writers, such as Arminjon[102] who maintains that political rights may be conserved but the wife should be aware that by marriage to a foreigner, her civil status follows that of her husband. This is true perhaps if her domicil is also that of the husband, but it does not seem ac-

[97] Cassation, July 6, 1922, Clunet, 1922, p. 714.

[98] Art. 8, see *post*, p. 186.

[99] Pillet, (1923) i, p. 636.

[100] See Flournoy & Hudson, A Collection of Nationality Laws of Various Countries (1929). The so called Cable Act of the United States relating to the nationality of married woman is given on p. 608.

[101] Art. 17, Introductory Stat. to German Civil Code.

[102] Arminjon, *Dr. int. privé* (1931) iii, p. 41.

ceptable where the matrimonial domicil is fixed in her own country.

An American woman married an Italian after the passage of the Cable Act. Under this statute she remained a citizen of the United States, but became Italian by Italian law. The French courts, the forum of her domicil, regarded her as an American and entertained her suit for divorce, which would have been denied had she been regarded as Italian. The court therefore, in a conflict between two alien nationalities, preferred the nationality of origin.[103]

Where there is a divergence in the nationality of the spouses, the jurisdiction of the last common *domicil* rather than the last common nationality, would seem to lead to a better result. It is an ascertainable unity avoiding the inconvenient conflict of two national systems. It also recognizes the equality of the sexes. At the same time, the common domicil is likely to be within the national state of one of the parties through the influence which both have in the choice of domicil. The endeavor to respect in part each of two systems is likely to deny even half justice to either. If the principle of the last common domicil had been accepted, it is probable that Switzerland would not have withdrawn from the convention, as she did in 1928. Italians living in Switzerland frequently marry Swiss women, especially in the Italian-speaking canton of Ticino. The husband of such a marriage might desert the wife, return to Italy and obtain a separation from bed and board on undefended allegations. Even though the wife re-acquired her Swiss citizenship, she would be prevented from obtaining a divorce as permitted by Swiss law because of Art. 8 of the convention, making the last common nationality (in this case Italian) authoritative. Switzerland therefore denounced the convention.[104]

### 3. Annulment of Marriage

The annulment of a void marriage is a proceeding distinguished from divorce in that it is based upon the assumption that the marriage by reason of some inherent defect was void *ab initio*. As marriage results from a contract entered into under the authority and with the sanction of the law of some particular jurisdiction, it seems reasonable to permit the same jurisdiction to declare that its laws

[103] Clunet, 1926, p. 663.
[104] Clunet, 1929, p. 813.

were not observed and that no valid marriage ever came into existence, even though the parties were domiciled elsewhere at the time of the suit.[105] It is equally reasonable to conclude that if the domicil of the parties, or indeed of only one of them, is not in the same state as the place of the marriage, the jurisdiction of the domicil at the time of marriage will also have power to nullify it. This follows from the doctrine that the law of the state of the domicil has control of the status of the persons domiciled within its territory. We are, of course, dealing with jurisdictional power in the international sense, not with the legislation of any particular state allowing it to assume jurisdiction upon some other ground, as for example, that of mere temporary residence within the jurisdiction of the forum. While such power may be assumed, a judgment under it will not be entitled to recognition in another sovereign jurisdiction.

The jurisdiction of the domicil of the parties at the time of the action has undoubted power also to decree annulment so far as to dissolve the tie from the time of the decree; but it is doubtful whether on principle it should have the power to declare the marriage void from the beginning, if the parties were not married or were not then domiciled within that state.[106] Bishop contends that annulment proceedings to declare a marriage void from the beginning "may and should be carried on in the courts of the domicil." [107] With this view Goodrich disagrees on principle and in a well-considered presentation contends also that in spite of broad statements of *dicta,* due in part to the failure to properly distinguish between annulment and divorce, no definite trend of authority has been established.[108] Ordinarily it is said that a marriage good where contracted, is good everywhere, if not repugnant to civilized conceptions of marriage. So that, for example, when a marriage entered into in a state where the marriage of first cousins is not prohibited, is sought to be annulled in the state of the petitioner's later domicil, where such marriages are prohibited, the petition will be denied.[109] As statutory prohibitions in the interest of good morals are considered to be coercive, there

[105] So held in Becker *v.* Becker, (1901) 58 A.D. N.Y. 374, though the New York Civil Practice Act does not lay down specific rules of jurisdiction for annulment.

[106] It was, however, so held in Avakian *v.* Avakian, (1905) 69 N.J. Eq. 89.

[107] Bishop, Marriage, Divorce and Separation (1891) ii, §73.

[108] Goodrich in 32 Harvard Law Rev. (1919) p. 806, 815.

[109] Garcia *v.* Garcia, (1910) 25 S.Dak. 645. *Accord:* Levy *v.* Downing, (1913) 213 Mass. 334.

is authority to the contrary. The extent to which public policy calls for opposition to established rules of conflict can seldom be predicted, or formulated by a fixed principle.[110]

The American Law Institute Restatement provides that a state can exercise through its courts jurisdiction to nullify a marriage, whether from its beginning or from the time of the decree, under the same circumstances as those which would enable it to dissolve the marriage by divorce.[111] This differs materially from the former draft of this section[112] and represents perhaps the only practical basis for uniformity where both judicial authority and statutory enactment have been so diverse. Its principle is made more acceptable by a further provision,[113] by which the substantive law governing the right to a decree of nullity is that of the state which determined the validity of the marriage with respect to the matter alleged to be the cause of nullity.

**Jurisdiction for Annulment in England.** The English courts have jurisdiction to declare an existing marriage to be null if it was celebrated in England, or if the respondent is resident in England and not a mere transitory sojourner at the date of the petition.[114] Whether this is to be accepted as more than a rule of local application is doubtful. It is to be remembered that jurisdiction in annulment was long a subject of contention between the ecclesiastical and the royal courts; and the statute which was intended to settle the dispute "is to be interpreted as applicable and as intended to apply only to matters within the jurisdiction of the legislature by which it is enacted."[115] On the other hand, it is sometimes said that a foreign decree annulling a marriage which took place in England would not be recognized even though the parties be domiciled at the place of the decree.[116] Ogden *v.* Ogden[117] involved the validity

[110] *Cf.* Pennegar *v.* State, (1889) 87 Tenn. 244. Goodrich in 32 Harv. Law Rev. at p. 814. See also *ante,* p. 38.

[111] Restatement, §115.

[112] *Cf.* 1931, Draft, §122.

[113] Restatement, §136.

[114] Matrimonial Causes Act of 1857, §6; Foote, Private International Law (Bellot's ed. 1925) p. 155.

[115] Brett, L. J., in Niboyet *v.* Niboyet, [1878] 4 P.D. 1 at p. 20. This case was one of divorce and its authority for assuming jurisdiction upon residence short of domicil is doubtful because the respondent was a foreign consul and incapacitated from acquiring a domicil in England during his official service. See also Roberts *v.* Brennan, [1902] p. 143.

[116] Foote, *ut cit.* p. 147.

[117] [1908] P. 46.

of a French decree which had declared a marriage celebrated in England to be void for lack of parental consent. The wife, an Englishwoman, had never followed the husband, a domiciled Frenchman, to France, but the refusal of the English court to recognize the decree caused Goodrich to complain of the unfortunate situation and to remark that it was not the only instance in which English courts refuse to recognize rights given under foreign law which are given under similar conditions by English law.[118] The criticism is all too true but in justice it cannot be aimed at English law alone. Unfortunately, all systems exercise greater power by legislation or by the jurisprudence of the courts than is conceded to foreign systems. The doctrine of Ogden *v.* Ogden has been sharply impugned by Salvesen *v.* Administrator of Austrian Property, in which a French marriage between a domiciled British woman and an Austrian was annulled by decree of a German court at the later domicil of the parties. The decree was upheld as valid by the House of Lords upon the ground that the court which regulates or determines the status, has power to decide conclusively with reference to the continuance of the status.[119] More narrowly interpreted, the decision's effect may be restricted to such cases wherein the ground is informality of the marriage, permitting the English court to entertain the suit and disregard the foreign decree in certain circumstances other than the informality of the original marriage.[120] But this decision in its broader implications has already exercised much influence upon later cases. In Inverclyde *v.* Inverclyde,[121] it is said that where the action is for the dissolution of a marriage alleged to be voidable on account of impotence of the respondent, there should be no doubt that the jurisdiction and law of the domicil of the parties should be deemed controlling. As the marriage was valid at the beginning and subject only to later voidance, the place of the marriage could not influence the choice of law for the divorce. A different problem is presented where nullity is sought on account of informality of the marriage through lack of consent of parents. The tendency is clearly to draw away from Ogden *v.* Ogden.[122]

Before leaving the subject of annulment of marriage, attention

[118] 32 Harvard Law Rev. at p. 818.

[119] [1927] A.C. 641, at p. 670.

[120] See Latey (1932) 17 Transactions of the Grotius Soc. 127.

[121] [1931] P. 29.

[122] See De Massa *v.* De Massa (decision of Lord Merrivale) an undefended case, Law Quar. Rev., Jan. 1932, p. 13. *Cf.* Cheshire, (1935) p. 254.

may be called to the suggestion of Goodrich that much difficulty might be avoided by giving up the concept that a decree of nullity relates back to the time of marriage. This results in bastardizing innocent children and otherwise ignores the existence of fact. He recommends that the common causes for annulment be bracketed under divorce.[123]

**Putative Marriage.** The evils attendant upon declaring a marriage null *ab initio* for all purposes, are avoided to some extent by the principle of "putative" marriage, by which a marriage declared null may nevertheless produce civil effects in respect to the spouses and their children, if it has been contracted in good faith. Though not recognized under Anglo-American law, it is admitted in France, Germany, Italy, Spain, Switzerland and other foreign countries.[124] Accordingly, though a marriage may be declared null by reason of not complying with the proper law, *e.g.*, the national law of the parties, the decree will not work the cruel injustice upon innocent parties which it often does when denying the marriage all validity whatsoever. An approach to this system has been sometimes made by judicial decision in the United States. In a New York case, the parties were married in Dakota after a divorce was obtained there *ex parte*. The children of the second marriage were recognized as legitimate in New York although the divorce and subsequent marriage were held to be void. The public policy which refused extraterritorial validity to the divorce and remarriage did not require the court to deny the status of legitimacy to the issue of a marriage valid in the State of Dakota.[125] The conflict of laws in respect to marriage produces many paradoxes. This one, so clearly in the interests of humane justice, will not be found objectionable.

**Proposed Uniformity of Legislation on Divorce and Annulment.** The National Conference of Commissioners on Uniform State Laws in 1907 approved the draft of an Act for Annulment of Marriage and Divorce. It related to annulment of marriage, separation from bed and board, jurisdiction for divorce and the grounds for divorce. In the twenty years that followed, only three States, Delaware, New Jersey and Wisconsin, adopted the law. Accordingly

[123] (1919) 32 Harvard Law Rev. 824.

[124] Burge, Commentaries on Colonial and Foreign Laws, (ed. 1910) iii, p. 113.

[125] *In re* Hall, (1901) 61 A.D. (N.Y.) 266.

the Conference again considered the matter and in 1930 recommended the adoption of a new draft restricted to the questions of jurisdiction and full faith and credit. The Uniform Divorce Jurisdiction Act as now recommended, provides (§1) that jurisdiction for the purposes of granting divorce shall not be exercised unless (*a*) the defendant is domiciled in the state, or the matrimonial domicil exists therein; or (*b*) the complainant has a separate domicil in that state justified by the consent or the conduct of the defendant. But a domicil acquired subsequent to the arising of the ground for divorce must have continued for one year prior to the bringing of the action. It is further provided (§2) that full faith and credit shall be given to a decree of divorce granted in another state, territory or possession of the United States under provisions not inconsistent with the foregoing, even if the decree is not entitled to full faith and credit under the Constitution of the United States.[126]

It would seem that a divorce granted under the proposed statute would be entitled to recognition even if the defendant was not personally served, provided the laws of the state permitted such service, as the statute does not affect the rules of law for obtaining jurisdiction over the person of a defendant.[127] The act therefore follows substantially the view of the minority of the Supreme Court in Haddock *v.* Haddock,[128] except that an uninterrupted domicil for one year is required, if acquired after the ground for divorce arose. Of course the statute would not apply to divorces granted in a foreign country. The state is left free in this respect.

### 4. Treaty Regulation of Conflicts Relating to Divorce and Separation

The conflicts in respect to the partial or total dissolution of the status of marriage are primarily conflicts of jurisdiction. Causes of action and defenses are dependent upon substantive law. The determination of the issue may and frequently does involve competition between the local and one or more systems of foreign law. In the well known case of the "Lotus" before the Permanent Court of International Justice, the issue involved the jurisdiction of Turkey

[126] Handbook of the Nat. Conference of Commissioners on Uniform State Laws, 1930, p. 502.
[127] §3, *ibid.*
[128] *Cf. ante*, p. 163.

to punish an alleged offense committed against her nationals upon the high seas by a French citizen. In seeking to establish whether or not such jurisdiction was opposed to any principle of international law the court said:

"Now the first and foremost restriction imposed by international law upon a state is that — failing the existence of a permissive rule to the contrary — it may not exercise its power in any form in the territory of another state. . . . It does not, however, follow that international law prohibits a state from exercising jurisdiction in its own territory, in respect to any case which relates to acts which have taken place abroad, and in which it cannot rely on some permissive rule of international law." The court proceeds to say that under existing international law, there is no prohibition against states to extend the application of their laws and the jurisdiction of their courts to persons, property and acts outside their territory. The court continues as follows: "This discretion left to states by international law explains the great variety of rules which they have been able to adopt without objections or complaints on the part of other states; it is in order to remedy the difficulties resulting from such variety that efforts have been made for many years past, both in Europe and America, to prepare conventions the effect of which would be precisely to limit the discretion at present left to states in this respect by international law, thus making good the existing lacunae in respect of jurisdiction or removing the conflicting jurisdictions arising from the diversity of the principles adopted by the various states." [129]

The alleged excess of jurisdiction resulted in the imprisonment of a foreign national by the Turkish court, leading to diplomatic intervention by France and the subsequent submission of the issue to the Hague tribunal. Had the excess of jurisdiction related to the status of persons by the decree of a partial or complete dissolution of some marriage tie between foreign nationals, there would not have been a diplomatic intervention and yet such excess might have had most unfortunate results upon the happiness, reputation and property of the persons concerned.

**Hague Convention on Divorce and Separation.** The nations of both continents have endeavored to avoid conflicts of jurisdiction by treaty. The Hague Conferences on Private International Law

[129] Collection of Judgments. Publications of the Permanent Court of Int. Justice, No. 10, (1927) pp. 18–19.

considered the subjects of a convention which, as amended at the conference of 1902, was ratified by nine nations.[130] The convention provides that a proceeding for divorce or judicial separation may be made only if the national law and the law of the forum both admit of divorce or separation, as the case may be.[131] The petition may be granted only for grounds sufficient by both systems. At first this was understood to signify that the grounds had to coincide, but a modification was made by the conference of 1902 to add the words *"encore que ce soit pour des causes différentes,"* so that the action must rest upon a ground recognized by each system even though the grounds are different.[132] These provisions in effect represent a compromise between the régimes of national and domiciliary law respectively, because jurisdiction is based on either the nationality or the domicil of the spouses. The convention prevents any change to a more favorable nationality by preventing a ground to be established by any fact which occurred prior to the change; similarly in case of desertion or a change of domicil after the ground arose, the jurisdiction may be laid at the last common domicil.[133] The convention also anticipates the case of a divergence in the nationality of the spouses, a possibility much more likely in the present period of legislation than at the time the convention was elaborated. In such event, the last system of law common to each is authoritative.[134] There is a certain ambiguity in this provision. At the time of the elaboration of the convention it was understood that all the contracting states recognized that at marriage the wife acquired the husband's nationality.[135] Accordingly, the provision then related to

[130] The Convention was ratified by Belgium, France, Germany, Italy, Luxemburg, Netherlands, Portugal, Sweden and Switzerland. Belgium and France withdrew prior to the World War, and the operation of the Convention was also affected between the belligerents by Art. 282 of the Versailles Treaty. Italy reinstated the Convention as to Germany in 1929. In the same year Switzerland withdrew. See Nussbaum, *op. cit.* (1932) p. 128. The Convention is contained in *Actes* of the Third Conference of the Hague, 1900, pp. 239–242. An English translation is given in Meili, Int. Civil and Commercial Law (1905) appendix ii, p. 532. It is discussed, *ibid.*, on p. 245, and by the same author in his address before the Universal Congress of Lawyers and Jurists at St. Louis in 1904, reprinted in "Progress of Continental Law in the 19th Century" (Cont. Legal History Series 1918) p. 483 *et seq.* Also by S. E. Baldwin in Yale Law Jour. 1903, p. 487, and by Baty, Polarized Law (1914) pp. 134–8.

[131] Art. 1.

[132] Art. 2.

[133] Arts. 4–5.

[134] Art. 8.

[135] *Actes*, 1900, p. 214.

the former common nationality. Under present legislation in some of the states, marriage does not have this effect unless the wife acquires the husband's nationality by this law; [136] so that in the event of divergence *ab initio,* there is a possible reference here to the last common domicil. Continental authorities are in doubt upon this point, and as there is no competent tribunal agreed upon to settle differences of interpretation, the courts of each contracting nation have developed a separate jurisprudence.[137]

Mutual recognition of decrees of divorce and separation is provided for, but at least one of the parties must be a national of a contracting state. In no event need a law be applied which is not that of one of the contracting states.[138]

It will be observed that the predominant law is national law. The application of the *lex fori et domicilii* is supplementary, or facultative. It does not at all represent the intended conciliation between the two systems recommended, for example, by the Institute of International Law in 1888, which provided for a reference to the national law only to determine whether divorce or separation was or was not recognized at all; if it was, then the grounds should be determined by the law of the forum.[139]

The Swiss jurist, Meili, approved of the solution of the Institute in preference to that of the convention, because it represents a compromise between national law and domiciliary law, besides respecting the Catholic view of the marriage relation. "The solution of the Institute is both practical and ingenious for the reason that the judge is not thus unnecessarily required to apply law strange to him." [140]

**Provisions of the Bustamante Code on Divorce and Separation.** The principle followed by the Bustamante Code in force in certain Latin-American countries distinguishes between the right or possibility of obtaining a separation or divorce and the grounds

[136] Belgium, Law of May 15, 1922, Art. 18. Portugal, Civil Code, Art. 22 (4). Flournoy & Hudson, Nationality Laws (1929) pp. 32, 492: Under the French Law of May 15, 1922, Art. 18, a French woman retains her nationality at marriage unless she declares her wish to acquire her husband's nationality according to his law. *Ibid.,* p. 249.

[137] *Cf.* the extended discussion in Walker, *Int. Privatrecht* (1924) p. 616 *et seq.* and in Meili and Mamelok. *ut cit.*

[138] Art. 9.

[139] 10 *Annuaire* of the Institute of Int. Law, 1888, p. 78 *et seq.*

[140] Meili (Kuhn's trans.) p. 246.

for the same. The former is regulated by the law of the matrimonial domicil while the latter, if arising before the acquisition of such domicil, must be recognized by the personal law of both spouses; otherwise the domiciliary law will prevail.[141] This is satisfactory to states in which the domiciliary law governs the personal status generally; but states which insist on the régime of national law are permitted to refuse recognition to divorce or separation decrees, with effects or for causes not admitted by the personal law of the spouses.[142] With this exception, the decrees produce their civil effects in all other contracting states.[143]

The rules of the Bustamante Code are a closer approach to the proposals of the Institute than are the provisions of the Hague Convention on Divorce and Separation. The Bustamante Code does not give recognition to the principle of the right of the wife to acquire a separate domicil as developed by the courts in the United States.

As a basis of possible future harmony between all of the various systems the author proposed the following solution at the session of the International Law Association in London in 1910: "A divorce granted by the court of a state in which either of the parties has a *bona fide* domicil according to international, not merely local, standards, should be recognized as valid in every other state, provided actual notice of the proceedings has been communicated to the other party, and the ground upon which such divorce has been granted is one recognized by the personal law of both of the parties."[144]

The personal law may be determined by domiciliary or by national law, according to whether the local state follows one or the other principle. The reservation of Art. 53 of the Bustamante Code makes the solution incomplete because even though the rules have been observed, there is still a right to refuse recognition by a state having a different theory of personal law. However, it is futile to expect complete uniformity of practice even by convention, because conventions of this nature, altering as they do the tenor of domestic legislation in a group of countries, are usually the result of compromise, for which different interpretations are possible.

[141] Art. 52, 54.
[142] Art. 53.
[143] Art. 56.
[144] Report of Proceedings of the 26th Conference of the Int. Law Assoc. (1910) p. 438.

## 5. Alimony

A decree of alimony so far as it seeks to create against the defendant a general pecuniary liability is not a disposition affecting the status of the parties but a decree *in personam*. If the court has obtained jurisdiction over the defendant by personal service within the state, or by voluntary appearance, the decree is entitled to recognition in another state. If the defendant's property can be reached and is seized in support of the application, the decree becomes *pro tanto* a valid decree *in rem*, even though only constructive service has been had against the defendant.[145]

Alimony may ordinarily be granted without a divorce and divorce may be decreed without alimony. It may happen that a court will recognize the extraterritorial validity of a divorce obtained without personal service in another state against the wife, and still grant alimony in her favor in a new proceeding. This follows the principle that "the (foreign) court took jurisdiction of nothing else but the marriage status," and that the judgment "established nothing except that the marriage relation has been condemned and destroyed by a judgment of divorce; all other questions are *res nova*."[146]

Without the seizure of property in support of the proceeding, a decree without personal service or appearance is void both within and without the jurisdiction. There is some question as to its validity if the defendant was domiciled within the state, but this circumstance would not seem adequate to give it extraterritorial validity.[147]

A contrary view is also maintained on the ground that the right to alimony has become *res judicata* by a foreign divorce granted without alimony and also upon the ground that the marriage having been dissolved, there remains no basis for alimony. But as we have seen, the court which may have jurisdiction to grant divorce may not have jurisdiction to award a binding decree for alimony. The defendant husband may have no property within the state of divorce; and if the divorce is procured by the husband, the wife may be foreclosed without even knowing of the pendency of the action. "To say the decree is *res judicata* as to the claim for alimony is to

[145] Rhoades *v.* Rhoades, (1907) 78 Neb. 495. Minor, §95.

[146] Thurston *v.* Thurston, (1894) 58 Minn. 279, quoted with approval in Toncray *v.* Toncray, (1910) 123 Tenn. 476.

[147] *Cf.* Goodrich, p. 309. Roberts *v.* Roberts, (1917) 135 Minn. 397. *Contra:* De la Montanya *v.* De la Montanya, (1896) 112 Cal. 101.

extinguish the claim without opportunity for its presentation."[148] The doctrine of non-severance of the issue of alimony from that of the divorce crept into our jurisprudence before the courts realized the hardship and injustice it often entails, especially in a country in which the State jurisdictions may be so widely separated geographically as to make the denial of alimony without divorce a practical if not a theoretical denial of justice. It arouses a strong sense of reaction against a rigid observance of *stare decisis* when a court will deny the right to adjudicate the question of alimony separately, though admitting its plausibility, its support by respectable authority and its appeal to the sense of equity.[149]

The Restatement[150] clearly declares: "No action for alimony can be maintained under the common law or the statutes of another state." It recognizes[151] that "Alimony can in its discretion be granted by a court under the law of its own state in favor of a spouse against any spouse who is personally subject or whose property is subject to the jurisdiction of the court." "A valid judgment for alimony granted in one state can be enforced in another state to the extent of the amount already due and unpaid on the decree, and not subject to reduction."

**Foreign Alimony Decrees in England.** The requirement of "finality and conclusiveness" which English courts apply to a decree of the divorce court before an action for alimony can be sustained in the regular law courts, applies *a fortiori* to foreign decrees of alimony. If under the foreign law the original judgment can be abrogated or varied by the court or judge which granted it, the proceeding will fail in England.[152] The question is therefore one of local procedure rather than of a conflict of jurisdiction. The English practice is therefore in substantial accord with the American rule. Instalments already due under a foreign decree may be recovered.[153]

**Foreign Conflict-of-Laws Rules relating to Alimony.** Alimony may be granted in *France* to the husband or wife as a provisional measure at the time of conciliation proceedings, or incidental to a final decree of divorce. The amount shall not exceed one-third of

148 Goodrich, p. 314 citing cases, *pro* and *contra*.
149 So held in McCoy *v.* McCoy (1921) 191 Ia. 973.
150 §462.
151 §§463–464.
152 Harrop *v.* Harrop [1920] 3 K.B. 386, 399.
153 Compare Beatty *v.* Beatty [1924] 1 K.B. 807, with the American Restatement, §464.

the income of the other and may be discontinued when no longer necessary.[154]

A foreign decree of divorce awarding alimony will be given execution to the same extent as any other judgment, though it awards a recurring payment. A Swiss married to an Englishwoman was divorced by an English decree awarding alimony against the husband in weekly payments. The husband removed to France and the payments being in arrears, the wife obtained an attachment of property of the husband located in France in a proceeding in execution of the English judgment. The court granted an order making the English judgment enforceable in France without pronouncing a new judgment. The court awarded a sum adequate to cover arrears (although under English law the plaintiff might have been held to have waived instalments), upon the principle that the *procedure* of execution is controlled by the *lex fori*.[155]

The *German* Introductory Statute[156] as we have seen, subjects the personal relations of husband and wife to German law even though the spouses are domiciled abroad. The husband owes support according to his station in life, the amount of his fortune and his earning ability; with a corresponding duty upon the wife to support the husband within her means and earning ability if he is unable to maintain himself.[157]

The rule of the Introductory Statute is applicable to foreigners by analogy, so that the duty of support is governed by the national law. Thus in the case of Danish spouses, alimony was refused in Germany, there being no alimony incidental to divorce under Danish law.[158] Where the spouses were Portuguese domiciled in Germany, the wife was not allowed to claim an annuity as permitted by German law.[159]

Alimony was sought in Germany pursuant to a decree of divorce obtained in New York by a German wife against her German husband. Recognition was refused on the ground that the effects of the divorce, including its prohibition against remarriage and the definitive fixing of alimony, were not consistent with German law; and that the effects of a foreign decree of divorce between German

[154] French Civil Code, Arts. 238, 301.
[155] Clunet, 1923, p. 872 and comment by J. Perroud.
[156] Art. 14.
[157] German Civil Code, §1360.
[158] *Landsgericht* Kiel, Dec. 3, 1926, Schleswig-Holstein *Anzeiger*, 1926, p. 97.
[159] *Reichsgericht*, Feb. 15, 1906, Clunet, 1907, 443.

nationals must be governed by German law in accordance with Art. 17 of the Introductory Statute.[160]

The Bustamante Code of Private International Law adopted by certain *Latin-American* nations approaches more nearly the Anglo-American view of alimony than do the European systems. It allows the law of the forum to determine the judicial consequences of an action of separation or divorce and to fix the terms of the judgment in respect to the spouses and the children.[161] This seems to be reinforced by the provision declaring that laws applicable to the duty of maintenance between relatives (ordinarily taken to include husband and wife) are declared to be of an "international public order" and therefore the court of the proceedings is free to apply its own law in this respect.[162]

[160] *Kammergericht* Berlin, Feb. 16, 1910; Clunet, 1911, p. 286.

[161] Art. 55.

[162] Art. 68. The provisions of the Code relating to the execution of judgments are broad enough to include a decree of alimony rendered in another state. *Cf.* Art. 423.

## Chapter VIII

# PARENT AND CHILD

### 1. Custody and Control

The relation of parent and child results normally from a marriage; but it may exist even without the marriage of the parents. Where the regulation and control of the relation of parent and child devolves upon more than one state, each state has the duty of promoting the highest welfare of the parties no matter where the status first arose, or where the parties are domiciled, or what may be the nationality of the parties. How may this be effected to the best advantage?

The relation of parent and child being a personal status, the system of law regulating it will be the system which controls the personal law generally, that of the domicil or of the nationality as the case may be. The domicil or nationality authoritative should be that of the parent at the time of birth of the child, because the relationship is established at that time. Civilized society recognizes and in large measure is founded upon the concept of the family. It gives control to the parent to a greater or less degree over minor children. Which parent? In the predominant ethnic practice of western civilization, it has been and still remains, the father, if living. What the social and legislative tendencies of the present will bring forth in "equalizing" the parental control of father and mother it is not necessary to discuss. This tendency to equality among the parents complicates the problem of ascertaining the nationality and domicil of children.

Although the relationship is governed by the personal law of the father, the personal control exercised through discipline or punishment must not exceed that recognized by the law of any state in which the parties happen to be. This follows from the superior right of all jurisdictions over matters of police upon a subject intimately connected with peace and order.[1]

**Parental Right of Custody.** The question of the right of custody of children by one parent as against the other parent is frequently tested in the United States under the writ of *habeas corpus*. Where the father is domiciled within the state, he may, of course, apply for the custody of a child living with the mother within the state; but if the child is living with the mother out of the state, the court will not have jurisdiction because of the nature of the writ, "as it is only when a person is detained in custody within this state that the writ of *habeas corpus* is applicable."[2] But if the domicil of the father (which at common law determines the domicil of the minor children in his custody) is not in the state of the application, even though the parties are temporarily within the jurisdiction, the court will not have "authority to adjudge a change of relation between the father and the child" by determining the right to custody as between contending parents.[3]

The tendency of modern legislation to give to the mother equal control over the children, by which the common-law rule of paternal domicil is modified, makes it increasingly difficult to determine the proper court for the award of custody. There is a lack of accord in the application of law. Where the mother is awarded custody incidental to a divorce obtained in a state in which the father was not domiciled, the decree has been accorded recognition; yet in the converse case, where the father obtains custody incidental to a divorce in the state in which both were domiciled, the same tribunal refused recognition on the ground that the court of the divorce may have had jurisdiction "but it is only for the purpose of changing the status of the complaining party and terminating the marriage."[4]

Of course this does not signify that the courts of the domicil of the parents is not the proper jurisdiction to settle the controversies between parents as to custody of the children, but simply that such controversies cannot be considered as finally settled by proceedings incidental to an undefended divorce case in another jurisdiction where the other spouse and the children are not before the court.

[1] "It has its origin in the protection that is due to the incompetent or helpless." Cardozo, J., in Finlay *v.* Finlay (1925) 240 N.Y. at p. 431.

[2] People *ex. rel.* Winston *v.* Winston, (1898) 52 N.Y.S. 816.

[3] Lanning *v.* Gregory, (1907) 100 Tex. 310.

[4] Compare Wakefield *v.* Ives, (1872) 35 Ia. 238, with Kline *v.* Kline (1881) 57 Ia. 386.

Cardozo, C. J., intimated that where the welfare of the child is not the issue, such controversies may not be brought before the jurisdiction of the mere residence of the child "as a pretense for the adjudication of the status of parents whose domicil is elsewhere, nor for the definition of parental rights dependent upon status." [5]

Where the right to the custody of a child has been determined and the parent and child change their domicil to another state, the second state then has control of the status of the child. Goodrich seems of the opinion that the first court's power is not lost as long as the question of custody remains to be passed upon; and yet with the welfare of the child as the prime consideration and the application of new facts and circumstances to the relation of the parties, the court of the new domicil will not hesitate to modify an earlier decree issued in the state of the old domicil.[6]

**Support of Children. Filiation Orders.** The duty of support of children by parents or of parents by children is likewise determinable by the courts of the domicil of the parties. The question as to what effect such a decree of support is entitled to receive in another state is another matter. It was presented in DeBrimont *v.* Penniman,[7] in which the plaintiff, a Frenchman, sought to enforce a French decree of support against the parents of his deceased wife obtained for the benefit of himself and the grandchild of defendants under French law, while they were residents of France. Apart from certain observations of the court that the obligation upon which the decree is founded is one strange to the common law, and not one recognized by all civilized nations like the duty of support of minor children, the decision held, upon demurrer, that such a decree is local and provisional, partaking of the nature of a police regulation and insuring against persons becoming a public charge. It was therefore not entitled to extraterritorial effect.

The Restatement provides [8] that no action can be maintained on a foreign bastardy statute. But a statute of the state of domicil of the

[5] Finlay *v.* Finlay, (1925) 240 N.Y. at p. 431. In this case it was held that the remedies for determining the right to custody were *habeas corpus* and petition in equity, and not by action at law. The chancellor (or a court of equity) acts "as *parens patriae* to do what is best for the interest of the child." *Ibid.*, see also (1907) 10 L.R.A. New Series, 690n.

[6] This is substantially the solution reached by the Restatement, §§144–148. Griffen *v.* Griffen (1920) 95 Ore. 78. Bishop on Marriage, Divorce and Separation (1891) ii, §1189.

[7] (1873) 10 Blatchf. U.S. 436.

[8] §§454–456.

father will be applied there to compel support, irrespective of the domicil of the mother, unless the statute provides otherwise. A statute of the state of domicil of the mother will be applied there to compel support by the father if the court obtains jurisdiction over him, unless the statute otherwise provides.

**Foreign Rules of Conflict relating to Parental Power.** Let us compare these doctrines with those recognized in other countries. Pillet agrees that the right of correction is territorial in France. There seems to be some authority for considering that in France, legislation which allows the parent to be superseded by a guardian in the exercise of parental authority where the interests of the child so require, is applicable to foreign as well as French children. Pillet, while not agreeing, would accept this by way of exception. But there is a well-reasoned view that as action putting an end to parental control affects the status, it may be taken only in accordance with the personal (national) law.[9] Pillet strenuously objects to the reliance upon the doctrine of public policy as tending to disturb the fixed application of rights and obligations growing out of parental power. In this he is in accord with the Swiss writer, Meili, who urges that it is sounder to relinquish this *deus ex machina* and recognize simply that national law cannot provide the extent to which parental authority may be exercised. He is, of course, referring to French practice, because in Switzerland the law of the domicil controls.[10] Swiss law differs from the law of France, Germany and Italy in that it permits parental power to be exercised jointly by both parents, the father's authority being decisive in the event of difference.[11]

German legislation contains the express provision that the legal relation between the parents and a legitimate child is determined by German law if the father is German; so also if he be dead, if the mother is German; and the same applies if the parents have lost German citizenship and the child remains German.[12] The principle is

[9] Clunet, 1896, p. 1055 and note p. 1060. Pillet, *Traité* (1923) i, p. 600.

[10] *Cf.* Clunet, 1913, p. 1266, in which the French court refused to consider the validity of an agreement made in England between English spouses, temporarily separated, which confined custody to the mother. Instead, the court granted custody to the father in accordance with French law. Meili, Int. Civil and Commercial Law (Kuhn's trans. 1905) p. 248.

[11] Swiss Civil Code, Art. 274. Italian courts will modify an agreement between foreign spouses domiciled in Italy as to custody of their child when conditions affecting the child's interest have changed. Clunet, 1913, p. 992.

[12] German Introductory Stat., Art. 19.

applied by analogy also to foreign parents and children unless there be a *renvoi* to German law.[13]

The courts in Germany are not permitted to exercise the discretion which they have in England and the United States, because the rule is fixed by statute. A change of nationality therefore may work a notable change in the scope of parental power. There is a certain similarity in practice, however, because facts and circumstances existing before the change will be recognized. A French father whose parental power was taken away in France before becoming a German, will be judged, in his relation to the child, by German law.[14]

An English or American father has no power of representation for his minor child in transferring land situated in Germany without a guardianship decree. He would have such power were German law applicable. The same applies in the purchase of land in behalf of the child. The contract of purchase would be governed by German law but the necessity of obtaining the consent of a court of guardianship is determined by the national law of the father.[15]

## 2. Legitimacy

Legitimacy is the legal kinship between a child and one or both of its parents. The status of a person as a legitimate child of its parents, or of one of them, may result from (*a*) the birth of the child in lawful wedlock, or (*b*) from some act or cause which entitles the child to be considered by law as though born in lawful wedlock. Under the second category the law may make or consider as legitimate a child that was not born in lawful wedlock. This act of the law is termed "legitimation." The concept of legitimacy, as the etymology of the word implies, is itself a creature of the law. Nature knows no legitimate children. It knows only children.

So far as concerns legitimacy as the result of birth in wedlock, no question will arise provided the marriage is recognized as lawful. But a marriage deemed valid in one state or country, may be deemed void or voidable elsewhere. We have already discussed to some extent the effect of the annulment of a marriage upon the

[13] Lewald, *Das deutsche int. Privatrecht* (1931) p. 132, citing decision of Bavarian *Oberlandesgericht* Feb. 13, 1912, in which German law was applied because the law of an American State adopted the domiciliary principle.

[14] Lewald, p. 134.

[15] Lewald, p. 135, citing (1925) 110 *Reichsger.* (Civ.) 173.

children.[16] At common law the issue of a marriage declared null and void are illegitimate; but in certain of the United States, a void marriage is regarded as valid to the extent of making the children of such marriage legitimate, if the marriage was entered into in good faith at least by one of the parties.[17] The fact that such statutes do not exist in all states and that their provisions are not uniform, have proved a fruitful source of conflicts of law.

**Legitimation by Statute from Time of Birth.** In California the children of a void marriage, even if such marriage is bigamous, are by statute considered legitimate. In Connecticut no similar statute exists but children born out of wedlock are deemed children of the mother and capable of inheriting from and through her. Children born in California of a bigamous marriage while the parents were domiciled there, were allowed to inherit as next of kin of the father in the distribution of an estate in Connecticut.[18] The court pointed out that public opinion in Connecticut would probably be opposed to a statute similar to that of California but that this did not furnish a test for a status created in the state of domicil. The court recognized that it would be in the highest degree inconvenient if a status of legitimacy were liable to fluctuate and change with time, place and circumstance. Once these relations have been established by the proper law, they remain fixed and unchangeable.

**Legitimation by Statute after Time of Birth.** Under the legislation of some states, *e.g.* North Dakota, public acknowledgment by the father of a child born out of wedlock, or action on his part toward the child deemed equivalent thereto, constitutes legitimation. In a North Dakota case, the father was a domiciled citizen of Norway where the children were also residing at the time the acts of recognition occurred. It was held that legitimation did not take place under North Dakota laws and therefore there could be no claim to the father's estate though he died domiciled in North Dakota. "Their own land attached to their status the stigma of illegitimacy. While so domiciled it was not within the power of another state to remove it." [19]

**Where Domicils of Parent and Child Differ.** It is quite possible that the domicil of the father differs from that of his child born out

[16] *Ante*, p. 184.
[17] See statutes collated in 5 Cycl. of Law and Proc. 632.
[18] Moore *v.* Saxton, (1916) 90 Conn. 164.
[19] Eddie *v.* Eddie, (1899) 8 N. Dak. 376.

of wedlock, because the child is often to be found with the mother. It is also possible that the child may be located in some third state when the act constituting legitimation takes place. Minor was of the opinion that legitimation would be held valid according to the domiciliary law of the father, or of the mother, provided the domicil of either were located at the forum. While this solution is largely speculative, it has the merit of aligning itself with social and humanitarian purposes.[20] It seems to be an attempt to forecast judicial decision rather than to formulate a principle. The Restatement prefers the domicil of the parent with whom kinship is in question, seemingly without regard to whether the question arises at such domicil or before the forum of another state.[21]

While the principles of private international law should not vary with each state of facts, it is quite probable that the courts may be inclined to broaden the rule of the Restatement in favor of the forecast of Minor, which would lead to recognition of legitimation in a larger number of cases. "Law," says Miraglia, "being an ethical principle, should not encourage illicit unions. It should, however, protect children born out of matrimony from the acts of the parents, in whom often love is lacking, or is smothered by the interest of their legitimate families or by conventionality. It should visit all the consequences of the fault upon its authors, and should not extend it to others." [22]

**Legitimation by Subsequent Marriage.** *Legitimatio per subsequens matrimonium* is an institution of the Roman law. Lord Fraser said that it was supposed to have been introduced by Constantine in order to put down the system of concubinage which had grown into almost universal favor throughout the Empire. It was later incorporated in the Justinian Code.[23] From the Roman law it passed into the Canon law and gradually became the law of practically all the countries of Continental Europe excepting Russia of the

[20] *Cf.* Minor, §98.

[21] §138. The legitimate kinship of a child to either parent from the time of the child's birth is determined by the law of the state of domicil of that parent at that time. §139. An act or event after the birth of a child who was born illegitimate may make it the legitimate child of either parent from birth, if the law of the state of domicil of that parent at the time of the child's birth and the law of the parent's domicil at the time of the legimating act so provides.

[22] Comparative Legal Philosophy Applied to Legal Institutions (1912, Lisle's trans.) p. 724.

[23] Fraser, Parent and Child (1906) p. 37. *Codex,* v. 27; 9, 11.

old régime. The institution was not adopted in England until 1926, but has long existed in Scotland and more recently in Australia and New Zealand, some of the Canadian provinces and many of the British overseas dominions.[24] It exists by statute in most of the United States though the conditions vary from state to state. By some statutes, acknowledgment is alone sufficient, in others, marriage alone, in still others, both are required. This again has been a fruitful cause of conflicts of law.

Although the validity of the subsequent intermarriage will be determined by the law of the state in which it is celebrated, the effect of such marriage on the question of legitimation will be determined by the domicil of the father. If the subsequent intermarriage has that effect by that law, the fact that it has no legitimating effect by the law of the state where it is celebrated, will not prevent the child from being regarded as legitimate even for the purpose of inheritance in a state which does not recognize the institute of legitimation by subsequent marriage. This was the conclusion reached in England before the present statute.[25]

In Blythe *v.* Ayres,[26] the mother and child were domiciled in England where the child was born. The father who was at all times a domiciled citizen of California publicly acknowledged it as his own within the meaning of the California statutes, so as to legitimate it from birth. The parties never married but the court by way of dictum expressly stated that the result is the same whether the act constituting legitimation is a subsequent marriage or a public acknowledgment. The court repudiated the fiction of the Canon law that in case of subsequent marriage the parents will be deemed to have been married when the child was born. Both cases must rest on justice and policy. In both cases the father's domicil at the time of the legitimating act must control, even though, as in the instant case, the mother and child had never been in the state of the father's domicil.

Conversely, if by the law of the father's domicil at the time of the subsequent intermarriage, such intermarriage has no legitimating effect, the fact that the parents afterwards acquire a domicil in a state in which the institution is recognized and one of them dies

[24] See J. D. White in Law Quarterly Rev. 1920, p. 255.

[25] Munro *v.* Munro, (1840) 17 Clark & F. 842; see also Lauderdale Peerage Case, (1885) L.R. 10 App. Cas. 692.

[26] (1892) 96 Cal. 532; *accord:* Ives *v.* McNicolls, (1899) 59 Ohio St. 402.

domiciled there, the child will not be entitled to succeed as legitimate to property, real or personal, located there.[27]

Although the English statute recognizing legitimation by subsequent marriage did not go into effect until January 1, 1927, yet if the parents were married at that time, or married after that date, and the father was, at the time of marriage, domiciled in England or Wales, the marriage renders the child legitimate from January 1, 1927, or the date of marriage, whichever happens last.[28] If the father was domiciled in a country other than England or Wales, by the law of which the child became legitimated by the marriage of the parents, it will be so recognized in England and Wales from a like date. It is immaterial that the father was not, at the time of the child's birth, domiciled in a country in which legitimation by subsequent marriage is recognized.[29] The statute grants the same rights to persons thus legitimated to succeed by intestacy to real or personal property as though they had been born legitimate.[30] Thus the peculiar doctrine which formerly prevailed in England came to an end. Subsequent marriage was permitted to legitimate only if the law of the domicil of the father at the birth of the child as well as at the time of the marriage concurred in conferring upon the child the capacity to become legitimated in this manner.[31] Upon principle, the capacity to become legitimated should be considered sufficient if it exists as of the time of the act constituting legitimation. Jurisdiction over the parties is complete and the law of the state in which the subsequent marriage is celebrated is effective to make a change in the status. It has, indeed, been properly suggested that where the legitimation is held to relate back to the time of birth, the domicil

[27] Smith *v.* Kelly, (1851) 23 Miss. 167. *Cf.* the learned note in 73 Amer. Law Rep. Ann. (1931) 941, and further cases there cited. The Restatement of the Amer. Law Institute provides: "§140. An act done after the birth of an illegitimate child will legitimize the child as to a parent from the time of the act if the law of the state of domicil of that parent at that time so provides." So far as concerns legitimation by subsequent marriage, a conflict between the father's and the mother's domiciliary law will be rare though possible. It is quite conceivable that as to legitimation by various forms of recognition, the statutes will differ as to the nature and degree of publicity required.

[28] Legitimacy Act, 1926, §1.

[29] *Ibid.*, §8 (1). The child must have been living on January 1, 1927, or at the time of marriage, whichever happens last. The statute does not legitimate the issue of a child deceased before such date. *Re* Lowe (1929) 2 Ch. 210.

[30] *Ibid.*, §4.

[31] Goodman *v.* Goodman (1862) 3 Giff, 643, 66 Eng. Reprint 565; *Re* Grove (1887) L.R. 40 Ch. D. 216; *In re* Grey's Trusts (1892) 3 Ch. 88.

of the parties at *that* time, is also essential.[32] But an examination of the English cases will show that in England the doctrine could not have been based upon this circumstance because there was often no retroactive effect claimed for the subsequent marriage. It was probably the result of a fictive assumption that what was equivalent to marriage, took place before the conception and birth of the child.[33]

**Legitimation and the Right to Inherit.** We have thus far considered the conditions upon which an illegitimate child receives the status of legitimacy and the proper law under which this status is acquired so as to be internationally recognizable. It does not necessarily follow, however, that a foreign state will permit a person so legitimated to inherit property within its territory even though it may recognize the status for other purposes. On the other hand, the foreign state may recognize a right in illegitimates to inherit, or at least in illegitimates acknowledged by one or both of the parents. This results from the conflict between jurisdiction over persons and the jurisdiction over property. In the celebrated case of Birtwhistle *v.* Vardill [34] twice argued before the House of Lords, it was held that a child born in Scotland, of unmarried parents domiciled in that country, and who afterwards intermarried there, is not by such marriage rendered capable of inheriting lands in England. Though of legitimate status, he was not "born in wedlock" within the meaning of the statute of Merton (20 Henry III, c. 9). Lord Brougham in his learned and forceful dissenting opinion pronounced the bounds of the law as applied, to be very narrow indeed. "I know, wherever I go in Europe, it is boldly denied to be the law. I know the opinion of Dr. Story and other American jurists is against us, and I do not think I could overstate the degree in which all these jurists dissent from the judgment in this case." [35]

The American viewpoint is, of course, free from the peculiar provisions of the Statute of Merton; so that ordinarily, children legitimated by marriage of parents, or by acknowledgment, may inherit

[32] Goodrich, Conflict of Laws, §136.

[33] *Cf.* Munro *v.* Munro (1840) 7 Cl. & F. 842, 872. In Hall *v.* Gabbert (1904) 213 Ill. 208 the doctrine is criticized as resulting from "a refinement of reasoning"; and in Blythe *v.* Ayres, (1892) 96 Cal. 532, the fiction is repudiated in the following terms: "Times are not what they once were, and we live in an age too practical to build our law upon the unstable foundation of fictions."

[34] (1830) 2 Cl. & F. 581; (1839–1840) 7 Cl. & F. 895, 940.

[35] 7 Cl. & F. at p. 915.

lands.[36] But the result follows from the rule of *lex rei sitae* applicable to the descent and title to land. The description which the law provides at the place of the situation of lands may be satisfied by a status elsewhere created. We have seen that under the old law of England, the description of "children," or "issue" did not suffice. It remains a question of the interpretation of the law of the territory within which the land is located. Thus where that law permits illegitimates to inherit, those who prove natural descent may inherit, whether domiciled within the jurisdiction or not.[37]

It is sometimes difficult to determine whether the law of the situs intends *its* requisite for legitimation to apply only to its domiciled subjects, or to those domiciled abroad as well. Ordinarily it does not, but requisites found in foreign inheritance laws do not of themselves serve to change the status of persons domiciled there. Thus a case in Oklahoma involved the right of a child to inherit as heir of the father. Oklahoma requires written recognition by the father in the presence of a competent witness. Does this apply to a child publicly recognized by the father in Kansas, but not by any writing? Both parent and child were domiciled in Kansas at the time, and such recognition would have been sufficient by Kansas law to constitute the child an heir. The court held the recognition to be ineffective because the Kansas statute was not one of legitimation but of inheritance.[38]

## 3. Adoption

Under the Roman law, from which the modern institution of adoption is principally derived, two proceedings were recognized, adoption strictly so called, and arrogation. The former related to persons already under the power of a *paterfamilias,* and had for its effect the transfer of his *potestas* to the *potestas* of the adopting

[36] Miller *v.* Miller (1883) 91 N.Y. 315. See (1922) 36 Harvard Law Rev. 83 and cases cited. *Contra,* Lingen *v.* Lingen (1871) 45 Ala.; 410.

[37] Van Horn *v.* Van Horn, (1899) 107 Ia. 247.

[38] Pfeifer *v.* Wright (1930) 41 Fed. 2nd Ser. 464. The unfortunate result reached in this case may be attributed to careless legislative drafting. The Restatement §246 provides: "A person who is heir by the law of the state where the land is, only if legitimate, is heir if, but only if, he is born legitimate as stated in §138 or has been legitimated as stated in §§139 and 140." The full-faith-and-credit clause is not effective to sustain the inheritance of lands by a child adopted under the decree of a sister state. Hood *v.* McGee, (1914) 237 U.S. 611.

parent. The latter brought under the *patria potestas* of the adopting parent, persons who, up to the time of the adoption, were independent. Under both systems, the adoptive child passed completely out of his previous family environment into that of the family of the adopter; but whereas adoption was effectuated by the consent of the parties evidenced by a declaration before the praetor, arrogation required the intervention of a public authority.[39] Under Justinian, adoption in the narrower sense of the term ceased to create *patria potestas* but merely gave the adopted child the same rights of succession as though he were a real child of the adopter.[40] The combined influence of the church, which frowned on adoption as a substitute for children through marriage, and feudalism, which favored conservation of property in the family, steadily tended to eliminate all vestiges of the institution in France and elsewhere, until it was revived, somewhat in the Justinian form, by the Napoleonic legislation and by the Prussian Code of 1791.

Adoption never found its way into the law of England until very recently. It is recognized by most of the Continental systems but not in the Netherlands, Norway or Sweden.[41]

By recent legislation in England, the adoption of minors is now permitted under careful restrictions. The adopter must be over twenty-five and be a resident and domiciled in England or Wales and the child must be a British subject.[42]

Adoption statutes seem to have been introduced in the United States through the example of Louisiana and Texas, where the institution was taken over from French and Spanish precedents. The first statute to be enacted in a common-law state was that of Massachusetts in 1851. The statute as now amended allows adoption by a person of full age, of a person younger than himself, except his or her wife or husband, brother, sister, uncle or aunt, of the whole or half blood. If the adopting person be married, the other spouse must join in the petition. The consent of the child must be obtained if over fourteen, and also that of the lawful parents or surviving parent or other person standing in a parental relation to the child. If the

[39] Burge, Commentaries on Colonial and Foreign Law (1908) ii, 392.

[40] Sohm, The Institutes (Ledlie's trans., 1901) p. 501.

[41] Burge, *op. cit.*, ii, p. 405.

[42] Adoption of Children Act, 1926, §§1–2. The statute entered into effect January 1, 1927. The courts are given discretion to apply or not to apply certain of the restrictions.

person to be adopted is of full age, such consents are not required. The adoption is consummated by the decree of a probate court after due notice to the parties in interest. An adopted person takes "the same share of the property which the adopting parent could dispose of by will as he would have taken if born to such parent in lawful wedlock." [43]

The first statute in New York dates from 1873 but the right of inheritance did not accrue to the adopted child until the amendment of 1887.

Adoption statutes exist in practically every state of the Union but with great divergence of detail both as to the requisites of adoption and as to the rights of inheritance, so that conflicts of law are frequent. The Restatement (§142) recognizes that: "The status of adoption is created by either: (*a*) the law of the state of domicil of the adopted child; or (*b*) the law of the state of domicil of the adoptive parent if it has jurisdiction over the custody of the child or if the child is a waif and subject to the jurisdiction of the state."

The primary question, as in the case of legitimation, is to determine whether the state in which an adoption is undertaken has jurisdiction in the international sense; the secondary question is as to the effects which will be recognized as flowing from an adoption undertaken in a foreign state where there is no question as to the jurisdiction of such foreign state. In the leading case of Ross *v.* Ross [44] there had been an adoption in Pennsylvania, where both parties were domiciled. The father afterwards removed to Massachusetts where he died intestate leaving real estate located in Massachusetts. In a learned opinion by Gray, P. J., it is said that status is to be determined by the law under which it was acquired if that state had jurisdiction; that personal property is to be distributed according to the law of the last domicil of the deceased and real property by the law of its situation; "but in either case, it is according to those provisions of that law which regulate the succession or the inheritance of persons having such a status." [45] The statutes were not in similar terms, there being no requirement in Pennsylvania for consent by the wife of the adopting father; furthermore the right of inheritance was limited to heirs of the body and from the kindred

[43] Mass. Gen. Laws, 1921, chap. 210, §7.
[44] (1880) 129 Mass. 243.
[45] At p. 246.

or through the children of the father. These provisions were not to be found in the Massachusetts statute but it was said that these differences were immaterial, the only question being whether the adopted child or a brother of the adopting father had the better title to the father's land. The adopted child was allowed to inherit as though adopted in Massachusetts.[46]

**Effect of Foreign Adoption where Local State does not have Adoption.** Let us suppose that a claim to inherit as a child arises in a state which has no statute providing for adoption. There was no statute for adoption in England prior to the legislation of 1926. Dicey was of the opinion that no effect should be given to a foreign adoption because it gives rise to a status not known to English law; although an English court in ascertaining who is entitled to an estate of a deceased person domiciled abroad might be compelled to apply a foreign law in which the status of adoption is recognized.[47] Phillimore was of the opinion that "whatever consequences affecting the status flow from them [adoption, arrogation, emancipation] according to the personal statute or law of the domicil, ought to be recognized in other countries."[48] So far as we are aware, the question has never been directly presented in the United States. In the American Law Institute Restatement it is assumed that the adoptive parent may claim the right of a domiciliary guardian in a state which does not recognize adoption if the child is a minor.[49] But it is also assumed that if there is no local statute for adoption, no recognition of a foreign adoption will be accorded.[50]

We have observed that the Restatement recognizes jurisdiction for adoption in a state in which the child is domiciled, even though the adoptive parent is domiciled elsewhere. Goodrich points out that as the relationship is intended to be of benefit to the child and does not seem to cause danger to social institutions at the domicil of the parents, there should be no objection by either of these states. The only persons to be adversely affected are blood relatives who otherwise might inherit property.[51] This is similar to the view of Pillet

[46] *Ibid.* at pp. 267–268. *Accord:* McNamara *v.* McNamara, (1922) 303 Ill. 191; Anderson *v.* French, (1915) 77 N.H. 509.

[47] Dicey, Conflict of Laws (1932) p. 950. *In re* Trufort, (1887) 36 Ch. D. 600.

[48] Phillimore, Commentaries upon Int. Law (1879–1889) iv. §531.

[49] Restatement, Comment *b.* to §143.

[50] Restatement, §143, Comment *a.*

[51] Goodrich, Conflict of Laws (1927) p. 328, citing Wolf's Appeal, 13 Addison, (Pa.) 760. Van Matre *v.* Sankey (1893) 148 Ill. 536. Fisher *v.* Browning (1914) 107 Miss. 729.

whose key to the solution of conflicts of law is to determine the social purpose of the laws which are in competition.[52]

**Adoption and the Right to Inherit.** Assuming the adoption to have been legally effected in a state having jurisdiction, will the adopted child have the rights of inheritance accorded to children? Here, as in the case of legitimation, the question is one of conflict between jurisdiction for status and jurisdiction for the title to property. As the jurisdiction competent to determine the devolution of land is the *lex rei sitae* and the jurisdiction competent for the distribution of personal property is that of the last domicil of the deceased, these laws must respectively govern. But what the law of the succession ought to decide is in turn often dependent upon an interpretation of the will of the legislature. Where the state in which the land lies provides that adopted children have all the privileges of a legitimate child to inherit and succeed to real and personal estate, the same right will be accorded to a child adopted abroad. This is the prevailing but not the universal law. A child adopted in Georgia was allowed to succeed to lands of his intestate adoptive father in Tennessee, but not in Alabama, although the statutes in all three states were similar.[53]

Let us suppose that the statute of the state under which adoption takes place (California) allows the adoption by the father of an illegitimate child through public acknowledgment and receiving it as his own with the consent of his wife, whereas the state of the inheritance of land (Illinois) provides only for adoption by a court-proceeding and also does not permit the adoption of illegitimates. Will the adopted child be permitted to inherit? It was held that he may and that "no narrow view of the relation will be taken to defeat the law." [54]

It is the foreign-created status which is recognized; but not any foreign-created right of succession. So that if the law of the state of adoption permits the adopted child to inherit through collaterals, but the law of the state of succession does not, the child cannot so inherit.[55] On the other hand where the rights granted by the state of the inheritance (South Dakota) are broader than that of the state

[52] Pillet, *Traité pratique de dr. int. privé* (1923) i, 644, 652.

[53] Finley *v.* Brown, (1909) 122 Tenn. 316; Brown *v.* Finley, (1908) 157 Ala. 424. The Alabama court recognized that the weight of authority was against its opinion but said that this had become a rule of property in Alabama.

[54] McNamara *v.* McNamara, (1922) 303 Ill. 191, 220.

[55] Van Matre *v.* Sankey, (1893) 148 Ill. 536.

of the adoption (Illinois) in allowing the adoptive father to inherit from the child, the law of the inheritance will again prevail.[56]

Whether an adopted child may be considered to be included in a class mentioned in a will is a question of interpretation to be determined by the principles which prevail in the state of the inheritance. A New York testatrix left a will with remainder to "the lawful issue" of one of her daughters. The daughter resided abroad and had adopted a child in Saxony. The court held that the testatrix did not intend to include an adopted child. The court recognized the status created abroad and indicated that if the Saxon law had declared that an adopted child should have the status of a descendant and all the legal consequences and incidents thereof, the same as though born in wedlock, there might have been a basis for concluding that the testatrix intended to include an adopted child within the term "lawful issue." [57]

**Comparative Study of Foreign Rules of Conflict relating to Legitimation and Adoption.** *French* law [58] differing from the provisions of derivative codes like that of Italy,[59] provides that the subsequent marriage of parents will legitimate children born out of wedlock only if recognized by the parents before marriage or in the certificate of celebration. Will a marriage of French parents in Italy where such requirement does not prevail, be sufficient? We have seen that questions of personal status are referred to national law. If national law prevails, marriage alone will not suffice and yet it has been maintained that such recognition is a formal act, required only if demanded by the law of the place where the act is celebrated. Despagnet sustains the view that the requirement of recognition is a substantive prerequisite of the status and not a mere formality and this view has received judicial approval.[60]

[56] Calhoun *v.* Bryant, (1911) 28 S.D. 268. At p. 275: "The relationship created, no more has its foundation in contract than has the relationship created by birth." At p. 276: "The right of inheritance does not grow out of the relationship of parent and child, though it may be created and conferred in the exercise of legislative wisdom, because of the existence of that relationship." *Contra:* Boaz *v.* Swinney, (1909) 79 Kas. 332.

[57] New York Life Ins. & Trust Co. *v.* Viele, (1897) 22 A.D. 80, affirmed (1899) 161 N.Y. 11.

[58] Civil Code, Art. 331.

[59] Italian Civ. Code, §194.

[60] Despagnet in Clunet, 1888, p. 594, citing Besancon, July 25, 1876. Conversely, legitimation by Italian or Spanish parents through subsequent marriage may take place in France without recognition until after the marriage. Seine, Aug. 21, 1876; Clunet, 1877, p. 330.

Let us suppose that the nationality of the father differs from that of the child and of the mother; let us assume that the child is born in France of a French mother and an English father. Could the child be legitimated prior to the recent English statute? The Court of Cassation said it could be legitimated because the French law was in execution of an elementary duty of parents and therefore was coercive in France.[61] But Pillet criticizes the result because the question is as to the right of the father to legitimate his child in a foreign country and force him into his family as a legitimate where, in the father's own country, the right would not have been recognized. He would permit the converse however, *viz.* legitimation in France of an English child born in England of an English mother and French father, because the family being French would not be concerned.[62] There seems to be no judicial sanction for these views and the courts in recent cases of legitimation by acknowledgment place the application of law squarely upon the requirement that the act of legitimation shall be lawful both by the law of the nationality of the father and of the child.[63]

Formerly, children of an adulterous union could not be legitimated in France by subsequent marriage after the divorce of one of the parents. This has now been changed by statute so as to permit such legitimation in almost all cases; not however where the father has legitimate children which are issue of the marriage during the continuance of which the illegitimate was born.[64]

France recognizes the institution of adoption under careful restrictions as to diversity in age of the adoptive parent and the child, the antecedent relations of the parties, the absence of legitimate or natural children and the consent of the spouse, if the parent be married, and of the actual parents of the child.[65] Adoption results from a solemn contract, but one in which the parties are not entirely free because, like marriage, it gives rise to a new status in which the legislator is deeply interested.[66]

Whether the contract requires the capacity of both parties has been a question much discussed by Belgian and French jurists. Rolin

[61] Cassation, Nov. 23, 1857.

[62] Pillet, *Traité* (1923) i, p. 644.

[63] Clunet, 1924, p. 410.

[64] French Law of Dec. 30, 1915. *Cf.* Surville in Clunet, 1916, p. 769, on the possible conflicts of law which may result.

[65] Civil Code, Arts. 343–346.

[66] Weiss, *Traité de Dr. int. privé,* iv, p. 118.

and Laurent support the view that capacity in accordance with the law of the adoptive parent will suffice because adoption entirely favors the child and therefore his personal law has no interest in restricting consummation. Weiss counters with the argument that it is the status of the child which is preponderantly affected and therefore his law should be observed. Pillet demands the observance of both laws.[67] But as adoption is regulated by special legislation, an adoption cannot be consummated merely by a solution of a conflict of laws. Thus under French law, the right to adopt or to be adopted is regarded as a civil right under Article 11 of the Civil Code, reserved for French citizens, and those foreigners whose rights have been homologated by "admission" to domicil or by diplomatic reciprocity. Therefore, a foreigner cannot adopt a French citizen nor be adopted by one, except in exceptional cases.[68]

Legitimation under *German* law may be effected either by subsequent marriage or by a declaration of the state of the Reich to which the father belongs, upon application of the father.[69]

Adoption under the German law is predicated upon a contract between one who has no legitimate descendants and the adoptive child, sometimes requiring consent of its parents, but always subject to confirmation by the court.[70] The German Introductory Statute (Art. 22) subjects legitimation and adoption to German law if the father at the time of the legitimation or the adopter at the time of the adoption be a German citizen. The legitimation or the adoption of a German child by a foreigner requires that German law be observed in respect to the requisites of consent by the child or that of a third person standing in a family relationship to the child. The fragmentary manner in which the article has been framed has given rise to much discussion as to whether it was intended as a rule of conflict so as to be applied analogously also in cases in which the father or the adopter, is not German, or (so far as concerns consent), to cases in which the child is not German. Lewald is of the opinion that the article applies in converse cases as well; also that the second provision supplements the first so that the personal law of both father or adopter, and the child, must both be observed. A difference is possible, however, between legitimation and adoption

[67] Rolin, *Principes du dr. int. privé,* ii, No. 604. Weiss, *op. cit.* iv, p. 118. Pillet, *Traité pratique de dr. int. privé,* i, p. 650.

[68] Pillet, p. 650 citing Rouen, Sept. 8, 1916. Clunet, 1917, p. 1009.

[69] German Civ. Code §§1719, 1723.

[70] *Ibid.,* §§1741–1772.

because in the former case the nationality of the child is changed under most systems, whereas the adopted child does not change nationality by reason of the adoption. Therefore, if the child is of a country which, *e.g.*, does not recognize the institution of adoption, it would surely not be just to permit the adopter's personal law to be controlling.[71] But this view has not been sustained in practice and the courts have restricted the application of the statute so far as the requirement of consent is concerned, to German children.[72] With regard to legitimation and adoption in general, the provision of the first part of Art. 22 is applied by analogy to foreigners as well. This results practically in the application of the personal law of the father or of the adopter, as the case may be. Thus if the adopter's personal law does not require judicial confirmation for adoption, none need be obtained in Germany. If that law requires a confirmation which can be analogously satisfied under the procedure of German law, a German court will carry it through, but not if the national law of the father requires a procedure requiring inquiry into the *good policy* of legitimation or the adoption. For this there is no parallel procedure under German law.[73]

So far as concerns legitimation by subsequent marriage of the parents, German law refers to the national law of the father, following Art. 22 of the Introductory Statute already mentioned. If the father is a German and the child an alien, German law will decide. If the father is an alien and the child a German, the father's national law will control. Some systems of law require the consent of the child if it has reached a certain age. This is quite understandable because of the duty of supporting indigent parents. German law does not require the child's consent so that German law is not involved in this case. Where the father and the child are both aliens, each belonging to a different state, the logic of the rule would also seem to require reference to the national law of the father alone; but there is a difference of opinion among German writers upon this point.[74]

[71] Lewald, *Das deutsche int. Privatrecht* (1931) pp. 152–154.

[72] *Reichsgericht,* Nov. 7, 1929; 125 *Reichsg. Zivilsachen* 265; *Oberlandesgericht,* Hamburg, Sept. 28, 1928. Adoption is not an institution recognized in the Netherlands. A Netherlands child may be adopted in Germany by a German, under the interpretation of the courts, although the adoption would probably not be recognized in the Netherlands. See Lewald, p. 155.

[73] Lewald, p. 158. *Kammergericht,* June 30, 1923, and Sept. 30, 1927. Walker, Int. *Privatrecht,* p. 734.

[74] Rappe, *Recueil de l'Acad. de dr. int.,* 1934, iv, p. 424.

*Switzerland* follows the principle that the national law and jurisdiction of the adoptive parent govern filiation, both legitimate and illegitimate, as well as the voluntary recognition of natural children and adoption, without reference to the personal law of the child.[75] The voluntary recognition of a natural child by a foreigner may be made in Switzerland by official deed or even *causa mortis* as provided by Art. 303 of the Civil Code, provided the national law of the father recognizes this procedure.[76]

A Swiss who had become naturalized in Chile without losing his Swiss nationality, adopted an illegitimate child in Switzerland (Zurich). An action for maintenance and support brought by the child was dismissed because adoption was not recognized under Chilean law. Later the child distrained certain property of the father in Switzerland in aid of the claim for maintenance. The Swiss court refused to be bound by the prior adjudication of the Chilean court on the ground that the adoption had created a valid legal relationship constituting a vested right to be recognized abroad even in a state where the act could not have been undertaken and that the failure to recognize it constituted a denial of justice.[77] While the national law of the father may be sufficient without observing any other law, it is always the part of wisdom to observe the requirements of the personal law of the child, if the child happens to be an alien at the place of adoption.

Under Art. 54 of the Swiss Federal Constitution, the subsequent marriage of parents constitutes a legitimation of children born antenuptially. In favoring the institution in so high a degree as to embody it in the fundamental law, the sovereign power has indicated a public policy against making any distinction between legitimate and illegitimate children of married persons.

The *Italian Disposizioni* makes no especial mention of legitimation or adoption but the usual broad interpretation given to Art. 6 leads to the application of national law and the observance of the conditions of the personal (national) law of both the adopter and the child. Legitimation by subsequent marriage is recognized under prescribed conditions; and where marriage is impossible, it is allowable only by royal decree. Application must first be made to a court of

[75] Fed. Stat. of 1891, Art. 8. Swiss Civ. Code, Final Title, Art. 61.

[76] Petitpierre in de Lapradelle and Niboyet, *Repertoire de dr. int.*, (1930) vii, p. 164.

[77] *H.E.*, x, p. 157.

appeal to pass upon the prescribed conditions.[78] A decree of a court of appeal is required also for adoption. Where an Italian has completed a proceeding for an adoption in a foreign country, it is necessary to obtain an *exequatur* of the foreign decree in order to make it effectual in Italy.[79]

As Italy follows the principle of national law with reference to questions of personal status, this principle is appropriately applicable to the question of legitimacy or illegitimacy. The national law of the father at the birth of the child determine the relative rights and obligations between father and child, whereas the national law of the mother will determine the relations between child and mother. Where the paternity of a natural child is not admitted, Italy follows the doctrine of the French codes, prohibiting action against a reputed father, except where pregnancy has been brought about through an act of violence (Art. 189, Italian Civil Code). Where the child and its mother are nationals of a state in which action against a reputed father is permitted, will such an action be permitted in Italy? Udina does not deny it categorically but indicates that it may readily be found objectionable upon the ground of public policy.[80]

The survey of these systems of Continental Europe furnishes some insight into the significance of the provisions of the *Bustamante Code* accepted by a large number of the *Latin-American* nations. The capacity to legitimate is governed by the personal law of the father; the capacity to be legitimated, by the personal law of the child. This results in requiring the concurrence of both. But where there is a prohibition against legitimation of children "not simply natural," this is to be taken to be of an "international public order." [81] We take this to refer not to the absence of any law relating to legitimacy but to special prohibitions such as those against legitimating children of an incestuous or adulterous union. These are coercive provisions which every state may properly see enforced within its territory.

The effects of legitimation and the right to impugn it are regulated by the personal law of the child except that the right to maintenance by a legitimated child is again a matter left to each state to apply the law of the forum. Under the rule of *locus regit actum,* the form by which and the circumstances under which the acknowledg-

[78] Italian Civ. Code, Arts. 198–200.
[79] Clunet, 1931, p. 756, Turin, Feb. 18, 1930.
[80] Udina, *Droit int. privé d'Italie* (1930) §154.
[81] Bustamante Code, Arts. 60–61.

ment of illegitimates takes place must follow the law of the forum.[82] Rights of inheritance are, of course, referred to the personal law of the deceased, be it the father or the child.[83]

A number of Latin-American countries do not recognize the institution of adoption. Accordingly, the Bustamante Code makes its provisions upon adoption applicable only within states which do recognize it. Again, the capacity to be adopted and the conditions and limitations under which it may take place require reference to the personal laws of both parties, the rights of inheritance being determined by that of the party whose estate is being administered.[84] Each state is free to apply its own law in determining the right to maintenance and also in respect to the establishment of solemn forms for the act of adoption.[85] It will be remembered that the Code leaves each state free to determine the personal law, either by reference to the law of the domicil or to national law, as the case may be.[86]

### 4. Guardianship

Under the term "guardianship" as applied to minors, Anglo-American law deals with two separate concepts for which a separate terminology is often found in other systems of law. Guardianship of the *person* of a minor is "an artificial extension of the parental power, and may be conferred by the last will of the parent, or by a deed executed by him, or by a judicial act, or by devolution on certain defined classes of relatives, or may vest in a tribunal, such as the Court of Chancery." [87] The guardianship of *property* results from the general inability of the minor to enter into valid contracts without the approval of some public authority, in order that his patrimony may be preserved until he is presumptively able to deal with it himself. Often the two functions of guardianship are united in a single person and yet, under the common law, a father, in his capacity of natural guardian of his child has no right to receive personal property of the child except earnings, nor to control real property. The parent's right of control is limited substantially to

[82] *Ibid.*, Arts. 59, 62, 66.
[83] *Ibid.*, Arts. 58, 65.
[84] *Ibid.*, Arts. 73–74.
[85] *Ibid.*, Art. 76.
[86] See comment of Judge de Bustamante in Tulane Law Review, June 1931, p. 539.
[87] Holland, Elements of Jurisprudence (1910) p. 178.

the person of the child. Some countries of Continental Europe give the father a usufruct in the property of the children until they reach maturity or prior emancipation.[88] The English common law and modern legislation in England and the United States do not give to the parent any control of or right in the child's property as such. A guardian must be appointed in order to collect and discharge claims due to the ward, to make contracts in regard to his estate, to sell land or personal property or to bring suit in his behalf.[89]

It is said "The status of guardian and ward is created and terminated by the state of the domicil of the ward." [90] The jurisdiction to appoint a guardian, whether of the person or of the property of a minor, or of one mentally incompetent, cannot be said to be confined to any one state because it does not effect a permanent status. The court of any state in which a minor happens to be found will exercise jurisdiction whenever necessary for his protection or best interests.[91] So also the court of any state in which property of a minor or of an incompetent is found, will appoint a guardian to deal with such property, whether or not the minor or incompetent is domiciled there. Indeed, a guardian appointed in one state will not have *eo nomine* power to deal with property of his ward in another state. It has not found its way into the law of the United States under the doctrine of comity as expounded by Story. Mr. Justice Bradley refers to the doctrine in his opinion in the leading case of Hoyt *v.* Sprague: [92] "One of the ordinary rules of comity exercised by some European States is to acknowledge the authority and power of foreign guardians, that is, guardians of minors and others appointed under the laws of their domicil in other states. But this rule of comity does not prevail to the same extent in England and the United States. In regard to real estate it is entirely disallowed; and it is rarely admitted in regard to personal property." He quotes Story, with approval as follows: "The rights and powers of guardians are considered as strictly local; and not as entitling them to exercise any authority over the person or personal property of their wards

[88] French Civil Code, Art. 384; Italian Civil Code, Art. 228.

[89] Peck, Law of Persons and of Domestic Relations (1930) pp. 410–411. When the word "guardian" is used by the legislature, as for example in a statute providing for workmen's compensation, a guardian appointed by the court and not a natural guardian is ordinarily intended. Matter of Decker, (1929) 252 N.Y. 1.

[90] Restatement, §149.

[91] Restatement, §150.

[92] (1880) 103 U.S. 613 at pp. 630–631.

in other states, upon the same general reasoning and policy which have circumscribed the rights and authorities of executors and administrators." [93] In the above case of Hoyt *v.* Sprague, the minors and their natural guardian were domiciled in New York; a guardian of their estate was appointed at the request of the natural guardian in Rhode Island where, by special act of the legislature and the approval of the court, the guardian was permitted to make an investment which would have been illegal in New York. The investment was held to be proper. In the case of Lamar *v.* Micou,[94] decided a few years later, the investment would not have been allowed in the state of appointment but was legal in the state of the domicil of the ward. The court again held the investment to be proper. The opinion quotes the prior decision with approval and yet the dicta seems to hold the domicil of the ward alone authoritative, a conclusion scarcely warranted by the established rules. The case is properly to be limited to the point that the guardian will not be held to the stricter rules of the place of appointment if at the ward's domicil the acts of the guardian would have been approved.[95]

Where the guardian has been appointed at the domicil of the ward, a foreign court will be more inclined to recognize his authority. In the exercise of such "comity," the authority of a foreign guardian over the person of his ward will often be enforced, and funds in the hands of a local guardian, not of the domicil, are often ordered to be transmitted to the guardian of the domicil.[96]

Occasionally a court at the domicil of an incompetent will be found unwilling to appoint a guardian when the incompetent is in fact in another state. But this cannot properly be ascribed to any want of jurisdiction but only to the difficulty of giving sufficient notice.[97]

[93] Story, §§499, 504, 504a.

[94] (1884) 112 U.S. 452.

[95] Goodrich suggests a possible acceptance of the decision under a still different interpretation, *viz.* that the property had been turned over by the local court to the guardian appointed at the ward's domicil. Conflict of Laws (1927) pp. 437–438.

[96] So decided in *Re* Benton, (1894) 92 Ia. 202. Under a statute, *habeas corpus* was granted to the foreign domiciliary guardian to enforce the right of custody of the ward in Grimes *v.* Butsch, (1895) 142 Ind. 113. It was denied in Hanrahan *v.* Sears, (1903) 72 N.H. 71, because the welfare of the ward did not justify it. *Accord:* Finlay *v.* Finlay, (1925) 240 N.Y. 429, 431, in which Cardozo, J. held that jurisdiction to regulate the custody of infants "has its origin in the protection that is due to the incompetent or helpless," rather than in the circumstance of parental domicil within the state.

[97] See note in 80 Univ. of Penna. Law Review (1932) p. 590, commenting upon McCormick *v.* Blaine, (1931) 178 N.E. 195 (Ill.)

The American Institute of Law's Restatement provides: "§150. A temporary guardian can be appointed in any state in which a defective person or a child is found." It further provides: "§151. A guardianship of the person created at the domicil of the ward will be given such effect in another state as would be given to such guardianship if it had been created in the latter state; but a temporary guardianship created in a state where a ward is found but not domiciled will not be given effect in another state."

The English and Scotch courts assume a characteristic attitude of realism without holding to any hard-and-fast rule in recognizing the authority of a foreign guardian either of the person or the property of a minor or an incompetent.[98] The interests of the ward will determine the extent of the recognition to be accorded.[99]

**Survey of Conventions on Guardianship.** The problems growing out of the conflicts of law and jurisdiction in respect to guardianship are principally problems of administration. The Swiss jurist, Meili, emphasized the point that it is not merely a question of determining the application of some objective system of law but of dealing with an organic medium functioning during a certain period.[100] The Hague Convention to regulate the Conflict of Law and Jurisdiction in regard to the Guardianship of Minors seems to recognize this because it provides not only for the competent *fora* but also for co-operation under certain circumstances between the various competing systems in the matter of supplying information.[101] The guardianship of a minor under the convention is governed by his national law, which also controls the beginning and the termination of the proceeding. The administration extends both to the person and to the movable property of the minor, but not to land, which is controlled by the *lex rei sitae*.[102] The state in which the minor happens to be, may take all necessary steps for the protection of his

[98] Johnstone *v.* Beattie, (1843) 10 Cl. and F. 43.

[99] Rudoyevitch *v.* Rudoyevitch, [1930] S.C. 619 (Scotland). Where a foreign guardian or curator demands property of his ward located in England, no special grant of authority is required unless proceedings in England prevent recognition of the effect of the proceedings completed at the domicil. Didisheim *v.* London & Westminster Bank, [1900] 2 Ch. 15. *Re* Larragotti, [1907] 1 Ch. 14. Pelegrin *v.* Coutts, [1915] 1 Ch. 696.

[100] Meili, Int. Civil and Commercial Law (1905, Kuhn's trans.) p. 250.

[101] The Convention was signed June 12, 1902, ratified by a majority of the States on June 1, 1904. An English translation is given in the English edition of Meili, Int. Civil and Commercial Law, p. 535.

[102] Arts. 1, 5, 6.

person and interests but if it becomes necessary to appoint a guardian, the national state must be promptly informed and the latter in turn will give information whether a guardian has been or will be appointed there.[103] Where the minor has his habitual residence abroad, the national state is empowered to institute the guardianship through its diplomatic or consular officials, if the law of the former state does not oppose it. If this is impossible, the state of habitual residence may itself institute and administer the guardianship. But this power is not exclusive and the national state may later appoint a guardian of its own, giving notice to the other state.[104]

The convention does not apply unless the minor is a national of *one* of the States. If he has double or multiple nationality, it does not apply because of the obvious impossibility of then applying its main principle of national law. The convention does not attempt to establish the system which shall be authoritative in respect to the execution of the guardianship, so as to determine the liability of the guardian or the administrative officials supervising the acts of the guardian. For a breach of their fiduciary obligations it is assumed that the law of the state which appointed the guardian will control, for the reason that under the law of European countries, we are dealing with the exercise of a public function.[105]

The Bustamante Code (1928) also recognizes the personal law of the ward but differs from the Hague Convention in regard to guardianship because, as we have seen, the personal law may be the national law or the domiciliary law or any other standard which domestic legislation may prescribe.[106] It would seem, however, that when one of the contracting states had assumed jurisdiction under the personal law as regulated by its domestic legislation, its acts would be entitled to extraterritorial effect in another state, even one in which the personal law was determined by a different standard, except as to those matters in which the law of the forum is strictly applied. To use the language of the Code, this occurs "when any of

[103] Art. 8.

[104] Arts. 3–4. The term *residence habituelle* is not synonymous with domicil. Its precise delimination has not been attempted but is left to factual determination. It was found desirable to avoid terms such as "legal residence" because of the divergence of meaning in the different countries. Meili and Mamelok, *Int. Priv. und Zivilprozessrecht* (1911) p. 258.

[105] *Ibid.*, p. 288.

[106] Arts. 7, 84–97. "The International Conferences of the American States" (ed. by James Brown Scott) 1931, p. 327.

their effects or consequences are in conflict with a rule of an international public order." [107]

The object, organization, and nature of the guardianship or curatorship, the security to be furnished, the manner of exercising the duties of the office, are all regulated by the personal law of the minor or of the incompetent.[108] The questions considered to be of international public order and controlled by local public policy are those which may properly be ascribed to matters of police, such as criminal penalties for infractions of a duty, the conditions under which public officials may request the declaration of the disability of alleged incompetents, the duty of the guardian or curator to support the ward and moderation of the power of personal correction. All these matters are free of the control of the personal law as, indeed, they would be under the principles of the common law.[109] If the guardian or curator is entitled to make an excuse for declining a duty which, under modern civil law is ordinarily regarded as compulsory, such excuse or incapacity is referable to the personal law of the proposed guardian or curator.[110]

[107] Art. 8.
[108] Arts. 84–85, 87–89.
[109] Arts. 90, 91, 93. A declaration of incapacity or interdiction will have extraterritorial effect. Art. 92.
[110] Art. 86.

## Chapter IX

# PROPERTY

### 1. The Separation in Law of Movables and Immovables

The peculiar system of land tenure which the Norman conquerors introduced into England after the Conquest seems to have been already partly developed among the Normans. The feudal mode of holding lands was subject to a strict definition of the duties of lord and tenant and carried out under a highly technical legal phraseology. The laws relating to the ownership or the use of land were especially designed to protect and perpetuate the military power of the king, and the state which he controlled. Land was regarded as *held* subject to some *service,* military or otherwise, the military service running always to the king, even though the grant came from one who himself was tenant of the king.[1] As the land was held directly or indirectly from the king and subject to service, it could not be freely disposed of. Restrictions upon the alienation of land even antedated the growth of feudal ideas but there seems to be no doubt that the prohibition of wills of land was of feudal origin. The feudal system devised further encroachments through the selfishness and avarice of the lords.[2] As alienation was not free, the procedure and remedies which were used in order to protect the tenant's qualified title were quite different from those used in order to regain chattels or to recover debts. A recent writer describing conditions in the fourteenth century refers to the fact that conveyances *inter vivos* were accompanied by such heavy burdens as to make it very unusual for the owner of land in fee simple to want to convey it; and as the right to devise land by will did not generally exist until the sixteenth

[1] Digby, An Introduction to the History of the Law of Real Property (1892) pp. 30, 40.

[2] *Ibid.,* p. 100.

century by the Statute of Wills, lands were usually held until death and passed to the heirs under the intestate laws.[3]

It is the peculiar history of the land-law of England which necessitates the distinction to be made between rights *in rem* to immovable or real property and rights *in rem* to movable or personal property. In Roman law and the systems derived from it, there is no such fundamental distinction and the property or "patrimony" of a person is for most purposes considered an *universum*. The development of the transfer of chattels by testament through the influence of the Church, and the function of the Church in acting as executor and often as the chief legatee of personal estates, also contributed greatly to the separation. Thus the ecclesiastical courts became seized of testamentary jurisdiction over movable property. The efforts of the royal courts seem to have been directed to a vigorous defense of all land-jurisdiction as against the Church.[4] With two different *kinds* of courts functioning separately over disputes regarding tenure of land and ownership in chattels respectively, it is not surprising that this cleavage grew more and more pronounced. Different forms and conditions were required for the transfer of each kind of property, both *inter vivos* and by will, after free disposition became permissible.

## 2. Rights in Immovables (Land)

There is perhaps no rule better settled under the common law than that the laws of the place where immovable property is situated "exclusively govern in respect to the rights of the parties, the mode of transfer, and the solemnities which should accompany them. The title, therefore, to real property, can be acquired, passed and lost only according to the *lex rei sitae*."[5] Sometimes the rule is stated to be "that to the law of the state in which land is situated must we look for the rules which govern its descent, alienation, and transfer, and for the effect and construction of conveyances."[6] But while there is agreement upon the rule thus generally stated, there is some vagueness

[3] R. D. Brown in Univ. of Penna. Law Rev., 1932, p. 523.

[4] Jenks, A Short History of English Law, (1913) pp. 61–62.

[5] Story, §424. "Story's statements with regard to the rules of the common law as regards the conflict of laws may be considered to some extent authoritative." Dicey, Conflict of Laws (1932) p. 583n. (b).

[6] McGoon *v.* Scales, (1869) 9 Wall. (76 U.S.) 23, 27; Platner *v.* Vincent, (1921) 187 Cal. 443.

discoverable as to its foundation in reason. It is, of course, obvious that the legal and the actual situs of immovables are identical. As Minor puts it: "By no fiction of law nor theory of public policy can land be regarded as constructively located at any other place than its actual situs. It naturally follows that every question affecting title to land must be governed by the law of the place where the land is situated." [7] Wharton thought that the rule is one for the protection of the state. "A sovereignty cannot safely permit the title to its land to be determined by a foreign power." [8] But it is difficult to see the danger unless aliens thus obtain title to large tracts. The application of some foreign law will not necessarily cause this result, which may be and often is prevented by express statute. Westlake derives the rule of *lex situs* from the importance attached to landed property and points out "that great confusion would have arisen if its tenure could have been interfered with by deeds in foreign form, or by matrimonial engagements tacitly entered into under and with reference to foreign laws." [9] Thus while the rule may be explained by the feudal nature of land tenure it is also justified as a rule of convenience to prevent "the innumerable diversities of foreign laws" from regulating titles to immovables in the local state.[10]

What constitutes an interest in immovables so as to be determined by the *lex situs?* The same public policy which would make an indeterminate or fee interest in land subject to the law of its location would seem to be required for interests which are of limited duration, such as estates for life or leaseholds for a term of years. This is indeed the rule followed in England. Leaseholds were not part of the heritable estate which went to the heir at common law and therefore were denominated "personal." Leasehold rights are nevertheless governed by the *lex situs*.[11] This has not always been followed in the United States. A testator domiciled in California dies possessed of certain leases of land in New York. By his will, valid in California, he disposes of the leases in a manner not permitted by New York law. The New York court sustained his disposition under the domiciliary law saying: "Personal property is subject to the law

[7] Minor, §119.

[8] Wharton, §278.

[9] Westlake, (1925) p. 9.

[10] Story, §440.

[11] Westlake, (1925) §219. Applied to succession—*Re* Gentili, (1875) Ir. L.R. 9 Eq. 541; to the limitations under the Mortmain Act, *In re* Moses, [1908] 2 Ch. 235.

which governs the person of the owner as to its transmission by last will and testament; and this principle, though arising in the exercise of international comity, has become obligatory as a rule of decision by the courts."[12]

A more difficult question is presented where particular chattels, such as farm implements, in fact movable, are declared to belong to the land or are referred to as "immovables" by statute. Story maintained that "every nation, having authority to prescribe rules for the disposition and arrangement of all the property within its own territory, may impress upon it any character which it shall choose; and no other nation can impugn or vary that character."[13] The doctrine thus stated would lead far afield, as it did indeed in Story's day. The designation of slaves as immovable by operation of law under Louisiana statutes were so regarded in Tennessee (where the slaves were located) for the purpose of descent and heirship.[14] The lengths to which a fiction of law may carry us is strikingly illustrated by this qualification of a human being as an immovable! "The law," says Mr. Justice Cardozo, "is no stranger to the philosophy of 'As if.' It has built up many of its doctrines by a make-believe that things are other than they are."[15] Undoubtedly, Story's doctrine is sound to the extent that rights which have become vested under a designation, however fictitious, given to tangible property at the time it was located in a particular state, will be respected in another state to which such property has been removed.

The Restatement provides: "Whether an interest in a tangible thing is classified as real or personal property is determined by the law of the state where the thing is."[16] A special note points out that civil-law systems employ the terms "movables" and "immovables" instead of "personal" and "real." Usually the terms are synonymous except with regard to "chattels real," including leaseholds, as already emphasized. We have retained the term "movables" because, as the special note points out, it is a convenient term to include all kinds of things, whether tangible or intangible, interests in which constitute

[12] Despard *v.* Churchill, (1873) 53 N.Y. 192. *Contra,* Beale, Treatise (1935) §249. 1, though admitting the rule of domicil for distribution.

[13] Story, §447.

[14] McCollum *v.* Smith, (1838) Meigs 342; 33 Am. Dec. 147. In Minor *v.* Cardwell, (1866) 37 Mo. 350, it was held that slaves taken from Kentucky, where they were regarded as real estate, into Missouri, lost their character as such and became personal property.

[15] Cardozo, The Paradoxes of Legal Science, (1930) pp. 33–34.

[16] Restatement, §208.

personal property; and this terminology is used also in the Restatement.[17]

**Contract Rights with respect to Foreign Land.** It may very well be that a contract concerning the conveyance of land in a foreign state may be ineffectual to transfer a valid title to the land because of the law of the foreign state and yet be enforceable as a valid covenant under the proper law of the contract. An action brought in Massachusetts in the early days upon a deed to lands in Pennsylvania was not sustained as to the covenant of warranty contained in the deed. The court intimated, however, that as to the consideration paid and the contracts collateral to the title, the agreements between the parties would not be deemed void.[18]

In the important English case of British South Africa Co. *v.* De Beers Consolidated Mines [19] the complainant was seeking to declare invalid an exclusive license for mining certain diamond mines in Northern and Southern Rhodesia because the contract was *ultra vires* the complainant; or alternatively that it was a "clog" on the equity of redemption, the loan upon which the license was granted as security having been paid. It was contended that the Roman-Dutch law was applicable at least to the part of the property in Southern Rhodesia and that, according to law there in force, the principle of clogging did not apply and that the license would continue valid even after the payment of the loan. It was held that English and not the Roman-Dutch law was applicable because the contract was made in England, in English form, and the loan was to be repaid in England. "The method and manner of performance abroad, so far as regards the grant of the license, the form of it, and the rights conferred by it, are to be governed by the law of the place where the land is situate, but the questions with regard to the validity of the stipulations in the contract itself must, in my opinion, be governed by English law." [20]

Contractual rights and liabilities not affecting the actual transfer of title are governed by the proper law of the contract. To illustrate: An executory contract for the conveyance of foreign land was made in Minnesota where the payment of the purchase price was to be made. Under Minnesota law, certain notice must be given to the vendee before forfeiture of amounts already paid could be validly

[17] *Ibid.*
[18] Phelps *v.* Decker, (1813) 10 Mass. 267.
[19] [1910] 1 Ch. 354; 2 Ch. 502.
[20] By Swinfen-Eady, J., in [1910] 1 Ch. at p. 386.

declared. No such requirement prevailed at the foreign situs of the land. Minnesota law was applied.[21]

The Restatement provides [22] that the law of the place of contracting determines the validity of a promise to transfer or to convey land. This rule must be taken in connection with the general principle accepted with regard to contracts. We shall see that the test adopted by the Restatement is not as elastic as the rule in England,[23] where the rule of the Restatement would probably not be followed. The Restatement further provides [24] that the law of the place where the deed is delivered determines the contractual duties of the grantor, while the *lex situs* determines the duties of the grantor which are not contractual. Here again we have a fixed test whereas the English court would regard the various elements, including the place of delivery of the deed, as bases for determining the proper law of the contract.[25]

**Covenants for Title.** The form of an instrument effective to pass title to immovables must conform to the law of the situs. This follows necessarily from the general principles already discussed.[26] A state is of course empowered to permit land within its borders to be transmitted by instruments made outside its territory according to the laws there in force. Statutes of a number of states of the Union have indeed accomplished this purpose within certain limitations.[27]

Should we say, therefore, that an instrument adequate to convey title under the law of the situs is to be construed according to that law also for the purpose of determining to what extent covenants of a personal nature have been validly created by the instrument. In Platner *v.* Vincent,[28] land in the State of Washington had been conveyed to plaintiff by "bargain and sale" deed, which under Washing-

[21] Finnes *v.* Selover, (1907) 102 Minn. 334. *Accord:* Walsh *v.* Selover, (1909) 109 Minn. 136; affirmed on the constitutional objection that the application of the law of the contract as opposed to that of the land did not deprive the vendor of due process of law or the equal protection of the laws. (1912) 226 U.S. 112.

[22] §340.

[23] See *post,* p. 282.

[24] §341.

[25] *Cf.* Cheshire (1935) p. 442.

[26] U.S. *v.* Crosby, (1812) 7 Cranch 115, in which a deed executed in Grenada, W.I., without a seal, was held ineffectual to pass real estate located in Mass., though valid where executed. See also L.R.A. 1916, A., 1020.

[27] See Lorenzen in (1911) 20 Yale Law Jour. 433: "The validity of Wills, Deeds and Contracts as Regards Form in the Conflict of Laws."

[28] (1921) 187 Cal. 443.

ton statutes is equivalent to an express covenant for quiet enjoyment and that the grantor was seized of the property in fee simple, free from incumbrances. The deed was executed in California where the grantors resided and where it was claimed such effect would not be given. It was held that the effect of the deed was to be determined by Washington laws. The problem is well expressed in Dalton *v.* Taliaferro,[29] as follows: "If a deed of land in Illinois be executed in Maine or Germany it would be unreasonable to say that while its sufficiency to transfer title must depend alone upon the laws of Illinois, yet we must resort to the laws of Maine or Germany to ascertain the existence and construction of covenants which are inseparable from the land, are annexed to the estate granted, can pass only with the grant of the land, and depend for their validity upon privity of estate between covenantor and covenantee." The law of the situs will determine whether the covenant "runs with the land," for that law affects the measure of title. But is the quality of running with the land to determine whether the covenant claimed is to be determined by the law of the situs or the law of the contract? It was so held in Bethell *v.* Bethell,[30] where land in Missouri was conveyed by bargain and sale deed in Indiana, all of the parties being domiciled in the latter state. There was no general warranty and according to Indiana law, no covenant of seizin can be implied. The court held that such a covenant does not run with the land where the grantor is not in possession; and if the grantor had no title, the covenant is at once broken and does not pass to a subsequent grantee. Upon this distinction it was held that Missouri law could not apply. The result has been criticized as undesirable, that it is based upon a technical distinction between "personal" and "real" covenants, which some courts have repudiated, and that a covenant like that of seizin is as inextricably connected with the conveyance as one of warranty.[31] There is much force in this criticism and yet where the parties are all domiciled in the foreign state where the instruments were drawn and delivered and the contract is completely executed (not executory) the measure of their personal obligations, even though it be in respect to land located elsewhere, should be determined by the law of the

[29] (1901) 101 Ill., 592, 596.
[30] (1876) 54 Ind. 428.
[31] Goodrich (1927) p. 341, citing Alcorn *v.* Epler, (1917) 206 Ill. App. 140. In that case, the grantee failed to allege that in the state of the situs, a covenant of seizin would have been read into the deed, and his action was dismissed on demurrer.

contract, at least *until* the distinction between personal and real covenants is abolished. The parties presumably intended to have the risk fall where it was placed by the law with which they were all familiar and under which the instrument was executed.

**Equitable Interests in Land.** As the law of the situs governs the title to land, it will also govern equitable interests in land. As the jurisdiction and the procedure of equity is a growth of English law, this question arises only where equity prevails either at the situs or in the forum. The legal owner and the beneficial owner alike are persons claiming upon the land; "whether they work out their rights through the sheriff or the chancellor is, after all, a question of procedure." [32]

Whether a trust of land has been validly created is determined by the law of the situs. Thus where a testator who died domiciled in New York left lands in California of which the will endeavored to create a trust, void by New York law, it was held that the California law and jurisdiction were alone competent to decide.[33]

Even though the creation of equitable interests in land is referred to the situs, equity will decree a conveyance. In *Ex parte* Pollard,[34] the petitioner was a creditor with whom a bankrupt had deposited as security, title-deeds to land in Scotland. In England, where the transaction took place, this would constitute a mortgage in equity, while in Scotland it would create no lien or equitable mortgage on the land. The court decreed that the land be charged with the debt upon the principle that so far as a court of equity can by decree *in personam* enforce its own idea of equity, it is not interfering with the *lex loci rei sitae,* unless that law actually forbids the enforcement of the decree. Beale maintains that the accurate way of describing these cases is that the court foreign to the land treats the defendant *as if* the plaintiff had an equitable right in the land.[35] But this seems to be just another way of avoiding the application of the proper conflict-of-laws rule and furnishes an opening for the court to extend its jurisdiction beyond its proper scope.

In countries of the common law, the conveyance by deed is sufficient to pass title though recording is usually necessary to protect such title against purchasers for value without notice. A court may

[32] Beale, "Equitable Interests in Foreign Property" in (1907) 20 Harvard Law Rev. 382.

[33] Knox *v.* Jones, (1872) 47 N.Y. 389.

[34] (1840) Mont. & C. 239.

[35] Beale in (1907) Harv. Law Rev. p. 386n.

thus effectuate a decree concerning foreign land situated in another common-law state. In civil-law countries the conveyance of any interest is usually ineffective unless registered and a foreign court would be unable to exercise control over the title. Lord Campbell said that "An English court ought not to pronounce a decree, even *in personam* which can have no specific operation without the intervention of a foreign court, and which in the country where the lands to be charged by it lie would probably be treated as *brutum fulmen.*"[36]

The American Law Institute Restatement furnishes a detailed elaboration in respect to rights in land under which all the following questions are governed by the law or the state of situs of the land, *viz.:*

The validity of a conveyance of an interest in land (§215).

Whether interests in land are to be treated as equitably converted into personal property (§209).

Capacity to make a valid conveyance of an interest in land (§216) and the capacity to take or hold the interest (§219).

The formalities necessary for the validity of a valid conveyance of an interest in land (§217).

Whether a conveyance is valid in substance (§218).

The effect of a conveyance upon the nature of the tenure or interest created (§§220–221).

The creation, transfer and termination of non-possessory interests in land (§222).

Whether an interest in land is transferred by operation of law (§223).

Whether an interest in land has been extinguished or acquired by adverse possession or prescription (§224).

The validity and effect of a mortgage or an assignment of a mortgage on land (§§225–226).

The method and effect of the foreclosure of a mortgage on land, the power to redeem and the validity of a discharge of a mortgage (§§227–229).

Liens and charges upon land (§§230–231).

Powers of attorney to convey land and the validity and effect of a power of appointment (§§233–234).

The effect of marriage upon interests in land owned by a spouse at the time of marriage or acquired by either or both after marriage (§§237–238).

[36] Norris *v.* Chambres, (1861) 2 De G. F. & J. 583 quoted by Beale *ut cit.* In Acker *v.* Priest, (1894) 92 Ia. 610, the court refused to declare an implied or constructive trust upon lands in Kansas where the facts would not have justified such a conclusion under Kansas laws.

Whether a person has an equitable interest in land and the validity of a trust in land (§§239–241).

Whether the interest of the beneficiary of a trust of land is to be treated as real estate or as personalty by reason of a direction to sell (§244).

**Analysis of Foreign Law relating to Property in Immovables.** The *Austrian* jurist, Gustav Walker, assures us that there are few principles of private international law so generally recognized as the rule that rights of property in immovables are to be determined by the laws which are in force at the situs. He believes that the rule is in accordance with the demands of public international law as well as the purposes which legislation pertaining to landed property necessarily subserves: [37] The grounds stated for the rule are those of public policy and the sovereignty of states. Savigny also bases the principle upon a voluntary submission to local laws implied in the holding of land. His argument covers all tangible things, not merely immovables. As they occupy space, the place in space in which the thing is located must be regarded as the situs of the legal relationship which is the subject of the property rights.[38]

The codified texts express the principle with general unanimity. The *French* Civil Code [39] declares that "Immovables, even those possessed by aliens, are governed by the French law." While in terms referring only to French lands, the usual acceptation of the rule in its converse form is implied. The principle though long established in the law of the *German* states [40] is not expressed in the German Civil Code nor its Introductory Statute which leaves to provincial laws a wide control over property in land.[41]

The *Italian Disposizioni* [42] declares that "Immovable property is governed by the law of the place where it is situated." The *Bustamante Code* [43] provides that "All property of whatever description, is subject to the law of the place where it is situated."

Notwithstanding these general phrases, a very great difference in the scope of application is to be observed outside the Anglo-American legal sphere. This is particularly true of the test of *capacity* to transmit property rights in land which in some countries is determined

[37] Walker, *Int. Privatrecht* (1924) p. 279.
[38] Savigny, *System des heutigen Römischen Rechts* (1849) vol. 8, p. 169.
[39] Art. 3.
[40] Lewald, (1931) p. 169.
[41] Arts. 100–129.
[42] Art. 7.
[43] Art. 105.

by the proper personal law, domiciliary or national as the case may be. This follows from the fact that the complete separation of personal from real property made by English law is not followed by civil-law countries. The French Civil Code in its laconic Art. 3, provides the rule for immovables and in the same article refers the capacity of persons to national law. The courts therefore consider the clause pertaining to immovables as an exception. An Italian who endeavored to make to his wife a gift *inter vivos* of movables and immovables located in France was admitted by the court to be under an incapacity so to do under Art. 1054 of the Italian Civil Code, but the Paris Court of Appeal refused to allow such incapacity under his national law to affect his transfer of immovables located in France. "It is according to French law that the validity of the act of transmission must be judged as well as of the stipulations included therein." [44]

In Italy, on the other hand, the rule of Art. 7 of the *Disposizioni* is taken only in conjunction with Arts. 6, 8 and 9, which regulate capacity; and therefore the capacity to transmit or to create rights in immovables is governed by the law governing capacity, the national law. The national law governs also the reciprocal rights of the spouses in each other's property, whether movable or immovable, and, as we shall see, also the rights to immovables through succession, testamentary or intestate.[45] Diena notices the marked difference in interpretation given in Italy to *Disposizioni,* Art. 7, from that given in France to the corresponding article of the Civil Code, and ascribes it to the influence of the old statutory theory. He also points out that the first paragraph of Art. 7 provides that "movables are governed by the national law of the owner, saving however contrary provisions of the law of the country in which they are found." From this he deduces that things considered by themselves or as the object of real (or property) rights are always subject to the law of the situs whether they be immovables or movables. Undoubtedly the spirit of Mancini has pervaded the interpretation given by both courts and jurisconsults. The difference in result can scarcely be derived from interpretation based upon the tenor of the respective codes and Diena admits that at the next revision of the Italian code, the language of Art. 7 of the *Disposizioni* is certain to be somewhat modified.[46]

The *German* Introductory Statute in Art. 7, par. 3, does not leave

[44] Clunet, 1901, pp. 775, 780. *Accord:* Clunet, 1925, p. 126.
[45] Udina, *Droit int. privé d'Italie* (1930) p. 115.
[46] Diena in *Recueil des Cours, Académie de Droit Int.,* 1927, ii, pp. 369–370.

room for much doubt because it expressly excludes the application of local (German) law in testing the capacity of one capable by German law, in respect to acts dealing with foreign land. As the application is excluded by way of *exception,* it leaves the rule of paragraph, 1, *viz.,* the national law, untouched in determining capacity to deal with foreign land. The importance of the rule is, of course, limited by the registration statutes in the place where the land is located. In Germany as in many other countries of Continental Europe, land cannot be effectively transferred without registration. The registration of a right affecting an immovable creates a presumption of the validity of the right and the title of the person in whose favor it is created. The cancellation of any such right on the register creates a presumption as to the release or extinction of such right.[47]

Lewald points out that in general, German private international law does not distinguish between movables and immovables in so far as the creation of real or property rights are concerned. In some cases, the Introductory Statute regulates the application of law by treating as a unity a whole group of questions relating to a single subject matter. Thus Art. 15 gives the rule for marital property rights, Art. 19 for the rights of parents in the estate of their legitimate children, Art. 24 and 25 for rights of succession. In other words, the rule applies to all the property rights falling within the designated category, irrespective of the location of the property.[48]

A similar result is reached in countries such as the *Netherlands,* still under the influence of the French Civil Code. Husband and wife, both Germans, were married in Germany where they also established the matrimonial domicil. Later the husband acquired land in Holland. After his death the wife claimed one half as her property under the rule of marital property prevailing in Holland according to which community of property exists between husband and wife if no special agreement is made at marriage. The Netherlands Court of Cassation held that notwithstanding the rule of Art. 3 of the French Civil Code reproduced in Art. 7 of the Law of General Provisions (1829) in force in the Netherlands, the German matrimonial law must apply, rather than the law of the situs. As the German law

[47] German Civ. Code, §891.

[48] Lewald, *ut cit.* p. 173. But this is subject to an important exception, unique, perhaps, in legislative practice, that the object must be within the state the laws of which are controlling; otherwise the *lex situs* itself may apply its special laws. Introductory Stat. Art. 28.

left the spouses each in enjoyment of their separate property in the absence of agreement at marriage, the land descended as part of the husband's inheritable estate.[49]

The *Bustamante Code* declares that the general rules relating to property and the manner of acquiring it or alienating it *inter vivos* are of an "international public order." [50] In the sense in which this term is used, the transfer of property is left to the local law having jurisdiction over it, which would be the law of its situs. Transfer by succession, both interstate and testamentary, are excluded, as the Code deals with all the property of an estate as a unit, "whatever may be the nature of the estate and the place where it is found." [51] The Code provides that the situation of debts is determined by the place in which they should be paid, and if that is not fixed, by the domicil of the debtor.[52] But whether this indicates their location or merely the law which is to indicate it, is not quite clear. Curiously enough, the Code locates other personal property at the domicil of the owner, or if he be absent from that place, in that of the property holder.[53] It seems to be for this reason that the Code refers any distinctions between real and personal property not to the situs, but to the "territorial" law, which would seem to allow any court which is able to sustain its jurisdiction over property to follow its own classifications and qualifications, without prejudice, however, to the rights acquired by third parties.[54]

### 3. Property in Movables

We have had occasion to refer to the especial significance attached during the Middle Ages to the ownership of land. It was a period which knew not mercantilism. Today the industrial system has penetrated almost everywhere with its vast mechanized productive capacity and its efficient means of transportation. Movable property has thus been brought from a secondary to a primary place as an object of wealth. The systems of credit and finance and the growth of corporations have created new kinds of personal property with

[49] Clunet, 1916, p. 308.
[50] Bustamante Code, Arts. 105, 117.
[51] *Ibid.*, Art. 144.
[52] *Ibid.*, Art. 107.
[53] *Ibid.*, Art. 110. Things given in pledge are situated at the domicil of the pledgor. Art. 111.
[54] *Ibid.*, Arts. 112–113.

which different systems of legislation have dealt differently, thus producing conflicts of great importance and difficulty. Furthermore, the convenience of representing property by documents, negotiable or otherwise, makes urgent the proper solution of conflicts of law in order that credit may be promoted.

The earliest writers in the United States begin their discussions with the same legal maxim as did the Continental authors: *mobilia sequuntur personam,* which implied that movables had no locality of their own.[55] Kent, more wary of early Continental casuistry, resisted the doctrine and maintained that where the interests of creditors were involved, title to personal property could not be governed by the domicil of the owner and that American jurisprudence had recognized the governing law of the actual locality of movables.[56] In analyzing the views of the seventeenth and eighteenth century, Livermore found that one set of writers adopted the fiction that movables have no situs in contemplation of law, and are attached to the person of the owner wherever he is, and being so adherent, are governed by the same laws which govern his person, namely the law of the domicil. This view was adopted by D'Argentré, Burgundus, Hertius and Bouhier. Another group in which were Paul Voet, Rodenburg and Boullenois recognized a situs for movables but placed it at the domicil of the owner. Both fictions lead to the same result. Story[57] accepted the principle that the owner's domicil governed the transfer of movables, subject to "some positive or customary law of the country where they are situate, providing for special cases (as is sometimes done) or from the nature of the particular property, it has a necessarily implied locality."[58] Indeed Story seems to have had serious misgivings about the old fictions without ever arriving at a more satisfactory result. For this he has been much criticized. Story called attention to the difference in the common law and the Roman civil law as it existed in Louisiana. By the former a sale of goods is complete without delivery, whereas in Louisiana delivery was essential. Where the owner was domiciled in a common-law state and there assumed to transfer movable property (part of a ship) located in Louisiana, the Louisiana court refused to recognize the transfer as against attaching creditors of the vendor; this on the

[55] Livermore, Dissertations, pp. 127–129. Story, §374 *et seq.*
[56] Kent, Commentaries, ii, p. 406.
[57] §377 *et seq.*
[58] §383.

ground of preventing injustice to local citizens and "What the law protects, it has a right to regulate."[59] He found no fault with the result but objected to the blow which it aimed at the rule that "personal property has no locality."[60]

Unfortunately, Story failed to observe the element which leads to logical and just results without the aid of fictions. This was developed later after a longer period of experience in the courts. Yet the old concepts are still met with from time to time. We are reminded of what Judge Cardozo has said of the "tyranny of concepts." "Concepts are useful, indeed indispensable, if kept within their place. We will press them quite a distance. Many a time they will give rise to rules which might just as well be the opposite were it not that in giving adherence to the opposite we should mutilate the symmetry of the legal order, the relation of its parts, its logical coherence. . . . A time comes, however, when the concepts carry us too far, or farther than we are ready to go with them, and behold, some other concept, with capacity to serve our needs, is waiting at the gate."[61]

This seems especially apposite with reference to the concept that movables have no locality. We have already seen (with reference to the capacity of persons) that the governing law is not that of the domicil for voluntary transactions.[62] Minor correctly points out that the domicil applies to the transfer of a movable by operation of law, for example by marriage, by involuntary assignments in bankruptcy, or by succession, because the law effectuates the involuntary transfer by its influence at the legal situs of the owner. In the case of a voluntary transfer, however, the owner deliberately submits himself to the sovereignty of the state in which the chattels are located.[63] Even Minor still uses the phraseology of the old rule but he points out the correct line of demarcation. Indeed it was precisely in connection with transfers by operation of law upon an entire patrimony or estate, as in the case of inheritance or by marriage, that the old rule was established. Von Bar, a sound analyst, declares that we can scarcely find one instance adduced by the old authors, of its application to a property right in a single or separate article or chattel. The principle of movables following the owner is applied in rights gained

[59] Olivier *v.* Townes, 14 Martin 93, 102.
[60] Story, §390.
[61] Cardozo, The Paradoxes of Legal Science (1927) pp. 62–63.
[62] See *ante*, p. 118.
[63] Minor, §120.

by inheritance and by marriage in order to avoid the result that would ensue by consistently applying the *lex rei sitae*. In this manner a different law might apply to each single movable article belonging to the estate. This was so absurd and impracticable that it was thought necessary to avoid it by the introduction of a fiction and a special rule of law.[64]

Modern conditions have led to the establishment of the principle that the *lex rei sitae* governs the determination of rights in movables, just as it does with respect to immovables. It will require an approach to the actual cases to observe the influence exerted by other systems, such as that of the domicil of the owner, or of the forum, when these are not identical with the situs. Movables are no longer so closely identified in fact with the person of the owner as they once were. Furthermore, as Goodrich points out, modern business is largely conducted through corporations, which frequently have not located their principal operations at the company's technical domicil. The character of the property itself, whether tangible or intangible, exerts an important influence upon the choice of law with reference to it. The *chose in action* represented by the creditor's right to collect his debt and the property represented by shares of stock and other securities is not movable in any physical sense, though the documents may be.

### 4. Tangibles of Transportation

Some things are by their nature and purpose destined to move over long distances and therefore often come under the control of more than one jurisdiction. Ships, aircraft and automobiles represent this class of movables. While it is not intended to suggest that any different rule should apply to the tangibles of transportation, the frequency with which conflicts of law arise with respect to property in these things and the complexity caused by the competition of interests created under different laws have motivated suggestions for a separate regime by which conflicts may be reduced or eliminated. The ownership of seagoing vessels is closely connected with registry in a particular port and the right to the flag. As such they are subjected to Admiralty jurisdiction and will not be dealt with here.

**Vessels in Inland Waters.** Conflicts in respect to the ownership of vessels upon inland waters are so frequent in Europe that a well

[64] Von Bar, The Theory and Practice of Private International Law (Gillespie's trans. 1892) pp. 489–490.

planned movement has been officially initiated to unify the choice of law by international convention. A diplomatic conference of 21 nations was held at Geneva at which three conventions were elaborated dealing with river navigation all of which were signed December 9, 1930. The second of these conventions refers to the registration of such vessels, property rights therein and connected matters.[65] Under the convention, the laws of the country of registration govern the transfer of ownership *inter vivos* and the effect of recording (Art. 20); the same law determines the effect of mortgages upon the vessel and the rights of preferred creditors (Art. 21). The effect of a seizure in aid of civil process made in a country other than that of registration is determined by the laws of the country in which the seizure is made (Art. 36).[66]

**Aircraft.** The choice of law with reference to aircraft may be considered still to be in the formative stage. There is some opinion in favor of homologating ownership to the rule applicable to ships. McNair is of the opinion that while there are certain resemblances in operation, there is no general analogy, and that aircraft are "goods" under the Sales Act.[67] The Air Commerce Regulations of the United States make provision for recording the transfer of ownership of licensed aircraft with the Aeronautics Branch of the Department of Commerce. That a person is the "recorded owner," however, signifies only that he has presented "evidence of ownership acceptable for the purpose of licensing."[68] On the other hand, in France, registration of property rights in aircraft is binding as against third parties. In Italy it constitutes ownership in an absolute sense.[69]

Lewald speaks of a widely-held opinion that ships and aircraft should represent an exception to the rules of private international law relative to property rights; that the *lex rei sitae* should not be made to apply to these things because of the impossibility of having property rights change with every change of local jurisdiction; that the conveniences of commerce demand that they be subjected to some constant system to which these means of transportation are more

[65] League of Nations Official Publications, 1931, viii, 2–5; Conf. 4 D.F. 57–60.

[66] See editorial comment by the author in (1932) 26 Amer. Jour. Int. Law, pp. 121–124.

[67] McNair, The Law of the Air (1932) pp. 132–143.

[68] Sec. 18, Air-Commerce Regulations, effective as amended Sept. 1, 1929, under the Federal Air Commerce Act of May 20, 1926: 44 Stat. 568.

[69] France, Law of May 31, 1924, Arts. 11–12; Italy, Decree of August 16, 1923, Art. 7.

definitely attached, *viz.*, to the law of the flag or the place of registration.[70] This view is, however, subject to the superior control of judicial process *in rem* against the ship or aircraft in a foreign port.[71]

**Property in Vessels Generally.** Dicta to be found in some English decisions rendered during the middle of the last century would seem to indicate that general maritime law governed the authority of the master to transfer property in a British ship while in foreign territorial waters. This was the basis upon which Lushington proceeded as admiralty judge in *The Segredo, otherwise Eliza Cornish.*[72] A British ship recaptured from pirates was on her way to England in charge of a master selected by the navy. She put into the port of Fayal for repairs and under Portuguese law she was condemned as unseaworthy and sold at auction on petition of the master. She was afterwards repaired and brought to England by the purchaser where she was arrested on process brought by the original owner. The court held the sale invalid under the general maritime law by which, as well as by English law, a sale by the master can only be made on the ground of urgent necessity. But there is no general maritime law with inherent force; and so far as the law of England as the owner's law was applied, the doctrine was soon repudiated as we shall presently see. Westlake points out that such a general law or custom only derives authority as English law,[73] and the United States Supreme Court in its decision in *The Scotland*[74] pointed out that the so-called general maritime law is only so far operative as law in any country as it is adopted by the laws and usages of that country.

**Other Tangibles.** The leading case of Cammel *v.* Sewell[75] removed all hesitancy upon the question of principle and may be considered authoritative especially because of later approval given to its dicta by the House of Lords in another case,[76] and its approval by the Restatement in the United States.[77] The action was brought to recover for part of a cargo of wooden deals shipped from Russia aboard a Prussian ship to consignees in England. The ship was wrecked on

[70] Lewald, *Das deutsche Int. Privatrecht* (1931) pp. 191–192.

[71] *Ibid.* p. 193.

[72] (1853) Spinks Eccl. & Adm. 36.

[73] Westlake, Private Int. Law (1925) p. 200.

[74] (1881) 105 U.S. 24, per Bradley, J.

[75] (1860) 5 Hurl. & N. 728.

[76] *Cf.* Castrique *v.* Imrie, (1860) 8 C.B., N.S. 405; affirmed 1870, L.R. 4 E. & I. A. 414.

[77] §50.

the coast of Norway. The cargo was sold by the master at public auction in Norway under protest of the plaintiffs, the underwriters, who endeavored to set aside the sale before a local court. The part of the cargo in suit was shipped by the purchaser to London and trover was brought upon arrival against defendants who had made advances to the new purchaser and who had received possession. The court below had decided for the defendants on the ground that the refusal of the Norse court to set aside the sale must be treated as a judgment *in rem;* but the court on appeal refused to so regard it and affirmed on the real merits as to the passing of the property. Considering the purchase as having been made in good faith, the court held the Norwegian law to be authoritative as the *lex situs* of the property, and this law recognized title in an innocent purchaser even though the master as between himself and the owners of the ship or the cargo could not justify the sale. The court did not find the law as thus stated to be so "barbarous" as not to be recognized. The court compared it to the English law of sale in market overt. The court approved the opinion of the Lord Chief Baron in the court below that "if personal property is disposed of in a manner binding according to the law of the country where it is, that disposition is binding everywhere"; overruling *The Segredo Case,* to which reference has already been made. The strength of the case lies in its application of the rule even where the goods reached the place of transfer by shipwreck and without the consent of the owner; its weakness, in that there was no proof of the Prussian law which was the law of the owner's domicil.

The English doctrine has had definite influence upon the development of the law in the United States. In Cooper *v.* Philadelphia Worsted Co.[78] the plaintiff represented the rights of a vendor of machinery delivered in Pennsylvania to the defendant company under a lease-and-purchase agreement, which the other defendants claimed to be void as against execution creditors in New Jersey. The property had been moved to New Jersey without the consent of the vendor and the vendor contended that the agreement would be construed as a conditional sale in New Jersey and held void for lack of registra-

[78] (1905) 68 N.J. Eq. 622. This case was decided before the adoption of the Uniform Conditional Sales Act which has been interpreted in New Jersey to require filing by a non-resident vendor within ten days of notice of the actual place of removal of the chattel. Non-compliance will defeat a title otherwise validly vested in the state of the original sale. Thayer Mfg. Co. *v.* Bank, (1922) 98 N.J. Law 29; 907.

tion. The court refused to apply the law of New Jersey as to the transfer of title, holding that as the property was located in Pennsylvania at the time of the agreement, and as that law regarded the agreement only as a bailment with an executory contract to purchase, the title remained in the bailor; further that the New Jersey registration statutes were not applicable where the property was brought into the state long after the transaction and without the bailor's consent. The court relied upon the English rule as laid down in the cases already discussed, upon the course of judicial decision in New Jersey consistently supporting the rule, and upon the decisions of the Federal courts, especially Green *v.* Van Buskirk[79] which, because of the frequency with which it is cited, requires our closer attention.

**Green v. Van Buskirk.** The property in question consisted of iron safes located in Illinois which the owner assumed to transfer to Van Buskirk by a chattel mortgage executed in New York. Several days later, Green caused an attachment to be levied on the safes in Illinois and obtained judgment, and the safes were finally sold in satisfaction of his debt against the original owner. Van Buskirk then sued Green in New York by levying upon property belonging to him (Van Buskirk) and the action being sustained by the highest court of New York, a writ of error was sued out in the Federal court under the full faith-and-credit clause. The Supreme Court upheld the validity of the Illinois attachment as a defense against the chattel mortgagee upon the ground that the Illinois court had full jurisdiction. "Attachment laws, to use the words of Chancellor Kent, are legal modes of acquiring title to property by operation of law. They exist in every state for the furtherance of justice, with more or less of liberality to creditors. And if the title acquired under the attachment laws of a state, and which is valid there, is not to be held valid in every other state, it were better that those laws were abolished, for they would prove to be but a snare and a delusion to the creditor." [80]

The case thus involved a conflict of laws in only the qualified sense expressed by Lord Blackburn in delivering the opinion of the judges to the House of Lords in Castrique *v.* Imrie.[81] The rule commonly expressed by English lawyers that a judgment *in rem* is binding everywhere, is in truth but a branch of the more general principle

[79] (1866) 5 Wall. (U.S. Sup. Ct.) 307; (1868) 7 Wall. 139.
[80] Davis, J., (1868) 7 Wall. at pp. 148–149.
[81] (1870) L.R. 4 E. & I. A. at p. 429.

that personal property disposed of in a manner binding at the situs is binding everywhere.

Much of the discussion of the earlier days, as for example by the New York court in Green *v.* Van Buskirk before Federal appeal [82] turns upon the supposed rule of comity to recognize the title obtained at the domicil of the owner, with a rectification if inconsistent with the law of the situs. This doctrine may be traced to Story.[83] It leads to confusion of thought when applied to voluntary transactions. It was originally applied to transfers by operation of law, as by succession or marriage. However, the courts of half a century ago were still trying to fit the doctrine to cases in which movables were surreptitiously removed from the state of domicil to another state wherein an interest is obtained by an innocent purchaser for value, good by the law of the latter state. Surely the jurisdiction of the later situs is paramount but the court says that its law should not be allowed to prevail because comity (always a convenient safety valve) does not require it.[84]

The automobile is *par excellence* a chattel of general utility intended to move speedily over long distances and yet because of its cost is frequently the subject of conditional sale, chattel mortgage or other qualified transfer of title. These conditions give frequent rise to conflicts of law. The following may be taken as a typical case. An automobile was sold and delivered in Tennessee on a part payment agreement, the purchaser giving a chattel mortgage duly recorded for the balance. The purchaser brought the automobile to Arkansas without the seller's consent where it was attached as the property of

[82] (1865) 2 Keyes 119. The court insisted that the jurisdiction of the Illinois court should not signify the application of Illinois law in the instant case.

[83] §§377, 390.

[84] Edgerly *v.* Bush, (1880) 81 N.Y. 199. Movables subject to a chattel mortgage in New York to a New York owner were taken without his consent to Canada and there sold to an innocent purchaser and again resold. The court sustained an action in conversion though title had passed by the law of Lower Canada. In Nichols *v.* Mase (1883) 94 N.Y. 160, the plaintiff as trustee for the holders of certain bonds secured by mortgage of a railroad and of real and personal property located in Connecticut was suing to prevent an attachment by the sheriff in New York upon personal property which had been brought into that state. It was contended that the mortgage was not valid in New York because it did not comply with the chattel mortgage laws. It was, however, valid to pass title to the property under Connecticut laws where the property was then situated. It was held that the mortgage was valid. The court quoted Folger, C. J., in Edgerly *v.* Bush to the effect that the law of the domicil of the owner determines the validity of the transfer of personal property; but the state of the domicil was also that of the situs of the property.

the purchaser. The Arkansas court held that the right of the Tennessee mortgage should be recognized as paramount because the change of situs was made without the mortgagee's consent.[85] The question here is really not so much between two possible governing laws as it is one of the recognition of an acquired or vested right. The conflict of laws, if indeed it can be called such in these cases, relates to two different moments of time. Both the plaintiff's and the defendant's rights have been acquired under a separate *lex situs,* each at a different time; so that the situation may be compared to that of a comet which has first come into range of the solar system, is drawn under the control of the sun, and later, due to its mobility and wide trajectory, drawn under the control of another star. The rights of ownership have been "polarized" in two states. In the instant case, the court yielded to the effects created at the first polarity and this is perhaps the prevailing rule.[86] It is even believed by some that permission by the vendor under a conditional sales agreement to remove the chattel to another state should not cause the owner to lose his prior interest in it, duly vested under the first state's law.[87] We believe, however, that this circumstance is sufficient to turn the equities in favor of an innocent purchaser in the second state. The vendor in fairness must be held to knowledge that the chattel may be the subject of commerce in the new situs under legal conditions different from that of the first state. The question is indeed a close one but the convenience of commerce would seem to place the burden upon the one of two innocent parties who made the deception possible. "Whoever sends personal property to this state or consents to its removal impliedly submits to the regulations of this state concerning its transfer here." [88]

The Restatement of the Law of Conflict of Laws prepared under the auspices of the American Law Institute adopts these conclusions

[85] Wray *v.* White Auto Co., (1922) 155 Ark. 153.

[86] *Cf.* Goetschius *v.* Brightman, (1927) 245 N.Y. 187 and cases cited in (1904) 64 L.R.A. 356, 833 note; *Contra:* Judy *v.* Evans, (1903) 109 Ill. App. 154; Snider *v.* Yates, (1904) 112 Tenn. 309 on the ground of "sound public policy."

[87] Goodrich, (1927) pp. 355, 358.

[88] Lehman, J., in Goetschius *v.* Brightman, *ut cit.* at p. 191 citing Hervey *v.* R.I. Locomotive Works (1876) 93 U.S. 664. See cases cited in 1917, A.L.R.A. 940. The Uniform Conditional Sales Act, §14, provides that the vendor must, within ten days after notice of removal to another state, refile the contract or a copy, in the filing district to which the goods have been removed, in order to protect his rights in that state. The statute has been adopted in nine States, including New Jersey (1919), New York (1922) and Pennsylvania (1925). Amer. Bar Assoc. Report, 1934, p. 745.

in respect to chattel mortgages and conditional sales. If the vendor has not consented to the removal of the chattel, his interest is not "divested as a result of any dealings with the chattel in the second state until the mortgagee (or vendor) has had a reasonable opportunity to remove it from the second state or until the period of adverse possession in the first state has elapsed." [89]

The Restatement further provides that if the mortgagee or conditional vendor has consented to the removal, his interest is not divested by process against or sale by the mortgagor or vendee in the second state unless the law of the second state so provides.[90] But, of course, if the second state does not so provide, there is no conflict.

## 5. Intangible Property

Having accepted the law of the situs as the governing principle in respect to the creation and loss of rights in tangible property, what shall be the rule in respect to intangible property? Where property is intangible, the situs cannot be physical. Where, therefore, shall we locate the proprietary right of creditor or obligee in ordinary debts, in bonds, in negotiable instruments? Where is the ownership in shares of stock? It is true that where the obligation is evidenced by a writing, the paper itself is tangible. The paper itself has no value, however, except as evidence of the right of the creditor or obligee to enforce the debt, or other obligation. A registered share represents the right of the shareholder to receive dividends and, at the proper time, distribution of the property of the corporation. Unless endorsed, it is not negotiable. The paper may only represent the *indicia* of ownership, not the actual property, which resides in that intangible thing which English law still designates by its Norman term, *chose in action,* and which modern Civil law still designates by its Latin term, *obligatio.*

**The Situs of Intangible Property.** The real problem, therefore, is to discover the situs. As Minor expresses it: "Such intangible rights can of course have no real situs, since they exist only in the mind's eye, but it frequently becomes necessary to assign them a situs somewhere, in order to ascertain the law properly applicable to them." [91]

In seeking the objects of taxation, the situs of intangible property of all kinds becomes a matter of judicial investigation but the situs

[89] §§288, 295.
[90] §§289–291; 296–298.
[91] Minor (1901) §121.

of such property for the determination of property rights as between private persons is not necessarily the situs for the determination of jurisdiction to tax. In the United States, as elsewhere, the courts are desirous of assisting the executive arm of government in collecting the revenue upon which all parts of the government depend for their very existence. Thus for the purpose of taxation, courts do not hesitate to regard a debt as located at the domicil of the creditor as well as at the domicil of the debtor. In the former case, it is taxed as property of the creditor; in the latter, as capital employed within the state, even though the owner be a non-resident. Similarly, shares of stock are taxed at the domicil of the shareholder and against the same owner at the domicil of the corporation. The mad race for new objects of taxation and the conflicts between the State and the Federal government and between the States *inter sese* have developed a jurisprudence which is illogical and confusing. It is primarily a question of public law and will not be dealt with here.

The entire subject of double and multiple taxation has been investigated by a committee of experts under the auspices of the Economic and Financial Committee of the League of Nations.[92]

**The Situs of Debts.** Having excluded from discussion jurisdiction over intangibles for the purpose of taxation, we must determine the extent to which an obligation may be considered as property at the domicil of the obligor, and whether it also exists at the domicil of the obligee. Where the obligor and the obligee are not in the same state, does the obligee's proprietary right follow him into that other jurisdiction?

The facts of a leading case may be stated as follows: A. domiciled in North Carolina owes a sum of money to B. domiciled in the same state. B. in turn owes a larger sum to C. domiciled in Maryland. A. makes a business journey to Maryland, and while there, C. causes him to be served with an attachment in an action which C. has brought against B. in Maryland, claiming this debt due to B. is property belonging to B. within the State of Maryland. A. does not contest this process as he admits the debt, and he afterwards pays the judgment entered against him in Maryland. He (A.) is, however, called into court again for the same debt, this time by B. himself in North Carolina. The highest court of North Carolina sustained judgment against him for a second payment upon the ground that Maryland had no jurisdiction over the debt because the debtor was

[92] League of Nations Official Pub., April, 1923, Report E.F.S. 73, F. 19.

never there domiciled. On writ of error, the United States Supreme Court held that A. need not pay again, because Maryland had obtained jurisdiction over the person of the debtor and hence of the debt, even though the debtor was not there domiciled. "The obligation of the debtor to pay his debt clings to and accompanies him wherever he goes. He is as much bound to pay his debt in a foreign state when therein sued upon his obligation by his creditor, as he was in the state where the debt was contracted." [93] It is to be observed that the court laid down what it considers to be a guiding principle of private international law, the "international rule" as it is sometimes designated. However, if the highest court of a state fails to apply the proper international rule in respect to the binding force of a foreign country's judgment as contracted with that of a sister state, there is no recourse on this ground to the Federal courts. Indeed, some State courts have held that the debtor must be domiciled as a basis of jurisdiction; but surely there is an obligation to pay wherever a competent court obtains jurisdiction over the person of the debtor.[94] Without the constitutional provision, the debtor would have been subjected to double payment through no fault of his own.

**The Equity Rule in England.** The Court of Appeal in England recognized the inequity of such a result in Martin *v.* Nadel,[95] where the obligation of a German bank to a judgment debtor was sought to be reached by a garnishee order upon the bank's London branch. The court refused the order, not upon the ground that the debt was contracted in Germany and *prima facie* governed by German law, but because by international law an execution acting thus *in rem* would not be entitled to extraterritorial recognition either by German law, or in the converse case, in England. As the debt would not be discharged it would be *inequitable* to order its payment in England; thus reaching the same conclusion through equity, which the Supreme Court reached through enforcement of the full-faith-and-credit clause of the Constitution.

**Jurisdiction rather than Situs.** The attachment of a debt outside the state in which it was contracted and in which the debtor and creditor are domiciled does not, strictly speaking, involve its true situs but the jurisdiction of the court to compel the debtor to pay it there, and thereupon to discharge the debt.[96] Possibly the concept

[93] Harris *v.* Balk, (1905) 198 U.S. 215.
[94] See Carpenter in (1918) 31 Harv. Law Rev. 905.
[95] (1906) 2 K.B. 26.
[96] See McShane *v.* Knox (1908) 103 Minn. 268.

of a situs for an intangible is in itself fictive. Justice Cardozo has said: "Concepts are useful, indeed indispensable if kept within their place."[97] He quotes John Dickinson as follows: "If we have not identities to work upon, we have at least resemblances; and on their basis can be constructed a legal system which, although far from attaining the inexorable and absolute certainty once thought possible, yet introduces a degree of beneficial order into a world that would be much worse without it."[98] It is some such value that we must ascribe to the concept of situs for such property as by its nature can enjoy a situs only "in the mind's eye." By what law then is a debt to be dealt with validly by its owner?

**The Law Governing Assignment of a Foreign Debt.** We have been considering the jurisdiction which may be exercised *in invitum* over the proprietary right of the creditor in a place foreign to the debtor. What shall be the rule governing a voluntary disposition by the creditor or obligee? The effect of an assignment of a foreign debt and the effect of the foreign assignment of a local debt have both occasioned much difference of opinion due in part to a confusion of ideas, in part to a confusion of terms. Story, with his keen appreciation of the importance of visualizing a conflict from some concrete variance in specific legislation, bases his discussion upon the difference between the law of Scotland, which requires a notice or "intimation" of the assignment to the debtor in order to vest title in the assignee, and the law of England and of the United States, in which title vests immediately. Both Story and Lord Kames, whose opinion he quotes, were inclined to the view that considering a debt as a subject of property in the creditor, an assignment by the creditor, good according to his law, should be valid as a good title for demanding payment in the country of the debtor.[99] Let us proceed to test this view by a leading case. An Australian mercantile company was being wound up in bankruptcy. Part of the winding-up took place in England. An Australian bank had underwritten the company's debentures and as security received a first charge equivalent to an assignment on the unpaid calls for subscriptions to capital stock. This transaction took place in Australia. There were shareholders in both England and Scotland, owing calls. A Scotch com-

[97] The Paradoxes of Legal Science (1930) p. 62.

[98] Dickinson, Administrative Justice and the Supremacy of Law in the United States, p. 131.

[99] Story, §§397–399.

pany commenced a suit against the Australian mercantile company in Scotland and arrested (attached) the obligations of various Scotch shareholders by process in aid of its action. The Australian bank claimed that its assignment, being prior in point of time to the arrestments, should be preferred. The Scotch company insisted that, as the assignment had not been intimated prior to the arrestments, the assignment was not to be preferred under Scotch law where the debtors resided. It was held that though no intimation was required under Australian or English law in order to complete title, an arresting creditor who duly acquired title "according to the law of the country where it is found and arrested, cannot be defeated by showing that if the property had been elsewhere, the title of the Union Bank (the assignee) might have been the preferable one." [100] Curiously enough, the court quotes at some length from the opinion of Lord Loughborough in the same case upon which Story, more than half a century before, had based his reasoning,[101] but does not refer to Story. Lord Loughborough repeats the old maxim that personal property has no locality and explains that this is equivalent only to predicating its subjection to the law which governs the person of the owner.

In the intervening period, as we have seen, a more correct principle came to be recognized.[102] The court acknowledged the principle that a transfer of movable property by the *lex rei sitae* will survive an attack made because of defect in title by the law of the owner's domicil. In other words, the court viewed the title as complete in the subsequent attaching creditor. But this assumes the very point in issue, *viz.*, whether there was anything to attach after a prior assignment of the debt good by the *lex contractus*. Perhaps the result is correct but there is a confusion of ideas which necessitates further analysis.

The term "debt" is often used to refer both to the right of action and to the obligation to pay. A *chose in action* was not assignable under early Roman or the early English law. The practical incon-

[100] *In re* Queensland Mercantile & Agency Co., (1891) 1 Ch. 536. Opinion by North, J. Aff'd, (1892) 1 Ch. 219, upon a different ground but the Court of Appeal did not question the soundness of the principles expressed by the court below.

[101] Sill *v.* Worswick, (1791) 1 H. Black 665, cited in Story §395n.; reprinted 126 Eng. Rep. 379. This case was decided upon the equitable principle that a creditor resident in England would not be allowed to obtain a preference with knowledge of the foreign bankruptcy by attachment in England.

[102] See *ante*, p. 239.

veniences of this rule, especially in periods of economic expansion, led both systems to modify it. The Roman system developed the *cessio actionum* by which the assignee brought the action in the name of the assignor. The English Court of Chancery, following the later Roman law, allowed the assignee to sue in his own name provided he had given consideration and the debtor had had notice, subject however, to all defenses against the assignor.[103] The Judicature Act of 1873, §25, recognizes the right to assign even without consideration if the transfer is in writing. An assignment by parol is valid in equity.[104] The New York Personal Property Act, §41, does not require the transfer of a claim or demand to be in writing. The transferee may sue in his own name, subject to any defense or counterclaim existing against the transferor, before notice of the transfer.

Even though the assignee may sue in his own name, all systems derived from both the common and the civil law regard the obligation as being derivative. *Nemo plus juris ad alienum transferre potest quam ipse haberet.* The assignment in itself does not constitute a new obligation. Minor has well pointed out in referring to debts that "though the right to enforce them follows the owner (the creditor) and his transfer is therefore to be governed by the law of his situs, actual or legal, yet his or his transferee's *ability* to enforce that right may depend upon another jurisdiction and system of law, if he has to resort to another state to sue the debtor." [105]

The courts frequently lose sight of the distinction so admirably expressed. It is sometimes said that the place of performance of the debt governs the validity of the assignment because the assignor and assignee contemplated the application of that law. A draft drawn on a New York bank in which the drawer had funds was made for valuable consideration in Illinois where the drawer was domiciled. Under Illinois law, this constituted an assignment of the account to the extent of the draft but not under New York law. It was held that the effect of the assignment was determinable by New York law because so contemplated.[106] Sometimes the dicta of the cases supports a situs at the domicil of the creditor, sometimes at that of the debtor.[107]

[103] Holland, Elements of Jurisprudence (1910) pp. 309–310.
[104] 4 Halsbury's Laws of England, §796.
[105] Minor, §121.
[106] Abt *v.* Amer. Trust & S. Bank, (1896) 159 Ill. 467.
[107] See (1907) 20 Harvard Law Rev. 637.

**Proprietary Rights in Life Insurance Policies.** In New York Life Insurance Co. *v.* Public Trustee,[108] the plaintiff was seeking a declaration that payments due to German nationals under life insurance policies payable in London were subject to a charge of the British Government under §1 of the Treaty of Peace Order, 1919, made pursuant to the Versailles Treaty. It was contended that these contract debts, in contradistinction to specialty debts, were not located in any other place than at the head office in New York. It was held, however, that as they were payable in London, and as the plaintiff had an office there, the debt was recoverable in London, hence "localized" there by the terms of the original obligation.[109] The difficulty with this conclusion is that the policyholders, the German nationals, were not before the court, and the judgment could therefore not be set up as *res judicata* if action were brought later upon the policies in New York. There was, indeed, some embarrassed recognition of the injustice thus made possible upon the innocent life-insurance company which was endeavoring to protect its other policyholders by avoiding double payment. The court, however, pacified any qualms it might have had on this score by referring to the clearing-office provisions of the Versailles Treaty.[110]

**The American Law Institute's Restatement** treats of the transfer of contractual rights under the heading of "Contracts" and not of "Property." The classification of contracts into "formal" and "informal" adopted in its Restatement of the Law of Contracts (§7) is carried over into its Restatement of the Law of Conflict of Laws. Formal contracts are contracts under seal, recognizances and negotiable instruments and other contracts made formal by statute.[111]

Whether a right under a contract can be transferred is determined by the law of the place where the contract to be transferred was made.[112] To the law of the place of assignment is allocated the determination of the validity of an assignment of an informal contract, the capacity to assign, the formalities necessary to make an effective assignment, its actual effect, and the operation of the assignment between assignor and assignee.[113] To the law of the place of per-

[108] (1924) 131 L.T. 438; reversing [1924] Ch. D. 15.

[109] See opinion by Pollock, M. R., at p. 442.

[110] The Master of the Rolls quotes with approval Dicey's rule that *choses in action* are "generally to be looked upon as situate in the country where they are properly recoverable or can be enforced." *Ibid.* at p. 440.

[111] Restatement, Conflict of Laws, §335.

[112] *Ibid.*, §378.

[113] *Ibid.*, §§380–383.

formance of an assigned contract is allocated the determination of whether the right of the assignee can be destroyed by payment to the assignor, and which of two or more successive assignments shall have priority.[114]

**Law governing Proprietary Rights in Shares of Stock.** Passing now from the relation between debtor and creditor, we have to consider the relation between corporation and shareholder. Here also we are dealing with intangible property although the property right itself is represented by documents called shares which pass readily from hand to hand. Of course where the shares are in bearer form, which is often the practice in Continental European countries, the statutes of the corporation practically identify the stockholder's right of property in the shares, with the document itself which is evidence of that right. In England and the United States, however, bearer shares are almost unknown. Shares are issued in the name of the owner and the by-laws of the corporation almost invariably provide that the shares may only be transferred on the books of the company by the owner himself or by his agent thereunto lawfully authorized. Indeed this is usually stated on the face of the certificate itself so that all parties have notice. Accordingly, a complete transfer of ownership can only take place at the seat of the company and according to the law there in force. Of course, as between the buyer and seller alone, property may be considered as having passed, but so far as the corporation is concerned, or third parties, such as creditors of the shareholder who wish to attach his rights at the seat of the corporation, the law of the seat of the corporation is alone competent to determine who is in fact the real owner of the shares in question.[115]

The stockholder's property is, however, also represented by the certificate itself. As Beale says: "His certificate of stock is by mercantile custom itself a document of value, and may be reached by a court which has control over the corporation itself. What effect a sale on execution would have upon membership in the corporation is a different question. If the certificate has been indorsed in blank by the owner, or is accompanied by such *indicia* of title that a transferee could take, and has been deposited with a resident bailee, the certificate may be reached by garnishment."[116]

[114] *Ibid.*, §§383A–383B.
[115] Jellenik *v.* Huron Copper Co., (1899) 177 U.S. 1.
[116] Beale, (1904) Foreign Corporations, pp. 483–485.

Before the World War, a number of German banks were doing business in England through branch houses. In the course of such business, they held certificates representing shares in various American corporations registered in the names of individuals, not the banks themselves. The shares were indorsed in blank by the persons registered as owners. After the outbreak of the war, the British Parliament enacted legislation appointing a so-called British Public Trustee as custodian of enemy property. Acting under these laws the proper authorities made certain "vesting orders" under which the certificates were actually seized by the Public Trustee and declared to be vested in him. At the close of the war, the British Public Trustee demanded of the American companies that he be registered as the true owner, while the German banks, the original owners, insisted that they alone be so recognized and that new certificates be issued in their name. There was some question as to the interpretation of the Treaty of Versailles but we may leave this aside for the purposes of our discussion. It was practically agreed that if these shares validly passed as property to the Trustee under British law, he was entitled to be registered as such on the books of the company. The German banks contended that the certificates were merely evidence of the shares; that the shares could have no locality except that of the domicil of the company and that they could only be transferred there by operation of law or decree of the court.

The Supreme Court, deciding specifically with respect to shares in the United States Steel Corporation and the law of New Jersey, in which the company was incorporated, said: "It allows an indorsement in blank, and by its law, as well as by the law of England, an indorsement in blank authorizes anyone who is the lawful owner of the paper to write in a name and thereby entitle the person so named to demand registration as owner in his turn upon the corporation's books. But the question who is the owner of the paper depends upon the law of the place where the paper is. It does not depend upon the holder's having given value or taking without notice of outstanding claims but upon the things done being sufficient by the law of the place to transfer title. An execution locally valid is as effectual as an ordinary purchase. The things done in England transferred the title to the Public Trustee by English Law." [117]

Where certificates of stock of a foreign corporation were pledged

[117] Direction der Disconto-Gesellschaft *v.* United States Steel Corp., (1925) 267 U.S. 22.

by the owner, it was held that his interest in the shares could be the subject of attachment in the state in which they are found. "Certificates of stock are treated by business men as property for all practical purposes. They are sold in the market and they are transferred as collateral security for loans, and they are used in various ways as property. They pass by delivery from hand to hand and they are the subject of larceny.[118] It did not appear in the record, however, that the shares had been indorsed in blank, and indeed the sheriff did not take the certificates into his custody. The dissenting opinion, and we believe with much force, emphasized the point that the attachment therefore did not reach "vendible property" within the state.[119] The case was cited later in Holmes *v.* Camp, (1916) 219 N.Y. at p. 368, and approved so far as to support the principle that the interest of a stockholder in a domestic corporation is property having its situs in the state.

In Union National Bank *v.* Hartwell,[120] the question was as to the power of a married woman to give her husband a power of attorney to pledge stock in an Alabama corporation, the parties being domiciled in Louisiana where the transaction took place. The court applied the general rule that the law of the domicil of the husband governs, unless the property, from its peculiar nature, necessarily has an implied locality, or unless the contract is made in the country where the property is situate. Accordingly, the power of attorney was held void under Louisiana law. The court did not regard the necessity for registration of stock in Alabama as compelling stockholders to conform to Alabama laws in respect to contracts dealing with the stock. "The mode of transfer and the capacity to contract in respect to such stocks are distinct and independent matters."[121]

In Loftus *v.* Farmers' & M. Nat. Bank,[122] the plaintiff, a married woman, was the owner of certain registered debts of the City of Philadelphia which she sought to transfer after her marriage, by power of attorney executed in Pennsylvania. She was domiciled abroad with her husband, an English subject, and the transfer agent refused the transfer contending that under English law she was without capacity to make the transfer without the authority of her husband. It was held, however, that as the wife was capable by the

[118] Gray, J., in Simpson *v.* Jersey City Contracting Co., (1900) 165 N.Y. 193.
[119] *Ibid.*, Dissenting opinion by Landon, J. at p. 203.
[120] (1887) 84 Ala. 379.
[121] At p. 382.
[122] (1890) 133 Pa. 97.

law of the situs of the obligation, the transfer was valid. The court (per Mitchell, J.) recognized the rule of the *lex domicilii,* but only to the extent that it was not inconsistent with the law of the situs. "Indeed it may be said that the tendency of modern authorities under the influence of the Continental European jurisprudence, is towards the recognition of the law of the situs, to such an extent that what was an exception is tending to become the rule." [123]

It is not necessary to conclude that the same rule applies to capacity to deal with personal property through agreements to sell or pledge. In the case just mentioned, there was a clear question of the transfer of the title itself upon the records of the debtor within the state.

**Law Governing Transfer of Rights Growing out of Negotiable Instruments.** As negotiable instruments are used by merchants to facilitate payments and as ready means of credit, they are, by their very nature, designed to be transferable by endorsement and delivery. "Doubtless bills of exchange," says Jenks, "which, as we have seen, were familiar to English eyes before the end of the sixteenth century, were popularly regarded as 'property' from an early date; but the Common Law persisted in treating them as mere rights of action, alienable only by reason of their inheritance from the Law Merchant. It was not till the advent of patents, copyright, stock, and shares, that the true importance of *choses in action* appeared. For these interests could not possibly be regarded as mere rights of action; they were far too positive and comprehensive, though the French term for a share (*'action'*) suggests that in one country, at least, the idea of procedural rights clung tenaciously." [124]

With the intimate identification of the right of action with the instrument itself, it would seem to follow that the rule applicable to tangible movables should apply to bills and notes. But the English Bills of Exchange Act (§72.2) provides that an inland bill indorsed in a foreign country shall be interpreted, as regards the payor, by the law of the United Kingdom. Thus if the indorsement is invalid by the foreign law, the holder may nevertheless recover if it was good by English law.[125]

What shall be the rule where the bill is not an inland bill and

[123] At p. 112, quoting Dicey on Domicil, Rule 57: "Where there is a conflict between a title, under the law of the country where a movable is situated and under the law of the owner's domicil, the *lex situs* will in general prevail."

[124] Jenks, A Short History of English Law, p. 275.

[125] So in Lebel *v.* Tucker, (1867) 3 Q.B. 77, decided prior to the Act.

where the parties must have contemplated the possibility of indorsement in countries foreign to the drawer or acceptor? A leading case will illustrate. A check was drawn by a Roumanian bank to plaintiffs, or order, on a London bank and was indorsed to G. E. & Co., a London firm, by the plaintiffs. The check was stolen and, on a forged indorsement of the name of G. E. & Co., cashed in good faith in Vienna by a Viennese firm, who, in turn, cashed it through defendants in London. The payees now sue for the conversion of the check. Under Austrian law, and indeed in Continental countries generally, the holder of a bill, note, or check, which he acquires bona fide for value and without gross negligence is entitled to recover thereon even though the instrument was stolen and the indorsement forged. It was held by way of analogy to the validity of a transfer of chattels, that the defendants were not guilty of conversion, having obtained a good title at the place of indorsement and delivery of the check.[126]

The New York Court of Appeals has held in an action by the indorsee against the drawee that a bill drawn abroad upon a drawee domiciled in New York, and therefore payable there, is validly indorsed if the indorsement conforms to New York law. The indorsement was made in New Granada where the law would have regarded an indorsement in the form actually used, to be only a power of attorney to collect. The court indicated that as between indorser and indorsee the conclusion would have been different but that the drawer must have contemplated that whatever would be understood to be the payee's order at the place of payment, was the thing intended by that expression in the bill.[127]

Two recent cases indicate that the trend of American judicial thought is away from Story's theoretical rule of domicil and toward the convenient rule of the *lex rei sitae*. In Weissman *v.* Banque de Bruxelles,[128] the plaintiffs were the assignees of the receiver of a New York bankrupt corporation. The defendant was a Belgian bank. A check drawn by the United States Treasury in favor of the bankrupt corporation for a refund of income taxes was surreptitiously indorsed by its former president in the name of the corporation and mailed to the defendant in Belgium who forwarded it to a bank in

[126] Embiricos *v.* Anglo-Austrian Bank, (1905) 1 K.B. Div. 677.

[127] Everett *v.* Vendryes, (1859) 19 N.Y. 436. Approved but distinguished in Amsinck *v.* Rogers, (1907) 189 N.Y. 261. *Accord:* Woodruff *v.* Hill, (1874) 116 Mass. 310.

[128] (1930) 254 N.Y. 488.

Washington for collection. The proceeds were thereafter appropriated to the personal use of the former president. Under Belgian law, there was no duty to inquire as to the legal title of the check, the indorsement being adequate on its face and the bank having no notice of the fraud. By New York law, the forged indorsement carried no title. The Court of Appeals decided that the defendant bank was only the agent of the indorser. There was no proof that the check was removed from New York without the consent of the true owner. When it went outside of Belgium to collect, it was in the same position as if the bank had sent its agent to New York to collect. In the absence of proof the law of the District of Columbia must be assumed to be the same as the common law of New York governing commercial transactions. Judge Pound quotes the rule tentatively adopted by the American Law Institute that where property is taken into another state without the consent of the owner, his title may not be divested by operation of its laws unless the chattel has become incorporated into the general mass of property located therein by failure to remove the chattel after a reasonable opportunity so to do, or if the statute of limitations has run, or if some other act or omission has rendered it inequitable for the owner to remove it.

Judge Pound did not apply this rule, however, because it did not appear affirmatively that the check was taken from New York without the consent of the corporation. The doctrine thus tentatively stated seems to have been derived from the older case of Edgerly *v.* Bush,[129] in which it was held that title to an owner of chattels in New York is not divested by the surreptitious removal of the thing into another state, and the sale of it there under different laws. Judge Pound adopts this as a satisfactory rule to apply to commercial specialties, such as bills, notes and checks, which is practically the doctrine of the Embiricos case. When the Restatement was finally adopted, the section was greatly altered so as to provide that except to the extent to which title to a chattel is embodied in a document (in which event the title is subject to the jurisdiction of the state having jurisdiction over the document), "a state can exercise through its courts jurisdiction over a chattel within the territory of the state, though a person owning or claiming the chattel or an interest in the chattel is not subject to the jurisdiction of the state." A caveat adds that the Institute expresses no opinion as to whether a state has

[129] (1891) 81 N.Y. 199.

jurisdiction over a chattel brought in without the consent of the owner.[130]

In a recent Supreme Court case, a United States Treasury check was sent to an American veteran in Jugoslavia where it was cashed by another person under a forged indorsement. The law of Jugoslavia, like that of many other European countries, recognizes title as passing by the delivery of a negotiable instrument under an indorsement apparently genuine where the indorsee has no notice of the forgery. The court held that the transfer of title to such an instrument must be governed by the *lex rei sitae,* as in the case of chattels generally, where the owner has consented to its removal to the country of transfer.[131] The government contended that the guarantee of prior indorsements made by the defendant Trust company on collecting from the Federal Reserve Bank of New York was an independent contract governed by New York law by which law the genuineness of the prior indorsements was guaranteed. The court (per Brandeis, J.) interpreted such guarantee as being only to the effect "that the indorsements were effective to give to the holder a legal title and the right to enforce payment of the check."

The American Law Institute in its Restatement follows the principle adopted by the Embiricos and Weissman cases.[132]

Lorenzen is of the opinion that so far as concerns the substantive law, it is merely a question of commercial policy as to whether the Anglo-American or the Continental rule is preferable. There is no moral issue. He suggested that the proposed international unification of the law of negotiable instruments should provide that the respective party should be held if the holder has acquired title either in accordance with the *lex contractus* or the law of the place of transfer.[133]

**The International Convention signed at Geneva, June 7, 1930,** provides, however, that the possessor of a bill, note or check is deemed the lawful holder if he establishes his title through an uninterrupted series of indorsements. Where a person has been dis-

[130] Restatement, §102. Where title is embodied in a document, jurisdiction is assigned to the state which has jurisdiction over the document, subject to the right of the state in which the chattel is located to enforce interests growing out of acts done to preserve the chattel, or by reason of the state's police and taxing powers and its power of eminent domain. §§50–52.

[131] United States *v.* Guaranty Trust Co., (1934) 293 U.S. 340.

[132] Restatement §349. "The validity and effect of a transfer of a negotiable instrument are determined by the law of the place where the instrument is at the time of the transfer."

[133] Lorenzen, Conflict of Laws relating to Bills and Notes (1919) p. 140.

possessed of a bill or note in any manner whatsoever, the holder who establishes his right as provided is not bound to give it up unless he acquired it in bad faith or with gross negligence.[134] The separate convention which regulates the conflict of laws, signed on the same day, provides that the effects of the obligations of the acceptor of a bill or the maker of a note shall be determined by the law of the place of payment, and the effect of the signatures of the parties, by the law of the country in which the signatures were affixed.[135] The law of the country in which the obligations arising out of a check have been assumed determines the effect of such obligations.[136] The conventions thus adopt what may be called the Continental system. The parties reserve the right not to apply the principles of private international law contained in the conflicts-of-law conventions so far as concerns an obligation undertaken outside the territory of one of the parties.[137] It would therefore seem that the conventions leave the application of the law in *statu quo* in respect to the effect of a forged indorsement, where the obligation to pay the bill, note, or check was undertaken in England or the United States.

**Comparison of Laws on Assignment of a Debt.** In France, Italy, Spain, many of the Latin-American countries and others following the system of the Napoleonic codes, an assignment of a claim or other incorporeal right against a third party becomes effective between the assignor and assignee at the time of the delivery of the instrument of transfer; but as against third parties, the assignee is seized of the right only upon notice of the assignment given to the debtor or by recognition of the assignment given by the debtor in an official instrument.[138] In Austria and Germany the assignee takes the place of the creditor from the moment of the agreement but the debtor is, of course, fully protected in his dealings with the former creditor even after the assignment, unless he had

[134] Convention providing a Uniform Law for Bills of Exchange and Promissory Notes. League of Nations Official Publications, C. 346, M. 142, 1930, ii, Art. 16 (bills), Art. 77 (notes). Convention providing a Uniform Law for Cheques, signed at Geneva, Mar. 19, 1931. League of Nations Official Publications, C. 458, M. 195, 1931, ii B., Arts. 19, 21, 35.

[135] Convention for the Settlement of Certain Conflicts of Laws in connection with Bills of Exchange and Promissory Notes, June 7, 1930. Official No. C. 347, M. 143, 1931, ii, Art. 4.

[136] Convention for the Settlement of Certain Conflicts of Laws in Connection with Cheques, Mar. 19, 1931. Official No. C. 459 M. 196, 1931, ii B., Art. 5.

[137] *Ibid.* Art. 10 (1) as to Bills and Notes, Art. 9 (1) as to Checks.

[138] France, Civ. Code, Arts. 1689–1691; Italy, Civ. Code, Arts. 1538–1540. Latin America: Argentine Civ. Code, Art. 1459; Brazil, Art. 1069; Chile, Art. 1902. See also E. Obregón, Latin-American Commercial Law (1921) p. 390.

knowledge of the assignment.[139] The same would appear to be the law in Switzerland except that the assignment must be in writing.[140]

**Foreign Rules of Conflicts in regard to Assignment of Debts.** The scope and nature of the original obligation created under the control of one system of law cannot be altered by its transfer within another system. If a debt is incurred under a system which does not permit the creditor to assign his rights, the assignment would not be valid even if made in a country where there is no such prohibition.[141] This result will be found in accordance with common-law conceptions but some writers are inclined to extend the control of the law of the original obligation, the debtor's law, to include also the conditions under which an assignable debt may be assigned. The French writer, Arminjon, and the Austrian, Walker, favor this principle even for determining whether it is necessary to give notice of the assignment to the debtor in order to complete its validity as against third parties. This is the principle which seems to be gaining ground in Continental Europe.[142] The courts have not always sustained this view. A leading case will illustrate the issues involved. The defendant, a domiciled German, bought some cotton at Havre, payable in ten days by acceptance of a draft against delivery of documents. The vendor drew upon the defendant at Havre for the sale price and indorsed the draft with the documents to a French bank which discounted it. Under French law this constituted an assignment of the underlying debt even before acceptance; under German law it did not. The bank sued defendant in Germany upon the assignment. The *Reichsgericht* held that the obligation of the debtor being determinable by German law, the validity of the assignment was also *prima facie* determinable by that law. German law however recognizes the autonomy of the parties in the assignment of an assignable debt and therefore the transaction between assignor and assignee having taken place in France, French law would be referred to in order to determine the implication to be drawn from the act of indorsing the draft.[143]

139 Austria, Civ. Code, 1395, 1396. German Civ. Code, 398–407.

140 Swiss Code of Obligations as revised by the Federal Act of Mar. 30, 1911, Arts. 165–166.

141 Meili, Int. Civil and Comm. Law (Kuhn's trans.) p. 320. German Civ. Code, §14.

142 Arminjon, *Précis de Droit int. privé* (1929) ii, p. 322. Walker, *Int. Privatrecht* (1924) p. 418.

143 *Reichsger.*, Mar. 19, 1907, Clunet, 1910, p. 227.

While the dictum of the foregoing decision may not appear entirely in harmony with the predominant principle, the case does not directly draw into issue a direct interest of third parties contesting the validity of the assignment completed under the foreign law. This occurred however in the following case. A German bought merchandise from a Frenchman in France and the vendor after delivery drew a draft for the purchase-price on the vendee and indorsed the draft to the plaintiff, a banker, at Paris. Before the draft was presented for acceptance, the debt was attached by another creditor, the vendor having been declared bankrupt in the interval. The bank thereupon sued the vendee for non-acceptance. The law of the obligation itself must determine whether the assignment validly passed title to the assignee of the creditor's rights, and as an indorsement of an unaccepted draft has no such effect in Germany, the complaint was dismissed.[144]

A different view is sometimes taken where the question is not the validity of the transfer itself but its consummation by notice to the debtor. Where the transfer takes place in a country which, like France, requires notice to be given to the debtor before the transfer becomes effective, the question arises whether the transfer will be regarded valid in the debtor's state where no such notice need be given. As the notice must proceed from the assignor, it is at his domicil that the act must be completed; therefore if required there, the assignment will not be considered valid, even by the debtor's law, unless notice is given.[145] Where the debtor's law requires notice to be given and the assignment would have been good, the formalities of notice required by the law of the obligation will be demanded even in the country of the assignment. A French life insurance policy transferred by an assignment in Germany good by German law was nevertheless seized under attachment and ordered delivered to a subsequent attaching creditor by the *Reichsgericht* because the formalities demanded by the French law (Art. 1690, Civil Code) had not been observed;[146] and the judgment was afterwards granted *exequatur* in France.[147]

[144] *Oberlandesger.*, Hamburg, Dec. 15, 1900, Clunet, 1905, p. 669.

[145] *Oberlandesger.*, Frankfort, Mar. 4, 1892; Clunet, 1894, p. 150. *Accord: Reichsger.* Dec. 3, 1891, Clunet, 1892, p. 1039 and note.

[146] *Reichsger.*, June 2, 1908, *Zeitschrift für Int. Privat. u. öffentliches Recht*, 1908, p. 449.

[147] Clunet, 1910, p. 162. *Accord:* Clunet, 1910, p. 155, in which the debtor was domiciled in France and the assignment was made in Germany.

A further source of conflict lies in the difference between the laws of some countries like Germany and Switzerland, and the laws of countries based upon the French Code. The transfer of a subjective right is regarded in Germany and Switzerland as an abstract or independent transaction, *i.e.*, not dependent for its validity upon any underlying *causa* or consideration passing between the parties, while in France the transfer is regarded as a causal or collateral transaction dependent for its validity upon the underlying transaction between the parties.[148] Lewald emphasizes the necessity of separating the transfer from the underlying transaction. Often they are both combined in the same instrument. Thus, where a debt is sold and assigned by the same instrument, the contractual relations between the parties are determined by the law applicable to the sale but the validity of the transfer depends upon the law of the debtor's obligation. A debt due by an Austrian to a German was sold and assigned by the German creditor to another German in Germany. Under Austrian law (Civ. Code §1397) the assignor would be held liable for the collectibility of the debt but not by German law. The *Reichsgericht* held that the liability of the assignor was determinable by German law as the law controlling the underlying relationship between the parties.[149]

The Bustamante Code ratified by 15 *Latin-American* countries adopts the principle of the *lex rei sitae* and allocates instruments evidencing credits of all kinds to "their ordinary or normal situation," and debts to the place of payment, and if that is not fixed, then to the domicil of the debtor.[150] This is not always identical with the law applicable to the debtor's obligation but in many cases it will coincide with it. Arminjon rightly warns against a reference to domiciliary law as such, when the question is not at all one of personal law.[151]

The Bustamante Code is in substantial accord with the Geneva Conventions for the Unification of the Law of Negotiable Instruments.[152] On the other hand, the provisions relating to the forgery, theft, or loss of credit-documents and bonds payable to bearer, if

[148] Lewald, *Int. Privatrecht* (1931) p. 271; Tuhr, *Schweiz. Obligationenrecht*, p. 719; De Ruggiero, *Istituzioni di diritto civ., ii,* p. 176. Planiol, *Traité élémentaire de Droit Civil,* (1905) ii, §§1026–1041.

[149] *Reichsger.*, Dec. 3, 1891, Clunet, 1892, p. 1039. Lewald, pp. 274–275.

[150] Arts. 106–107. English translation in "The International Conferences of American States 1889–1928" (1931) p. 337. Arts. 110, 111 and 113 would seem to be ambiguous without authoritative interpretation.

[151] Arminjon, ii, p. 322.

[152] See *ante*, p. 256.

intended to cover acquisition of title by those not claiming through the original owner, depart from the principles we have been discussing in that laws dealing with these subjects are declared to be of an "international public order," which would seem to eliminate reference to the law of the country in which alleged title is acquired, unless it be in the country of the forum.[153]

**Foreign Rules of Conflict as to Acquisition of Lost or Stolen Securities.** A sharp conflict of legislation exists in respect to title which may be acquired in bearer securities which have been lost or stolen and afterwards acquired in good faith by a purchaser for value. The French Civil Code (Arts. 2279–2280) while establishing the principle that "possession is equivalent to title with respect to personal property," still allows the claim to possession of the original owner within three years from the loss or theft. If the purchaser acquired it at a fair or market or at public sale, or from a tradesman selling similar goods, the original owner must reimburse the price paid. By the German Civil Code (§§932, 935) and the Swiss Civil Code (§935) however, a sale in good faith confers ownership even though the thing does not belong to the seller, so far as concerns money, bearer securities, or (in Germany) things sold at public auction. By the Italian Commercial Code (Art. 57) bearer securities which have been lost or stolen cannot be reclaimed except from the finder or thief or from one who has received them in bad faith.

A leading case will illustrate the problems to which this divergence of legislation gives rise. Bonds of a French railway, payable to bearer, were stolen in France and carried to Italy, where they were bought in good faith after a lapse of two years. The purchaser sent the bonds to France for sale where they were seized under a revindication proceeding brought within three years as permitted by French law. The purchaser maintained that complete title had been acquired in Italy before the securities were sent back to France. The court held, however, that even though title may have been perfected under the law of the situs in Italy, it was divested again under French law by the return of the securities to France followed by the proceeding of revindication allowed by French law.[154] The court proceeds upon the assumption that shares and bonds of corporations, even

[153] Art. 272. Art 273 requires the observance of the law of the place of the theft or forgery as well as of the place of negotiation and of the place of payment. But this article manifestly refers to administrative requisites for cancellation or re-issue and not to laws of title.

[154] Clunet, 1910, p. 898.

though in bearer form, must be deemed located at the debtor's domicil, *i.e.*, the seat of the company. Although this is opposed to the general view, it sufficiently explains the unsatisfactory result, because the title was therefore, in the view of French jurisprudence, never completed in Italy.[155]

A more logical doctrine has been applied by the German *Reichsgericht*. Bearer bonds which had been stolen in England, had been negotiated through several transactions in England, and finally sold to the defendant. The claim of the original owner was rejected upon the ground that title had been perfected pursuant to English law and that the measure of the good faith of the last purchaser was that of the English and not of the German law.[156]

The Institute of International Law at its Ghent session in 1906 recommended the application of the law of the place of negotiation in respect to the acquisition of title in bearer securities, lost by or stolen from the original owner, without regard to the domicil or seat of the debtor company. If a good title has been obtained by the purchaser under the law in force at the place of negotiation, the subsequent removal to another jurisdiction will not entitle the owner to claim; conversely, if no title was obtained at the place of purchase, the owner may reclaim even though the securities have been removed to a jurisdiction in which a good title might have been obtained if purchased there.[157] Whereas there may be some doubt as to whether the phrase "place of negotiation" assumes that the instrument was in that place, the context would seem to so indicate and the provision is therefore substantially in accord with the Restatement of the American Law Institute.[158]

The French statutes of June 15, 1872, and February 8, 1902, permit the owner of a lost or stolen bearer-security to publish an "opposition against negotiation" in a bulletin indicated by the statute, so that even a purchaser for value shall not subsequently acquire a good title. The obligor of the bond or the maker of the negotiable instrument or the corporation issuing the shares, as the case may be, may be served with an "opposition against payment." Suppose the security was lost or stolen in France and acquired by an innocent purchaser in Germany. Under German law, the purchaser would have

[155] *Cf.* Clunet, 1889, p. 688; 1893, p. 596; 1910, p. 902 note.
[156] Clunet, 1898, p. 378.
[157] Clunet, 1907, p. 323.
[158] §349.

obtained a good title because of the rule of *lex rei sitae,* but the French statutes would bar the practical benefits of title. The German law would still permit a right of recourse against the vendor.[159]

**Law Applicable to Transfer of Literary and Artistic Property.** An unusual problem was presented to the French courts with respect to the literary and artistic property of the Russian composers Moussorgsky and Rimsky-Korsakoff, especially as to the exclusive right of representation in France of their well known opera *"Boris Godounov."* The rights of the composers for exclusive production in France had been sold and assigned to a Belgian national, by contracts valid by Russian law, made in Russia as early as 1874, 1875 and 1886. The first public representation was made in Russia. The Soviet government in 1918, having "nationalized" the works of the composers then long since dead, and having denounced the treaties with France relating to literary and artistic property, the heirs of the assignee were obliged to rely upon the common law of France. The court held that by publicly producing the work, the authors had not renounced their rights in France. With this part of the decision, however, we are not here concerned.[160] The court further held that the right of authorship resembles a right *in rem* and is not a purely personal right; that it would therefore be improper to apply the personal law of the author in determining the validity of transfer; that situs of the property-right in a musical work is transferred to France every time it is produced there; that a right was thus created in France born of the representation itself, and that this was independent of the law of origin; that therefore the French law was applicable.[161]

The conclusion reached would seem to be amply sustainable on the ground that the transfer of the composer's rights was validly accomplished under Russian law, creating an acquired right in the purchaser over which the Russian state no longer had jurisdiction at the time of the nationalization decree of 1918. It cannot be cogently maintained that the right was independent of the law of origin (Russia) as the court based the right of representation upon

[159] German Civ. Code, §437, (1). *Cf.* Nussbaum, *op. cit.,* (1932) pp. 333–334. Clunet, 1930, p. 688.

[160] This ruling is contrary to the decision of the Court of Cassation rendered in 1857 in respect to the operas of Verdi, which having been first produced in Italy, were not accorded protection in France. This branch of the case is criticized by Boucher in Clunet, 1932, p. 26.

[161] Civil Trib. of the Seine, Feb. 14, 1931, Clunet, 1932, p. 114 at p. 140.

the original contracts with the composers. Having once established that Russian law had created an assignable right and that this right had been exercised in France so as to give it recognition as an enforceable right also in France, the Russian law could no more reinvest the original owners or their successors with the right, than it could declare that goods sold and delivered abroad before the decree should become the property of the Russian state.

## Chapter X

# CONTRACTS

### 1. Formal Validity

It is indeed a striking paradox that in a period in which technical facilities for international commerce are increasing by leaps and bounds, the political and legal barriers to international commerce are likewise increasing. The ease and rapidity of communication and transportation by land, by sea and through the air, open the way for the most extended variety of contractual relations. Acts connected with the making and the performance of a contract frequently take place in more than one country so that the interpretation and enforcement of the contract are frequently subject to determination by two or more possible systems of law.

Story treats of conflicts of law in respect to contracts under the heading "Foreign Contracts," but it is often not a simple matter to determine when a contract is foreign and when it is domestic.[1]

**Early Nature of Contracts.** An obligatory contract is a species of agreement; but many agreements produce no legal effect upon the relations of the parties one to another. It is only to those promises of which the state sees fit to take cognizance that it will lend its force to assure performance.[2] Sir Henry Maine informs us that neither ancient law nor any other source discloses a society entirely destitute of the conception of contract. "At first, nothing is seen like the interposition of law to compel the performance of a promise. That which the law arms with its sanctions is not a promise, but a promise accompanied with a solemn ceremonial."[3] The formal

[1] Story, §231 *et seq.*

[2] Holland, Elements of Jurisprudence (1910) p. 257.

[3] Maine, Ancient Law (1864) p. 303. Holland points out that there has been some controversy as to whether formal or informal contracts are historically earlier, but recent investigators are led to the conclusion that complexity rather than simplicity is the characteristic of primitive customs. *Op. cit.*, p. 275.

contract of the classic period of the Roman law was the *stipulatio* or solemn question and answer. The form in the classic period consisted of certain words or a ceremony, while in later periods, emphasis was laid upon a writing, often with the addition of a seal or the authentication by some public official.

**Form of the Contract.** It is clear that if the forms and ceremonies prescribed at the place where the agreement is made are essential to its validity, no contract can be constituted without their observance. On the other hand, if the forms and ceremonies required at the place of celebration have been complied with, the omission of other or different forms required by the law of the place of performance, or at the place where it is sought to enforce the contract, will not affect its validity. Whether the courts of such other state will enforce the contract is another matter.

We shall later observe the principle prevailing in Anglo-American jurisdictions according to which the requirement that certain contracts be in writing is viewed as a rule of evidence and are therefore regulated by the law of the forum governing procedure.[4]

The English Bills of Exchange Act,[5] expressly adopts the rule that "the validity of a bill as regards form is determined by the law of the place of issue and the validity as regards requisites in form of the supervening contracts, such as acceptance or endorsement, or acceptance supra protest, is determined by the law of the place where such contract was made." Where a bill issued abroad complies with the formal requisites of the law of the United Kingdom, it is validly enforceable as between persons who there negotiate, hold or become parties to it.[6]

In the United States there has been some confusion and two leading cases decided before the adoption of the Negotiable Instruments Law relating to the validity of oral acceptances have left doubt as to the correct principle applicable to the form of contracts generally. In Scudder *v.* Union National Bank,[7] action was brought upon a bill drawn in Illinois upon a Missouri firm payable in Missouri to an Illinois bank. The partner of the Missouri firm had orally promised in Illinois to accept the bill. It was held that though an oral promise to accept a bill was invalid in Missouri, yet the law of the

[4] See *post*, p. 273.
[5] §72. The Negotiable Instruments Law does not contain a parallel provision.
[6] *Ibid.*, §72 (1) b.
[7] (1875) 91 U.S. 406.

place of making the promise recognized its validity and the payee could recover. The court treated the promise to accept as an actual acceptance under Illinois law and hence "no question of jurisdiction or of conflict of law arises."[8] In Hall *v.* Cordell,[9] however, the promise to accept was made by an Illinois firm in Missouri where an agreement to accept must be in writing, and the same court held that as the place of performance was to be in Illinois, the parties must have contemplated Illinois law with reference to the performance of the contract. The dicta of the cases would seem inconsistent but in the earlier case the contract to accept was equivalent to acceptance; hence it was an executed contract in Illinois; in the later case, the contract was executory and there is nothing in the Missouri statute to make invalid such a promise although no person within the state could be charged thereon. The confusion lies in the court's reference to the will of the parties, which could not validate that to which the law at inception gave no recognition. Lorenzen suggests that the cases may be harmonized if *locus regit actum* is to be viewed as permissive; so that the formal validity may rest either upon the *lex loci celebrationis* or the law which governs the validity of the transaction in other respects.[10]

Support has been given to the view taken in the Hall-Cordell case by English courts. The greater formality required by the laws of Continental countries for the execution of bills and notes has given us English precedents. Bills were drawn in the English form in France and in the French language on an English company which duly accepted them. The drawer indorsed the bills in France in form good by English law but not by the French, under which the indorsement would not make the bills negotiable and free from equities. The court held that the bills being payable in England in English form and likewise indorsed in English form, the bill in question was "intended to be" an English bill "for all purposes, at all events as regards the acceptors of the bill."[11] Accordingly, the acceptor was held liable although its contracts and those of the indorser would have been invalid according to French law.

Similarly a marriage settlement invalid in the country where made, has been upheld in England "if it relates to the regulation of property

[8] At pp. 412–413.

[9] (1891) 142 U.S. 116. *Accord:* Hubbard *v.* Exchange Bank, (1896) 76 Fed. 234; Bank of Laddonia *v.* Bright-Coy C. Co., (1909) 139 Mo. App. 110.

[10] Lorenzen, Conflict of Laws relating to Bills and Notes (1919) p. 89.

[11] *In re* Marseilles Extension R. & L. Co., (1885) 30 Ch. D. 598, at p. 602.

subject to the laws and within the jurisdiction of" that country.[12]

There seem to be no decisions or dicta in England or the United States subjecting the requisites of form to an exclusive system. Lorenzen points out that the question as to what law shall govern seems still to be regarded as a part of the larger and more complex problem relating generally to the obligation and validity of contracts, and subject to the same uncertainty.[13] We shall presently consider how far the intention of the parties should be permitted to function in regard to the selection of law governing the form of contracts.[14]

**The Place of Contracting.** A preliminary question presents itself. In what state has the contract come into existence? The parties need not be in each other's presence and are therefore frequently within different states at the time of negotiation. The place of the agreement may be determinative of the law controlling its interpretation and effect. It may even be determinative of whether a legally binding contract has come into existence at all. Holland, with his accustomed clarity, says: "That which gives validity to a legal right is, in every case, the force which is lent to it by the state. Anything else may be the occasion, but is not the cause, of its obligatory character." [15] Negotiations carried on by exchange of letters, by telegrams, by telephone or radiophone, may result in an agreement to which the state in which one of the parties was located would give legal sanction, whereas the state in which the other party was located would not.

An intrastate case will illustrate the principles of contract which remain applicable also where there is a conflict of law. In Bank of Yolo *v.* Sperry Flour Co.,[16] the cashier of the plaintiff called up the agent of the defendant on the long-distance telephone and offered to advance money to a prospective purchaser of defendant's wheat if the defendant would honor the purchaser's draft in an amount stated, to which the defendant's agent agreed. To the question whether the contract was made in the plaintiff's or the defendant's county, the court answered as follows: "A contract is supposed to be made at some place, and the place where it becomes complete is the place where it is made. If a contract is made by exchange of letters

[12] Van Grutten *v.* Digby, (1862) 32 L.J. Ch. 179. *Accord: Re* Bankes, Reynolds *v.* Ellis, [1902] Ch. 333.

[13] Lorenzen in 20 Yale Law Jour. (1911) 427, 442.

[14] See *post*, p. 272.

[15] Holland, Elements of Jurisprudence, (11th ed., 1910) p. 82.

[16] (1903) 141 Cal. 314.

or telegrams, it is held to have been made at the place where the letter is mailed, or telegram filed, containing an unconditional acceptance by one party of the offer of the other. If the communications are oral, either with or without the telephone, between parties on opposite sides of a county line, the same principle would seem to require that the contract should be deemed to have been made in the county where the offer of one is accepted by the other—in this case in Sacramento." The place where the last act necessary to complete it was done will determine the place of execution.

The Restatement expresses the view of the court in the case last cited by declaring: "In case of an informal unilateral contract, the place of contracting is where the event takes place which makes the promise binding."[17]

Under the Restatement, the place of contracting is determined by the law of the forum. This place is determined by the law of contracts in force in the forum, not by the conflict-of-laws rule. It may be that the law of the forum may not regard the particular state of facts to be such as to constitute a contract; yet if the place of contracting is not at the forum it may be that the law of some other state will determine whether or not a contract has come into existence.[18] It may therefore be that at the place of contracting, no valid contract came into existence. Whether a contract exists is a question of the substantive law of the forum. Whether the alleged contract will be recognized and enforced by other states is a question of conflict of laws.[19]

Formal contracts are contracts under seal, recognizances and negotiable instruments, and other contracts given by statute the character of formal contracts. Where the contract is formal and becomes effective on delivery, the place of contracting is where the delivery is made.[20] When a document embodying a contract is to be delivered by mail or common carrier, the place of contracting is where the document is posted or is received by the carrier.[21]

**Principles of Foreign Systems as to Place of Contracting.** A contract is therefore considered made at the place where the letter

[17] §323. Where an informal contract is to guarantee future credits to be given by the promisee, the place of contracting is where the credit is given in reliance on the guaranty. §324.

[18] Restatement, §311.

[19] *Cf.* Restatement. Scope-note to Ch. 8.

[20] Restatement, §313.

[21] *Ibid.*, §315.

of acceptance was mailed or the telegram of acceptance delivered for transmission. While this has been declared "a rule of very general application," [22] it has been by no means accepted in all countries. Miraglia vigorously contests its validity on philosophic and logical grounds. He maintains: "We cannot allow a contract to exist where one of the contractors does not know of the acceptance of the other, and therefore has no knowledge of his own obligations. Offer and acceptance are necessary to a contract, and they should be governed by the same rules." [23] He excepts, of course, those cases in which by custom no notice of acceptance is expected. Even legal philosophers are influenced by the environment of the law with which they are most familiar and Miraglia practically adopts the principles of the *Italian law* in this respect.[24] There has been considerable difference of opinion upon this question in European countries even within the same jurisdiction but an important distinction should be emphasized which will explain the seeming inconsistency of some of the decisions. France and Switzerland, for example, follow the theory of reception of acceptance in order to determine whether the parties are legally bound; but they follow the theory of declaration to the extent that the law of the place from which the acceptance was transmitted will determine the import of the contract.[25] This solution, more subtile and more scientific, has received approval in recent cases in *Germany*.[26] Thus the question as to how long an offer sent from Germany remained open to acceptance was determined by the law at the place of the offer and not at that of the acceptance.[27] Lewald cites these cases in contrast with others [28] which hold the proper law of the contract itself applicable to determine whether a contract actually came into existence. The application of the law in force

[22] Emerson *v.* Proctor, (1903) 97 Me. 360, 364.

[23] Miraglia, Comparative Legal Philosophy. (Trans. by Lisle, 1912) pp. 574–575.

[24] Italian Commercial Code, Art. 36. Bartin ascribes the divergence between the French and the Italian law in this respect to reasoning based not on the French text of Art. 420, French Code of Civ. Procedure, but on its Italian adaptation. *Académie de Dr. Int., Recueil de Cours,* 1930, i, p. 583.

[25] Merlin, *Repertoire de Jurisprudence,* (1887) tit. *vente* 1, art. iii, no. xi. Meili, International Civil and Commercial Law (Kuhn's trans. 1905) p. 329.

[26] *Reichsgericht,* Dec. 4, 1926, *Jurist. Wochenschrift,* 1927, p. 693.

[27] *Oberlandesger. Augsburg,* April 22, 1914, *Leipziger Zeitschrift für d. Recht,* 1914, Sp. 1138. *Accord:* where a telegraphic offer sent from Austria was wrongly transmitted, and was accepted in Germany in accordance with its apparent tenor. *Oberlandesger. Bamberg,* March 14, 1908.

[28] *Cf.* Lewald, pp. 232–238.

at the place from which the acceptance was sent leads to complications in countries which, like Germany, regard the place of performance as the proper law of the contract (with certain exceptions). Lewald favors the principle of the offeror's law because of its simplicity and employs an example given by Lorenzen.[29] A New York merchant sends an offer by letter to a German in Germany. After the offer is received but before acceptance, he telegraphs a withdrawal, but the offeree accepts, which he would be entitled to do according to German law. Lewald would recognize the application of New York law no matter where the proper law of the contract would be, and favors recognition of the making of a contract only at the moment when the laws applicable to the declaration of each of the parties recognize the creation of a binding obligation.

A similar conception is intended to be expressed by the provision of the Bustamante Code of Latin-American countries relating to commercial contracts. "Contracts by correspondence shall be complete only when the conditions prescribed for the purpose by the legislation of all the contracting parties have been duly complied with." [30]

**The Rule "locus regit actum."** The development of a body of law from decided cases rather than from general principles to be found in codifications has doubtless influenced the common law in developing rules of form to particular transactions rather than to transactions generally. English and American courts speak of the form of contracts, of wills, of deeds, while Continental authorities discuss in general terms of the "form of legal transactions." They are confirmed in this by the rule of *locus regit actum* which has been recognized as a rule of customary law as early as the sixteenth century. Von Bar gives us a reasonable account of its origin. *Statuta* were binding only upon subjects but the rule of *locus regit actum* was an exception because the solemnities of an act belong to *jurisdictio voluntaria* and transactions attested before one court must be held by all other courts to be well attested. Contracts concluded in the presence of the judge or recorded on the books of the court were given recognition elsewhere although the forms varied greatly; otherwise the benefit of public instruments would have been much restricted.[31] Later the application of the rule of *locus regit actum*

[29] (1921) 31 Yale Law Jour. 53.

[30] Bustamante Code, Art. 245. Int. Conferences of American States (1931) p. 350.

[31] Von Bar, Theory and Practice of Private Int. Law. (Gillespie's trans. 1892) pp. 264–266.

was much extended. Bartolus and Baldus applied it to wills. Dumoulin applied it to other formal transactions.

What is the scope of the rule in modern times? Some authors assert that form is the dress of a transaction, and being a part of it, should be subject to the same law as the transaction itself; that for practical reasons, the observance of this form is often impossible and therefore the observance of the form prevailing at the place of entering into the transaction will suffice. In other words, the rule is permissive and not coercive.[32]

But the statement of the rule in its permissive form is likely to be misleading in common-law jurisdictions where the concept prevails that the voluntary agreement of the parties requires the authority of a territorial sovereign to give it the character of a binding contract.[33] We have purposely refrained from saying *the* territorial sovereign because a contract made in one state may very well have validly come into existence under the law of another state. It would indeed be a barbarous system of law which would recognize only contracts which came into existence within its own territory. On the other hand, if State A is willing to give validity to a contract made in State B according to its laws, it is likely also to hold the contract valid in its inception if the parties have observed the forms required by State A. A distinction between the form required for contracting and the substantial requirements of a binding contract is made by civil-law countries. Dicey distinguishes between the "formal validity" and "essential validity" of contracts, but Beale is of the opinion that the common law would not support such a distinction, or at least that the decisions of common-law courts have seldom turned on this difference.[34] Lorenzen says: "The thought that the parties had an option in regard to the formal requirements of contracts to comply either with the laws of the place of making or with that of the place of performance did not occur to any court."[35]

Story quotes from Boullenois, Burgundus, Dumoulin, Hertius and

[32] Meili frames the rule as follows: "The observance of that form is sufficient which is provided by law at the place where the transaction was entered into. However, that form may also be employed which is provided by the substantive law to which the transaction is subject." Int. Civil and Commercial Law, (Kuhn's trans. 1905) p. 162. Walker, *Int. Privatrecht* (1924) p. 190.

[33] See *ante*, p. 265.

[34] (1909) 23 Harvard Law Rev., pp. 3-4.

[35] (1910) 20 Yale Law J. 442.

other writers from the sixteenth to the eighteenth century to show the various terms into which the maxim *locus regit actum* was subsequently moulded, adding that "it seems fully established in the common law." [36] The examples given are, however, meager and conflicting and Beale denies acceptance of the rule in the common law. There seem to be no decisions or dicta in England or the United States by which formal validity is referred to a distinct system of law; so that the question as to what law shall govern the formal validity of contracts is still regarded by the English and American courts as a part of the larger and more complex problem relating to the obligation and validity of contracts in general.

Of course, matters of form which in other systems of law would be deemed to affect the validity of a contract are frequently, under the Anglo-American system, part of the requisites by which the contract must be proved. The leading case of Leroux *v.* Brown [37] originally suggested a distinction between that part (§4) of the English Statute of Frauds providing that "no action shall be brought" upon contracts not to be performed within one year unless made in writing as required by the statute, and that part (§17) which allowed no contract for the sale of merchandise "to be good" if over a certain value and not in writing as provided. A contract made in France under the former section and good by French law could not be sued upon in England. The decision has been followed by American courts.[38]

The English Sale of Goods Act of 1893 as well as the Uniform Sales Act of the American States [39] now contain a formula by which an oral contract for the sale of goods or choses in action above the value allowed, "shall not be enforceable by action." This throws the formality of a writing into the domain of procedure. It becomes a method of proof, a form of evidence, not a requisite of validity, and thus the necessity for the writing will be determined by the forum and not by the proper law of the contract.

[36] Story, §260 and note.

[37] (1852) 12 C.B. 801.

[38] Heaton *v.* Eldridge (1897) 56 Ohio St. 87. An oral contract made in Pennsylvania not within the statute there, was not allowed to be proved in evidence in Ohio, where the statute prevailed. It is interesting to observe that the court regarded also the legislative intent to make the statute applicable to foreign contracts and referred to the statute as "a peremptory rule of procedure." *Accord:* Third Nat. Bank *v.* Steele, (1902) 129 Mich. 434. Matthews *v.* Matthews, (1897) 154 N.Y. 288.

[39] The New York text is found in the Personal Property Law, §85.

This does not apply to specialty contract such as bills and notes, because the formal nature of these contracts is recognized everywhere; their utility as means of credit and exchange and their ready negotiability under fixed commercial practices make it imperative that the law of the place of making the particular contract must determine its validity as to form. The English Bills of Exchange Act[40] provides that "the validity of a bill as regards requisites in form is determined by the law of the place of issue" and as to the form of the supervening contracts, such as acceptance and endorsement, by the law of the place where made. To this rule two exceptions are made, one which gives validity to foreign bills even though they do not comply with the stamp laws of the place of issue; and the second allows a foreign bill to be treated valid as between persons who negotiate, hold or become parties to it in the United Kingdom. The Uniform Negotiable Instruments Law does not contain any provision allocating the requirements of form to any particular jurisdiction.

The Restatement[41] declares that the law of the place of contracting determines the formalities required for making a contract. That law therefore determines:

(§335) whether an instrument is effectively sealed; whether it is duly executed and delivered; whether it is valid without consideration, and if not, whether consideration has been given.

(§336) whether a mercantile instrument is negotiable; whether it is duly executed and delivered; whether it is valid without consideration, and if not, whether consideration has been given.

(§337) the duties of the carrier when passengers or goods are accepted for carriage pursuant to a contract.

(§338) the validity of a contract limiting the carrier's liability.

(§339) whether mutual assent has been expressed, whether a promise is valid without consideration and if not, whether consideration has been given.

**"Locus regit actum" in Foreign Systems of Law.** The separation of the form of a contract from its other requisites of validity is quite characteristic of the genius of the Roman law. The tendency to define and to subdivide led the medieval writers to speak separately of the *solemnitates* of a transaction apart from its other phases. Bartolus states the rule in No. 32 as follows: *"In solemnitatibus sem-*

[40] §72.
[41] §334.

*per inspicimus locum ubi res agitur . . . tam circa contractus quam circa ultimas voluntates.*" It is curious that though Bartolus was among the earliest writers on the conflict of laws, he should have expressed the contrast in such modern terms—"rather the (place of) contract than the (place of) ultimate intent."

The practical question by the law of European countries is to determine in each jurisdiction whether the rule is to be considered imperative or facultative. Lainé reviews the history of the maxim in *France,* pointing out that the original intention was to embody it in the Civil Code but that finally it was omitted. He insists, however, that the intention was to give it a facultative character and that the object of the maxim was to extend the powers of the individual, not to restrict them.[42]

The *German* Civil Code leaves no doubt upon the subject because it provides: "The form of a legal transaction is governed by the laws which are authoritative for the relationship constituting the subject of the transaction. However, compliance with the laws of the place where the transaction was entered into will suffice."[43] It has been decided that a contract completed by correspondence is considered as having been executed at the place in which the acceptance of the offer was made and the meeting of the minds occurred.[44] Walker points out that if the formal requisite under the law of either place is for the contract as a whole, it will not suffice to comply only as to the part of the correspondence issuing from that place. Thus if the law of the place of the offer requires a notarial document and that of the acceptor only a written instrument, both sides must comply with the notarial requisite because the provision applies to the contract as a whole.[45]

Under §313 of the German Civil Code, a contract for the sale of land requires a notarial or judicial authentication. Can action upon a contract executed in Germany without such authentication, for the sale of land located in a foreign country, be sustained before a German court? The answer depends upon whether the "relationship constituting the subject of the transaction," *i.e.,* the *causa,* is located in Germany or at the place of the land. The doctrine of most of the cases seems to be that the *lex causae* is the foreign law but unless

[42] Lainé in Clunet, 1908, pp. 336–339.

[43] Art. 11, par. 1, Intro. Stat. Ger. Civ. Code. The rule does not apply to transactions affecting title to property. *Ibid.,* par. 2.

[44] *Reichsger.,* Feb. 12, 1906, R.G. (1906) p. 379.

[45] Walker, *Int. Privatrecht* (1924) p. 195.

the transaction contemplates an immediate right of property in the land, the German law would seem on principle to be indicated as controlling the contractual relationship of the parties.[46]

The *Italian* Civil Code[47] provides that the extrinsic form of acts, both *inter vivos* and by will, are governed by the law of the place in which they are made. This provision is confirmed for commercial transactions by the Commercial Code[48] which provides that the forms and essential requisites of commercial obligations are also governed by the laws or usages of the place in which the obligation was created. There is a saving clause in Art. 9 of the Civil Code permitting the parties to follow the form of the national law provided this is common to all the parties. In this connection it is important to note that under Italian law, a contract does not become perfected until the acceptance of the offeree has been made known to the offeror. Accordingly, the question arises with respect to contracts by correspondence between a party in Italy and a party abroad, as to whether the contract has been perfected even though the acceptance was sent from a country in which the law recognizes a contract from the time of mailing acceptance. Italian courts seem to apply Italian law here. Even where both parties were located abroad at the time of the acceptance, the law applicable, according to some authorities, is that of the Italian forum because the forum is competent to determine where the contract actually came into force.[49] This does not seem to be reasonable upon principle as it practically allows the court to circumvent the effect of the rule *locus regit actum*.

**Place of Contracting by an Agent or Partner.** An important consideration in determining the place of making a contract by one acting only in a representative capacity is whether full authority to act was delegated or whether approval by the principal was required. If the agent has full authority, the classic dictum of Lord Lyndhurst is determinative of the place as well as of the binding character of the agreement: "If I, residing in England, send down my agent to Scotland, and he makes contracts for me there, it is the same as if I myself went there and made them."[50] If the agent exceeds his

[46] So *Deutsche Juristen Zeitung*, 1905, Sp. 864; *contra, Reichsger*. March 3, 1906, Clunet, 1907, p. 779; *Kammerger.*, March 19, 1925. Lewald, *Das deutsche int. Privatr.* 1931, p. 67.

[47] *Disposizioni*, Art. 9 (1).

[48] Art. 58.

[49] Udina (1930) p. 126, relying upon Cavaglieri; and Diena giving other grounds.

[50] Pattison *v.* Mills, (1828) 1 Dow & Cl., 342, 363.

authority, no contract has come into existence either at the alleged place of making by the agent or at the place of the principal. Of course, if the principal thereafter ratifies the act, it becomes valid *ab initio* and the contract has come about at the place of the original transaction.[51] But suppose there be no ratification and the third party relies upon some authority implied at the place of the agent's transaction. Even if the law of the place in which the agent has acted would have implied a wider authority under which the principal would have been made liable, its imputations must necessarily be based upon some conduct of the *principal,* not of the agent, warranting a legal presumption of agency. Accordingly the law of the place where the relationship between principal and agent was created must determine the legal implications of that relationship. The cogency of this principle is convincingly stated by Story in an opinion as a Justice of the Supreme Court. The question involved the authority of the master of a ship to bind the owner by certain bottomry bonds in a foreign port: "Any other rule would subject the principal to the most alarming responsibility, and be inconsistent with that just comity and public convenience, which lies at the foundation of international private law."[52]

An analogous principle applies in determination of the scope of the authority of a partner to bind the partnership of other members of it individually. A Cuban limited partnership became indebted to persons in New York through contracts made in New York by the general partners. In an action in New York to hold the limited partner, it was held that the authority of the general partners to bind the limited partner was referable to the Spanish law then in force in Cuba. The law to limit the partner's liability having been complied with in Cuba where the partnership was created, no such liability could be predicated.[53]

A sharp distinction is therefore to be noticed between the case of testing the capacity of a person to enter into a contract in a country foreign to his domicil and measuring the authority of an agent

[51] Hill *v.* Chase, (1886) 143 Mass. 129; McMaster *v.* N.Y. Life Ins. Co., (1897) 78 Fed. 33.

[52] Pope *v.* Nickerson, (1844) 3 Story 465, at p. 476. The use of the term "international private law" in deciding a case before the Supreme Court as early as 1844 is notable. Story maintained that the extent of the authority of the principal must be measured by the law of the place where it is given, not by the laws of the foreign country, "of which the principal is or may be wholly ignorant, and by whose regulations he is not bound." *Ibid.*

[53] King *v.* Sarria, (1877) 69 N.Y. 24.

in a country foreign to the place of origin of the agency. We have seen that on the basis of justice and convenience, the prevailing principle, at least in the United States, determines personal capacity by the *lex loci actus*.[54] In considering the authority of a mandatory, however, we are not dealing with his capacity *sui juris*, but only vicariously. His capacity is derivative and dependent upon a legal relationship constituted under the aegis of another system of law. Third parties may properly insist that persons of legal age within the territory shall be so considered, whether or not of foreign domicil, or origin; and that married women shall have the powers attributed to them at the place in which they contract. But this is not conclusive upon the powers conferred upon an agent abroad and exercised within the territory. It is just as much the duty of third parties to inquire into their actual or implied powers under the foreign law as it would be if their powers had been created wholly within the territory.

A more difficult problem is presented where a power created abroad, itself emanated from one having capacity limited by the foreign law, though capable by the *lex loci actus*. Thus in Milliken *v. Pratt*, to which we have previously referred,[55] a guaranty was executed by defendant, a married woman, in Massachusetts, delivered to her husband and by him sent by mail to the plaintiffs in Maine. The law of Massachusetts did not permit a married woman to enter into a contract of this nature but the court held that the guaranty was complete only when it had been received and acted on by the plaintiffs in Maine and therefore good because the defendant's capacity was not restricted by the law of Maine. The court apparently failed to consider that the delivery of the instrument was made through an agent, the defendant's husband, and as such agency was constituted, if at all, in Massachusetts, the agent's power was lacking. This lack of authority was emphasized in a well-considered Connecticut case. The facts were similar except that the guaranty, signed in Connecticut, was there given to the husband who mailed it to his partner in Illinois where it was delivered to the claimant-bank. In holding the contract void under Connecticut law, Judge Baldwin said: "It is not the place of delivery that counts, but the power of delivery."[56] In other words, a married woman could not delegate a power in

[54] See *ante*, p. 118.
[55] *Ante*, pp. 32, 119.
[56] Appeal of Freeman, (1897) 68 Conn. 533 at p. 543.

Connecticut to do that which she herself was incapable of doing.

The Restatement[57] solves the problem with reference to acceptance sent by an agent by considering the place where an agent delivers the acceptance to be the place of contracting; but if the acceptance is sent by any other means, the place of contracting is the state from which the acceptance is sent.

## 2. Substantive Validity

Whether or not the separation of formal from essential validity is justified by the common law rules of contract, there is need for a distinction between form and substance where a contract made in one jurisdiction is claimed to be invalid in another. If we regard a contract as being a legally enforceable agreement, the agreement has never evolved into a contract if the forms requisite for legality at the time and place of the agreement were not observed. Forms and ceremonies are considered local in their application. They are the mandatory rules of a territorial sovereign. We have seen that religious forms and ceremonies are sometimes considered to be applicable without regard to place,[58] but this is only when the temporal and the spiritual sovereignty coincide. It is not consistent with the modern system of territorial sovereignty. The formal requisites of contracts are no longer connected with religious sanctions as they were in ancient times. The formal requisites of mercantile contracts serve social purposes, especially in regard to the transfer of title to real or personal property, the maintenance of credit and the prevention of fraud.

When the parties to an agreement have expressed their will in accordance with the legal forms prevailing at the place of their agreement, a contract has come into existence even though some other or different form be required in another state, such as that of the place of performance where the validity of the contract may be challenged. Is this true also in respect to the validity of the *provisions* of the contract itself? If the provisions of the agreement render the contract invalid at the place of the agreement, should the contract nevertheless be valid if it is so regarded in some other jurisdiction such as at the place of performance, or the domicil of the parties, when the validity of the contract is challenged there?

[57] §326.

[58] See *ante*, pp. 139–140.

The United States Supreme Court had to consider this question in Pritchard *v.* Norton.[59] The defendant executed *in New York* to the plaintiff's testator, Pritchard, an idemnity bond to hold him harmless against any loss which might arise from an appeal bond which Pritchard *had already* executed in Louisiana as surety upon an appeal of a case pending there. Judgment was rendered in the Louisiana case and Pritchard was obliged to pay as surety. The executrix of his estate sued in the Federal court of Louisiana to recover upon the indemnity bond. The defendant asserted that he was not liable because of the lack of consideration under New York law, where a pre-existing liability will not support the promise of indemnity. In Louisiana the bond would not have been void if executed there. There was some question as to whether the place of performance was New York or Louisiana, but the Supreme Court found that the obligation of the bond was to repay the surety in the place where he was bound and where he did actually discharge his own liability. We have therefore a contract valid in form but void as to a substantial requisite at the place of making, yet valid in both respects at the place of performance. The court sustained the validity of the agreement by reference to the Louisiana law, that law being the law "which the parties have, either expressly or presumptively, incorporated into their contract as constituting its obligation." The opinion of the court referred to the well known dictum of Chief Justice Marshall in Wayman *v.* Southard,[60] in which he stated, "a principle of universal law; the principle that in every forum a contract is governed by the law with a view to which it was made." It is curious that a dictum so widely removed from the point involved should have had such an enormous influence in American jurisprudence. The will of the parties determines the place of performance and the parties probably intended to enter into a valid agreement. We may also agree with Phillimore that "the parties cannot be presumed to have contemplated a law which would defeat their engagements."[61] But is this decisive of the case on principle? Can the will of the parties vary the legal requisites of a binding promise so as to dispense with the necessity for a valid considera-

[59] (1882) 106 U.S. 124.

[60] (1825) 10 Wheat. 1, at p. 48. The case did not deal with the application of law to a contract, but involved the validity of a state statute regulating executions, when applied to executions upon judgments of the United States courts.

[61] (1889) 4 International Law §654.

tion by the law of the state in which the parties made their agreement? If they can do that, the parties may substitute their own will for that of the legislature. In the Pritchard case, the court was sitting as a Louisiana court. Undoubtedly it had the power to hold that a contract could be made in New York, good by Louisiana law, though it lacked the requisites of a good New York contract; but in doing so, it determined the requisites of agreement by a law which the Louisiana legislature primarily intended to apply to agreements made within the jurisdiction of the state, not to agreements made outside the state. The fact that performance was contemplated to be made within the state should not be decisive of a requisite which has nothing whatever to do with the place of performance.

The case has been widely followed, though rather in its dictum than in the logical application of the rule which might ordinarily be derived from its peculiar facts. When it is said that a contract is "governed" by the law with a view to which it was made, it should not be assumed that either its formal or its substantive validity is to be determined by that law, though the validity of the acts done or to be done under the contract may well be determined by the law intended by the parties. To illustrate: A conditional sale is entered into in the State of Washington, delivery to be made in Alaska. The contract was not recorded as required by Washington laws though it was so recorded in Alaska where recording is not necessary to retain title in the vendor. After delivery took place in Alaska, bankruptcy intervened before payment; and the vendor claimed the property from the trustee. It was held that the contemplated performance was to be in Alaska and the transfer of title must be judged by that law. The court relied upon Pritchard *v.* Norton, but clearly there was no question of the validity of the contract itself but only of the effect of acts done under the contract.[62]

We may say therefore that the law which determines the effect of performance is that which prevails at the place of performance. Persons who agreed in Pennsylvania to lend money to a business carried on in New York with the understanding that they were to receive a share in the profits until the money was repaid, were sued before a Pennsylvania court as partners in that business. The New York law must decide, because it is that law which determines the

[62] *In re* Hood Bay Packing Co., (1922) 280 Fed. 866. *Accord:* Carnegie *v.* Morrison, (1841) 2 Metc. (Mass.) 381.

effect of their performance,[63] and the same is true where an act is relied upon to discharge performance.[64]

**Autonomy of the Parties.** As the determination of what is the "proper" law of the contract may be affected or indeed controlled by acts done or circumstances created by the parties themselves, it becomes immediately pertinent to discover whether the parties may expressly choose the system of law which shall govern the validity or interpretation of the content of the contract. We have seen that the parties cannot under English or American law give to an agreement the binding character of a contract by mere reference to another legal system, if at the place where the agreement was undertaken, there was no contract in the eye of the law. If the formalities were not observed at that place, the acts of the parties even for the purpose of reference to another system are ineffective.[65] It may very well be, however, that some system of law other than that of the place of celebration may by the force of its own sovereign legislative power regard the agreement valid by *its* law, though void at the place of making. Let us illustrate: Two British subjects domiciled in England entered into a marriage settlement in France in contemplation of a marriage ceremony to be celebrated first at the British Embassy in English form and afterwards according to French law. It was agreed that the parties should have community of property and acquests "according to the disposition of the custom of Paris, which shall regulate their future community, and the other clauses of the present marriage contract." The contract also provided that certain funds of the wife charged on her brother's property in England should be settled as a *dot* upon the husband but for which amount he should be chargeable to his intended wife. Only the English ceremony was ever performed and there was doubt as to the validity of the marriage under French law, especially as the parties never cohabited but ever afterwards lived separately. The husband claimed a right of survivorship in funds against the executor of the wife's will probated in England. It was held by Sir John Romilly,

[63] First Nat. Bank *v.* Hall, (1892) 150 Penn. St. 466.

[64] Dickinson *v.* Edwards, (1879) 77 N.Y. 573. In the celebrated case of Youssoupoff *v.* Widener, (1927) 246 N.Y. 174, paintings were sold and delivered in England with a limited right of repurchase in the seller after their removal to Pennsylvania. The New York court held that though performance of this part of the contract was contemplated in Pennsylvania, the nature of the transfer was already determined by English law and Pennsylvania law could not convert the transaction from a sale into a mortgage by the latter law.

[65] See *ante*, p. 272.

M.R., that although the contract might be invalid by French law because no valid marriage was contracted under that law, the contract was valid as to English property and would be construed "exactly in the same manner as the French law would regulate the rights between two married French persons under a similar contract." The court therefore held that the wife could dispose of the property by will. Reference was made to Story's statement that the *lex loci contractus* governs the validity of the contract but as the contract was made to be operative in England over English property, its validity by English law was sufficient, even though it might be invalid in France. The choice of law was therefore regarded as relating to its interpretation and not to its validity under French law.[66]

**The "Proper" Law of the Contract.** The principle applicable to contracts in general is well illustrated in Wilson *v.* Lewiston Mill Co.[67] An agreement for the sale of goods though resulting from correspondence between the sellers at New York and the purchasers in Maine was actually consummated by the seller's agent's oral acceptance of a bid from the purchasers in Maine. The sellers sued the purchasers in New York and a general denial was interposed. Under the New York rule, the Statute of Frauds must be specially pleaded. Under the Maine statute, oral agreements for the sale of goods of a value over thirty dollars were declared void. The court held that the mere place of acceptance will not alone determine the place of making; that the place of performance and the place of making must both be taken into consideration "in connection with the whole contract, and the circumstances under which the parties acted in determining the question of their intent." [68] It was further held that the parties intended to consummate a Maine contract and as the contract was void as to form in Maine, its validity was properly pleaded under a general denial.[69]

The significance of the case lies in the intimation of the court that the intent of the parties determines the place and therefore the law of contract as to its formal validity. This may be taken to be dictum because the final act undoubtedly took place in Maine and the

[66] Este *v.* Smyth, (1854) 18 Beav. 112. Haudek believes this case to be the earliest dealing with the concept of a voluntary choice of substantive law. *Die Bedeutung des Parteiwillens im int. Privatrecht,* (1931) p. 5n.

[67] (1896) 150 N.Y. 314.

[68] *Ibid.*, p. 323.

[69] Citing Jenness *v.* Mt. Hope Iron Co., (1864) 53 Me. 20 which was read in evidence at the trial.

intent of the parties as to place of contracting coincided with the rule of law.[70]

The converse case is presented by Reilly *v.* Steinhart,[71] in which plaintiff was suing for the balance of moneys agreed to be paid for an option. The agreement was made in Cuba in writing but was not a public document. Under Cuban law a contract of this kind must be "protocolized" before action may be brought, but the contract was not invalid and the plaintiff could maintain an action to compel defendant to authenticate it. It was held that the contract was valid in form, and actionable in New York. "The law of New York follows the law of Cuba in recognition of the contract, but prescribes its own remedy, and pursues its own procedure." [72]

**Maritime Shipping Contracts.** A closer analogy to problems of substantive validity is presented by certain leading cases of maritime contracts. In *In re* Missouri Steamship Co.,[73] a Massachusetts citizen sued to recover for the loss, by negligence of master and crew, of a shipment upon a British vessel under a contract and bills of lading executed in Boston, in which the carrier was exempted from liability for such negligence. Under Massachusetts law, the clause was void though good by English law. The circumstances that the ship and destination were English and that the forms for the contract and bills of lading were English forms, all contributed to the conclusion that the parties intended the application of English law. The court under a lead given by Sir Walter Phillimore (afterwards Lord Phillimore) at Nisi Prius, considered whether the contract was void or the exemption merely unenforceable under the Massachusetts law. For the better decision of this point, the case seems to have been held over by the Court of Appeal until the decision of the United States Supreme Court in the case of *The Montana.*[74] There the exemption clause was similar and the contracts were made in New York State, by the law of which the clause was valid if judged by the decisions of the highest tribunal of the State, but void by the rule of the Federal courts; and as the question was one of mercantile law but not one of local statute or usage, Federal law was held to be final.[75] The bill of lading did not indicate that the owners

[70] See *ante,* p. 268.
[71] (1916) 217 N.Y. 549.
[72] *Ibid.,* p. 554, per Cardozo, J.
[73] (1889) 42 Ch. D. 321.
[74] Liverpool & G. W. Steam Co. *v.* Phenix Ins. Co., (1889) 129 U.S. 397.
[75] *Ibid.,* p. 443.

of the ship were English or that their principal place of business was in England and the court called attention to the circumstances that transhipment might have been made into a non-British vessel and that the contract also included a general-average clause according to York-Antwerp rules as drawn by the International Law Association, thus giving the contract an international rather than an English form. The court therefore held the contract to be "with a view to" New York and not to English law. A review of both English and American decisions led the court to state the general rule to be "that the nature, the obligation, and the interpretation of a contract are to be governed by the law of the place where it is made, unless the parties at the time of making it have some other law in view." [76] The rule thus stated was expressly adopted by the English court though the slight variations of fact led it to find that the parties contemplated English and not the American law. The rule has been amply confirmed by later English cases.[77]

In the later case of *The Kensington*,[78] the Supreme Court had to decide the validity of an exemption clause in a contract made in Belgium for transportation of passengers and baggage to New York. Although valid at the place of making, the court held that public policy demanded that enforcement should be nevertheless refused in the courts of the United States.

The maritime cases we have just discussed do no violence to the principle we believe to be correct, *viz.*, that the contract must not be illegal or void *qua* contract at the place of making. They indicate, however, that the rule of intent, the autonomy rule, even when restricted so as to determine only the enforceability of clauses of a contract otherwise valid, allows much leeway to the court to apply the law of the forum through interpretation of what the will of the parties really was, or may be presumed to have been. Where enforcement is deemed to violate a coercive principle of public policy at the forum, intent would seem then to be immaterial.

### 3. Legality of Performance

How far shall the illegality of the act constituting performance of a contract, react upon the validity of the contract itself? Contracts

[76] Gray, J., at p. 458.

[77] Hamlyn *v.* Talisker Distillery, (1894) A.C. 202; Jones *v.* Oceanic Steam Navigation Co. Ltd., L.R. 1924, K.B.D. vol. 2, 731.

[78] (1902) 183 U.S. 263.

made on Sunday are considered void in some states but not in others. If made in a state where they are valid, they may be sued upon even in a state in which such contracts are void because the evil aimed at by the statute is to prevent acts done within the territory, but not elsewhere.[79] But what of contracts valid where made but to be performed on Sunday in a state where such performance is prohibited? Let us illustrate: The maker and payee of the notes in suit had an incidental meeting in New York with regard to the sale of real estate in Florida. The notes were executed on Sunday in New York, where an executory contract is not void on that account. The maker was domiciled in Massachusetts, the payee in Wisconsin. Performance on both sides was contemplated in Massachusetts under the law of which all executory contracts for the payment of money made and delivered on Sunday are void. It was held that the contract was void.[80] Conversely, where a bond was given to secure the faithful performance of duties in Kentucky in connection with the sale of lottery tickets authorized by a Kentucky statute but illegal in New York, it was held that as the bond was valid at the place where consideration was to be performed the courts of New York would enforce it.[81] But where notes were made on Sunday in Michigan where the act was not only a penal offense but where the parties were considered to be without legal capacity to make a contract on that day, the fact that payment was to be in Ohio was not sufficient to cure the inherent vice of the contract at its inception.[82]

It would be unsatisfactory to attempt to draw a definite principle from these cases except to the extent of saying that if the contract is not void at inception in the place of making, the illegality of performance, if intended to be carried out there, will not void the contract if performance is in good faith contemplated in another state where such performance is not deemed illegal.

**Usury.** A neat application of the principles we have been discussing is presented by contracts in which the interest agreed to be paid is considered usurious by statute at the place of making or at the place of performance (payment) or both. Usury statutes vary greatly in different states and countries. New York has a drastic statute which provides that such contracts shall be void, that prosecution shall be

[79] McKee *v.* Jones, (1889) 67 Miss. 405; Brown *v.* Browning, (1886) 15 R.I. 422.

[80] Brown *v.* Gates, (1903) 120 Wis. 349.

[81] Kentucky *v.* Bosford, (1843) 6 Hill, (N.Y.) 526.

[82] Arbuckle *v.* Reaume, (1893) 96 Mich. 243.

enjoined thereon and that usurious contracts may be ordered to be surrendered and canceled.[83] If the contract is valid at the place of making, the fact that performance is to be in a state in which it would be void for usury if made there, should not prevent recovery even if action is brought in the latter state. The court seeks to determine the proper law of the contract by circumstances connecting the transaction with one or the other jurisdiction. For example, where usurious notes were given in exchange for moneys collected at the place of making (Illinois) and remitted by mail to the payee in the state of performance (New York) it was held that what occurred between the parties was equivalent to a transaction consummated in Illinois.[84] Where the note specifies no interest but is made and payable in New York, the fact that it is discounted in another state where the rate would not be usurious will not save the note if usurious by New York law.[85]

Conversely, if the note was made and delivered in a state in which it would be void for usury, payable in a state in which the contract is not usurious, the fact that the security (real estate) is also located there, should not revive a contract void at its inception. It can doubtless be admitted that the parties contemplated the law of the latter state, that they acted in good faith and did not intend to evade the law of the place of making. But is this material? In Arnold *v.* Potter,[86] the court deemed the good faith of the parties to be decisive, holding that they had contemplated the law of the latter state without intending any evasion. Goodrich wisely asks when the parties are to be deemed guilty in specifying a place of performance. If they do so with knowledge that the contract is not usurious at that place, are they evading the law at the place of making? If so, "can there be a transaction of this type in good faith unless the parties are in fact ignorant of usury laws?" [87]

[83] N.Y. Gen. Business Law, §373, amended to 1935; a less drastic statute has been proposed.

[84] Sheldon *v.* Haxtun, (1883) 91 N.Y. 124.

[85] Dickinson *v.* Edwards, (1879) 77 N.Y. 573.

[86] (1867) 22 Ia. 194.

[87] Goodrich, Handbook on the Conflict of Laws (1927) p. 239. (1921) 21 Columbia Law Rev. 585. In Shannon *v.* Georgia State Building & Loan Assoc. (1901) 78 Miss. 955, the payments were to be made in Georgia where the contract was delivered if not actually executed. Payments in fact were made to the defendant's local agent in Mississippi where the borrower resided. In an action to recover interest paid, deemed usurious by Mississippi law, the court regarded the recital of Georgia as the place of payment to be an evasion, though the home office of the lender was in that state.

In the same case in which the United States Supreme Court declared that contracts made in one place to be performed in another are "governed" by the law of the latter place, it also correctly made its dictum more precise by explaining that the rule applies only to agreements "permitted by the *lex loci contractus*"; and that "the same rule cannot be applied to contracts forbidden by its laws and designed to evade them." [88] In later cases the Court still demands "that the parties act in good faith," [89] though it is difficult to see how good faith can cure a contract void *ab initio,* or how bad faith may be ascribed to parties who make a choice of law within limits which the law allows. The requirement of good faith should properly be applied in limiting the choice of law to one with which the contract has a substantial connection, such as the place of making, or payment, of the location of security, or even of the domicil of either of the parties, provided, of course, that the contract was valid *ab initio* at the place of making.[90]

Minor draws the conclusion in this class of cases that the validity of the contract will depend not on the law of the place of making or of that of performance as such, but on the law of the place where consideration is furnished. He bases this upon the premise that the policy of the usury laws is aimed against the exaction of usurious interest by the lender, not against the promise by the debtor to pay usurious interest.[91] The distinction is important only if the circumstances of the transaction were the criterion of the proper law; but we have already seen that the decided cases allow the parties within a limited sphere to make a choice of the law. The difficulty in finding agreement in the decided cases may perhaps be ascribed to the discretion which all courts exercise in their interpretation of the territorial scope of statutes establishing a public policy of a prohibitory nature.

**Performance Made Illegal After Making of the Contract.** Differing from the prohibition against usury, is a class of cases in which performance is valid everywhere at the time of making the

[88] Andrews *v.* Pond, (1839) 13 Pet. 65.

[89] Miller *v.* Tiffany, (1863) 1 Wall, 298.

[90] "In thus holding, we, of course, do not decide that two citizens of Massachusetts could make a contract in that state, payable there or in New York, agree to be governed by the laws of Iowa or California, and thereby avoid the consequences of the usury." Wright, J., in Arnold *v.* Potter, (1867) 22 Ia. 194, at p. 200.

[91] Minor, Conflict of Laws (1901) pp. 432–433.

contract but becomes illegal and is prohibited by reason of some supervening event before performance is due. Problems of this kind arose at the outbreak of the World War in connection with the export of grain from the United States and countries of South America. Much business of this kind was done by contracts made in London on forms of the London Corn Trade Association which contained the following clause:

> "Buyer and seller agree that, for the purpose of proceedings, either legal or by arbitration, this contract shall be deemed to have been made in England and to be performed there, any correspondence in reference to the offer, the acceptance, the place of payment or otherwise notwithstanding; . . . Such disputes shall be settled according to the law of England, whatever the domicil, residence, or place of business of the parties to this contract may be or become."

The contracts also provided that any dispute should be referred to arbitration in England and that English courts should have exclusive jurisdiction. There was extreme difficulty in obtaining ships for European ports due to the feverish demand for war supplies, the extra hazards and the almost prohibitive prices for insurance. Accordingly, many contracts were broken. Now there is a notable distinction between the English common law and modern Roman law in respect to impossibility of performance. The common law does not recognize relative impossibility as an excuse. Only an impossibility caused by act of God or the public enemy will excuse performance. The United States, as well as the South American countries, was still neutral. The obligation of contracts in this respect is much more strict and positive under English law than under the Continental codes. Thus under French law, performance is excused by *force majeure;*[92] under German law, performance is excused if prevented by a circumstance for which neither party is responsible;[93] the Swiss, by a circumstance for which the obligor is not responsible.[94]

The Continental rule thus adopts a subjective or relative impossibility, while under English law the seller would not be excused by impossibility to ship due to war. This would be true even if the parties agree, in a contract for the sale of goods to be shipped by vessel between certain dates, that the contract shall be void if the

[92] French Civil Code, Art. 1048.
[93] German Civil Code, §320.
[94] Swiss Civil Code, Art. 119.

goods do not arrive because of loss of the vessel or other unavoidable cause.[95] The question presented itself under a new phase, however, because at the very beginning of the war, by Trading with the Enemy Proclamations of August 5th and 12th, 1914, it was made unlawful to trade in or carry any goods destined for Germany or Austria, or for any person resident, carrying on business, or being therein. The doctrine of continuous voyage greatly extended the scope of these decrees to shipments destined for neutral European ports.[96] The fact that the American shipper was a neutral becomes immaterial both because the parties expressly made a choice of English law and because the buyer's performance having been made unlawful, the seller is also relieved. Wharton points out that the expressed or presumed intention of the parties as to the governing law of the obligation of the contract determines not only so far as it depends upon the interpretation of the language used by the parties "but also so far as it depends upon local laws which add to, or subtract from the rights and duties of the parties to the contract as fixed by its terms." [97] It was certainly not anticipated that a clause ostensibly made for the benefit of the English or Continental purchaser acting through his London agents would have just the contrary effect. But this would seem to follow inevitably from the drastic character of war legislation, coupled with the principle of mutuality in contracts.[98]

**Confusion of Theories as to Law Governing Substantive Validity.** It seems to be hopeless to arrive at a fixed principle from the decided cases alone, to determine the system of law by which the substantive validity of a contract is to be governed. Goodrich regards this subject as the most confused of all.[99] Beale classifies the cases into three categories of the governing law, *viz.*, 1. the place of making; 2. the place of performance; 3. the place intended by the parties; to which may be added the class of cases in which presumptions of intent are drawn. He holds Story responsible for much of

[95] Ashman *v.* Cox, 1899, 1 Q.B.D. 439. If impossibility results from a contingency which, if it had been contemplated by the parties, would have been regarded as "so obviously terminating the obligation as not to require expression," it has been held that performance may be excused. See Columbia Law Rev. 1900, p. 533; Kinzer Construction Co. *v.* the State (1910) 125 N.Y. Supp. 46. But this does not apply to an outbreak of war.

[96] See Baty in Law Quarterly Rev. 1915, p. 30.

[97] Wharton, Conflict of Laws, (1905) ii, p. 901.

[98] See Kuhn, "The War and Commercial Contracts in Neutral Countries" in *Festschrift für Georg Cohn* (Zurich, 1918).

[99] Goodrich (1927) p. 228.

the confusion because he first applied the law of the place of making, and then qualified the rule by applying it only when contracts are made and to be performed in the same place. Beale maintains that Story only wished to point out that the law of the forum did not apply to contracts made elsewhere but the inference drawn by the courts frequently leads to the application of the law of the place of performance.[100] Further confusion has been introduced by making the assumption that the law of the place of performance represents the law which the parties themselves intended to govern their contract. This is traceable to the dictum of Lord Mansfield in Robinson *v.* Bland,[101] which applied to one of the counts upon a bill drawn in France and payable in England for money lost at play in France. Although the law of both countries was substantially the same, Lord Mansfield maintained that the parties had a view to the laws of England. "The law of the place can never be the rule, where the transaction is entered into with an express view to the law of another country, as the rule by which it is to be governed." [102]

We shall not attempt to harmonize the principles of the cases relating to the substantive validity of contracts because we believe that such a task is impossible. It will be more advantageous to accept the principle of the law of the place of making as a basic rule, at the same time recognizing that the law of the place of performance must be observed in a large category of cases intimately bound up with performance. We shall see that the law of the place of performance is referred to for the measurement and interpretation of the contract rather than the determination of its substantive validity.

### 4. Performance of the Contract

**Place of Performance.** Agreements are made with a view to performance, if the parties have acted in good faith. Accordingly the place of performance and the law prevailing there, will be important considerations in determining the rights and obligations of the parties. Often the parties will designate the place of performance. If they fail to do so, the place of performance must be derived "by interpretation of the language of the promise." [103]

[100] Beale in (1919) 23 Harvard Law Rev., 100–103.

[101] (1760) 2 Burr. 1077.

[102] *Ibid.*, p. 1078, with reliance upon Huber.

[103] Restatement, §355. When the parties have an option to do one thing in one place, or another in a different place, the place of performance can only be determined when the option is exercised. *Ibid.*, §§356–357.

We have already discussed the influence which the law of the place of performance exerts upon the legality of the agreement or the legality of the performance which constitutes its consideration.[104] Assuming a valid contract to have been made, by what law shall the respective obligation of the parties be interpreted? Much of the confusion which has prevailed with regard to the competition between the law of the place of making and the law of the place of performance has been caused by the failure of judges and jurists to distinguish between the validity of agreements and their interpretation. Story established the principle of the *lex loci contractus* upon the supposition that the performance of the contract is to be in the place where it is made, either expressly or by tacit implication. But he maintained that where the contract is either expressly or tacitly to be performed in any other place, then the general rule applied, *viz.*, that its "validity, nature, obligation and interpretation is to be governed by the law of the place of performance."[105] This is a confusing statement due to the failure properly to analyze prior cases and discussions applicable only to interpretation. The Netherlanders, Voet and Huber, upon whom Story relied, often used general terms although discussing only a specific application. Thus P. Voet[106] speaks of a general rule of looking to the law of the place where the performance was intended to be made. But Voet, quoted by Story,[107] was considering the measure of performance in money or goods.

**Interpretation of Performance.** This presents quite a different question. It does not involve the validity of the agreement *ab initio* but of its interpretation. The parties are free to express their intent as to the nature and circumstances of their respective promises, assuming the performance of these promises does not violate the law of place of making or of performance. If they fail to express such intent and the law of the place of making proves to be at variance with the law of the place of performance, the court at the forum must arrive at its own conclusion by implication or presumption as to how the contract shall be performed. To illustrate: A promise was made to pay in New York the purchase price of an executed contract of sale. The promise was to be performed by payment part in cash and part by note made in Massachusetts and payable there. By Massachusetts law, a negotiable note taken for an antecedent debt is deemed

[104] See *ante*, p. 285 *et seq.*
[105] Story, §280.
[106] *De Statutis*, §§15–16.
[107] §281.

payment unless a contrary intention is shown; not so, however, by New York law. The action was brought on the original contract and the court of Massachusetts properly held that the New York law must determine what is equivalent to complete performance.[108]

An interesting case grew out of a shipment of merchandise by the plaintiff in New York to Sweden during the World War. The plaintiff delivered to the defendant drafts, with documents attached, with direction to present the same to the consignees against payment. The defendant's correspondent in London notified the plaintiff that it would undertake to deliver the documents to the consignees only upon their signing and delivering the British form of neutrality declaration to the effect that the goods would not be shipped to the Central Powers. This was agreed to by plaintiff. The consignees refused to accept the goods because a statute in Sweden made the British form illegal and substituted a Swedish form of somewhat different tenor. The court held that the defendant was negligent in not notifying the plaintiff that the British form could not be signed. By way of dictum, however, the court pointed out that: "The performance of the details of the arrangement between the plaintiff and the bank as to the certificate of neutrality was to be in Sweden and was regulated by the law there in force." [109]

A contract made in Pennsylvania provided for a loan to be used in an enterprise to be carried on in New York. The lender was to obtain part of the profits of the business but was not to take any part in its management nor be considered a partner. This would have made the lender liable as a partner by statute in Pennsylvania but not in New York. The question of such liability "would necessarily be connected with or grow out of such performance in New York" and, therefore, the lender was absolved from liability to a creditor of the borrower.[110]

The Restatement of the American Law Institute provides that the law of the place of performance determines the following questions:

(§358) Discharge with respect to (*a*) the manner and (*b*) the time and locality of performance; (*c*) the person by whom or to whom performance shall be made or rendered; (*d*) the sufficiency of performance; (*e*) excuse for non-performance.

[108] Tarbox *v.* Childs, (1896) 165 Mass. 408.
[109] Bown Bros. Inc., *v.* Merchants Bank, (1926) 243 N.Y. 366, 372.
[110] First Nat. Bk. of Waverly *v.* Hall, (1892) 150 Pa. 466.

(§361) The details of the manner of performing the duty imposed by the contract.

(§362) When performance is due.

(§363) The postponement of performance by operation of law.

(§364) The medium of payment.

(§365) Whether the obligation is satisfied by the giving and acceptance of a bill or note.

(§366) The person to whom performance shall be rendered.

(§367) The exact spot of performance.

(§368) The application of the payment to one or another of several debts.

(§370) Whether a breach has occurred.

(§372) The right to damages for a breach and the measure of damages.

(§374) Whether release of one party to a contract, or extending the time for performance in favor of the principal, or surrendering security, discharges the other parties.

**Gold Clause Cases.** The Joint Resolution of Congress of June 5, 1933, declared that every obligation which purports to require payment in gold or a particular kind of coin or currency of the United States, or in an amount in money of the United States measured thereby, to be against public policy. It further provided that every obligation whether containing any such provision or not, "shall be discharged upon payment, dollar for dollar, in any coin or currency which at the time of payment is legal tender for public and private debts."

We are not here concerned with the constitutionality of these provisions, nor with their interpretation as applied to obligations payable in the United States. An important question arises, however, as to whether they are applicable to a contract payable in a foreign country. The Restatement (§364) declares the general principle that the law of the place of performance determines the medium of payment in which a contract to pay money is to be performed. Obligations of American corporations were payable at the option of the bearer at a certain place in the United States in an amount of dollars of United States gold coin, or in London in sterling, or in Amsterdam in guilders, at a fixed ratio mentioned in the bonds. A bond of this kind was involved in the case of City Bank Farmers Trust Co. *v.* Bethlehem Steel Co.[111] The plaintiff held a bond of this tenor the coupons of which it presented for payment to defendant's agent in

[111] (1935) 244 A.D. N.Y. 634.

Amsterdam and demanded the dollar equivalent of Dutch guilders. It was not denied that the place of performance would ordinarily control the medium of payment. The court, however, gave judgment only for the equivalent amount of dollars stipulated, in legal tender, upon the ground that "the citizens of our country are controlled by the terms of the Joint Resolution particularly where, as here, the bonds were purchased in the United States by citizens thereof." The decision seems unsound and the vigorous dissent by Merrel, J., upon the ground that the Joint Resolution was not intended to control payments made in foreign countries in money not of the United States, may be sustained on appeal.

In Anglo-Continentale Treuhand A. G. *v.* St. Louis Southwestern Railway Co.,[112] a loan of the defendant was made payable in United States gold coin in New York, or in a specific number of other foreign currencies in the respective foreign places named. In an appeal from a judgment below, awarding only dollars equivalent to the foreign currency at the rate of exchange prevailing in New York at the time of the judgment, the Circuit Court of Appeals (per L. Hand, C. J.) decided that as the contract was to be performed abroad and was lawful there, the defendant should be held to the terms of the obligation, without regard to the Joint Resolution. To hold otherwise would be an "invasion of the prerogative of other states." The court also held that if the law did not apply to bonds held by aliens, it could not apply to citizens where performance was agreed to be made abroad.

The English courts were presented with a similar clause in the case of International Trustee for the Protection of Bondholders, Vaduz *v.* the King.[113] The court (per Branson, J.) held that the clause was to be construed as a gold-coin clause rather than a gold-value clause. The obligor of the bond was the British Government and as payment was made illegal within the United States, the equivalent of dollars at a fixed rate at time of judgment would have been in depreciated dollars. This was reversed, the court taking the view that the clause was a gold-value clause. As the defendant could not have been sued in the United States, the law applied was necessarily English law as laid down in the Feist Case.[114] Accordingly, it was held that the prohibition of the Joint Resolution did not

[112] (1936) 81 Fed. (2nd) 11.
[113] (1935) 52 T.L.R. 82.
[114] Feist *v.* Société Intercommunale Belge d'Electricité, [1934] A.C. 161.

apply. However, the House of Lords upon final appeal, though agreeing that the clause was a gold-value clause, reversed the judgment upon the ground that the United States law and not English law should apply because inferentially contemplated, thus giving judgment only for the equivalent of devalued dollars.[115]

**Foreign Conflict-of-Laws Rules Relating to Contracts.** With the exception of the provision as to form to which reference has already been made,[116] the *German* Civil Code fails to provide any general norm for the system of law which shall govern contracts. The Gebhard draft and the draft of the Second Preparatory Commission had both set up a series of rules for contracts which were, however, not included in the Introductory Statute. So that the modern law of Germany represents a throw-back to Savigny with the numerous modifications and the discordant decisions which we find in other systems. Savigny, with his perpetual search for the "seat" of the transaction, recognized the invisible and intangible nature of contracts. Separating the contract into the elements of obligation on the one side and right on the other, he found that the place of performance of each obligor, was the "seat" of each respective obligation. If the parties have fixed the place of performance, there will ordinarily be no difficulty; otherwise the place of performance must be determined by the circumstances inherent in the contract. The obligor's place of business is presumptively the place of performance.[117]

From these principles, later German practice has developed the rule that any specific agreement (autonomy) of the parties fixes the system of law in the first instance, and in the absence of such agreement, the place of performance is controlling;[118] and this may be taken to be the prevailing rule in Germany at the present time with the limitations we shall indicate.[119] The freedom of contract has wide limits but it is not unlimited because the binding character of the agreement is itself derived from law and not from the will of the parties. As one German writer has expressed it: what the parties have agreed to is legally inconsequential if there were no precedent

[115] (1936) N.Y. Law Jour. 1849; reversed in House of Lords, (1937) 53 T.L.R. 507.

[116] *Ante*, p. 275.

[117] Savigny, Private Int. Law, Guthrie's trans. (1880) pp. 194–195; 209–210.

[118] Decision of *Ober-Landesgericht*, Stuttgart, Aug. 2, 1894, cited by Lewald, *Das deutsche int. Privatrecht* (1931) p. 198.

[119] Lewald, p. 199.

system of law with power to create a legal effect from such agreement.[120]

The *Reichsgericht* had come to this conclusion in the period immediately preceding the adoption of the Civil Code, which, as a federal statute, unified the civil law of the Empire. A contract executed in Saxony provided for a marriage broker's commission. The parties were domiciled in Saxony where such an agreement is void. In Prussia it was valid and the agreement provided that Prussian law and jurisdiction should be applicable. The court dismissed the action, holding that the autonomy of the parties was permissible only within the limits of the law itself; and a violation of the coercive provisions of the law by the choice of a foreign law is itself illegal and void.[121]

Notwithstanding the logical reasoning of the court, the question is by no means simple. By what system of law is the will of the parties to be limited? Beale would say, by the law of the place of making,[122] but this assumes that the coercive provisions of the law of the place of making applies to every agreement entered into upon the territory of that state, no matter what the circumstances of the agreement may be. Legislation is seldom specific enough to leave no room for interpretation; especially where the forum is not in the country of making. To illustrate: The plaintiff and defendant were domiciled subjects of Soviet Russia. The defendant gave the plaintiff in Russia an order on a bank in New York for the payment of a sum in American dollars and guaranteed the payment to the plaintiff if the bank failed to pay. Afterwards the defendant escaped from Soviet Russia and settled permanently in Germany. The plaintiff presented the order to the bank in New York, but payment was refused because of a countermand by the defendant. The plaintiff then sued in Germany, the defense being the prohibition by Soviet law of all transactions in foreign exchange. The *Reichsgericht* sustained the validity of the contract because of an implied choice of the law of the place of performance, derived from the circumstance that both parties had intended to escape from Russia at that time and settle abroad.[123] Lewald criticizes this result as unsatisfactory but concedes that the question is whether Soviet law or the law of the place of

[120] Neumeyer, *Int. Verwaltungsrecht,* vol. ii, p. 456.
[121] *Reichsger.,* Sept. 21, 1899, 44 *R.G.Civ.* 300.
[122] See Beale, Treatise (1935) ii, pp. 1082–83.
[123] *Reichsger.,* Oct. 3, 1923, 108 *R.G.Civ.* 241.

performance is to determine the validity of the contract in the first instance. If the latter, then the will of the parties as to the application of law becomes quite irrelevant as the Soviet law had no control over the contract. The *Reichsgericht* followed Savigny's rule making the place of performance applicable to determine the validity of the contract. Therefore the decision may be sustained without the court's dicta relating to choice of law by the parties.[124] The *Reichsgericht* has frequently decided that in the absence of an express agreement of the parties, the validity of the contract is governed by the law of the place of performance.[125]

The principle of the autonomy of the parties has been subjected to a similar limitation in *France*. The provision of the Civil Code, Art. 1134, provides that "contracts lawfully entered into take the place of the law for those who have made them." This is accepted as establishing the autonomy of the parties in the choice of law. The general principle may be traced back to Dumoulin.[126] On the other hand, Arminjon maintains: "It is the law and not the will of the parties which gives to contracts the force which is accorded to them by Art. 1134." [127] Arminjon has been influenced not alone by the futility of following the vicious circle which the unlimited exercise of autonomy creates, but to some extent also directly by English authority. He quotes Dicey: The validity of a contract cannot be secured by apparently subjecting it to a law by which it is not properly governed.[128] Arminjon puts the case of an agreement made in the country of the parties' nationality and domicil where the interest rate is limited to 5%. The contract provided for the interest rate allowed by X, a foreign country, with which the parties never had any connection. The law of X permitted interest up to 10%. "Would the courts consider this clause more valid than if the parties had simply copied the article [of the law] into their contract?" [129] Pillet reinforces the argument by emphasizing that the code does not speak of *all* contracts, but only of contracts lawfully created (*légalement formées*), and maintains that the will of the parties can never be

[124] Lewald, p. 206.

[125] (1911) 78 *Reichsger*. Civ. 59; (1919) 95 *Reichsger*. Civ. 165. Swiss courts apply the *lex loci contractus*. Schnitzer, *Handbuch des int. Privatrechts* (1937) pp. 281–282.

[126] Weiss, *Traité de droit int. privé*. (1901) iv, p. 335.

[127] Arminjon, *Précis de droit int. pr.* (1934) ii, p. 260. *Cf.* Gény, *Méthodes d'interpretation*, p. 529.

[128] Dicey, (1916) p. 561. See also 1932 ed., p. 965.

[129] Arminjon, ii, p. 193.

equivalent to a law. Nevertheless he admits that the French Court of Cassation has only too often treated the voluntary choice of a foreign law as though it were equivalent to law and hence has annulled judgments below for failure to apply such choice.[130] A compulsory arbitration clause in a contract entered into in France according to English law, between a French citizen and an alien, has been held valid, though it would be void by French law.[131] It is to avoid a possible conflict of laws that the agreement was upheld. But if an agreement of this kind is made between two French citizens, choosing English law, recognition would not be accorded even if the agreement were signed in England, because the agreement would not be to avoid a conflict of laws but simply to avoid the local law of France.[132] Niboyet remarks that international life has thus become more elastic than life within a single state and has infringed to that extent the authority of coercive laws.[133]

From the point of view of positive law, Niboyet mentions four restrictions upon the autonomy of the parties: (1) there must be a possible conflict of laws; (2) the contract must represent one of purely private interest; (3) it must not relate to an act of inheritance; (4) it must not violate public policy (*ordre public*).[134] While these categories may be found to be convenient in the classification of decided cases, it is difficult to see that any neat criterion is thereby fixed. The fourth category may easily be conceived of as embracing all the others for the question in itself is the extent to which the law of the forum is willing to permit the parties to derogate from the ordinary rules of private international law prevailing in the country of the forum. Two illustrations may be made from French law. Clauses exempting carriers from liability or limiting their liability, as in the well known Harter Act of the United States, represent a clear legislative intent to limit the freedom of contract; yet French law in this matter applies the law which the parties have expressly or presumptively chosen.[135]

Another example is presented by the liberty permitted to the parties

130 Pillet, *Traité* (1924) ii, pp. 164–165 citing Court of Cassation, June 4, 1878, 1 Sirey, 1878, 428.

131 Clunet, 1910, p. 867; *Accord:* Clunet, 1926, p. 926.

132 Court of Cassation, May 17, 1927. *Gaz. du Palais* 1927, ii, p. 173.

133 Niboyet, *Acad. de Droit Int.*, 1927, *Recueil des Cours,* i, p. 31.

134 *Ibid.*, p. 18.

135 Court of Cassation, Feb. 23, 1864; 1864 Sirey i, p. 385; Dec. 5, 1910, *Rev. de droit int. privé,* 1911, p. 395. Niboyet himself regards this to be somewhat startling. Niboyet, pp. 29–30.

to choose the law of prescription applicable to the obligation created by their contract. The outlawing of a right of action under a statute of limitation is, of course, a rule of procedure in the view of English law, while under the law of France and certain other jurisdictions, prescription of a right is incorporated in the right itself and is governed by the same system of law which determines the nature and effect of the right.[136] Even with this concept quite well understood, it is curious that French law permits the parties freedom in the choice of law applicable to the statute of limitations.[137] The actual system of law applicable to limitation of action, in the absence of choice,—whether the personal law of the debtor or of the creditor, or the system which determines the nature and effect of the contract generally,—is still a matter of difference in French doctrine and jurisprudence. The prevailing opinion seems to favor the latter system, giving then a freedom of the parties to shorten the term by reference to another system but not to lengthen it beyond the term allowed by the *lex fori.*[138] Audinet [139] points out with great force, however, that the Code has indicated the legislative will by providing that a person cannot renounce prescription before it has taken effect,[140] and that therefore it is against public order to permit the parties freedom of choice in respect of prescription.

The plaintiff, a French citizen, obtained a policy of marine insurance in London for the safe arrival of a ship belonging to his debtor, on a voyage between two foreign ports, in which his only interest was the freight guaranteed for the payment of his debt. The insurance company was British and when sued in France, defended upon the ground that the plaintiff had no insurable interest under French law. The court sustained the defense upon the ground of French public order, although it was not doubted that the contract was valid by English law where the contract was made.[141] The result cannot be sustained upon the general principles of conflict in respect to contracts because the contract was valid where made and the intent of the parties was clearly that English law should apply. The contract was also beneficial to the plaintiff, a French citizen, suing in a French court. But the rule of public policy as already pointed out, is

[136] See *ante,* p. 91.
[137] Clunet, 1883, p. 145 at p. 155.
[138] Weiss, iv, pp. 385–386; Niboyet, p. 24.
[139] Clunet, 1896, pp. 475–476.
[140] Civil Code, Art. 2220.
[141] Clunet, 1899, p. 340.

a negation of international standards in the application of law. It has been characterized by Pillet and Niboyet as the most vague concept of private international law.[142] Perhaps French courts will regard contracts of this kind as equivalent to gambling contracts, which should be, though obviously are not, considered void everywhere.

These illustrations demonstrate that Niboyet's four categories may be quite true by a negation method but they fail to set up a measure of the parties' freedom of choice because the rules are themselves indefinite in scope. Obviously the four categories refer only to express choice. The parties, however, in the vast majority of cases, do not make an express choice of law. Are the courts then obliged to find an implied choice from the circumstances or should they adopt a system of the proper law of the contract in the absence of such choice? In French law as in other systems, these two concepts are often confused. The principle of English law which applies the law with a view to which the contract was made, rests upon an implied choice and often this concept is found in French decisions as well. For example, where a contract is executed abroad between parties both of French nationality, it is customary for the court to say that they would have wished French law to apply, especially where they were ignorant of the local law.[143]

Ordinarily, however, it may be said that the rule in France is to apply the law of the place of contracting. The rule is derived historically from Bartolus and the Post-glossators but it is also founded upon the reasons which have influenced its adoption in whole or in part elsewhere, *viz.,* that it is the common ground for the meeting of the minds,[144] and that it is a system which is fixed at the moment of entering into the contract as contrasted with the place of performance, which may or may not be known at that time. Art. 1159 of the French Civil Code which provides that "what is ambiguous shall be interpreted according to the customs of the country in which the contract was made" is not to be underrated as an analogy, although the article was not intended to lay down the international rule.[145] The law of the place of contracting governs the nature and scope of the obligation,

[142] Pillet and Niboyet, *Manuel de dr. int. privé.* (1924) pp. 167, 283. So also Healy in *Recueil des Cours,* 1925, iv, p. 471.

[143] Clunet, 1926, p. 643 at p. 645.

[144] Weiss, iv, p. 346 calls it *"la loi commune de leur entente"*; Von Bar, ii, p. 8: *"Einen gemeinsame Boden des Verständnisses."*

[145] Weiss, iv, pp. 346–348 citing numerous cases in which the rule has been accepted. See also Court of Cassation, June 21, 1904, Sirey 1906, i, 22.

the conditions which suspend or dissolve it, whether it is voidable on account of mistake, duress or fraud, and generally as to the methods by which the obligation may be discharged.[146] There are certain exceptions. French courts accept a designation of the place of payment as also fixing the character of the money in which the obligation is to be paid.[147]

The *Italian* law has adopted by statute substantially the result reached by French courts. "The substance and effect of obligations shall be deemed governed by the law of the place where the transactions took place, and if the contractants belong to the same nation [then] by their national law, provided however, that proof of a different intent may be made in any case." [148]

The law of *Poland* is entitled to especial mention upon this subject because of its detailed content and progressive character. In the absence of express agreement, contracts are governed by the following systems of law:

(*a*) Contracts made upon a stock exchange, by the law of the place of exchange;

(*b*) contracts relating to land, by the *lex rei sitae;*

(*c*) retail sales, by the personal law of the vendor;

(*d*) contracts with public entities (states, provinces, municipalities) by the law of the place of these entities;

(*e*) insurance contracts, by the law existing at the seat of the insurer, or of a branch;

(*f*) labor contracts, by the law of the place where the labor is to be performed.

(*g*) In all other cases, law of the common domicil of the parties. If there be no common domicil, then the law of the domicil of the obligor if the contract be unilateral; or the law of the place of contracting, if bilateral.[149]

The Bustamante Code for *Latin-American countries* accepts as the general conflict-of-laws rule applicable to contracts, the personal law common to the contracting parties, and in the absence of such law, the law of the place of contracting.[150] The author of the Code apparently did not accept as a primary principle the express or im-

[146] Weiss, iv, 371–375. See Clunet, 1920, p. 777.

[147] Clunet, 1922, p. 999.

[148] Italian Civil Code, *Disposizioni*, Art. 9.

[149] Law of Aug. 2, 1926, summarized by Niboyet, *Académie de droit int., Recueil des Cours*, 1927, i, 48–49.

[150] Art. 186.

plied will of the parties. The interpretation of contracts is to be made in accordance with the law "by which they are governed." "Only when that law is in dispute and should appear from the implied will of the parties" may the rule already stated be "presumptively applied although it may result in applying to the contract a different law." [151]

These two provisions are not completely co-ordinated because the first restricts the application of the second to cases in which the governing law is in dispute and the second applies to a residuary without a specification of particular contracts, such as the Polish statute clearly does.[152]

The Bustamante Code declares the rules relating to legality ("clauses and conditions in conflict with the law, morality and public policy") to be of an "international public order," as that term has previously been explained.[153]

[151] *Ibid.*, Art. 184.
[152] Art. 186 begins with the words: "In all other contracts" . . .
[153] Arts. 175, 179.

## CHAPTER XI

# FOREIGN TORTS

JUSTICE demands that wrongs be redressed even if they occur outside the jurisdiction. If this were not so, the guilty party could easily escape liability because of the facility of movement in modern life, and the increase in the number of sovereign jurisdictions. We are not here considering crimes, or wrongs against the state as such. At common law, an injury done to the person or personal property of another was said to be transitory in the sense that the right of redress followed the guilty party wherever he might go. An injury to real property was local, localized by the *res* itself, which was stationary. The wrong and the redress involved an inquiry into the ownership of the land in question, which only a local court could determine. Ordinarily, an injury caused to a person abroad may constitute a cause of action in a local court. Of course, if the recognition of the cause of action is repugnant to the law of the forum, the cause of action will not be enforced there. The phrase "against public policy" is often used in this connection as though it had a defined or definable significance; but nothing is settled by its use. It remains to establish the reasons for such repugnance and to classify the specific applications.

Originally, tort actions in England were grounded upon a breach of the king's peace "with force and arms."[1] As this was a jurisdictional fact, it had to be laid within the kingdom. When the new action "on the case" was developing, the same forms continued to be used. Even when the tort arose *out* of England, the specific allegation of being against the peace of the king was not allowed to be disputed. A similar result was reached in the American colonies without employing the fiction.[2]

[1] Jenks, A Short History of English Law (1913) p. 136.

[2] *Cf.* Kuhn, "Local and Transitory Actions in Private Int. Law" in (1918) 66 Univ. of Penna. Law Rev. 301. Goodrich, Conflict of Laws (1927) §95. Beale in (1912) 26 Harvard Law Rev. 290.

The distinction between local and transitory actions was made however, not to determine whether an English court as opposed to a foreign court had cognizance, but only to determine venue *within* the realm. When an injury to land located abroad was sought to be redressed in England, it was held that the plaintiff was "not relievable in any ordinary court of law."[3] Lord Mansfield went out of his way in Mostyn *v.* Fabrigas[4] to refer to two earlier decisions (not directly reported) in which he had entertained damages to real estate in Nova Scotia and Labrador, where no local courts had yet been instituted. The plaintiff in the case before him was suing for assault and false imprisonment, so that his remarks were *obiter;* but he characterized the distinction between local and transitory actions as a fiction invented simply for the mode of trial. His opinion did not prevail and the old rule was established in Doulson *v.* Matthews.[5] Even Chief Justice Marshall, sitting as Circuit Judge in Virginia, in an action against Thomas Jefferson for a trespass alleged to have been committed in New Orleans before annexation, found the rule too firmly intrenched to change, though he complimented Lord Mansfield on his effort to do so.[6] It has been remarked as strange that Marshall should have given more weight to English decisions rendered after the American Revolution than to those of Lord Mansfield rendered before it. Indeed the courts of some of our highest State tribunals have refused to be slavishly bound by these limitations,[7] and will take jurisdiction to an injury to foreign land. In some jurisdictions the old rule has been repealed by statute.[8] In England and in many American jurisdictions, the old rule still prevails.[9]

If the action is for an injury committed abroad but recognized as such at common law, the local forum will recognize and redress the injury. Hence, if one brings a civil action for false imprisonment for an assault and battery committed abroad, he need not, in the first instance, offer any proof that such acts are unlawful and that they

[3] Skinner *v.* East India Co., (1665) 6 Howell's State Trials, 710, 719.

[4] (1774) 1 Cowp. 161; 1 Smith's Leading Cas. 591.

[5] (1793) 4 Term R. 503.

[6] Livingston *v.* Jefferson, (1811) 1 Brock. 203; Fed. Cas. 8411.

[7] Little *v.* Chicago & St. Paul Ry., (1896) 65 Minn. 48.

[8] *Cf.* Kuhn, *ut cit.* (1918) 66 Univ. of Penna. Law Rev. 306. The rule in New York was changed after Brisbane *v.* Penna. R.R., (1913) 205 N.Y. 431.

[9] British South Africa Co. *v.* Cia. de Mocambique (1893) A.C. 602. Kuhn, *ut* cit. 306n. We would here seem to have another instance of the survival of a rule of law long after the historical conditions which gave rise to it had disappeared.

entitle the injured party to a recompense in damages in the place where they were inflicted.[10]

Where the tort is one not familiar to the common law, where *e.g.*, (*a*) it is not recognized as a wrong in the local jurisdictions, or (*b*) the right of action is created by statute in the foreign court though the act itself causing the injury is recognized as a wrong by the law of the forum, the question arises whether the action may be maintained. The principles adopted in England and in the United States vary greatly and it is best to illustrate. In *The Halley*[11] the plaintiffs were the owners of a Norwegian ship damaged by a collision with the ship of the defendants in Belgian or Dutch waters and while in charge of a compulsory pilot. The English law recognized no liability for negligence in the owners under such circumstances because of the lack of relationship of master and servant between defendants and the pilot. The Privy Council decided that it was "alike contrary to principle and to authority to hold that an English court of justice will enforce a foreign municipal law, and will give a remedy in the shape of damages in respect of an act which, according to its own principles, imposes no liability on the person from whom the damages are claimed."[12] The doctrine was carried still further in Machado *v.* Fontes[13] where an action was brought in England for damages because of the publication of an alleged libel in Brazil. Such a publication was not actionable by the plaintiff under Brazilian law though it was "wrongful," and on appeal the plea on the Brazilian law was disallowed. The forum is asked to enforce an action *in personam.* If it did not exist in the foreign state, it cannot be pursued in the local. No case in the United States has been found where recovery in tort has been allowed for what was not the basis of action by the *lex loci delicti.*[14] Goodrich suggests that the real source of difficulty in cases like *The Halley* may be the notion that in giving redress for the foreign wrong, the forum is allowing the foreign law an extraterritorial operation.[15] But if this be the difficulty, how explain Machado *v.* Fontes?

In the class of cases referred to above under (*b*), there is a wide

[10] Whitford *v.* Panama R.R., (1861) 23 N.Y. 468.
[11] (1868) L.R. 2 P.C. 193.
[12] *Ibid.*, p. 204.
[13] (1897) 2 Q.B. 221.
[14] Goodrich, (1927) p. 190.
[15] *Ibid.*, p. 198.

diversity of opinion and authority due to the varying statutes in amendment of the old common law rule allowing no survivorship of actions for negligence where the injury caused death. The old rule "was a great and admitted defeat in the law." [16] Lord Campbell's Act of 1846, which was intended to cure the defect, was not everywhere adopted and the legislatures of the various states enacted laws greatly at variance with each other. Some limit the amount of recovery, others do not. Some provide for a survival of the original cause of action, others give a new right to certain designated beneficiaries not always identical. A Massachusetts statute provides for the assessment of damages against the defendant in proportion to his degree of culpability.[17] As to this, Judge Cardozo, writing for the Court of Appeals in Loucks *v.* Standard Oil Co., said: [18] "We shall not feel the pricks of conscience if the offender pays the survivors in proportion to the measure of his offense." The court allowed the parties designated by the Massachusetts statute to recover in New York even though the measure of damages differed, the case not being one in which special remedies established by the foreign law were not capable of enforcement in the home tribunals. The court observed a growing tendency to admit that only exceptional circumstances should lead one of the states to refuse to enforce a right acquired in another.[19]

The Federal Supreme Court has long since drawn away from the earlier doctrine that a cause of action created by statute can be enforced only in the state of the statute.[20]

A final illustration of the extent to which a foreign tort will be redressed in the forum even though requiring a procedure unknown by the local law is furnished by a recent case in New York. An accident occurred upon the Canadian side of the Niagara Gorge. Under the laws of Ontario, where the plea of contributory negligence is allowed, the jury must find the entire amount of damages to which the plaintiff would have been entitled had there been no such con-

[16] Cooley; A Treatise on the Law of Torts, 4th ed., 1932, §210.

[17] *Ibid.*, §211.

[18] (1918) 224 N.Y. 99 at p. 112.

[19] *Ibid.*, p. 111. "The misleading word 'comity' has been responsible for much of the trouble. It has been fertile in suggesting a discretion unregulated by general principles."

[20] Dennick *v.* Central R.R. of N.J., (1880) 103 U.S. 11; Stewart *v.* B. & O. R.R., (1897) 168 U.S. 445; *Contra:* Texas & P. R.R. *v.* Richards, 68 Texas 375.

tributory fault; and "the plaintiff shall have judgment only for so much thereof as is proportionate to the degree of fault imputable to the defendant."[21] The jury was instructed, pursuant to the statute, that the burden of proving contributory negligence was on the defendant and the jury found the plaintiff was guilty of contributory negligence to the degree of ten percent. Under the law of New York in a common law action such as this, the burden of proof of freedom from contributory negligence is on the plaintiff. The defendant on appeal urged that this was a rule of procedure. The Court of Appeals unanimously held the appellant "wrong according to reason and authority" and decided the question of freedom from contributory negligence to be a substantive part of plaintiff's right; also that the New York court would enforce the right of recovery to the extent granted by Ontario law, although this was unknown to the common law.[22]

**Torts Committed on the High Seas.** The rule that the *lex loci delicti* governs the right of action creates difficulty when the tort occurred on the high seas. Ordinarily the law of the flag will determine the existence and measure of the right. Where a right to sue for wrongful killing was not given under the existing maritime law of the United States, but was given by the law of the flag, the right was nevertheless recognized.[23]

Undoubtedly, the law of the forum may limit the recovery upon a foreign tort. Where the tort occurs on the high seas, the result of a limiting statute may work injustice. The owner of the *Titanic,* a British vessel which foundered upon her maiden voyage to the United States, tendered a few lifeboats as being the limit of its alleged liability for negligence by reason of the disaster. The Supreme Court allowed the limitation under United States law not because the foundation of the tort was any other than British law (which permitted a greater recovery) but because it regarded the limitation as in the nature of a domestic policy. This result seems indeed bizarre, for the principle thus forces the application of a *domestic* statute to the liability arising in respect of a *foreign* vessel foundering upon the *high seas* before she had ever been within the jurisdiction. Thus the exemption might be granted in favor of an *alien* shipowner as against

[21] Laws of Ontario, 1924, chap. 32.

[22] Fitzpatrick *v.* International Ry. Co. (1929) 252 N.Y. 127. In the Federal courts the burden of establishing contributory negligence is on the defendant. Inland & Seaboard Coasting Co. *v.* Tolson, (1891) 139 U.S. 551.

[23] *The Hamilton,* (1907) 207 U.S. 398.

rights of action of *American* citizens duly acquired under *British* law.[24]

**The Restatement Rules relating to Torts.** The Restatement of Conflict of Laws relating to wrongs committed in foreign jurisdictions must be considered with reference to the Restatement of the Law of Torts, as adopted and promulgated by the American Law Institute. The phraseology in both Restatements distinguishes between "wrongs" and "torts." If the right is that of a private person, the wrong is considered to be a tort. If it is in favor of the state, the wrong is a crime. If a tort has been committed by the law of a state, the question whether other states will recognize it and enforce a duty of compensation for the injury is a question of the conflict of laws. To constitute a tort there must be an injury to the plaintiff legally caused by an actor whose conduct is tortious in character.[25] If the law of any state imposes a tort liability, the law of the place where the last event necessary to make an actor liable for an alleged tort is considered as the place of the wrong;[26] and the place of the wrong determines whether the person is responsible for the harm he has caused by intention or negligence.[27] If the law of the place of wrong imposes the doing of a particular act or the happening of a certain event as a condition of liability, such condition must be satisfied to enable a plaintiff to recover for a tort in the forum. If the act was privileged at the place where it was performed, there will be no liability in the forum.[28] On the other hand, if a cause of action is created at the place of wrong, a cause of action will be recognized in other states, subject however to the general exceptions to recognition of foreign causes of action, such as the lack of a form of action in the forum, action to recover a penalty given by the law of another state or upon a right created by the foreign state as a method of furthering its own governmental interests, or actions upon a cause "created in another state, the enforcement of which is contrary to the strong public policy of the forum."[29] Actions of trespass to foreign land cannot be maintained.[30]

[24] (1914) 233 U.S. 718. *Cf.* Kuhn, (1915) 9 Amer. Jour. of International Law, 336.

[25] Restatement of Torts, §§6–7.

[26] Restatement of Conflict of Laws, §377.

[27] §379.

[28] §§381–382.

[29] §§384, 608–612.

[30] §614.

With the general principle stated as above, the Restatement refers to the law of the place of the wrong in order to determine the following:

Whether contributory negligence precludes recovery in whole or in part (§385);

Whether a master is liable to a servant for a wrong caused by a fellow-servant (§386);

Whether the master or principal is liable for the acts of a person authorized to act for him (§387);

Whether a claim for damages survives the death of the tortfeasor or of the injured person (§390);

Whether there is a right of action for wrongful death, and the amount of possible recovery (§391);

The distribution of the amount of damages recovered (§393);

The person or persons who have the right to sue for wrongful death (§§394–5); however, where the foreign law designates the personal representative of the deceased, his qualification as such is, of course, determined by the law of the forum (§396);

The statute of limitations for recovery for wrongful death (§397); however, where the limitation imposed by the law of the forum may be interpreted as applying to all actions for death, the limitation of the forum must also be respected (§605).

**Foreign Conflict-of-Laws Rules relating to Torts.** The terminology of Continental Europe in respect to torts is not always equivalent to the English terms. All systems agree that torts give rise to an "obligation." The *French* codes speak of *"delits,"* which are crimes as well as civil torts. *"Quasi delits"* are violations of rights without willful intent.[31] The *Italian* codes employ the terms *"delitti"* and *"quasi delitti"* in a similar sense. The *German* Civil Code treats of torts under the head of *"Unerlaubte Handlungen"* (acts not permitted).[32] The *Austrian* Civil Code uses the term *"wiederrechtliche Beschädigung"* (unlawful injury).[33] The *Swiss* Code of Obligations treats the subject under the title: *"Die Entstehung durch unerlaubte Handlungen."*[34]

**French Law.** The influence of Savigny was felt far beyond the confines of his own country. He maintained that the principles of obligation arising from wrongful acts are *moral* principles and therefore should be conceived of as strictly coercive. Therefore, the "seat"

[31] *Cf.* Weiss, *Traité* (1901) iv, p. 386. French Civ. Code, §1382.

[32] 25th Title.

[33] Austrian Civ. Code, Art. 1294.

[34] Arts. 41–61.

of the obligation should lie at the forum and be governed by that law. This view gained acceptance for a time not only in Germany but also in Belgium, though not in France.[35] The courts in France recognize that the law of the place of the act must determine whether it constitutes a wrong, the person entitled to redress and the amount of damages.[36]

Where a tort is committed on the high seas against a French citizen, the courts still apply the *lex fori* in order that there shall always be a redress of grievance before a French court. To illustrate: A British ship was in collision with a French ship upon the high seas. When sued in a French court, the British owners sought to limit their liability by abandoning the ship and freight as permitted by French law to French shipowners but not to foreign shipowners. The British law allowed a less favorable limitation of liability. The French court applied the British law.[37] The theory of the decision is not clearly expressed but seems to rest upon the theory that the law of the flag is tacitly accepted by the owners as to the extent of liability. Curiously enough, the rule was applied by the United States Supreme Court in *favor* of the owner of the ill-fated British ship *Titanic*,[38] but of course upon the entirely different principle that the right to limit liability is a rule of procedure and therefore governed by the *lex fori* under common-law principles.[39]

**German Law.** The doctrine of Savigny was definitely reversed in favor of the *lex loci delicti commissi* by the *Reichsgericht* at the turn of the century. A fraud committed in Ohio formed the basis of an action in Hamburg. The *Reichsgericht* approved the application of Ohio law in the court below.[40] On the other hand, the Introductory Statute to the Civil Code[41] provides that no greater claims may be maintained against a German for a tort committed abroad than are recognized by German law.[42]

[35] Weiss, (1901) iv, p. 391, Clunet, 1889, p. 664; Belgian Court of Cassation, Nov. 26, 1908, Clunet, 1909, p. 241, p. 1178. See Savigny (Guthrie's trans. 1880) p. 253.

[36] Pillet, *Traité* (1924) ii, p. 313.

[37] Court of Cassation, May 4, 1891. Clunet, 1892, p. 153.

[38] See *ante*, p. 308.

[39] *The Titanic*, (1914) 233 U.S. 718.

[40] *Reichsger.*, Feb. 5, 1900. Clunet, 1900, p. 812.

[41] Art. 12. The same principle is to be found stated in Art. 11 of the Japanese Statute of 1898 upon the Application of the Laws in General.

[42] Lewald doubts the justice of this limitation. *Das deutsche int. Privatr.* (1931) p. 269. Arminjon accepts it only when necessary to prevent gross injustice. *Précis de dr. int. privé* (1929) ii, p. 273.

A difficult question presents itself under German law where certain acts constitute a tort in the foreign country in which the acts occurred, but would not be so considered or classified under German law. Lewald supposes the case of a foreign system of law which regards an action for the maintenance of an illegitimate child to be an action sounding in tort. Could an action upon the foreign cause of action be brought before a German court? Lewald believes that the case should be resolved by the proper rule of conflict applicable to the circumstances as they are classified by German law. Art. 21 of the Introductory Statute determines the obligation for maintenance by the father of an illegitimate child according to the laws of the state to which the mother belonged at the birth of the child (with a limitation of redress to the damages allowed by German law). Lewald adds that the legal system of the place of the injurious act cannot force its "qualification," *i.e.*, its conception in law, to be accepted by a German judge.[43]

The application given to Art. 12 seems to require that both the cause of action and the nature and measure of damages as provided by the foreign and the German law must coincide. The *Reichsgericht* expresses the rule in this sense in an action brought by the husband of a woman injured while visiting the German division of an architectural exhibition in Ghent, Belgium. The action was brought against the president of the division upon the ground of negligence and breach of contract. The judgment below was reversed and the case remanded to determine whether an action on contract was permitted in the circumstances by both the Belgian and the German law.[44] But it would seem that if the foreign law gives a wider claim sounding in tort than the German, it may be sustained provided an equivalent redress is given in contract or quasi-contract.[45]

The *Italian* and *Swiss* systems adopt the principle of the *lex loci delicti* without the limitation of the *lex fori*.[46] The legislative and legal justification of the rule without such limitation was made the subject of a scholarly study by the late Pasquale Fiore.[47]

The Bustamante Code adopted by some of the *Latin-American* states declares that obligations arising by operation of law are gov-

[43] Lewald, (1931) p. 266.

[44] (1919) 96 *Reichsgericht* 96, 100.

[45] Lewald, *op. cit.*, p. 269 citing *Ober Landesger.* Frankfort, July 5, 1923.

[46] Udina, *Droit int. privé d'Italie* (1930) pp. 127–128. Schnitzer, *Handbuch des int. Privatrechts* (1937) p. 288.

[47] Clunet, 1900, pp. 449 *et seq.*; pp. 717 *et seq.*

erned by the law which has created them; that those arising from crimes or offenses are subject to the same law as the crime or offense from which they arise; and that those arising from actions or omissions involving guilt or negligence not punishable by law shall be governed by the law of the place in which the negligence occurred or in which the guilt became obligatory.[48]

[48] Code of Private Int. Law, Arts. 165, 167–168. Int. Conferences of American States (1931) p. 343.

## Chapter XII

# SUCCESSION UPON DEATH

### 1. Comparison of the English and the Roman Systems

We have previously (Chapter IX) called attention to the complete separation maintained in English law and the systems derived from it, between the transfer of and acquisition of rights of ownership in real property and the transfer of and acquisition of rights in personal property. This separation profoundly affects the transfer of property by the death of the owner because not only the inheritance of the property but also the right to administer property is determined by its character as real or personal as the case may be. Under the common law, only real property, *i.e.*, land and rights homologated to the use and possession of land, passed to the heir direct. After the period when testamentary dispositions of real property were permitted, it passed direct to the devisee. No interposition of a public authority, judicial or otherwise, was required. In this respect English law followed the Roman system except that by the law of Rome the *entire* property of whatever nature passed as an *universum* to the heirs, subject to the payment of the debts of the deceased. From the Justinian period onward, however, the estate could be accepted with a "benefit of inventory," in which event the liability was limited to the extent of the property received.[1] The Roman conception was based upon the continuity of the personality of the deceased in his heirs, a concept deriving from the more ancient idea of the collectivity of the family. The English system of landholding was based upon feudal service or homage to the overlord. Under this system an estate could not pass as an *universum*. When wills of land were first permitted, they operated as declarations of uses taking effect after the testator's death.[2] Under the modern systems of the Roman law, property of

[1] Sohm, The Institutes (Ledlie's trans.) §§108, 114.

[2] Digby, An Introduction to the History of the Law of Real Property, 4th ed. pp. 379–380.

a deceased person, both real and personal, passes direct to the heir or heirs. The English system requires a public grant after death to an executor named in the will, or to an administrator appointed by a court of probate in the event of intestacy, or failure to name an executor. To the extent of personal property, the executor or administrator is invested with the legal character, *persona* or *status,* of the decedent, and is therefore spoken of as his "personal representative." [3] Since the English Land Transfer Act 1897,[4] the real or immovable property also passes through the hands of the executor or administrator. This legislation has not been generally adopted in the United States.

The distinctive manner of dealing with the personal property of deceased persons by probate and appointment was developed by the Church in order to protect and encourage, indeed almost to enforce the making of death-bed gifts. It "insisted strenuously upon the duty of making a will, and almost stigmatized as doomed to perdition the unlucky man who omitted this duty." [5]

The ecclesiastical courts had no jurisdiction over land though they had sole jurisdiction over death-bed gifts of personalty and hence the rules relating to the different categories ceased to be similar.

The complete separation which exists in Anglo-American jurisprudence between the succession to land and the succession to chattels does not exist at all in some European countries and is followed only to a modified degree in others. The Roman theory of universal succession or succession as a unit, under which the legal personality of the deceased passes over to his heir, still exists in the civil-law countries of Europe, except that certain countries recognize a separate regime for immovables, although still adhering to the Roman theory as to all other property. In the latter group of countries, succession to immovables is determined by the *lex rei sitae*.[6] The group which regulates succession by one and the same system for all kinds of property includes Germany [7] and Italy.[8]

[3] *Ibid.,* p. 380.

[4] 60 and 61 Vict. c. 65.

[5] Jenks, A Short History of English Law, p. 61. "If intestacy was admitted, the Church appointed an 'administrator'; and it was long before the next-of-kin could make him answerable for the 'dead's part.'" *Ibid.,* p. 62.

[6] To this group belong Austria, Imperial Decree of Aug. 9, 1854, regulating Judicial Procedure, §23; Belgium, Civ. Code, Art. 3; France, Civ. Code, Art. 3; and the Netherlands, Civ. Code, Art. 7.

[7] Introductory Statute, Arts. 24–25.

[8] *Disposizioni,* Art. 8.

The *German* Introductory Statute provides that succession to the estate of a German citizen, even though dying abroad, is governed by German law, and an alien domiciled in Germany, by his foreign law. But Art. 27 of this Statute makes the peculiar doctrine with which we have become familiar under the head of capacity to act, capacity to marry, and divorce, applicable also to matters of succession. The *lex patriae* is recognized as authoritative in the first instance, but if the particular *lex patriae* itself refers to German law, that law shall govern.

It follows, therefore, that the estate of a citizen of a country supporting the doctrine of domiciliary law in regard to succession, as, for example, England, the American States, or Switzerland, will be administered according to German law, if the deceased was domiciled in Germany at the time of his death. Conversely, the estate of a German citizen domiciled in such a state will be subjected to the domiciliary law by the doctrine supported there. Art. 27 of the Introductory Statute does not refer to the converse case, and therefore a German court would apply the main principle of *lex patriae.* This is a case of absolute conflict. It would, of course, be solved in favor of the law of the country whose courts actually obtain jurisdiction of the parties and of the property.

The law of *Switzerland* follows a middle doctrine. Although the domiciliary law is applicable, a testator has the right to choose the law of his canton of origin by will or in a contract for succession; and this provision is made applicable by analogy to aliens domiciled in Switzerland. This election is subject, however, to the separation between movables and immovables, the latter being governed by the *lex situs.* Furthermore, Swiss law is applicable to Swiss subjects domiciled abroad if the foreign law and forum is not applicable by its own terms in regard to succession.[9]

## 2. Intestate Succession to Land

Property in land is determined by the law of its location.[10] This necessarily includes the transmission of ownership by the death of the owner, whether to the heirs by intestate succession, or to devisees under a will.[11]

[9] Swiss "N. & A.," Arts. 22, 28. Schnitzer, *Handbuch des int. Privatr.* (1937) pp. 233–236.

[10] See *ante,* p. 222.

[11] Clarke *v.* Clarke (1900) 178 U.S. 186.

The selection of those entitled to succeed, however, may involve a question of personal status already fixed by circumstances established abroad, or procedure completed under the law of a foreign state. Thus for example the question may arise whether a person legitimated or adopted under the law of a foreign country in which he and his parents were domiciled, or of which they were nationals, may inherit as an heir? We have already discussed this question when considering Legitimacy and Adoption.[12] It is only necessary to emphasize that the application of the *lex situs* does not require more than the determination of the prerequisites for inheriting. As Westlake points out in discussing the early case of Birtwhistle *v.* Vardill,[13] English law required birth after marriage as a condition for the inheritance of English land. It did not require legitimacy to be determined by the *lex situs.*[14] Expressed in another way, the Anglo-American rule of intestate succession to land is determined by the object, not by the subject of ownership.

### 3. Intestate Succession to Movables

A different principle applies to intestate succession to movables. Here the prevailing rule is to apply the law of the last domicil of the deceased. The United States Supreme Court referred to the rule as having existed for several hundred years, not only in England but also on the Continent. "It has been universal for so long a time that it may now be said to be a part of the *jus gentium.*" So spake Mr. Justice Wayne writing the opinion in Ennis *v.* Smith.[15] The case involved the distribution of part of the estate of the Polish patriot, General Kosciusko, who participated in the War of the American Revolution. Kosciusko died domiciled in Switzerland leaving several wills, but he made no disposition of certain personal investments in the United States. The rule of domicil, said the court, prevails in the ascertainment of the person who is entitled to take as heir or distributee. The law of the domicil, therefore, is to decide, whether primogeniture gives a right of preference, or an exclusive right to succession, and whether a person is legitimate, or not, to take the succession. So whether persons are to take *per capita,* or *per stirpes;*

[12] See *ante,* pp. 202, 208.
[13] (1830–1835) 2 Cl. & F. 571, 582; (1839–40) 7 Cl. & F. 895, 940.
[14] Westlake, Private Int. Law (1925) §178.
[15] (1852) 14 How. 400.

and the nature and extent of the right of representation."[16] Since the decision was rendered (1852), the assumed universality of the rule has been broken, as we shall see, by certain European countries. It remains, of course, the Anglo-American rule. What is the principle upon which it is founded? Story bases it in great measure upon the legal fiction that movables have no situs but follow the person of the owner and inhere in his very bones. *Mobilia sequuntur personam et ejus ossibus inhaerent.* Story suggests that the rule may also be based upon its general convenience and utility, and its tendency to avoid endless embarrassments and conflicts where personal property has often changed locations.[17] It is sometimes based upon the presumed intent of the deceased. However this may be as to a person who leaves a will, it is certainly illogical to adopt a "presumed" intent of one who has not even expressed an intention concerning his beneficiaries. A more logical presumption is, we believe, drawn by Minor. The deceased wished his estate to be distributed according to the general provisions *of the law.* The transfer is to be effected "by act of the law and therefore it is the owner's *legal* situs or domicil that furnishes the proper law; and the transfer being effected at the time of his death, it is his domicil *at that time* that is to be looked to."[18] Where the legal situs of the person is determined by nationality, the distribution of personal property will follow the national law.

Another ground given for the rule is that the law of the domicil is given an extraterritorial effect by the law of the (foreign) country in which the movables may be situated.[19] Goodrich doubts this explanation and aptly remarks that there would seem to be no reason why the law of the situs should allow the law of the domicil to displace its own legislative enactments on the subject.[20] But Goodrich draws a further conclusion to which we are unable to agree. He believes that the distribution of the decedent's property is in every case governed by the law of the situs of the property.[21] This view seems to confound situs with jurisdiction. True, they are frequently identical, but not necessarily so, as the property may have been removed after the death of the owner. In *In re* Barton's Estate,[22] a

[16] Story, §481, quoted in Ennis *v.* Smith at p. 424.
[17] *Ibid.*, §481b.
[18] Minor, (1901) §139.
[19] Morton, J., in Frothingham *v.* Shaw, (1899) 175 Mass. 59.
[20] Goodrich, (1927) p. 370.
[21] *Ibid.*, p. 371.
[22] (1925) 238 Pac. 681.

will was probated in California upon the jurisdictional fact of the domicil in California. The testator had left a legacy of personal property, a considerable portion of which was located in Rhode Island. The legatee died before the testator and under Rhode Island law the legatee's heirs would have been entitled to succeed to his interest in the legacy. Under California law, however, the legacy had lapsed. Some effort was made to prove that the testator had in fact been domiciled in Rhode Island, but the court considered the allegations and finding of a California domicil to be *res judicata* by the probate proceedings. Accordingly, the court held that California law governed and not the law of Rhode Island, the *lex situs*. Curiously enough, the California Civil Code (§946) provides: "If there is no law to the contrary in the place where personal property is situated, it is deemed to follow the person of its owner and is governed by the law of his domicil." By this the court interpreted the phrase "no law to the contrary" to refer to some general or specific law which might provide that the domiciliary law shall not govern; in other words, the California statute enacts a *renvoi* to the conflict-of-laws rule of the situs and not to the substantive law of the situs. The interpretation seems reasonable only because the section is dealing with the conflict of laws. The point to be emphasized, however, is that the application of the domiciliary rule followed from the fact that California had taken *jurisdiction* of the estate, the situs of the property being in another state.[23]

Another indication that the domiciliary law is not applied through any extraterritorial force ascribed to it, is afforded by the exercise of sovereign jurisdiction over *bona vacantia* for the succession to which no next of kin can be found. A claim to such property under a law of the domicil of the deceased owner which assumes to make it revert to the state of the domicil will be ignored in favor of the state in which such property is found.[24]

Treaties are sometimes entered into to preserve the right of the national state to reclaim such property. Such a treaty with Italy

[23] In Vogel *v.* New York Life Ins. Co., (1932) 55 Fed. (2nd) 205 at p. 208 it is said: "while a state may undoubtedly assert power also over personal property actually within its borders, 248 U.S. 115, 39 S. Ct. 33, 33 L. Ed. 158, it is a rule so general as to be esteemed a settled principle of private international law that, unless it affirmatively does so, personal property of a decedent, following the person, passes and is distributed according to the law of his domicil at death, no matter where the property may be . . ."

[24] "*In re* Barnett's Trust, [1902] 1 Ch. 847.

has been sustained by the United States Supreme Court against the power of an individual state to apply the law of the situs, even where the last domicil was also within that state.[25]

**Foreign Conflict-of-Laws Rules relating to Succession.** Countries of the Roman-law tradition do not require the interposition of a grant by state authority through an administrator or executor to the beneficiaries designated by law upon intestacy or by the decedent through testamentary disposition. Legacies and devises have the force of "inserting an heir" in the civil-law sense. The proper law (whatever that may be) governing the estate generally, will apply to such questions as the degree of relationship required for intestate succession and the order of preference; to the rights of succession of legitimated or adopted children; and to peremptory rights of succession through limitations upon the testator in favor of certain protected persons such as children or spouse. The same applies to rights of succession in movable property. The principle applicable to intestate succession will also apply to wills. Now what is the proper law applicable?

**French Law.** French jurisprudence has shown hesitancy in answering this question and a tendency to shift principles and policies so that even today it would be difficult to say that the rule is fixed. France is one of the countries of the Continent of Europe which recognizes a separation between movables and immovables in contradistinction to the Roman unity of succession. Art. 3 of the Civil Code provides that immovables even when owned by foreigners are governed by French law. Although this legislation does not specifically refer to rights of succession, it cannot be doubted that the intention was to place control with the *lex rei sitae*.[26] French writers of the highest authority have been strongly opposed to the separation of movables and immovables, preferring the symmetry of the Roman universal or unitary succession.[27] The rule of *lex rei sitae* is applied in conjunction with the application of *renvoi*. The curious result to which this may lead is well illustrated by the case of an Algerian Israelite of French nationality who died intestate in Egypt, leaving land and movables situated there. The Cour d'Appel of Aix decided that the law of Egypt was applicable to determine succession to the land, and the French law to the movables. But because Egyp-

[25] Santavincenzo *v.* Egan, (1931) 284 U.S. 30. See editorial comment by the author in Amer. Jour. of Int. Law, 1932, p. 348.

[26] Pillet, *Traité*, (1924) ii, p. 346.

[27] Renault in Clunet, 1875, pp. 329, 422; 1876, p. 15.

tian law by definition or "qualification" made the succession to land equally controlled by the personal law of the deceased (which was the Mosaic law), the same law would be applied by a French court in determining succession to land.[28] Perroud in commenting upon the decision finds the result to be "perfectly shocking" and illustrative of the effects of *renvoi,* a doctrine opposed by many French authors. But Perroud admits that the decision is a logical deduction from French jurisprudence.[29]

The French rules for the choice of law in the intestate succession to movables distinguished between (*a*) the succession of movables of a French national domiciled in France or of a foreigner with an *authorized* domicil in France; and (*b*) the succession to movables of a foreigner domiciled abroad or having only a *de facto* domicil in France. In the case of (*a*), French law was applied; while in (*b*), the foreigner's national law was applied. Two ancient theories lead to different results. The maxim *mobilia sequuntur personam* was interpreted by Dumoulin and his partisans as confirming a fiction that movables were situated at the domicil of the owner. D'Argentré on the other hand regarded ownership in movables as an attribute of personality. This theoretical difference did not give rise to any practical difference so long as domicil governed the personal law, which indeed it did in France until the adoption of the Civil Code. Art. 3(3) changed the situation by providing that laws relating to the status and capacity of persons apply to French nationals even when residing in a foreign country. Dumoulin's principle finally triumphed so that the law of the last domicil became applicable to Frenchmen at home and abroad.[30]

If we were to follow the analogy, foreigners domiciled in fact in France, even though not authorized to acquire a domicil as provided by the Code, should likewise have their movable property distributed at death according to French law. In the celebrated case of Forgo, to which reference has been made,[31] the fiction that the location of movables is at the domicil of the owner was seemingly superimposed upon another fiction, *viz.,* that unless the deceased has homologated himself to French nationality by authorization, he must

[28] Bitton *v.* Bitton, Jan. 28, 1920, Clunet, 1923, p. 99. *Semble:* Bouvier *v.* Fleury, Clunet, 1925, p. 116.

[29] *Ibid.,* p. 105.

[30] Pillet, *op. cit.* ii, p. 353, citing Court of Cassation, 27 April, 1869, Sirey, v. 68, pt. 1, p. 257.

[31] See *ante,* p. 53.

be considered as intending to retain his domicil of origin. This frequently leads to the application of national law. So that D'Argentré's doctrine of personality finally gained qualified admission through the intricacies of the Forgo case.[32] This resulted from two causes, *viz.*, a repercussion of the intricacies of the old statutory theory and the fragmentary character of the conflict-of-laws rules contained in the Civil Code.[33] D'Argentré interprets the rule as indicating that the succession to movables is determined by the same law which regulates the personal status of the owner, while the school of Dumoulin interprets the maxim as justifying only the application of the law prevailing at the place where the person is to be considered as physically established, *i.e.*, his domicil. Where the personal law was governed by domicil, as indeed it was prior to the Code, both doctrines centered in the law of the domicil. Art. 3 (3), however, applies French law to French citizens with regard to status and capacity. It becomes necessary therefore to judge whether devolution of rights in movables through death is part of the personal "statute," in which case French law applies, or of the real "statute," in which case the law at the physical center of ownership, *viz.*, the domicil, is applicable. Where a French decedent was domiciled abroad, the courts formerly refused the application of national law and applied the law of his foreign domicil.[34] At the time this decision was rendered, it was perhaps not inconsistent with the rule of the French courts which applied the national law of persons having only a factual domicil in France to determine succession to their movable property. At that time the system of "authorized" domicil prevailed in France. If the domicil was not authorized, it remained at the domicil of origin.[35] There were indeed errors in dicta and occasionally the courts believed that they were applying the personal law as such.[36]

Niboyet believes that the courts applied the law of the last domicil in some cases where by an error of terminology the decision speaks of national law. Lepaulle denies this.[37] In a leading case decided in the Court of Cassation in 1909, the definite statement is made that the national law applies to the transmission of movables, testate or intestate, of foreigners residing in France without authorized

[32] Court of Cassation, May 15, 1875.

[33] See Brault in Clunet, 1933, p. 311.

[34] Jeannin Case, Sirey, 1868, 1, 260; Cass. April 27, 1869.

[35] See Brault in Clunet, 1933, p. 311. Forgo Case, May 5, 1875, Sirey 1, 875, 1, 409.

[36] Sirey, 1872, 2, 313.

[37] *Cf.* Clunet, 1933, pp. 819, 821.

domicil.[38] The procurator-general justifies this choice of law because, unless the foreigner has asked for admission to domicil, he has shown an intention of retaining his national customs.[39]

The law of August 10, 1927, abolished the institution of admission to domicil or "authorized" domicil. As a result, the courts now seem to be inclined to draw away from the former rule of origin and to decide in favor of the law of the last domicil. In Mondet *v.* Rouxel,[40] an Italian died domiciled in France leaving movables situated there. It was held that the abolition of admission to domicil "transformed into a domicil by law that which was formerly only an establishment in fact." The legislature must be taken to have wished to grant foreigners the right to a legal domicil without the authorization previously required. This reversal of the previous rule has received the approval of contemporary writers especially because the difficulties and inconsistencies of the *renvoi* doctrine will be much reduced. The domicil will in most cases coincide with the place of administering the property.[41]

**Right of Deduction (Prélèvement).** Before leaving the consideration of French law, a peculiarity of this system must be observed. Under the Law of July 14, 1819, a right of deduction or *prélèvement* is given to French citizens where an estate is divided between alien and French heirs or legatees and part of the property situated in France. This deduction amounts to the value of any property situated in a foreign country from which the French beneficiaries may be excluded by the foreign law or custom.[42]

An interesting example of a recent application of this law is furnished in Bernet *v.* Phily.[43] The testator, a French citizen, emigrated to the United States with his first wife. He obtained a divorce and remarried in the United States. He died while on a visit to France, leaving his entire property to his second wife by a will executed in accordance with the law of New Jersey where he was domiciled. His first wife claimed certain community property situated in France. His son by the former marriage claimed the same property as a compulsory portion under French law and also under

[38] Clunet, 1909, p. 773.
[39] *Ibid.*, p. 783.
[40] Clunet, 1933, p. 970.
[41] Lepaulle in Clunet, 1933, p. 833.
[42] A similar system has been adopted in Belgium, (Civil Code, Art. 726 as amended) the Netherlands, (Civil Code, Art. 884 as amended) and the Argentine, (Civil Code, 3470).
[43] Clunet, 1932, p. 930.

the benefit of the Law of 1819 relating to deduction. The Court of Appeal of Lyons decided that the succession to the movable estate must be determined according to the last domicil of this French decedent under Arts. 3 and 110 of the Code. But the court also accorded the son a right of preference through deduction under the Law of 1819, interpreting this law as applying even where the competition was between French beneficiaries, *i.e.,* not between French nationals and foreigners. The law therefore has a coercive character quite apart from the proper law applicable to the estate generally.[44]

**German Law.** The Introductory Statute to the German Civil Code answers categorically some of the questions left in doubt under French law. Art. 24 provides that succession to the estate of a German is determined in accordance with German law though he had his domicil in a foreign country. But his heirs may rely upon the application of the law of his domicil with respect to the liability for his debts. Art. 25 provides that the succession to the estate of a foreigner domiciled in Germany is determined according to the law of the state to which he belonged at the time of his death. However, a German may assert a right of inheritance under German law unless the national law of the foreign decedent would recognize German law as exclusively applicable to the succession of a German domiciled in such state. In other words, a preference for German law will be exercised in favor of a German claimant unless reciprocity is granted by the laws of the decedent's country. Art. 25 fails to provide for the event of a foreigner dying domiciled in a third state leaving property in Germany. The decisions of the courts have drawn the logical analogy and have applied the decedent's national law in such a case as well.[45]

*German law* follows the civil-law principle by which estate of deceased persons is regarded as an *universum* or single entity, no matter whether the property be movable or immovable or where it be located. German law formerly regarded succession to be governed by the law of the domicil as the decedent's personal law. During the nineteenth century, national law was gradually accepted by statute in the various provinces and finally also by the Introductory Statute to the Reich's Civil Code.[46]

[44] See Brault in Clunet, 1932, p. 308. This writer does not seem to favor withdrawal from the old rule of national law.

[45] 91 *Reichsgericht,* Civ. cases 139; Aug. 11, 1917.

[46] Lewald, *Das deutsche int. Privatrecht* (1931) p. 285. Where, however, land is located in a state which applies the *lex rei sitae,* German law withdraws in favor of that law. Intro. Stat., Art. 28.

We have already called attention to the adoption of *renvoi* by German statutory law with reference to succession.[47] Art. 27 of the Introductory Statute specifically refers to Art. 25 as subject to *renvoi.* So that where an American or Englishman dies domiciled in Germany, his property in Germany will be subject to the inheritance provisions of German laws because the decedent's national law itself applies the law of the last domicil.[48]

**Italian Law.** The national law is made applicable by Art. 8 of the *Disposizioni* or Preliminary Title to the Civil Code. The article specifically makes the national law applicable to both intestate and testamentary succession, the order of succession, the *quantum* of the rights to inheritance and the intrinsic validity of the dispositions of the testator. Italy has adopted the *universum* principle with reference to succession. The inconvenience, if not the impossibility, of allowing national law to control the succession to land by a law not that of its location leads to considerable modification of the strict rule through the safety valve of the doctrine of "public order." Of course foreign forms or conditions of tenure or possession would not be recognized by the law of the situs. This is recognized even in Italy where the principle of national law has become almost a fetish.[49]

In the Bustamante Code accepted by many *Latin-American* countries,[50] "personal law" is substituted for "national law" under the well-known compromise permitting each state to apply either the law of the domicil, or the national law, as its own legislation may prescribe.[51]

## 4. Wills

In view of the principles for the choice of law applicable to intestate succession to movables, should there be a different rule for determining the formal validity of a document presented as a will of personal property? The making of a will is a voluntary act and as such it may be urged that the same rules should govern the application of law to determine its validity, as are applied to any other formal voluntary act for the transfer of personal property, such as a contract

[47] See *ante,* p. 54.

[48] Lewald, *op. cit.,* citing *Oberlandesger.,* Karlsruhe, Dec. 13, 1919, Civil Cases vol. 40, p. 270; *Oberlandesger.,* Dresden, Mar. 4, 1923, Saxony, Annals of *Oberlandesger.,* vol. 35, p. 63, etc.

[49] See Udina, *Droit int. privé d'Italie* (1930) pp. 148–149.

[50] Arts. 144, 154–155. International Conference of American States, 1931, p. 341 *et seq.*

[51] *Ibid.,* Art. 7.

under seal or a deed. However, the will alone does not of itself accomplish a succession. It is the incident of death which gives force to the will. Minor prefers to refer to death as an "involuntary act" and therefore looks to the legal situs of the property, which is the domicil of the decedent. We prefer to say that as the law of the domicil governs succession *ab intestato,* it would seem reasonable to have the laws of the same country determine whether or not, in a given case, there is an intestacy.

Let us illustrate. A person domiciled in South Carolina executed a will there, according to the laws of that state, which did not require any declaration in the presence of the witnesses to the effect that it was his last will. He subsequently changed his domicil to New York where such declaration was and is required. He subsequently died domiciled in New York. The South Carolina will was presented for probate in New York. It was held that the will had not become a "consummate and perfect transaction" until his death; just as a deed does not become effective for the transmission of property until delivery. Therefore the law of New York was alone competent to determine whether the will was validly executed or whether the deceased had died intestate.[52] Judge Denio referred to the rule of *locus regit actum* applied under these circumstances by French authorities such as Tollier, Felix, Malin and Pothier. He found the common-law rule to be as already stated and followed it as it had been handed down from Voet through Story.

**"Locus regit actum" Applied to Wills.** The result forces a testator to consider the execution of a new will with every change of domicil. Fortunately the rule has been modified both in New York and in other states by specific legislation which so often has to rescue us from the inconvenience caused by the relentless logic of jurists. Accordingly, in many states the application of law in determining the validity of the execution of a will of personal property or the construction of its provisions is no longer affected by a change of domicil after execution of the will.[53] Attention should also be called to legislation which provides that a will executed in another state of the Union, or in Canada, or in the British Isles, according to the local law, will be received for probate; or indeed the will of

[52] Moultrie *v.* Hunt, (1861) 23 N.Y. 394. *Accord: In re* Beaumont's Estate, (1907) 216 Pa. 350.

[53] New York Decedent Estate Law, §24. Uniform Foreign Executed Wills Act, adopted in eleven States, Amer. Bar Assoc. Rep. (1934) p. 746. English Wills Act of 1861, §§1–3.

any *non*-resident executed according to the laws of his residence.[54]

A very reasonable rule has been adopted by the Commissioners on Uniform State Laws in their uniform statute which provides that a will of real or personal property executed without the state in the mode prescribed either by the law of the place where executed or of the testator's domicil shall be valid provided it is in writing and subscribed by the testator.[55]

## 5. Testamentary Capacity

There can be no doubt that the exigencies of modern commerce due to the greater fluidity of populations and the rapidity of transportation and communication tend toward the requirement of uniformity and certainty in the tests of capacity to enter into transactions within a given territory. The same considerations do not apply where the rights of other parties are not affected by any act which the person has done within the territory of the local state. Judge Gray in a leading Massachusetts case said: "The capacity or qualification to inherit or succeed to property, which is an incident of the status or condition, requiring *no action* to give it effect, is to be distinguished from the capacity or competency to enter into contracts that confer rights upon others. A capacity to take and to have, differs from a capacity to do and contract; in short, a capacity of holding, from a capacity to act." [56] From this dictum, Minor derived his classification of capacity for "voluntary" transactions and that for "involuntary" transactions. Of the latter class, typical illustrations are the capacity to make a will and to be a beneficiary thereunder, the capacity to receive and give acquittance for property as one of full age under personal law even though not so considered in the state where the property is located.[57] An illustration is furnished by an English case in which a domiciled Englishman bequeathed legacies to two children of a German domiciled in Germany, a girl aged 18 and a boy aged 17. By the German law then existing, a

[54] N.Y. Decedent Estate Law, §23. Lorenzen in (1911) Yale Law Jour. 427, 435–437.

[55] Adopted by N.Y. Decedent Estate Law §§22a–23. The statute was interpreted as retroactive; so that a holographic will of a New York resident, executed in Italy before the statute, was allowed to be probated although it disposed of real estate. Matter of Tinker, (1925) 209 N.Y.S. 723; aff'd (1926) 216 N.Y.S. 689.

[56] Ross *v.* Ross, (1880) 129 Mass. 243, at p. 246.

[57] Minor, §69. See Memphis Trust Co. *v.* Blessing (1899) 103 Tenn. 237. The converse case is found in Kohne's Estate (1850) 1 Pars. Eq. (Pa.) 399.

female attained her majority at 18, a male at 22. The legacy was held payable to the girl on her own receipt because of full age by her domiciliary law.[58]

The capacity to make a will is an unilateral transaction and does not affect the contractual rights of others. The capacity to dispose of land by will is not here considered because of the distinction between land and movable property and for other reasons to which we shall later give attention.[59] Minor, loyal to his classification, points out that the will takes effect at the death of the testator, which is involuntary. Hence the law of the testator's domicil at the time of death will govern.[60] The classification seems, however, to be somewhat strained at this point. Death is not always involuntary and one is apt to think of the gravedigger in Shakespeare's *Hamlet:* "For here lies the point; if I drown myself wittingly, it argues an act; and an act hath three branches; it is to act, to do, and to perform; argal, she drowned herself wittingly." (Act V, Scene I.) The fact is that the capacity to dispose of property by will is a special capacity inseparably bound up with the law of succession. It is usually specially regulated by statute, while the capacity to act in general, refers to acts *inter vivos*. It is not necessary, however, to conceive of the capacity to make a will as referring to an act taking effect with death. It is the will which takes effect with death but the act of making it is complete when the will is executed. Where there is no conflict of laws, the testator's capacity is determined at the time of executing the will, and if capable then, the will is entitled to recognition even though a later incapacity supervenes. Probate granted by the court of last domicil will be recognized elsewhere, except as to land.[61]

**Effect of a Change of Domicil upon Testamentary Capacity.** The same rule would seem to be reasonable in the case of a conflict of law and indeed the legislation of some countries has expressly adopted it.

Under the English statute known as Lord Kingsdown's Act[62] "no will or other testamentary instrument shall be held to be revoked or to have become invalid, nor shall the construction thereof be altered, by reason of any subsequent change of domicil by the person

[58] *In re* Hellman, (1866) L.R. 2 Eq. 363; *Accord: In re* Schnapper [1928] Ch. 420.

[59] See *post*, pp. 329–330.

[60] Minor, §70.

[61] Thompson, (1936) The Law of Wills, §90.

[62] 24 and 25 Vict. chap. 114, §3.

making the same." This was not the common law and the statute, while substantially copied in some of the United States, does not prevail in all.[63]

Indeed the Restatement[64] provides: "The validity and effect of a will of movables is determined by the law of the state in which the deceased died domiciled." The comments (*b.* and *d.*) indicate that this rule refers to capacity and that the law of the state of domicil at death is preferred to that of the time of execution.

In view of the hardship which the old common law principle entails, most testators being ignorant of the influence which a change of domicil may have upon the validity and effect of a will already executed, the crystallizing of the old rule into the Restatement cannot be approved as a progressive adaptation of the law to the facts of life.[65]

The Argentine Civil Code provides that "the law of the place where the testator is domiciled at the time of making his will determines his capacity so to do," while the effect of the will, its validity or its invalidity, is governed by the law existing there at the time of his death.[66]

**Testamentary Incapacity Distinguished from Illegality of Certain Dispositions.** It is not always a simple matter to determine the proper scope of laws relating to testamentary capacity so as to be able to say that this or that provision should be governed by the personal law of the testator as distinguished from the law applicable to the succession as a whole. Minor points out that in order to create a true testamentary incapacity, the policy of the prohibiting law must be directed against the capacity of the testator considered as a power of disposition, "not against some particular form of disposition he may desire to make, nor against the right of his beneficiary to hold the property bequeathed."[67] A statute of New York prohibits

[63] Higgins *v.* Eaton, (1911) 188 F. 938; Shaw *v.* Grimes, (1920) 187 Ky. 250.

[64] §306.

[65] The decision in Moultrie *v.* Hunt (1861) 23 N.Y. 394. followed the common law rule upon the principle that "everyone must be supposed to know the law under which he lives, and conform his acts to it." Lord Kingsdown's Act applies only to British subjects; as to other persons the common law rule still applies. Bloxam *v.* Favre, (1884) L.R. 9 P.D. 130.

[66] Arts. 3611–3612. A similar provision is to be found in the Swiss Federal Statute of 1891 "N. & A.," Art. 7. It is implied also in the provisions of the German Introductory Act, Art. 24, to the extent that an alien testator acquires German citizenship since the execution of the will. The view of the text is upheld for German law generally by Walker, p. 803.

[67] Minor, §70.

a testator from disposing of more than half of his estate to charity provided he or she leave surviving a wife or husband, a child or parent. If a person domiciled in New York makes a will in another state disposing of property in that other state, where such prohibition does not exist, the legacy is not valid, at least to the extent that it contravenes the domiciliary law. The law relating to the capacity of the testator has been enacted for the protection of members of his family and in support of the family as an institution. It is therefore properly within the jurisdiction of the state of the domicil, where the family life of the testator is centered, to provide for its protection by pronouncing an incapacity in the testator to that extent. It is not a prohibition against the legatee. The law of the domicil of the testator, not at the time of executing the will, but at the time of death, will control because the partial incapacity is determined only when the succession takes effect.[68]

**Testamentary Capacity Distinguished from Restrictions Caused by Reserved Portions.** Meili earnestly warns against the confusion caused by viewing rules which reserve certain portions of an estate in favor of certain relatives as being rules of capacity. It is confusing to speak of the "capacity" to receive a gift and the "capacity" to inherit, when referring to the objective and substantive requisites for these processes. The preliminary question is: Can a certain person undertake transactions with binding effect, or is he in whole or in part incompetent? When once this question is determined, we then have to deal with the requisites of the substantive general law, otherwise all the subjective rights of an individual could finally be denoted *jura status* and referred to the same law which governs personal status.[69]

**French Law of Reserved Portion.** This principle is recognized in France in respect to prohibitions against disposing by will of certain portions or proportions of the estate to the disadvantage of certain members of the family (*la réserve*). Though often spoken of as imposing an incapacity, the reserve is rightly conceived of as part of the disposition of the estate as a whole and governed as to movables, by the last domicil of the testator, and as to immovables,

[68] Healy *v.* Reed, (1891) 153 Mass. 197. A similar result would probably be reached under the recent New York statute in effect from September 1, 1930, giving to a surviving husband or wife, "a personal right of election . . . to take his or her share of the estate as in intestacy." . . . N.Y. Laws of 1929, chap. 229, §4, amending §18 of the Decedent Estate Law.

[69] Meili (Kuhn's trans.) p. 174.

by the *lex rei sitae*.[70] But there is a sharp conflict when the capacity of the testator has been restricted in his own behalf and not in behalf of any particular legatee, as for example, the prohibition under French law (Art. 907, Civil Code) against disposing of property by a minor in favor of his guardian, even though the minor be otherwise capable of disposing by will. Weiss denotes this as an active incapacity and allows the personal law to control. He reaches the same result where (under Art. 909) physicians who have treated the testator in his last illness, and ministers, are prohibited from receiving donations or bequests made during the last illness. This is often called "passive incapacity." In both cases, however, though the personal law of the testator recognizes no such prohibition, the prohibition will operate if the personal law of the beneficiary be French.[71] Pillet, on the other hand, and we think rightly, maintains that only the personal law of the testator should govern, because the prohibition is for his benefit and is in recognition of the natural feebleness of will accompanying his last illness.[72]

## 6. Capacity to Receive by Will or Intestacy

The term "capacity" with reference to inheritance by will is used in two senses which it is important to distinguish. There is the capacity of the testator to make a will, which is the capacity of performing an act-in-the-law, and the capacity to succeed which is a "capacity" to receive or enjoy an inheritance. A "capacity" of the latter nature may be questioned by an interested party both in respect to intestate and testamentary succession. It is not always a simple matter to determine whether a prohibition against making certain kinds of dispositions by will, or to certain persons, is a prohibition against testamentary capacity. Minor very rightly emphasizes the point that in order to create a true testamentary incapacity, "the policy of the prohibiting law must be directed against the right of the testator to dispose of his property, not against some particular form of disposition he may desire to make, nor against the right of his beneficiary to hold the property bequeathed." [73] This distinction

[70] Weiss, *Traité* (1901) iv, p. 643, citing numerous French cases.
[71] Weiss, *ut. cit.* iv, p. 617.
[72] Pillet, *Traité* (1924) ii, p. 442. Yet where the testatrix and beneficiary were both German, a French court applied the French prohibition as a matter of public policy. Clunet, 1904, p. 713.
[73] Minor, (1901) §70.

is of very great importance; for if the prohibition exists by reason of the personal quality or status of the testator, such as infancy, mental incompetency, or coverture, it is the personal law of the testator which determines if and to what extent such qualities affect testamentary capacity. A statute of Pennsylvania provided that a gift to charity by deed or will was required to be made at least one month before the decease of the testator or donor. A New York court construed the statute to restrain both the capacity of the donor and of the donee and declared a legacy to a Pennsylvania charity void on this account.[74] The decision rests upon an interpretation of a specific Pennsylvania statute. Ordinarily such restrictions are considered to be only upon the testator and governed by the law of his domicil and the authority of the decision has been questioned.[75]

An intermediate class of prohibitions are those which do not bear upon the power of the person to make any kind of a will but upon his power to make it at a particular time, *e.g.*, within a certain time before his death, or in favor of a witness to the will. There are also prohibitions such as .those to be found in French law against dispositions in favor of the physician who attended the testator in his last illness, the notary who drew his will, or the priest who administered the last rites.[76]

What is to be thought of laws limiting the power of disposition by will, not as to time nor as to particular persons which may be presumed to have an undue influence upon the testator immediately prior to death, but of the amount of property of which the testator may dispose? It would be improper to conclude that all such limitations bear upon the capacity of the testator and it is necessary to distinguish between the various cases. Lord Cranworth in Whicker *v.* Hume,[77] supposes a case in which the law of some foreign country in which the testator was domiciled, limited disposition by will to one-half his property. Even though probated in England, the law of the domicil would preclude passing more than one-half under the will. The restriction is a limitation of the testator's capacity. Similarly, legislation in New York providing that no person having a husband, wife, child, or parent, shall devise or bequeath more than one-half the net estate to charities, is properly considered as a pro-

[74] Kerr *v.* Dougherty, (1880) 79 N.Y. 327.
[75] Beale, Treatise (1935) p. 796 note 2.
[76] See Art. 909, French Civil Code.
[77] (1858) 7 H.L. Cas. 124, 156.

hibition which "operates upon the testator's capacity to give, rather than upon the power of the legatees to take."[78] Accordingly, the legacy of a Massachusetts testator disposing of more than the permitted amount to a New York religious society was upheld in Massachusetts where the restriction did not prevail.[79]

Another class of cases is that in which the restriction is not primarily intended to protect the testator against possible undue influence (although this may represent a secondary purpose of the legislature), but which affirmatively provides that certain near relatives of the testator, the surviving spouse, children, or parents, shall receive a certain fixed proportion of his estate under certain conditions. These legislative provisions establish what is generally referred to in Continental Europe as the "legitimate portion." Statutes such as these vary greatly in the various jurisdictions. They have only recently begun to find their way into the legislation of some of the American States. Thus the Decedent Estate Law of New York,[80] provides that a surviving spouse has a personal right of election to take his or her share as in intestacy in preference to the benefits provided by will, but in no event more than one-half the net estate of the decedent.

A will made by the testatrix, a Netherlands subject, in Holland, prior to her marriage, appointed her intended husband as heir, "with reservation only to the legitimate portion of the lawful share coming to her relatives in a direct line . . ." After the marriage, the testatrix removed to England with her husband who afterwards became naturalized as a British subject. Under the Netherlands law, only one fourth of the estate could be disposed of; the other portion would go to her children. The court interpreted the will as disposing of the entire estate to her husband subject to the legitimate portion, but as she died domiciled in England, where no such legitimate portion existed at the time of her death, the entire estate was awarded to the husband.[81]

### 7. Substantive Validity

The provisions of a will may be so vague as to be rendered illegal by virtue of legislative provisions having to do with an orderly ad-

[78] Chamberlain *v.* Chamberlain, (1871) 43 N.Y. 424, 440.
[79] Healy *v.* Reed, (1890) 153 Mass. 197.
[80] §18 by amendment applicable from Sept. 1, 1930.
[81] *In re* Groos, [1915] 1 Ch. Div. 572.

ministration of inheritances. The provisions of a will may also violate a rule of the state relating to property-holding in general. In these cases, the instrument is entitled to be considered as a will, but its substantive provisions may not be permitted to be carried out at the place of probate. Suppose, however, that the execution of the testator's design is to take place in a foreign country where such provisions could be carried out. Will the provisions be upheld? If the restraints bear upon the testator's capacity to do these things or are designed to protect his freedom of will in the larger sense, his personal law should control and the place of executing the provisions should not be material; if the restraints do not relate to the testator's capacity, they should prevent execution of the will where execution is allowed. Under the will of a New York resident, the residuary estate was directly to be converted into money and paid over to trustees in Scotland to establish and administer a certain charitable trust there. There was, however, no defined beneficiary either named or ascertainable and the trust would therefore have been invalid by New York law. The charity could be validly carried out in Scotland. The New York court decided that the policy of the statute applied only to New York trusts as the trustees were definitely named in the will and had power to receive the money. The statutes "were intended to operate within and promote the welfare of people of each particular state and it was not contemplated that they should have any extraterritorial effect." [82]

The doctrine of Hope *v.* Brewer has recently received renewed support in a case in which a trust *inter vivos* created in Canada (Quebec) and invalid by that law, was nevertheless valid by New York law where the trust property was located and the trust administered. "Our courts have sought whenever possible to sustain the validity even of testamentary trusts to be administered in a jurisdiction other than the domicil of the testator." [83] The court drew attention to the statute of New York passed in 1930 providing that when a trust of personal property to be administered within the state under New York law is created either by a citizen or alien, resident or non-resident, the validity and effect of such trust shall be determined by

[82] Hope *v.* Brewer, (1892) 136 N.Y. 126, 137. Seemingly *contra* is Lozier *v.* Lozier, (1919) 99 Ohio St. 254. A trust created by an Ohio will was to be administered in New York by testamentary trustees. The beneficiary made an assignment of his interest in the trust, which is forbidden by New York law but allowed in Ohio. The assignment was upheld. The court was endeavoring to carry out the presumed intent of the testatrix but the conclusion is strained as the provisions of the will were to be executed in New York.

[83] Hutchinson *v.* Ross, (1933) 262 N.Y. 381, at p. 394, per Lehman, J.

such law.[84] Although the statute was passed after the creation of the trust, the court took notice of the creator's implied intention and regarded the statute as establishing a definite public policy in a field in which the rules of law were still fluid and undefined.

**Foreign Conflict-of-Laws Rules concerning Wills.** In Continental European systems, testamentary capacity is governed by the personal law of the testator. Accordingly, in countries such as France, Germany and Italy, where capacity to act is governed by national law, a foreigner may make a will abroad, valid by his own law, although a native citizen under the same conditions would not enjoy such capacity at the same place. A German of 17 may make a will in "authentic" form in Italy although an Italian cannot do so until the age of 18. A French married woman may make a will abroad even in a country which requires the consent of her husband.[85] Lewald raises the curious question whether a German minor over 17, forbidden to make other than a will in "authentic" form, *i.e.*, by oral declaration before witnesses to a judge or notary, can do so if he be a mute. If this be a limitation upon his capacity he could not make a will of any kind abroad. If the rule is simply one of form, the minor could make a will abroad, good by local law under the principle *locus regit actum*. This seems to be a reasonable conclusion.[86]

The prohibitions of French law to which we have referred[87] are clearly motivated by the desire to restrain the testator to his own advantage and Pillet rightly refers them to the national law of the testator under the accepted rule of capacity. A German woman left a legacy to a German physician who had attended her during her last illness. The German law does not contain any prohibition analogous to that of Art. 909 of the French Civil Code. Ordinarily the capacity of the testatrix would have been determined by German law. The court considered the legacy void for reasons of public or social policy (*ordre social*).[88] Pillet correctly disapproves of the application of any other principle than that of the testator's personal law.[89] A similar restraint is placed upon a guardian,[90] and upon the notary with whom

[84] N.Y. Personal Property Law; Cons. Laws ch. 41, §12a.

[85] Clunet, 1874, p. 128.

[86] Lewald in *Recueil des Cours, Académie de dr. int.* 1925, iv, p. 108.

[87] *Ante*, p. 332.

[88] Clunet, 1903, p. 713. There seems to have been sufficient evidence of undue influence exerted by the physician.

[89] Pillet, *Traité*, (1924) ii, p. 442.

[90] French Civil Code, Art. 907; Italian Civ. Code, Art. 769; Netherlands Civ. Code, Art. 951.

the will is filed.[91] Some authors, such as the French jurist André Weiss, regard such provisions as an incapacity to receive as well as to give, and refuse validity to legacies to such persons even if the testator's personal law does not prohibit it. A legacy by a French ward in favor of his English guardian would, of course, be invalid under Art. 907, but Weiss would also apply the rule conversely to the legacy of an English ward in favor of his French guardian.[92] Even some English writers favor this viewpoint. Baty, in his usual epigrammatic style exclaims: "If you throw a stone in the air, you depress the earth. If you regulate the legal status of a subject you affect the position of everybody else";[93] and he quotes Vareilles-Sommières to the effect that it is preferable to apply the personal law of the successors: "Were I to choose between them, I would rather decide for the law of the living than that of the dead."[94] These arguments would appear to be rather more specious than sound when it is realized that the validity of testamentary dispositions might thus be subjected to as many rules as there were heirs and legatees. The certainty of the amount distributable to each beneficiary as well as the uniformity of administration would thus be frustrated.

On the other hand, a prohibition such as those contained in the French Civil Code, Art. 908, and the Italian Civil Code, Art. 768, which prevent children born of adulterous or incestuous unions from receiving more by will than necessary for their maintenance, has for its purpose (whatever may be its justification) not the protection of the testator but of the family or society in general. Lewald, Fedozzi and others would judge such provisions by the law applicable to the succession as a whole. Weiss maintained that no French tribunal would give effect to a foreign will which violated a provision of this kind. Indeed, with its strongly moral incentive, it would appear to be within the category of laws coercive by reason of public policy.[95]

**Trusts under French Law.** It is interesting to observe that trusts do not ordinarily fall within the prohibition of French law against substitutions. Under Art. 896 of the French Civil Code, every provision by which a donee or legatee shall be required to keep property and return it to a third person shall be void. The devolution of property

[91] Germany, §2235; Italy, Art. 771; Netherlands, Art. 954.
[92] Weiss, *Traité*, iv (1901) p. 643.
[93] Baty, Polarized Law (1914) pp. 159–160.
[94] *Ibid.*, p. 159n.
[95] Lewald in *Recueil des Cours* (1925) p. 113. Weiss, *ut cit.*

envisaged by a testamentary trust does not ordinarily militate against this provision. If it did, it would be void in France even though created under a will probated in England or the United States and valid there. A complicated state of facts was presented by the settlement of the estate of the French composer Hervé, who was naturalized in England, and was probably domiciled there at his decease, though he died in France. Under his will probated in England he left his entire property to two trustees for the benefit of one of them, his alleged second wife, with remainder over on certain contingencies. It was decided that this was not such a substitution as was prohibited by the French Code, as the trustees were not truly substituted heirs but simply testamentary executors within the meaning of French law.[96]

**Change of Domicil or Nationality after Making Will.** A difference is to be noted between Continental European systems and those of England and America with respect to the policy of Lord Kingsdown's Act and American legislation derived from it. By this statute a change of domicil by the testator after making his will does not have the effect of revoking it or rendering it invalid, nor is its construction to be changed. Westlake presumes that this applies to every circumstance on which a will may depend except the testator's capacity, which continues to be determined by the domicil at time of death.[97] Story, writing at a time before the statute, assumes that under the common law, testamentary capacity was determined as of the time of making the will.[98] It is not the general rule on the Continent. Weiss insists that the testator must have had testamentary capacity both according to his personal law at the time of making the will and at the time of his death. So *e.g.*, if a change of nationality intervenes, he may be under age by the law of his new citizenship; and vice versa, if he be of age by the law of his new allegiance, it would not correct his lack of capacity at the time of execution.[99]

The *German* Introductory Statute attempts to avoid this difficulty by providing that where a person alters his nationality after having made a testamentary disposition, the validity of such disposition or

[96] Clunet, 1911, pp. 594, 597. See also Lepaulle, "The Resident of France in Face of the Trust Problem." In Proc. Amer. Foreign Law Assoc., May 21, 1931, No. 11, p. 10.

[97] Westlake, Treatise (1925) §86.

[98] Story, §465. This is specifically made the rule by the Argentine Civil Code, Art. 3611 and the Swiss Statute "N. & A.," §7. *Cf.* Schnitzer, *ut cit.* (1937) p. 233.

[99] Weiss, *op. cit.* iv, 618–619.

its revocation is governed by the law of his former citizenship. The capacity to make a will, if possessed before the change, continues, although he has not attained the age required by German law.[100] The converse of the position presented by the case of a German having testamentary capacity at the time of making a will but afterwards changing his nationality, is not specifically covered. The question does not seem to have been presented to the courts but Lewald favors an analogous solution.[101]

*Italian* law still looks to the old nationality under which a will has been made in order to determine both the capacity of the testator and the interpretation of the instrument.[102]

The *Bustamante Code* adopted in certain Latin-American states makes no special provision applicable in the event of a change of the testator's nationality or domicil after the making of the will, but the large number of questions declared by the code to be of an "international public order" make it probable also that the rules relating to capacity of the country of personal law at death, which would also be the presumptive jurisdiction of administering its provisions, would have to be satisfied. Thus the local law determines whether the will of an insane testator was made during a lucid interval.[103]

## 8. Interpretation of Wills

We have been considering the effect of certain restraints upon the testator's capacity to dispose of his property by will. Certain of these restraints result from qualities inherent in the person of the testator; others, from a legislative intent to protect him, or his family, or society in general, from making dispositions by will of a particular nature or to certain classes of persons. These restraints are independent of the actual will of the testator because imposed by law. We have now to consider by what system of law the intention of the testator is to be determined either as expressed in the will, or presumed from his acts, expressed or presumed, with reference to the will.

**Interpretation of Intent as Expressed in the Will.** Story lays it down that "if the question should arise, whether the terms of a

100 German Introductory Stat., §24 (3).

101 Lewald, *Das deutsche int. Privatr.* (1931) pp. 306–7.

102 Udina, *Droit int. pr. d'Italie* (1930) p. 154.

103 Code of Private Int. Law, Art. 147. Int. Conferences of Amer. States 1889–1928. (1931) p. 341.

will include a bequest of real estate, or show on the part of the testator an intention to bequeath real estate, as well as personal estate, the question must be decided according to the law of the place of his domicil, and where the will was made; and the same interpretation must be put upon those terms in every other country which would be put upon them by the law of that domicil." This seems to have been a condensation of the decision of Lord Lyndhurst in Trotter *v.* Trotter,[104] in which a Scotsman domiciled in English dominions in India made his will there, but died domiciled in Scotland, leaving a will which by Scotch law was ineffectual to carry Scotch heritable bonds regarded as real estate going to the heir under Scotch law. The will also contained a legacy of movables in favor of the heir and the question arose as to whether the heir took the heritable bonds by intestate succession, in which case he would have been put to an election as to the legacy, or whether he took them under the will. It was held that the will was to be interpreted by English law under which the language was considered sufficient also to carry real estate; accordingly the heir was held entitled to the bonds as well as to the legacy.

Under Lord Kingsdown's Act and legislation in the United States to which reference has been made, a change of domicil after the making of the will, will not change the construction of the will according to the law of the domicil at the time of making will. "Interpretation being a question of fact, the law which decides on the validity of a bequest when it has been construed may well look beyond itself for aid in construing it." [105] In other words, the rule applicable to the interpretation of wills would seem more soundly expressed if we take the standard applicable in contracts. In the absence of an absolute rule, that law will be applied with reference to which it may be inferred that the testator expressed his will.[106] Ordinarily, the context of the document will give the intent; but often technical legal words are used, such as "heir," "heir at law," "next of kin," or a word of ordinary use having different significations in the law of different countries, such as "children," or a bequest of money is made in a currency having the same nominal unit but a different value in different countries, such as "dollars," "francs" and "pounds." "The general proposition may be laid down that the interpretation of such

[104] (1829) 4 Bligh R. (N.S.) 502; 3 Wils. & Shaw 407.
[105] Westlake, (1925) §122.
[106] Thompson, The Law of Wills (1936) §92.

ambiguous phrases should be determined in accordance with the laws and customs of that state most probably in the mind of the grantor or testator when he used the words, and with which he is presumed to be most familiar." [107]

A Maine testator devised and bequeathed a portion of his residuary estate to a trustee in trust for his two sons for life, the proportionate principal at the death of each, respectively, "to go to his heirs at law." One of the sons died domiciled in Massachusetts and was so domiciled at the time of his father's will. The son left no children but by his will made his widow sole legatee. Under Massachusetts law, the widow would be, in the circumstances, considered his heir at law but not under Maine law. Here the common law rule applying the law of the last domicil should control, because the testator was presumptively using phraseology according to its accepted usage in the state in which he was then and thereafter domiciled and with the laws of which he was most familiar.[108]

The question whether the domicil at the time of making the will or at the death of the testator will control, when these are not the same, was discussed but not decided in Harrison *v.* Nixon.[109] The case is of particular interest because the majority opinion was written by Mr. Justice Story. A native of Pennsylvania went to England in 1776 returning to Pennsylvania after the Revolutionary War and in 1791 made his will dated at Philadelphia. He subsequently made several voyages back and forth, and died in England in 1824. The will bequeathing all his estate to his "heirs at law" was proved in England, but persons claiming to be the heirs at law under Pennsylvania law began proceedings in Pennsylvania. The court remanded the bill for further proceedings because the bill did not aver where the testator was domiciled at the time of making his will or at his death. Mr. Justice Story remarked that a will of personalty speaks according to the law of the testator's domicil unless he had reference to the laws of another place. But he specifically refrained from expressing any opinion upon what would be the effect upon the interpretation of the will, if the domicil was in one country at the time of making his will, and in another country at the time of his death." [110] Mr. Justice Baldwin dissenting, urged with considerable force, that the

[107] Minor, (1901) §145.
[108] Houghton *v.* Hughes, (1911) 108 Me. 233.
[109] (1835) 9 Pet. U.S. 483.
[110] At p. 505.

bill should not have been dismissed because the domicil of the testator "is only a circumstance from which to draw an inference of intention." [111]

A testator by will drawn in Rhode Island where he was then domiciled left certain real and personal property to his widow, without declaration that the provision was to be in lieu of dower. Certain other land passed to other devisees under the residuary clause in which the widow claimed dower. The testator removed his domicil to Massachusetts, where he died. It was claimed that the will should be construed by Massachusetts law under which the widow was not entitled to dower in addition to the provisions of the will "unless such plainly appears by the will to have been the intention of the testator." The court decided that Rhode Island law should govern, saying: "Since the purpose of interpretation is to ascertain what meaning was intended to be conveyed by the testator by the words which he saw fit to use, we certainly can look only to the meaning of these words according to the use in the place where he was domiciled when he made the will." [112]

The interpretation of the kind of currency referred to is quite different from the interpretation of the value to be assigned to a currency mentioned in the will, whose kind is not disputed, but whose value has changed. A native of Germany, domiciled in New York, left to certain near relatives a number of legacies in marks. There was no dispute that German marks were intended but it was claimed that the testator intended to make the bequests in marks at the current rate of exchange on the day of the execution of the will. This would have amounted to about one and one-half cents per mark. After the making of the will, the German paper-mark became practically worthless and was withdrawn from circulation. At the time of the testator's death the mark had been re-established on a gold basis. It was decided that the bequest in marks was intended not as a measure of value but as a commodity, to be satisfied in kind, or the equivalent, as of the time of his death.[113] This is an entirely reasonable conclusion because if the legacies were payable in marks having a value as of the time of making the will, he would probably have made them payable in dollars.

[111] *Ibid.*, at p. 515.
[112] Atkinson *v.* Staigg, (1882) 13 R.I. 725, 728.
[113] Matter of Lendle, (1929) 250 N.Y. 502. "Fluctuations were the symptoms of a disease which might be fatal but from which the patient might recover." Pound, J., at p. 506.

A different question of interpretation is presented by conflicts of law as to the validity and construction of a power of appointment exercised by will where the domicil of the donee of the power is in one state and the domicil of the donor of the power is in another state. The property is not vested in the donee, but in the donor, and construction must revert back to the instrument creating the power. Let us assume that the power is attempted to be exercised by a general bequest without mention of the power of appointment. Even if by the law of the donee's domicil this is ineffective, it will be upheld if valid by the law of the domicil of the testator granting the power.

In *In re* Lewal's Settlement Trusts,[114] an English woman, about to marry a domiciled Frenchman, was given a power of appointment over certain property to be exercised either by deed or will so as to be valid by English law or by the law of her domicil. Later, when still only 19 years of age, she signed a holographic will making her husband her universal legatee. She died domiciled in France. The court held the appointment good because the will was valid by French though not by English law. The court invoked the English Wills Act for the purpose of interpreting the will and held that the power was effectually exercised. However, the testamentary capacity of the wife being limited at the time of making the will to only one-half her property under French law, her will operated only to the extent of one-half the funds subject to the power.[115]

**Interpretation of Wills of Land.** Should the rule of interpretation be different with reference to a devise of real property? If the question were such as to affect the system of tenure or the transfer of title to real property, the answer would require an unqualified reference to the law of the situs. If, however, it is merely a matter of interpreting whether the devise is in favor of one person or group, rather than of another, the interpretation given by the law of the domicil does not violate any of the rules of title at the situs, even though a like interpretation would not be given in the country of the situs. Goodrich favors the situs rule principally because of public convenience.[116] While this may be cogent with reference to a rule of property it does not apply where the question is simply as to the

[114] [1918] 2 Ch. 391.

[115] *Semble:* Matter of N.Y. Life Ins. and Trust Co., (1913) 209 N.Y. 585; Sewall *v.* Wilmor, (1882) 132 Mass. 131. See also Murphy *v.* Deichler, (1909) App. C. 446.

[116] Goodrich, (1927) p. 376 citing article by C. D. Hening in 41 Am. Law Reg. (N.S.) 623 and 718.

testator's intention upon a matter upon which he was free to choose both by the law of his domicil and by the law of the situs. The law of the situs will execute his intention and the fact that its own courts might draw a conclusion different from the courts of his domicil does not justify the situs rule. Minor favors the law of the domicil applied as to land as well as to personalty because that law is the one "with which the testator is supposed to be most familiar." [117] In cases appearing to establish a contrary doctrine, a distinction is drawn between a will in which ambiguous words or phrases have been used having a local or domiciliary meaning and a will which is not ambiguous on its face but to which it is attempted to give a construction by reason of the after-birth of a child or other circumstance assumed to have changed the testator's intent. Thus in Peet *v.* Peet,[118] the testator was domiciled in New York by the laws of which state a portion is raised for an after-born child unprovided for in the will, equal to his share if the parent had died intestate. There was no such provision by Illinois law where the land was situated. The court applied the Illinois law making the distinction to which we have just referred, and which appears to be entirely reasonable because the construction is *ex lege*. It is not in pursuance of any language of the will, express or implied and, indeed, is a result of laws of a coercive character bearing upon the distribution of the estate.

## 9. Revocation

Where a will is executed in one state and revoked in another in which the testator died domiciled, the revocation being by an act such as tearing off the signature with intent to revoke, no serious question arises even though the state of execution regards such an act as an insufficient revocation. The proper law by which transfer at death is regulated, *viz.*, the law of the last domicil, gives force and effect to the revocation.[119] Suppose, however, that the act of tearing, though effective at the place where it occurred, was not performed at the last domicil, and was not considered a revocation there. A serious conflict is presented because, by the effect of the law at the

[117] Minor, (1901) §145, followed in Keith *v.* Eaton, (1897) 58 Kas. 832; Guerard *v.* Guerard, (1884) 73 Ga. 506.

[118] (1907) 229 Ill. 341.

[119] Restatement, §307, as to a will of movables. "The effectiveness of an intended revocation of a will of an interest in land is determined by the law of the state where the land is." Restatement, §250.

place of tearing, the will had become *non est*. As Minor puts it: "whether the revoking will is to operate an *immediate* revocation of the former, or is to operate only *post mortem*, must be determined by the law of the testator's domicil at the time of the *execution* of the last will; for if the first is thereby revoked immediately, no subsequent change of domicil will revive it." [120] Some authors oppose this view, holding that if the decedent made a distribution of his property, good by the law of his domicil and by the same law never effectively revoked, that direction should stand as his will.[121] But this assumes the very question to be decided. Should the law of the last domicil apply its law of revocation to a will revoked in another state when the decedent was domiciled there? To do so is to deny to that other state the power to determine the validity and effect of an act completed by a person domiciled there, under which the instrument ceased to exist as a will. In many states a prior will is revoked by the execution of a second, if the later will contains an express revocatory clause, even though the second never becomes active as a will. In other states, revocation, whether express or implied, becomes effective only when the subsequent will becomes operative at the death of the testator.[122] Suppose A. makes his will in State X. while domiciled there, expressly revoking a prior will. He dies domiciled in State Y. The subsequent will cannot be admitted in State Y. because it did not dispose of any property. Under the law of X. the second instrument is nevertheless good as a revocation, but in Y. it is not.[123] It would indeed seem to be an unjust intervention in respect to an act completed in State X. to say that the testator must be held to have dealt with his property with a view to the laws of State Y., before he had any thought of ever being domiciled there. A will may be considered an ambulatory instrument but so far as it works a revocation of a prior will, its effect must be considered as immediately active.

**Revocation by Subsequent Event.** Suppose, however, the act or event deemed a revocation by the law of the state where the act or event occurred was not expressly intended by the testator as a revocation, such as the marriage of the testator, or the birth of a child after the making of the will. What law shall determine, where there is a conflict between the law of the place where the testator was domiciled

[120] Minor, (1901) §149.

[121] Goodrich, (1927) §162.

[122] See the authorities cited in (1915) 64 U. of Penn. Law Rev. 218.

[123] The facts are suggested by Gose, J., in *In re* Pierce's Est. (1911) 115 Pac. 835.

at the time of the event, and the law of the testator's last domicil. The question here is *ex lege* and quite independent of, perhaps even contrary to, the testator's actual intent and should be governed by the same law which determines succession to his estate generally, *viz.*, the law of the last domicil.[124]

What then is the effect of Lord Kingsdown's Act and similar legislation upon the change of domicil in working a revocation by the law of a new and last domicil? In *In re* Coburn (*supra*) the court construed §2612 of the New York Code of Civil Procedure (now §24 Decedent Estate Law) and decided that the effect of the New York statute did not prevent a change of domicil from destroying the instrument's existence as a will; the statute merely insures that the right to have a valid will admitted to probate, the form for the execution thereof, or the validity or construction of any of its provisions shall not be affected by a change of domicil. The third section of Lord Kingsdown's Act, on the other hand, specifically provides that no will or other testamentary instrument "shall be held to be revoked" by reason of a change of domicil.[125]

**Foreign Conflict-of-Laws Rules relating to Revocation of Wills.** As the particular system of law, national, domiciliary, or territorial, recognized by a particular country for succession, determines testamentary as well as intestate succession, it follows that the same system must also determine the portion of the estate, if any, which is reserved by law for certain beneficiaries; also whether revocation of a will must be expressed or whether certain facts or certain conduct by the deceased is to be taken as equivalent to revocation. Accordingly the successoral law determines whether a subsequent will revokes a prior will *ipso facto,* or only to the extent that its provisions are inconsistent with a prior will. The will of a domiciled Netherlander was considered by a *Belgian* court to be impliedly revoked by a subsequent marriage-contract entered into in Belgium, for the reason that Netherlands law so provides.[126]

Under Art. 892 of the *Italian* Civil Code, every alienation of a

[124] *In re* Coburn (1894) 30 N.Y. Supp. 383. In Bloomer *v.* Bloomer (1853) 2 Bradf. 339, the principle was similarly applied to gifts *causa mortis.*

[125] Applied in *In re* Goods of Reid, (1866) L. R. 1 P. & D. 74, to an antenuptial settlement operating in Scotland as a valid testamentary instrument, made in Scotland by a domiciled Scotsman who afterwards died domiciled in England. *Accord: In re* Groos's Est. [1904] P. 269.

[126] Lewald, (1925) 9 *Recueil, Acad. de dr. int.* p. 121, citing Court of Bois-le-Duc, Oct. 17, 1922.

thing bequeathed, constitutes a revocation of the legacy, even though the thing is again found in the possession of the testator at the time of his decease. A domiciled Englishman devised land in Italy and after making the will transferred the land to another. Lewald believes that the devise would not be considered revoked by an Italian court because Italian law makes the national law of the testator govern succession to his entire estate, both land and movables. But this would seem to be correct only if an Italian court would not accept a *renvoi,* because the English rule with regard to land is that of *lex rei sitae.* We have seen that *renvoi* is still a disputed doctrine in Italy.[127] A *German* court would consider the will of an Italian, domiciled in Germany, revoked by the birth of a child after the making of the will, under Art. 888 of the Italian Civil Code. Art. 25 of the German Introductory Statute to the Civil Code makes the national law of the testator applicable to domiciled foreigners on the basis of legislative reciprocity. We have just observed that the Italian *Disposizioni* apply the national law of foreigners domiciled in Italy for succession to all classes of property.

A domiciled citizen of the Netherlands who died in *France,* had made a gift under the disguise of a contract transferring to certain persons, subject to a usufruct, land and movables located in France. The gift left his remaining estate below the value of the legitimate portion reserved by French law, to his grandchildren. This portion was therefore awarded to the heirs so far as the land was concerned, as though it were a separate estate, and without waiting for the liquidation of his entire estate under the Netherlands law. The Netherlands law was admitted to be competent as to the personal property.[128]

**Reserved Portion.** German law makes the reserved or legitimate portion (*Pflichtteil*) depend upon the general successoral law. An important difference is to be noted between the rights of the heir to a reserved portion in France and those accorded in Austria and Germany. In France, the heir enjoys a direct right to a portion of the estate, whereas in Austria and Germany he may simply bring suit as a creditor for the money value of his reserved portion against those who have received it under the will. Where land located in Germany formed part of the estate of a French testator, German law was ap-

[127] See *Disposizioni* of Civ. Code, Art. 8.

[128] Clunet, 1912, p. 550. In *In re* Coleman, Clunet, 1918, p. 280, a French tribunal interpreted the will of a French subject who became American through marriage (and remained such though domiciled in France at her decease), according to the law of Pennsylvania, of which state her husband was a citizen.

plied under a presumed *renvoi* to the German law *rei sitae,* the French heir being relegated to his right as a creditor only.[129]

The case of an implied revocation of a will by acts considered as such in a jurisdiction not that of the successoral law seems not yet to have presented itself to German courts. Lewald believes that the successoral law must determine, although Art. 24, par. 3 (1) of the Introductory Statute provides that if a foreigner who has executed or revoked a disposition to take effect with death, acquires German citizenship, the validity of the execution or revocation is determined according to the laws of the state to which he belonged at the time of the execution or revocation. The tenor of this provision might presumably be limited to voluntary acts, thus making the distinction which we have ventured to support on principle.[130] Lewald on the other hand is insistent that the provision refers only to the capacity of the testator and the form of the revocation.[131]

The Bustamante Code of *Latin-American states* contains a novel provision with regard to the revocation of wills. It provides:[132] "The procedure, conditions and effects of the revocation of a will are subject to the personal law of the testator, but the presumption of revocation is determined by the local law." A reference to the local or foral law to determine a presumption of revocation from certain stated facts is quite comparable to the Anglo-American principle of determining procedural rules by the *lex fori,* provided the presumption is *prima facie* and not conclusive. A conclusive presumption partakes of a substantive rule of law.[133]

129 Dec. of *Reichsgcr.,* Apr. 14, 1891, Clunet, 1893, p. 605. The Swiss rule which permits a choice of national law by will, applies also to the reserved portion. Schnitzer, *ut cit.* (1937) p. 236.

130 *Ante,* p. 344.

131 Lewald, *Das deutsche int. Privatrecht* (1931) p. 318.

132 Art. 151, Code of Private Int. Law. Int. Conferences of Amer. States, 1889–1928, (1931) p. 342.

133 *Cf.* Beale (1935) iii, p. 1611.

# TABLE OF CASES

(References are to Pages)

# INDEX

C

G

R

U



V



W

## Z